MW01143222

Learning Mathematics and Logo

Learning Mathematics and Logo

edited by
Celia Hoyles and Richard Noss

The MIT Press
Cambridge, Massachusetts
London, England

© 1992 Massachusetts Institute of Technology

All rights reserved. No part of this book may be reproduced in any form by any electronic or mechanical means (including photocopying, recording, or information storage and retrieval) without permission in writing from the publisher.

The book was set in Times Roman and Helvetica by Asco Trade Typesetting Ltd., Hong Kong and was printed and bound in the United States of America.

Library of Congress Cataloging-in-Publication Data

Learning mathematics and logo / edited by Celia Hoyles and Richard Noss.
   p. cm.—(Exploring with Logo)
 Includes bibliographical references and index.
 ISBN 0-262-08207-1
 1. Mathematics—Computer-assisted instruction. 2. LOGO (Computer program language) I. Hoyles, Celia, 1946– . II. Noss, Richard.
III. Series.
QA20.C65L43   1992
510′.285′5262—dc20   91-33382
                                                    CIP

Contents

Contributors

Laurie D. Edwards   Department of Education
Crown College
University of California
Santa Cruz, CA 95064

Trevor Fletcher   44 Cleveland Avenue
Darlington
DL3 7HG
UK

Jean-Luc Gurtner   Institute de Psychologie
University of Fribourg
CH-1701
Switzerland

Brian Harvey   Faculty of Computer Science
University of California
Berkeley, CA 94720

Joel Hillel   Department of Mathematics
Concordia University
Montreal
Quebec, H4B 1R6
Canada

Celia Hoyles   Department of Mathematics, Statistics & Computing
Institute of Education, University of London
London, WC1H 0AL
UK

Thomas E. Kieren   Department of Secondary Education
University of Alberta
Edmonton, T6G 2G5
Canada

Chronis Kynigos   19 Kleomenous Street
Athens 10676
Greece

Tamara Lemerise   Department de Psychologie
Université de Quebec à Montreal
Montreal PQ, H3C 3P8
Canada

Uri Leron   Department of Science Education
Technion-Institute of Technology
Haifa 3200
Israel

Herbert Loethe   Paedagogische Hochschule
D-7140 Ludwigsburg
Germany

Richard Noss   Department of Mathematics, Statistics & Computing
Institute of Education, University of London
London, WC1H 0AL
UK

Rosamund Sutherland   Department of Mathematics, Statistics & Computing
Institute of Education, University of London
London, WC1H 0AL
UK

Bruno Vitale   University of Geneva
LDES-FPSE
Meyrin
CH 1217
Switzerland

Sylvia Weir   TERC
2067 Massachusetts Avenue
Cambridge, MA 02140

Rina Zazkis   Department of Science Education
Technion-Institute of Technology
Haifa 3200
Israel

Series Foreword

The aim of this series is to enhance the study of topics in the arts, humanities, mathematics, and sciences with ideas and techniques drawn from the world of artificial intelligence—specifically, the notion that in building a computer model of a construct, one gains tremendous insight into that construct.

Each volume in the series presents a penetrating yet playful excursion through a single subject area—such as linguistics, visual modeling, music, number theory, or physics—written for a general audience.

E. Paul Goldenberg

Foreword
by Seymour Papert

As an inveterately concrete thinker I will ground what I want to say about this book by first telling a story from my own experience. As a Logophile I will show my fondness for recursive self-reference by choosing as my story the story of writing the story.

My first pass at this preface started something like this: I am delighted to be asked, etc., but there is such a wealth of material in the book that anything I could add in the number of words that is reasonable to use in a foreword (other than REPEAT COUNT text [Bravo]) would be carrying chips to Nippon.

As I stared at the words on the computer screen, the jokes quickly wore thin, and a certain pooh-bah tone became painfully assertive. I thought of deleting the file and starting afresh. But another strategy for pursuing a project in trouble is apparent even to children, as you will read in this book. There is a saying: Beware of first impressions; they are often right. A related heuristic for dealing with a project in trouble suggests sticking with your instincts in the hope of finding out what you were really trying to do. Your "first go" in starting a project often expresses an inchoate idea that has been waiting for an opportunity to form, or perhaps an idea that worked once in another context. Sometimes if you play with and nurture your project, it will come to life; not always but with experience, and only with experience, you can learn to get a feel for when there is something there. Giving children the opportunity to develop this empowering sense is central to the philosophy of learning I associate with Logo.

In the unfolding of this story, sticking with my first approach *does seem to be* leading to something that feels better. If you pressed me, I would have to agree that this example is at least slightly strained. Although I want to believe that what I am now writing confirms my sense that there was "something there" all along, the transition used what might appear to be the "cheap trick" of evading the specific problem (developing that first shaky paragraph into something more substantial) by changing the subject. In my mind's ear mathematics educators are protesting that such tricks might work in expressive writing ("where you can go from anywhere to anywhere") but have no place in mathematics ("where there are real constraints"). But I think I can get away with it since I am only trying to draw attention to a question, not offer proof of anything, and for this purpose the more salient and provocative the example the better it will serve. In fact the outraged protest is grist to inciting you to think, as you read *Learning Mathematics and Logo*, about whether such differences between "writing" and "mathematics" derive from an artificial and schoolish delimitation of what counts as doing mathematics. Less extreme examples, with more recognizable mathematical content, abound in the book where you will find much rich material to fuel your own attempts to rethink (which does not mean abolish) the line between mathematics and other components of the child's intellectual life. As for myself, I will avoid invidious choices by continuing to use my personal case to develop my argument.

Looking behind the Logo statement in my first paragraph at its evolution yields a more focused case of straddling the line. I had first written a single "Bravo" in plain English. Then I thought it would be more dramatic (and a more generous reflection of what I actually felt) to say: REPEAT 100 [Bravo]. In so doing, I also felt I was making an in-joke that might, despite its feebleness, help establish a connection with readers from the Logo community. Once formulated, the joke took on a life of its own and led quickly to the idea of inserting, instead of 100, the actual number of words in the preface. This would deepen the joke by a reference to self-reference, for reasons that anyone who knows the Logo culture will immediately recognize. But since I couldn't know in advance what that number would be, I wrote REPEAT 1729 [Bravo], using the number from Hardy's story as a placeholder. But the presence of this number out of its context made looking at the screen even more irksome and led me (in between writing and revising early versions of this very paragraph) to worry at the situation a little more. REPEAT X assuaged the worry but took away the immediate concrete presence of the self-reference. And so my mental peregrination (including a sidetrack into thinking that the number of characters was a better measure for the age of the computer) continued and gave rise to the following sequence of versions: REPEAT TEXTLENGTH/6 [Bravo]. . .REPEAT TEXTLENGTH/ (1 + COUNT "Bravo)[Bravo]. . .and, finally, with a relieved sense that this had been there all along trying to get out: REPEAT COUNT :TEXT [Bravo]

These Logo statements have the "look" of mathematics, but it is still tempting to argue that the "feel" of the activity from which they emerged is more in the spirit of literary work than mathematical and that I simply used mathematical metaphors in the course of doing something essentially unmathematical. On the other hand, one could also argue that something akin to the notion of "variable" or to the notion of function or algorithm is being used here in a playful, personal, even if not completely "mathematical," way. And, more important, one could argue that the literary feel is or ought to be appropriate at least sometimes in mathematical work. My conclusion is not that one side or the other is right but that like many other Logo situations, this incident is somewhere in between, not only straddling the ambiguous boundary but making us aware of its degree of arbitrariness. I suspect that a poll of the authors of this book would show that some do and some do not want to count this as doing math. But I conjecture that this imaginary (*gedanken*) dispute is rooted in taking the idea of mathematics too seriously, excluding amateurish play and jokes and setting up boundaries with such care, so pompously, that young minds enter with difficulty. Perhaps what I did with REPEAT is merely a mathematical metaphor, but perhaps greater opportunity to make mathematical metaphors is exactly what is needed to make mathematics more appropriable.

I find that the issue becomes easier to discuss in another frame of reference. There has been much talk recently about a shift in vision of the learning of mathematics from accumulating skills and concepts to acquiring a culture. Using this language, I ask: What kind of a culture should this be? Will it be one that permits only rigorous and literal thinking? Or will it encompass and value jokes, tricks, and metaphors? Will it have a place for ideas that are unorthodox or even plainly wrong in the standard culture of professional mathematicians? An interesting aspect of this wider conceptual frame is that many who would refuse to count my playing with REPEAT [Bravo] as doing mathematics might allow that it should be recognized as a valued genre of activity in children's mathematics culture.

I read much of the discussion in *Learning Mathematics and Logo* as contributing (though often not explicitly) to the emergence of an appropriate mathematical culture by exploring a variety of ways in which Logo and Logo research bear on relocating the boundary between what is and what is not to be counted as mathematics in the lives of children. The variations sometimes appear as differences about where to place Logo in relation to this boundary: Some of the authors take as given that Logo is a kind of mathematics, some ask whether it is mathematics, and others talk of bridging between Logo and mathematics, thereby implying that they are distinct. But these are not like differences about whether dinosaurs were green, subject to resolution through scientific investigation; they are more constructively seen as turbulence (or better, as the signs of work in progress) on the shifting boundaries between the cultures of mathematics and the cultures of everyday life. From this point of view the experiments described in the book appear to be less a quest for truth (though of course many are that as well) than happenings in the evolution of a culture, and similarly the chapters that discuss the experiments appear more in the tradition of cultural commentatary, such as literary criticism, than in the tradition of educational psychology. For example, a thread of articulating, asserting, and defending mathematical values runs through recurrent discussion in the book about whether children doing Logo are really doing mathematics or, on the contrary, using the exploratory power of the computer to avoid mathematical thinking. I see this discussion of values as most clearly akin to a T. S. Eliot or a Jacques Derrida—or a Leopold Senghor or the feminist scholars and activists—articulating, debating, and so participating in the evolution of the cultural issues that pervade our lives. But the shift in perspective produced by thinking about Logo research in terms of the evolution of cultures is more far-reaching than the discussion of values.

Indeed, what was most new, fascinating, and thought-provoking for me in reading this book was experiencing very much more fully than ever before the breadth of the encounter of Logo with the culture of mathematics education research. I do not mean that my interest was engaged only by issues that are best understood in terms of cultures. On the contrary, I scarcely paid attention to them on my first reading because I was so entirely gripped by other aspects of the book: For me the plums in the cake were stories about children and new mathematical ideas. I savored these at length in their own right before even noticing that in the book they are embedded in a matrix of concerns and ideas whose texture represents the intersection of the two cultures.

Hoyles and Noss raise a problem about the timing of this encounter. Since the earliest publications about Logo were really about mathematics education, it does seem odd that until recently Logo research and mathematics education research went their own separate ways. Although I do not by any means have a complete explanation, the book has provoked me to rethink my own development in a way that has a bearing on the larger problem of how these two cultures developed and on why I think that this book is a significant marker in the evolution of both of them. So I will tell another story.

In a brief and highly schematized version, the story of my relationship with the mathematics education culture is as follows. *Chapter 1, sixties:* I was formulating ideas that would develop into Logo and its turtle. I was an active mathematician, and my thinking was imbued with mathematical values not radically different from those I rediscover today in *Learning Mathematics and Logo*. I conjecture that if the authors of the book had been around and thinking as they do now, I would have been with them. But as I saw it at the time, the mathematics education research community was thinking in the radically incompatible spirit that gave rise to the New Math. There emphasis was on mathematics as formal system. The Logo/turtle conception insisted also on mathematics as related to the self, the body, material and social objects, and activities. *Chapter 2, seventies:* Isolation from the mathematics education community allowed my thinking to become more radical and more futuristic. I thought increasingly in terms of bypassing rather than of reforming or supporting math ed. A favorite slogan was "Let's stop trying to make kids learn math; let's make mathematics for kids to learn." Since it seemed inconceivable that in the computer-rich future world children would learn the math (as opposed to mathematics) of today's curriculum, it was obvious that a new paradigm for research was needed. The math ed community defined itself as dispensing rather than creating mathematical knowledge which it took as given from above. I thought of turtle geometry as an exercise in creating a new piece of mathematics expressly for its learnability. In my dream (which I still believe for ten or twenty years hence) many other mathematicians would create many other, and quite different, pieces of really new mathematics for children. *Chapter 3, eighties:* Computers enter the world of learning in sufficient numbers to create pressure to focus on the present but still not in sufficient numbers (by a long way) to support the dream of a radically different learning environment and the creation of radically new mathematics for children. The dream goes on the back burner, and I (and others in a rapidly growing movement of Logo users) look for things to do with Logo that have a better chance of success in the short run than recreating mathematics. The movement through these three phases has resulted in a situation in which the mainstream of Logo work is cut off from the quest for real change in learning mathematics. Small groups, such as the kernel of contributors to *Learning Mathematics and Logo*, continue to keep the Logo-mathematics connection alive. However, in the meantime, and slightly ironically, a widespread cultural movement begins that turns away from formal and abstract ways of knowing in favor of relational ones, and away from propositions in favor of objects as carriers of knowledge. The movements comes from many sources among which feminist scholarship and radical movements, as well as trends in the sociology of science, are much more prominent than mathematics education. But its influence is already discrediting the image of the formal and abstract mathematics of the

New Math period in favor of something more like the Logo/turtle image. *Chapter 4, the nineties:* Many currents are coming together to favor a period of transformation of the culture of mathematics education. The most important is the more favorable cultural ambiance. Then there is the continued growth of the computer presence. And the intellectual kernels of a Logo culture including *Learning Mathematics and Logo* have come to a sufficient degree of maturity to be able to channel the other currents.

The story is couched largely in terms of one person's history. But like my earlier one, and like the cases studies scattered throughout *Learning Mathematics and Logo*, it should be read as what Hoyles and Noss call a "situated abstraction" and I call an "object to think with." These phrases refer to the fact that something can be concrete in its form but general enough to be used as a reference marker in other situations. I tried to write so that it would be personal enough to be real and yet show clearly that the main events did not just happen or depend only on idiosyncratic conditions. In doing so, I am exercising self-referentiality one last time: for I hope that these stories will seem convincing enough to you to strengthen the epistemological basis that makes them convincing. But you do not have to be convinced. What I really want to request is borrowed from Warren McCulloch: "Don't bite my finger (or lick it)—look where I'm pointing." I am pointing to *Learning Mathematics and Logo*. I hope these words will contribute a little to how you see it.

Preface

In this volume we draw together the fruits of research and curriculum development for the learning of mathematics through Logo programming. We outline where this work has been and where it might be going, we highlight key themes from both theoretical and practical points of view, and we look at the implications for mathematics education that reach out beyond Logo.

We begin by asking an obvious question: Why Logo? It is ten years since Logo was implemented on a microcomputer and the first implementations found their way into classrooms. In that time much has been written, many classrooms equipped, and Logo has entered various curricula in a variety of guises. Yet surprisingly the effort expended in seriously developing Logo as a medium for mathematics education has only been a small part of the total enterprise— surprising because Logo was originally developed with the intention of building a computational system for the exploration and learning of mathematics. More surprisingly still, it is clear that though reports of Logo-based investigation can be found throughout the educational literature, it is only recently that researchers in the field of mathematics education have begun to accept Logo as a valid setting in which to investigate and promote children's mathematical activities.

We observe that there is an established literature, stretching back some twenty-five years, that has investigated the role that computer programming (by students) might have in the learning and teaching of mathematics. Not unnaturally, until the early 1980s when Logo became widely available, the majority of this was in languages like BASIC. Nevertheless, much was learned, and it is worth summarizing what this preexisting (and continuing) research effort has offered to the teaching and learning of mathematics:

1. Programming is difficult and time-consuming to learn for most students; it takes time and is a significant overhead as an adjunct to existing mathematics curricula.
2. There *may* be some problem-solving skills that can be learned through programming, but there is no agreement about what these might be, and no uniformity in the findings.
3. It is unreasonable to expect that students will transfer knowledge acquired in a programming context to standard school-mathematics skills and concepts.

Logo was developed in the late 1960s and early 1970s by Seymour Papert and his colleagues, first at BBN[1] and then at MIT. From the first, Logo set out to represent more than simply another programming language: It was designed within a coherent educational framework, a "language for learning."[2] With the publication of *Mindstorms* in 1980, Papert offered a vision not just of how mathematics teaching might be improved but of a different kind of mathematical learning altogether, one in which the medium of expression—Logo—crucially influences the kinds of mathematical thinking and learning that might take place. In the same year Harold Abelson and Andrea diSessa published *Turtle Geometry*, setting out the rich mathematical potential of the Logo turtle idea. However, neither of these seminal works attempted to map out an alternative curriculum or a practical guide to the realization of their ideas.

Educational researchers in the early 1980s devoted considerable energy in attempting to rework with Logo what had achieved only moderate success with less sophisticated and powerful languages. At the same time a few educators, understandably impatient with the conservatism of this approach, allowed themselves to make ever more extravagant claims for what Logo could do for children and teachers. Nevertheless, by the middle of the decade, there were a number of mathematics educators who were prepared to reject both euphoria and conservatism and to accept Papert's view as a challenge to begin the task of creating and evaluating mathematical learning environments that could operationalize his vision.

So why Logo? After all computer science tells us that all languages are formally equivalent, and yet we seem to be claiming that a particular style of investigation and innovation is tied to a specific programming language. One answer has to do with epistemology. As a derivative of LISP—still a major contender for the programming language of computer science and artificial intelligence—Logo is a programming language with mathematical integrity: For example, programs can be written as collections of free-standing procedures that behave like mathematical functions, and ideas expressed as programs can be layered on each other. It encourages the programmer to use notions that resonate with

---

1. Bolt, Beranek and Newman—an independent high-tech communications research organization where Papert and Wallace Feurzeig developed the first implementation of Logo.

2. As Abelson and diSessa put it in their book *Turtle Geometry* (MIT Press, 1980): "Logo is the name for a philosophy of education and for a continually evolving family of computer languages that aid its realization." (p. 412)

mathematical concepts and ways of thinking. And of course, in responding to the commands FORWARD and RIGHT, the turtle offers not just a visually attractive and comprehensible introduction to programming but an entry into differential geometry as well.

This perspective allows us to justify our concentration on Logo and to explain how research with Logo can differ qualitatively from that which involves other languages: We recall the three broad findings that we outlined above. First, it is true that programming takes time to learn, but this difficulty is subtly transformed if we begin to think of programming as a medium for expressing mathematics rather than as a tool for learning it. Second, given the plasticity of the Logo environment, we can permit ourselves to be less interested in the identification of generalized problem-solving skills that are developed by the medium and to focus more closely on the ways in which a range of styles and approaches are allowed to surface. Third, the question of transfer of understandings from one domain (programming) to another (school mathematics) becomes less important compared to the opportunity to rethink what mathematics might be made accessible and how it might be expressed. Taken together, these three points give meaning to the idea created by the juxtaposition of the two words *Logo mathematics*.

None of this is sufficient to predict how Logo might be used for learning. Of course it is possible to claim that such a language carries with it the seeds of an alternative philosophy of education or the potential for a more human kind of mathematical learning. In our view such claims are interesting. They have certainly formed an important part of Logo's appeal, and they underpin the contributions of this volume. However, they can hardly be accepted as unproblematic, and they cannot be seen merely as attributes of Logo's structural features. It is a mistake to propose that the educational value of a programming language—or indeed any technological innovation—can be assessed by its epistemological features or that there is any causal linkage between a piece of software and a way of learning. Instead, we need careful investigation of the ways students use the computer, how it enters into the educational domain, and how it might structure and be structured by the classroom setting into which it is inserted.

Our intention in drawing together the contributions in this volume is to collect writing that expresses a range of issues from a perspective that synthesizes the theoretical and the practical, research and curriculum development. We see these two domains as complementary: Research only flourishes if it is informed by the creation of environments that have been developed for and used by children. On the other hand, it makes no sense to create curricula that ignore the epistemology of mathematics, what is known of children's understandings or the settings in which they are developed. For this reason, if for no other, the reader will not find in any of the subsequent chapters research that aims to investigate the effects of Logo "treatments," or "curriculum development" that consists of examples of hierarchical sequences of Logo tasks. Such approaches seem to us to be fundamentally misguided in that they guarantee at their outset the impossibility of real change and effectively marginalize the innovatory potential of the technology they seek to investigate.

The contributions in this volume—all of them original—attempt to synthesize the computer into its pedagogical, cultural, and social setting. Although the individual chapters vary in focus and emphasis, the book embodies a uniformity of spirit around such notions as pupil autonomy and the need for pupil engagement in challenging mathematical environments. We have divided the book into three main themes that broadly reflect the issues we outlined at the beginning of this foreword, themes that problematize the areas of *curriculum, learning, and mathematics*.

The chapters in part I, "Logo in the Curriculum," discuss the linkages between Logo and school mathematics. Although there are plenty of ideas for classroom implementation to interest the reader, the focus is not restricted to the classroom; rather, the contributions of part I concentrate on broadening our understandings of the ways in which Logo activities bear on (and influence) the ideas pupils encounter in school algebra and geometry.

In part II, "Styles and Strategies," the authors turn our attention from the cognitive to the metacognitive and affective domains. What range of learning styles can the Logo setting accommodate? How can we make sense of pupils' preferred strategies? Pedagogy also takes on a more prominent profile. How, for example, can we help pupils to reflect on the strategies they are using? The chapters within this part range widely and sometimes controversially.

In part III, "Expressing Mathematical Structures," we return to mathematical concerns, this time not so much in connection with curriculum or pedagogy but more with the mathematical structures themselves. A central claim for Logo has been that pupils are able to express new (to them) mathematical ideas and to express old mathematical ideas in new ways. The contributors consider a variety of mathematical ideas and draw out relationships between mathematics and computing. The focus is on the ways in which constructing Logo programs helps (or not) to illuminate the underlying mathematics.

In the afterword we attempt to draw together some of the important issues raised in the volume by reflecting on the successes and failures of research in Logo mathematics and setting out ideas for work to be done in the future.

We intend that this book will be of interest to an audience that includes researchers and teachers but extends beyond both. We hope that it will further the analytical work on the role of computers in mathematics, and equally that there is sufficient material here to inform classroom practice. Ten years ago we were inspired by Logo: It represented an oasis in the desert of drill-and-practice programs founded on untenable and anachronistic behavioristic psychology, or the arid dryness of the AI community who threatened to add intelligence to their tutorial programs. We share Papert's vision of the computer as a means to reappraise what children can do mathematically. There are some who say that Logo has outlived its role as a beacon and others who never saw it that way in the first place. We think that Logo *does* point in new directions. Yet the vision of what the computer might offer the educational endeavor is still both tantalizing and distant. It is certain that at some point before our collective arrival, Logo will have been replaced by considerably more powerful computational environments. It is equally certain that whatever replaces Logo will not come ready-made with all of the interesting social, psychological, and pedagogical problems solved. Our hope is that by subjecting the vision to the critical interrogation of research, we might aid in the process of transforming the vision into curricular reality.

Celia Hoyles
Richard Noss
London

Acknowledgments

In the last five years the field of Logo mathematics education has become a small but viable community, and we are well aware of the debt we owe to the teachers and researchers within it. We would like to express our thanks to all the contributors to this volume for their patience and willingness to accede to our always urgent requests, to Hal Abelson for his support and critical insight, to David Pimm for his helpful editorial comments, and to Ann McDougal for her invaluable secretarial assistance.

Logo in the Curriculum

The chapters in this part examine the role that Logo can play within school algebra and geometry. The authors are not constrained by the boundaries of existing curricula, and most point to ways in which the curriculum could be transformed by the introduction of Logo. Nevertheless, the discussion does center on "conventional" school-mathematical content, and there is no doubt that the curricular proposals the authors make *could* be implemented without much rethinking of the role and status of mathematics in schools. Although all the contributors recognize the need to consider pedagogical issues, these are not the object of discussion in this part. Pedagogy is given a more explicit focus in part II.

Focusing on algebra, Joel Hillel (chapter 1) synthesizes the findings of his research work with children (aged eight to fifteen years) in Canada in order to present a conceptual analysis of the notions of procedure and variable. Rosamund Sutherland (chapter 2) extends the research undertaken as part of her doctoral thesis from the University of London to discuss how experience with Logo programming can help children toward an algebraic approach to problem solving.

Turning to geometry, Herbert Loethe (chapter 3) describes research from Germany on the advanced use of Logo at the teacher education and high school levels. Chronis Kynigos (chapter 4) provides an overview of work with children's learning of geometry with Logo in a Greek school and summarizes the findings of his doctoral thesis (submitted to the University of London) on understanding different pupil views of turtle-geometric knowledge. Finally, Laurie Edwards (chapter 5) reports research that formed the core of her doctoral thesis, this time from the University of California at Berkeley. She describes the development of a Logo-based microworld concerned with transformation geometry and its evaluation by reference to the activities of a group of middle-school pupils (aged eleven to fourteen years).

In our view school algebra and geometry, cannot realistically be separated. Algebra—at least in its broad meaning of formalized generalizations of relationships—lies at the heart of the programming enterprise. Similarly turtle graphics serves as the vehicle for both Hillel's and Sutherland's algebraic research. Nevertheless, there are theoretical and pragmatic differences, so we organize our commentary by considering first the contributions focusing on geometry and second those concerned with algebra.

We are aware that we might have chosen other cuts between the five contributions of this part. For example, both Loethe and Hillel start from an epistemological analysis of geometrical and algebraic concepts, respectively, and only subsequently discuss the implications and possibilities of children's behavior. Kynigos, Edwards, and Sutherland, on the other hand, base their approach more closely on curricular priorities, and on their knowledge of children's understandings and misunderstandings of the ideas under consideration during their Logo activities.

The first two contributions by Hillel and by Sutherland are concerned with children's strategies for working with variables. They give examples of children being introduced to generalized procedures and how they come to discover what varies and what does not. Both agree that children's spontaneous projects often do not involve the use of variable and that children have to be initiated into it (Hillel proposes that this be in a wide variety of contexts). Both agree that there are many complicating factors: Hillel mentions difficulties with interfacing; Sutherland comments on the difficulties children have with decimals.

Hillel, however, is more concerned with cognitive obstacles in children's understanding of variable (in contrast with Sutherland who is more interested in comparing this understanding with more traditional algebraic content). Hillel points out that the notion of procedure itself is problematic for students—even fixed procedures (i.e., procedures without inputs). We might note the algebraic nature of naming a procedure: giving a name to an entity (even if this is in some sense "known") is in large part an algebraic act. Thus it is not surprising that children often do not appreciate the full power of the idea. In fact he goes further; by analyzing the minutiae of the concept, he indicates just how complex it is. For example, he shows that using a procedure as a building block involves the *identification* of what is varying, the *assignment* of appropriate values to the variable, and the *construction of interfaces*—which is no mean task!

Two other issues stand out as being of general interest. The first concerns the difficulty children have with knowing just what an input actually does. Hillel points out that the naming of an input is problematic where the relation between cause and effect of the variable is not obvious. Contrary to accepted Logo wisdom, in such cases it is not clear that "meaningful" names (e.g., LENGTH and ANGLE) are the best kinds of words to use. Hillel even suggests that there might be a case for using, for example, x and y!

The second point concerns the difficulty children have in seeing figures the way we would like them to see them: We know that many children are extremely reluctant to adopt a modular strategy for their program design. Hillel cites the literature that suggests that young children tend to see figures in terms of "primary contour structures" in which overlapping line segments are avoided. This is a salutary lesson as it seems to illustrate clearly that what has often been taken as a conceptual programming bug (or, indeed, an illustration of the difficulty of programming itself) is in fact something much more complex, something that the computer has raised to our awareness rather effectively. In summary, Hillel argues that children's understanding of variable in Logo is both multilayered, and complex. That is, before we make too glib prognoses about what children do and do not understand, we should be careful to specify what we mean.

Sutherland is concerned with a broader category of algebraic thinking, namely, that of expressing generality in a symbolic form. She starts from the premise that there exists a fundamental paradox at the center of children's algebraic thinking. On the one hand, algebra derives its power from the ability of its practitioners to suspend referential meaning; on the other hand, it is precisely the absence of such referential meaning that makes algebra so difficult for pupils. Sutherland argues that algebraic thinking is qualitatively different from arithmetic thought and that explicit algebraic activities have to be given to children in order to develop algebraic intuitions. Of course her findings are open to an alternative interpretation, namely, that less sophisticated activities of an essentially arithmetic nature *do* develop intuitions, although these take time to develop and are difficult to evaluate.

Sutherland carefully plots the growth in understanding of variable within structured Logo environments and illustrates how fundamental notions—such as unknowns standing for a *range* of numbers, or *closure* of expressions—seem to be developed, at least by students some three or four years older than Hillel's. Her main pedagogical conclusion is that algebraic understandings are closely related to the types of computational situations into which the pupils have been placed: This is not an unreasonable claim, and quite likely it applies to other domains as well. Thus, for Sutherland, as with the other contributions in this part, the teacher's role is critical in developing the required intuitions. Sutherland argues that the Logo setting offers a means for pupils to accept and use abstract symbols, two aspects that have posed the most intransigent barriers in developing algebraic understandings.

The next three contributions by Loethe, Kynigos, and Edwards shift our focus from algebra to geometry and are concerned with the development of microworlds that tap into learners' existing intuitions of space. All three bear heavily on the notion of constructing means to express geometrical ideas in a "natural" way. But it is clear that *making available* the tools with which to express specific ideas is not the same as finding ways to get learners to avail themselves of them—a point explored by all three authors.

Loethe's contribution starts from the premise that by endowing the turtle with a variety of carefully chosen "extra" properties such as the ability to mark and signpost a point, it is possible to build new means of expressing the properties of different geometrical systems. Loethe presents us with a wealth of data collected from different settings—from both teacher-education and pupil activities.[1]

Loethe predicates his approach on the belief that the key to children's understandings lies in the provision of helpful "didactical models," both literally and metaphorically. That is, he places at center stage the necessity for learners (teachers and pupils) to play with *physical* models of the ideas they are dealing with and helps them to construct *mental* models of the turtle's behavior. Loethe wants to tap into the use of tools in a handicraft sense. To do so beyond the realm of body syntony (i.e., the standard identification of body movement with the [standard] turtle), he wants to build these intuitions by the provision of models.

It is clear that Loethe does not regard the construction of his intelligent turtles as determined by pedagogical considerations alone. On the contrary, he is at pains to point out the essential mathematical integrity of the environments. For example, a primary motivation for his construction of new primitives that record "total turn" and "total distance" (which he calls a *rotameter* and *odometer*, respectively) is precisely that "unreflective mixing" of intrinsic commands (FD, RT) and global ones (e.g., SETPOS) results in an "awful mixture" of local and global systems. This is what we mean by mathematical integrity: Loethe's concern is to provide clean and consistent geometrical or computational systems that simultaneously provide the learner with the tools for the job.[2]

---

1. It is worth noting that Loethe's contribution belongs to the German school system and curriculum and that this may differ in a number of respects and emphases from some of the other contributions to the book (which are mainly from the UK and US educational tradition). One example of this is Loethe's use of the word "didactics" which may not be familiar to anglophone readers and which we have found almost impossible to translate. The nearest we can come is "science of pedagogy," which we are aware is not much of a translation.

2. For example, using the rotameter and odometer of his first illustration, this integrity is ensured by the mathematical fact that a curve is completely defined by expressing its curvature as a function of arc length.

Loethe also raises the question of pedagogical agenda. He provides a nice example of a point where teachers have to decide *on pedagogic grounds* whether to encourage a generalizable strategy that only pays off in the longer term (this concerns ways of programming the turtle to produce complex solids). Thus he argues that the means of expressing an idea is dependent not only on the medium available, or on the teacher's or pupils' intuitions but on the teacher's own agenda. He suggests the importance of making connections with teachers' views of and priorities for the mathematics curriculum. These issues are both complex and mutually interacting—there is no guarantee of shared meaning between teacher and pupil (a point addressed by Sylvia Weir in part II). Certainly this contributes to the difficulties that Loethe refers to in developing a stable pedagogical approach.

Loethe addresses the issue of 3-D exploration, which is clearly far from trivial. However, it appears that an unequivocal investment in developing this repertoire can pay off, and Loethe claims that children who have built simple figures in 3-D Logo have no difficulty in interpreting the pictures on the screen— this is due in part to the slowness (it is not clear whether this was a design feature or a limitation) of the turtle, which allowed learners to watch the construction process on the screen, and in part to their experience of playing with real objects before going on to write procedures. This is a bold claim, particularly since we know from elsewhere that many learners have considerable difficulty in interpreting three-dimensional figures when presented in paper-and-pencil mode.

However, Loethe points out that it is impossible to construct complex Platonic solids (e.g., the icosahedron) by a process of trying and debugging from the visual feedback. This activity raised difficult issues of teacher intervention, as Loethe points out, because the teacher needed considerable (and unavailable) time to interpret her pupils' mistakes—which made it next to impossible for her to be of any assistance in the debugging process. In these activities (at least with the tools provided) it was *essential* for the teacher to analyze the situation and to confront head-on the mathematical structure of the problem. This stands in marked contrast to the normal situation of turtle-geometric activities, at least for beginners, and it is clearly an issue that deserves considerable attention.

Kynigos's contribution is concerned with asking what frameworks children actually use in turtle geometry and whether their ideas can be exploited to build conceptual frameworks beyond the boundaries of intrinsic (turtle) geometry. Kynigos makes the assertion that Logo is "lacking in density" of embedded notions, which may explain the difficulties children have in synthesizing ideas that they derive from schooling with those they encounter in Logo. His claim is that the available intrinsic notions are rather restrictive for children. This may be true for the range of directly accessible figures, although it is hardly the case for higher-level constructions, as the chapters in part III amply testify. In this restriction, he claims, may be found one of the origins of children's preference for what Hillel calls, earlier in this part, *perceptual* rather than *analytic* strategies. Of course Kynigos is not arguing that Logo cannot provide appropriate frameworks: On the contrary, he tries to construct learning environments that overcome the problem, drawing heavily on Loethe's ideas of providing new primitives that are not strictly intrinsic.

Kynigos argues that as a tight deductive system, geometry is out of favor, at least in the United Kingdom, and that there is little opportunity to engage in inductive thinking within the framework of school mathematics: He sees Logo as a possible way to remediate this. (In a similar way Sutherland looks at some of the major misconceptions that children have in dealing with algebraic objects and points to the gap between arithmetical and algebraic thought.)

For Kynigos the body syntony of turtle geometry is not the primary issue. Here his work contrasts strongly with Loethe's, who is interested in tapping in to intrinsic notions even when he is trying to build systems that go beyond strictly intrinsic ones. Kynigos is more concerned to develop children's thinking *beyond* these intuitions, to build intuitions explicitly about coordinate and cartesian geometrical ideas that do *not* hinge on the intuitions built around the turtle. Like Loethe, he is involved in designing linguistic fragments to increase the expressive power of the language. But he too is forced to the conclusion that the pedagogical issues are paramount: Reading Kynigos' accounts, one does not get the feeling of open-ended exploration that one gets from reading similar accounts of interactions with raw turtle graphics (note that Loethe explicitly makes the same point).

Edwards discusses the ways in which children made use of a transformation geometry microworld in order to express their own ideas about geometry. Her intention is not primarily group theoretic but geometric (which is why we place her contribution in this part rather than in part II). Edwards's agenda is the exploration of transformation geometry, to encourage a "working understanding" of the underlying notions from this domain in the children with whom she works.

She discusses in detail the ways in which the children expressed their ideas within her microworld. One of the interesting results was that children mobilized intuitions derived from their experience with turtle motions in their interpretation of the primitives of her microworld. Where these primitives effected *local* transformations (which she calls *PIVOT* and *SLIDE*), they fitted with the agenda of the microworld itself: For these primitives, children had no need to see them as effecting a transformation of the whole plane. On the other hand, there were misconceptions that derived from these turtle-based intuitions. A good example is her *rotate bug* which illustrates just how difficult it is to view the plane as a conceptual entity. These kinds of difficulties raise more general problems, those of how new knowledge displaces old and how existing intuitions bear on the learning of new knowledge. These are deep issues that cannot be addressed in this chapter, although they are touched on elsewhere in this volume (see the afterword by Noss and Hoyles).

Edwards's claim is that by operating within her microworld, her students acquired a language with which to express ideas about transformations, and some chose to represent such ideas by reference to the microworld primitives when talking about them after their Logo experiences. Her microworld primitives are opaque, and children did not choose to access them (although they could, in principle, have done so because these were Logo procedures). An interesting research endeavor would attempt to modify Edwards's project by providing primitives at a lower level (or even base level) so that the symbolic representations of the primitives would be more visible for the students and could be used as a vehicle for discussion of the nature of the transformations and pupils' difficulties with them.

Finally, we mention here two further issues. First, all the contributions in this part have argued in different ways for a more explicit structuring of the Logo environment to highlight the "embedded" mathematics by restricting the repertoire of "permitted commands" or of careful task construction. This raises a contentious issue: To what sense is such a restriction legitimate?

The second issue relates to the question of learning style. Loethe's model of three-dimensional turtle actions is designed to tap into the idea of the pupil as spaceship commander. This is an appealing and powerful notion. Yet there are implications here that range beyond merely the gender issue of whether the metaphor is equally appealing to boys and girls: What, for example, are the implications in terms of children's identification with objects of thought? There is little doubt that some children clearly do identify with the turtle as if they were the driver, others as if they were the turtle itself. Still others seem to find it more intuitive to maintain a boundary between themselves and the turtle, to think of themselves steering the turtle, but from their position in front of the screen, as separated from it. Both of these issues are touched on in part II, and we revisit them in our afterword, chapter 14.

The Notion of Variable in the Context of Turtle Graphics

Joel Hillel

1 INTRODUCTION

In this chapter I examine aspects of the concept of variable in Logo. The variable concept is multifarious, and its acquisition by children brings into play different psychological, mathematical, and programming issues. Consequently my analysis of the concept, and the ensuing discussion of children's understanding of it, will be restricted in several ways. I will consider only local variables and their use in turtle graphics,[1] that is, their use with (nonrecursive) procedures that output screen graphics. The focus of the chapter is on questions of variable use that are particularly relevant for children at the elementary school level. While I look at how children gain understanding of the variable concept and at the cognitive obstacles that arise, there is an equally important question of how children might link this understanding with more traditional forms of algebraic thinking. This topic will be taken up by Rosamund Sutherland in chapter 2.

2 A CONCEPTUAL ANALYSIS OF THE NOTIONS OF PROCEDURE AND VARIABLE

In general terms any programming solution to a given problem demands the coordination of several sorts of knowledge:

1. *Domain-specific knowledge about the problem to be solved.* In turtle graphics such knowledge may be about properties of distance and angle or about symmetry and similarity of geometric objects.
2. *Knowledge of programming techniques.* Such knowledge may be of syntax or of programming concepts such as sequentiality,[2] modularity, repetition, variable, recursion, and the calling of subprocedures.

---

1. I prefer to use the term *turtle graphics* rather than *turtle geometry*. The latter seems to convey a specific kind of geometry, namely, an intrinsic geometry. Associated with it is a whole range of issues about children's understanding of the intrinsic aspect of the geometry (understanding what class of figures is defined by a single procedure, separation of the procedure definition of a figure from the location of the figure on the screen, the use of command HOME, etc.). These issues are mostly independent of variable use.

2. The linear sequencing of Logo commands.

3. *Knowledge about the general operating system.* This category includes knowledge about the different modes of the computer screen (workspace, editor), file management, saving-and-calling procedures, and the disk operating system.

Clearly, depending on the type and level of complexity of the problem at hand, these different aspects of knowledge play a greater or lesser role. Some of the difficulties in arriving at a programming solution are language independent; other obstacles are specific to a particular (family of) language(s). The problem of planning a program can take different shape with compiled languages such as PASCAL from interpreted languages such as Logo. In particular, in Logo one can use *direct mode* (each command is executed immediately after it is entered), so the temporal lag between planning and execution is brief. The user has access to intermediate results of operations and hence can adopt a "local" approach to arriving at a particular result (*planning in action* rather than *action planning*).

The Conceptual Field in Turtle Graphics

Vergnaud (1983) describes a conceptual field as a "large set of situations for handling different interconnected concepts, procedures and representations." In this respect turtle graphics is a conceptual field for handling different programming concepts. Figure 1 highlights some of the relationships among various programming constructs, their underlying concepts, and the cognitive demands created by their use. I elaborate, first of all, on some of the terms used in this figure.

By *primitives*, we mean the set of Logo commands to the turtle that is initially given to children. Typically these commands include FD, BK, LT, and RT, but they can also include "primitives," such as CIRCLE or TRIANGLE, which output more elaborate constructions. The available primitives are assimilated by a child as a *scheme of actions* that corresponds to these primitives: For example move the turtle, turn the turtle, or draw a circle. These we have termed *elementary actions*. A *simple procedure* is a procedure made up only of primitives. If a procedure contains another (sub)procedure, we refer to it as a *composed procedure* (or superprocedure).

From the perspective of a child, writing a simple program involves only elementary actions. These actions must be coordinated in order to respect the *intraprocedural* relations, the most obvious of which is that of *sequentiality*. Other intraprocedural relations include *inversion* of operations, as apparent in

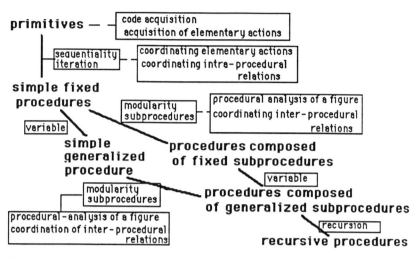

Figure 1 Relationships among programming constructs, their underlying concepts, and the cognitive demands created by their use

sequences of commands such as PU, . . . , PD or RT X, . . . , LT X and *additive properties* such as FD X, . . . , FD Y, . . . , (X + Y).

Writing a composed procedure involving several other procedures demands mental operations of greater cognitive complexity. Here the child has to coordinate not only elementary actions but also procedures that are themselves coordinations of actions. For composed procedures we speak of *interprocedural* relations, and in particular of the *interface* relations between (sub)procedures.

The Notions of Procedure and Variable in Turtle Graphics

The variable concept is introduced in Logo through *generalized procedures*[3] (as opposed to *fixed procedures* which do not require an input); thus it encompasses both the concept of procedure and the concept of variable. In particular, for children to construct meaning for the concept of variable, they need to have reasonable fluency with using procedures. The fact that even experienced Logo children have often not developed "procedural thinking" (Leron 1983; Hillel 1986) points to some inherent difficulties, even with the notion of procedure.

---

3. The term *generalized procedure*, though not standard, seems more appropriate than *procedure with input*. The latter use of "input" confuses the variable name with the numerical values assigned to the variable.

I begin by discussing several aspects of procedural use in turtle graphics. In particular, it is important to delineate the different reasons for defining a procedure:

1. Procedures defined solely as a *saving* device for the purpose of saving a graphical output (i.e., procedures play the role of a SAVEPICTURE command).
2. Procedures defined for an *editing* purpose, so as to be able to debug, modify, and extend a production.
3. Procedures defined as a *programming technique.* In this case the definition of a procedure is motivated by its *functionality*, since it can call on the use of procedural mechanisms such as subprocedure, variable, and recursion.

This last aspect of procedure includes both the case where the definition is functionally tied to a specific construction (e.g., LEFT-ARM, CHIMNEY, WING) and the case where the procedure is intended to be used as a general utility, often through the introduction of a variable (e.g., MOVE.TO.NEXT, POLYGON, SLIDE.RIGHT).

Several comments are in order. First, the status of a procedure definition is of course changeable over time. A procedure initially defined, *post factum*, to save a particular figure, may later on be identified as a useful subprocedure in a more complex production or even as a useful building block for many potential projects. It may be generalized so as to increase the flexibility of its use.

Second, the central idea of a procedure resides in its utility rather than simply in its capacity as a label attached to some production. Surely this is the sense in which Papert (1980) talks about "procedural thinking" as a problem-solving heuristic. We have noted, though, that some children seem to conceptualize procedures in Logo only as a way of saving their productions (which often consist of long lists of FD and RT commands to describe, say, a "spaceship"). Clearly turtle graphical activity with its "drawing-with-the-turtle" metaphor contributes substantially to such linking of procedures with saving a picture. We have argued elsewhere (Hillel 1986) that the "drawing schema" developed by children is in conflict with the the use of procedural mechanisms such as subprocedure. It seems to us important to provide children with Logo experiences that will evoke a changed conceptualization of the purpose of procedures.

Third, there are several obstacles in the way of changing a specialized (sub)-procedure into a general purpose one. One obstacle is related to the functional naming of a procedure (e.g., CHIMNEY instead of RECTANGLE), and another is the often observed tendency to *incorporate an interface move into the*

Figure 2 CHIMNEY bound to a specific construction HOUSE

procedure definition (e.g., the procedure CHIMNEY may include the interface move from position *A* to position *B*, as shown in figure 2). This renders the procedure bound to a specific construction and hence lacking in flexibility.

From a cognitive psychology viewpoint the concept of variable represents, as do the concepts of iteration and recursion, an *invariant.* By that we mean that in the case of a variable, changing the values of the inputs in a procedure still leaves both the inter- and intraprocedural relations invariant. This invariance is characterized by the attribution of a name to the variable and by the control of its value. This is particularly true in Logo programming where the attribution of a name to an object in a procedure can be used as a substitute for the particular values taken by the object.

Activites with Generalized Procedures

I now differentiate between turtle graphics activities that call only on the *use* of an already defined generalized procedure and activities that also involve the *definition* of a generalized procedure.

The Use of Generalized Procedures

A child in possession of a generalized procedure (independently of whether or not the procedure was initially defined by the child) may engage in situations requiring the following:

1. *Trying out specific instances of the procedure (specializing).* An example of this activity would be of a child trying out RECT 40 20 after being given a generalized procedure RECT :SIDE1 :SIDE2 for a rectangle.
2. *Using instances of a generalized procedure as building blocks in a more elaborate project.* An example of this activity would be using the given procedure RECT for producing a flag such as the one shown in figure 3. Implicit here is the idea that the availability of the generalized procedure suggested a suitable project.

Figure 3 A flag created with RECT

The Definition of a Generalized Procedure

Defining a generalized procedure is an activity that may or may not be tied to a specific graphical production. It encompasses: (1) generalizing a fixed procedure to increase its scope (the generalization may affect attributes of a figure such as its size, its shape, or both) and (2) defining a generalized procedure as a subprocedure for a production of an elaborate project. The second activity encompasses all of the previous activities as subgoals. It is a programming solution for producing a complex figure that involves the decomposition of the figure into appropriate subfigures, recognizing that some of the subfigures can be defined as special instances of a generalized procedure(s), defining the procedure(s), and then using specific instances of the procedures as building blocks for the figure (e.g., as in the pyramid project discussed in section 3).

Cognitive Demands of Activities Involving Variables

Here I elaborate on the cognitive demands of the different programming activities with generalized procedures.

Trying out Specific Instances of a Procedure

We refer here to an initial exploratory activity with a procedure (that can be constructed by a child) and that is often characterized by planning in action and the lack of explicit goals. The focus of the activity is more on the output than on the process by which the procedure is defined. When such activity involves generalized procedures, it requires the *assignment* of values to the variable name. This does not generally pose any difficulty for children, at least after the first few instances of "forgetting" to make the assignment (after all, children have been using generalized procedures from the moment they started with FD and RT).

Using Procedures as Building Blocks

The availability of procedures suggests that they can be used in combination to create more elaborate complexes. Children engaged in such "synthetic" activity need to attend to *interface* features as well as to question the size of each building block (both for the purpose of appropriate matching of different components and for working within the size limitation imposed by the screen). Such activity with generalized procedures, particularly if it is *preplanned*, calls for (1) *identification* of what is varying, (2) *assignment* of appropriate values to the variable, and (3) *construction of the interface(s)*.

Identification of What Is Varying When using a generalized procedure, it is not always transparent what part(s) of the resulting figure(s) is (are) varying. When a generalized procedure is given to children as a primitive (hence the actual procedure definition may be inaccessible), they may use the procedure without necessarily understanding what the inputs signify. Children often operate on the implicit assumption that "bigger inputs make bigger shapes." For example, in our initial study eight-year-olds were given a generalized procedure CIRCLE with diameter as an input of a primitive. Even though they used CIRCLE repeatedly, and the nature of the input was discussed with them, its significance was not understood. More recently twelve-year-olds were given a generalized procedure for an isosceles triangle that was parametrized by the base and the base angles. After twelve weeks of intensive work with the procedure, some of the children still mistakenly assumed that the variables were the base and the altitude (Kieran and Hillel 1990). This can be the case even with procedures defined by the children themselves since, once defined, their content is not often reexamined. Thus, when there is a temporal lag between the definition of a procedure and subsequent use, children identify what is controlling the variation based on their perception of global changes in size, length, or shape of the figure.

Assignment of Appropriate Values Even when the components of a figure that are varying are properly identified, it may not be obvious how the variable assignment controls these components. The input may be passed on to several commands in the procedure, and it may be *transformed* by arithmetic operations. We will discuss an activity in the next section in which children defined a state-transparent procedure for a rectangle of variable base and a fixed height, as shown in figure 4. The variable name LENGTH signified half the base (the initial displacement of the turtle from the midpoint of the base to an adjacent vertex). Children then had to realize that RECT 100 would produce a rectangle with base length of 200. Such relations between the input to the variable and the output of the procedure have to be understood in order to be able to use a generalized procedure as a building block.

Figure 4 A state-transparent rectangle of variable base and fixed height

Figure 5 Construction of the interface between SQUAREs

Construction of the Interface   Children have often been observed to have difficulty in anticipating an interface construction. The reason for it is explained in cognitive terms as a lack of representation of a procedure as a process, so procedures are identified as screen figures with, at best, only a partial regard for the associated turtle states. The interface issue is compounded here by the fact that, in using generalized procedures, interfaces are often a covariant (i.e., interfaces are *input dependent*). For example, using the usual generalized SQUARE procedure to construct figure 5 results in displacements *ab* and *bc* (part of the interface between the two squares) which correspondingly vary with the inputs to the procedure. In fact *ab* = input1 and *bc* = 1/2 (input1 − input2).

Defining New Procedures
When defining a generalized procedure (either directly or by *generalizing* a fixed procedure) children have to coordinate the actions of (1) *identifying* what varies, what is a covariant, and what is invariant; (2) *naming* and *declaring* the variable; and (3) *operating* on the variable.

Identifying What Is Varying   We have already mentioned that children tend to identify variation in a set of geometric figures by referring to the global effect of the variation, generally the size of the figure. However, to define a generalized procedure, children need to look more carefully at all the components of the figure that are varying and then to identify the commands within the procedure to which they need to assign a variable input. The relation between the external variation of the output figure and the internal variation within the procedure is not always obvious. For example, a procedure for varying the *length* of an arc of a fixed curvature involves varying the *number of repetitions* of the sequence RT

Figure 6 A chain of variable-size VEEs

1, FD 1 within the procedure. In the construction of spiral figures, the key activity in their procedural definition is the identification of what actually is varying.

Identification of what varies and what remains fixed is not simply a programming issue; it also involves domain-specific knowledge. To define a generalized procedure VEE :SIZE in order to construct a chain of similar vees, as in figure 6, a child needs to know that only the length of the arms of the vee varies while the central angle remains fixed.

Naming and Declaring the Variable   It is generally assumed that when introducing children to the notion of generalized procedures, it is better to use variable names rather than letters to designate the variable. However, in situations where the relation between the cause and the effect of the variation is not obvious, naming the variable becomes problematic. In defining a generalized procedure for circles via changing the input to RT in the repeated sequence FD __, RT __, neither SIZE nor ANGLE seems like an appropriate variable name. (The signifier SIZE would have to input to the rotation RT, and the signifier ANGLE seems to obscure the obvious variation in size of the circle.) Children are sometimes confused about how they should name a variable. This is partly because they attach undue importance to the name as determining the function of the input. (While conventional Logo wisdom is to use variable names rather than letters, there might be situations in which the use of X and Y may actually remove some conceptual problems. The use of letters for variables sounds "school-ish", but if the context in which they appear here as generalized numbers is understood by children, it may give legitimacy to their use.) The declaration of the variable is of course part of the construction of a general procedure.

Operating on the Variable within the Procedure   We refer to operating on the variable as both the action of passing the variable as a parameter to other commands and the action of modifying the variable within the procedure. We note that in a generalized procedure, the input can be passed to one or several commands, which may be either primitives or other generalized (sub)procedures (including the procedure itself, in case of recursion). Furthermore a variable X may be modified by arithmetic operations such as $X + 3$, $2 * X$, or $180 - X$. In operating on the variable, children need to be aware of all the parts of the procedure that become variable dependent: for example, in generalizing a procedure for a triangle to a procedure for a regular N-gon, varying the number of repetitions (N) necessitates varying the corresponding angle of rotation as well ($360/N$).

Children have been observed to bypass the operation of transforming the variable by simply adding on new variables (Hillel 1987; Noss and Hoyles 1987; Sutherland 1987). A procedure for a regular N-gon with its side length fixed at 30 is often written as

```
TO POLY :N :A
    REPEAT :N [FD 30 RT :A]
END
```

A child writing the above procedure has understood that both the number of repetitions and the angle of rotation vary but might not have understood the relation between the two (possibly because of a lack of domain-specific knowledge about the role of 360). However, on some occasions it has been observed that children can handle the relation between N and A numerically (e.g., they would write POLY 10 36 or POLY 7 51), but their difficulty resides in not being able to deal with an explicit generalized relationship such as $A = 360/N$. In chapter 2 Sutherland gives some further examples of this kind of behavior.

Another aspect of operating on a variable is understanding the type of relation between a covariant and a variable. In the above example of POLY, the relation is one of inverse proportionality (which might account for the difficulty in expressing it). More common to children's projects are situations where they need to sort out additive or subtractive relationships from direct proportionality (e.g., see Hoyles 1987).

Procedural Analysis of Figures

The definition of a generalized procedure as part of a solution of a turtle graphics task requires an a priori identification of some parts of the figure as definable in terms of autonomous procedures. We call such analysis of a figure a *procedural analysis*, and we remark that it requires a particular perceptual organization. Even when children have a fair amount of experience in composing elaborate figures using existing procedures as building blocks, their spontaneous perceptual organization of a figure is in terms of primary contour structures (Vurpillot 1972). The salient characteristics of such an organization is the avoidance of

Figure 7 An example of a figure with different perceptual organizations: a triangle with six horizontal bars or seven embedded triangles?

overlapping line segments (i.e., no two subfigures share the same line segment) and the treatment of line segments as undivided units (i.e., no subfigure contains only part of a line segment). Consequently a solution to a problem such as figure 7 may involve neither the definition of a generalized procedure for an equilateral triangle (if not already available) nor its full use (if it is available), simply because the solver's perceptual organization of the figure is in terms of a triangle with six horizontal bars rather than seven embedded triangles.

3 CHILDREN'S UNDERSTANDING OF THE NOTION OF VARIABLE

In this section I discuss some of the research findings on children's understanding of variable in turtle graphics. My own longitudinal observations of four children (over sixty hours, spanning a period of over two years) allows me to elaborate both on the conceptual difficulties and on the genesis of the variable concept.[4] Similar findings were also reported by Sutherland (1987) who observed eight pupils (eleven to fourteen years old) during their first three years in secondary school.

Description of the Experimental Setting

Since the use of a variable is unlikely to emerge spontaneously out of the children's familiar activities, a child's acquisition of the concept requires an instructional sequence organized in a fairly explicit way. Consistent with our theoretical analysis of the previous section, we designed the experimental sessions to include the different kinds of activities involving generalized procedures described in the previous section.

4. The research discussed here was supported by the Ministère de l'Éucation du Québec, FCAR Grant #EQ. 2539. Dr. Renan Samurçay of the Centre National de Recherche Scientifique, Paris, was the principal research collaborator. For a complete report of the research, see "Analysis of a Logo Environment for Learning the Concept of Procedures with Variable." Research Report #2, Concordia University, Montreal (1985).

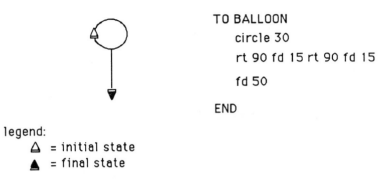

```
TO BALLOON
    circle 30
    rt 90 fd 15 rt 90 fd 15
    fd 50
END
```

legend:
  △ = initial state
  ▲ = final state

Figure 8 BALLOON: a fixed procedure

Introducing Generalized Procedures

The two pairs of children (nine to ten years old) were introduced to generalized procedures on about their fifteenth session of turtle graphics activities. Each pair was shown how a procedure that they have already written can be generalized to take a variable input. For example, the fixed procedure BALLOON, shown in figure 8, which used an available CIRCLE primitive (parameterized by the diameter), was generalized so that the length of the "string" became a variable. The children were shown the mechanics of generalizing a fixed procedure, beginning with the identification of what is to be varying (the length of the string), the naming the variable (LENGTH), the declaration of variable ("I want to tell the turtle that I will be changing the length of the string"), and, finally, operating on the variable inside the procedure (FD :LENGTH). An analogy was then made with the FD command ("What would happen if you only type FD?" "What does the 'not enough inputs' message mean?").

This rather directive activity was followed by an exploratory activity whereby the children experimented with the effects of assigning specific values for the variable name LENGTH.

Using Generalized Procedures

To demonstrate to the children the *utility* of generalized procedures, we gave them several projects requiring the use of such procedures as building blocks. The children were also encouraged to come up with, and to plan ahead, other projects that would require the use of an available generalized procedure.

One of the first projects that was given was that of "flowers" (figure 9). This project involved specializing the generalized procedure BALLOON by assigning

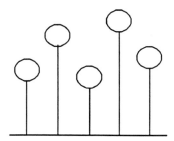

Figure 9 The flowers project

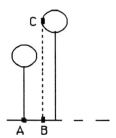

Figure 10 Interfaces in the flowers project

several specific inputs and constructing an appropriate "interface" between successive subprocedures.

To use the procedure, the children needed to be aware of (1) what the variable name LENGTH signifies and how the figure defined by BALLOON varies with the input and (2) the process of the balloon construction, in particular the initial and final state of the turtle.

Because of the way that the fixed procedure BALLOON was defined by the children (see figure 8), the flowers project required interfaces that involved 90-degree turns, a fixed horizontal displacement AB, and a covariant vertical displacement BC from the ground up, with the property that $BC =$ (length of string) + (radius of circle), as shown in figure 10.

The main obstacle to a solution was related to interface. Progressive attempts by the children evolved through

1.   an implicit assumption that the procedure BALLOON was state transparent, with the turtle positioned at the bottom of the string and heading toward the center of the circle;

2.   a correct analysis of the initial and final turtle states, assuming a fixed interface between the BALLOON subprocedures;

3.   an awareness that the interface is a covariant.

The last stage was followed by a visual assessment of how the vertical displacements *BC* vary with the input and led to fixing each as twice the length of input. However, paper-and-pencil planning led to a more careful analysis and resulted in the correct relation.

This progression in the solution was typical of all other projects calling on the use of a generalized procedure. The assignment of appropriate values to the variable was not problematic; whether fixed or input dependent, the interface aspect remained an obstacle. (We note that in this case the complication with interface was partly an artifact of the definition of BALLOON. Another production of a balloon figure that is state transparent and begins at the base of the string would have made the project a lot simpler. The fixed procedure initially defined as a "stand alone" procedure was not the most suitable building block for the project. In retrospect we can question the pedagogical merit of generalizing that procedure; the interface "noise" might have confused the issue of the utility of a generalized procedure.)

Defining Generalized Procedures

Among the projects whose solutions could have been facilitated by the definition of a generalized procedure was the pyramid figure (figure 11). It was presented to the children after six sessions of work on the use of generalized procedures. We will discuss this task and the children's solutions in some depth, since it provided some valuable insights about the obstacles to the use of variable by children of that age group and experience.

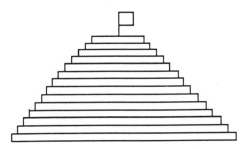

Figure 11 The pyramid figure

Figure 12 The construction of each layer of the pyramid figure

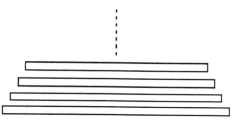

Figure 13 The pyramid viewed as a stack of rectangles

Figure 14 The interface between layers in the pyramid figure

The Pyramid Project   The pyramid project was presented to the children as a program that we had written. The program was executed on the screen several times, in slow mode and with the turtle showing. It indicated that the pyramid was built from the bottom up, with each rectangular layer being constructed starting and ending at the midpoint of the base and in the sequence $A–B–C–D–E–A$ (figure 12). The children were then asked if they could write their own program to produce the same figure.

Several observations about the project are in order:

1. The pyramid was chosen because it could be viewed from a variable perspective (as a "stack" of rectangles of varying base and uniform height); hence its program description can involve a generalized procedure (figure 13).
2. Our order of construction was meant to simplify the interface between successive rectangles by reducing it to a fixed forward displacement (figure 14). The more natural Logo construction of a rectangle would have begun at one of the vertices and would have resulted in a harder, input-dependent interface for centering the successive layers.
3. In constructing the rectangle beginning at the midpoint of the base, the turtle traverses both the full base and half the base of the rectangle. In other words, two

Figure 15 Bill, Elaine, and Robert's perception of the pyramid as a stairway

varying lengths *A B* and *CD* (figure 12) have to be accounted for in the procedure, though they are in a rather obvious relation to each other.

Thus, in giving this activity, our aim was to see whether the children would spontaneously analyze the figure in terms of rectangular building blocks with a varying component and whether they could write a generalized procedure for such a rectangle.

The Children's Solutions

Initial Perceptual Organization of the Task

Three of the children—Bill, Elaine, and Robert—initially perceived the pyramid as comprising a stairway rather than a rectangular stack (figure 15). The stairway was a typical perceptual organization of the figure in terms of primary contour structures, since it avoided any overlap of components. Nevertheless, it had aspects of a procedural analysis because a fixed procedure named STEPS, which produced a stairway, was something the children had written in the past. Thus these children spontaneously connected with concrete procedures that they had already done, even though six months had elapsed in the interim.

The remaining child, Norm, immediately viewed the pyramid as comprising a rectangle of varying "size"

Norm: Make a procedure for this thing [*rectangle*], and we change.

Bill: Remember our STAIRS procedure from last year? We can load it and join the lines.

Norm (ignoring Bill's suggestion):   One problem, the size of the screen.

Bill (pursuing his STAIRS idea and suggesting the plain in action):   I'll do the bottom line, and then we will take turns.

Norm: "No, remember what we did with FLOWERS ? We can do the same, a procedure that changes length . . . it is just rectangle one, rectangle two. We may have to go RT 90, FD 5, RECTANGLE and keep on going like that.

To bring in the concept of variable, the other children were told of Norm's idea of viewing the pyramid as a stack of rectangles, and then they were asked if they could write the program for it.

Some Attempted Solutions

Using a Simple Procedure   Elaine and Robert began by writing a lengthy simple procedure (using only primitives), starting with a rectangle of base 100. In the process they resolved several aspects of the construction such as the number of rectangles (13) and their height and by how much to decrease the base of each successive rectangle (less than 5), given that 100 was chosen as the base of the first one,

Elaine: "We have to minus every time . . . if 10 [*less*] on each side then 20 less for each rectangle. Then 100, 80, 60, 40, 20, 0.

Using REPEAT   To evoke the idea of a variable, Elaine and Robert were asked what was changing in going from one rectangle to the next. They were then reminded of the flowers project and were asked if they could construct the same type of procedure.

Robert: Use REPEAT?

However, the idea was ruled out by Elaine:

Elaine: But they [*the rectangles*] are getting smaller every time.

Norm, on the other hand, tried to incorporate a variable into his plan right from the start. His attempted generalized procedure for a rectangle (with the turtle's initial state at the lower left vertex) was

```
TO RECT :LONG
      REPEAT 4[FD 10 RT 90]
END
```

It seems that Norm wanted to combine the two features of the pyramid, a varying rectangle and a repetition of rectangles. He identified length (of what?) as varying, named the variable LONG, and declared it. He did not, however, operate on the variable within the procedure.

Bill had nearly an identical procedure. Possibly because he remembered that the variable had to appear within the procedure as well, he wrote REPEAT 4[FD 10 RT 90 LONG]. After being questioned about the purpose of LONG inside the REPEAT statement, Bill modified it to FD LONG.

Defining a Fixed Procedure   In his next attempt Bill defined a fixed procedure REC for a 120×10 rectangle. When Norm told him that it is not a procedure that "can change the size," Bill replied, "you can do that in the editor." He then went on to demonstrate his strategy by going into the editor and making several changes that he believed would output a 100×10 rectangle. He seemed to have adopted this strategy as a substitute for the definition of generalized procedures (and this strategy resurfaced several times during the forty subsequent sessions)—namely, that of using the editor to vary a fixed procedure.

After cleaning up his fixed procedure REC (children of that age still have lateralization "bugs" in their programs that are not always picked up as the cause of a production gone awry), Bill returned to the next session with his composed procedure PYRAMID. The procedure called the subprocedures REC 120, REC 110, and so on, even though REC was still a *fixed* procedure. He was puzzled at the error message, "I don't know what to do with 120," and asked Norm for help. Norm tried to bring up the question of a variable:

Norm: Instead of putting LONG, you put 120, 60 and things like that.

Bill: I went from 120 [*for the size of the base*] to 110.

Norm: I'll show you. You put 120, I put LONG.

Bill seemingly assumed that the computer would "understand" the intention of his instructions (Pea 1984 referred to to such notions as "egocentrism bugs"). He would need a lot of individual help before he could sort out some of his misconceptions on the definition and use of generalized procedures.

Defining a Generalized Procedure   Since Elaine and Bill were at a loss of how to go about writing the generalized procedure, they were shown figure 16. Elaine immediately started a (state-transparent) procedure named RECT which included FD :LENGTH to designate the displacements *AB*, *CD*, and *EA* (see figure 12), where LENGTH signified two unequal displacements. When Elaine was asked how the program would run if LENGTH were set at 50, she mentally went through the instructions, saying "go 50 here" at the first instance of LENGTH (displacement *AB*) and "go 100 here" at the second instance (displacement *CD*).

Figure 16 An intervention to assist Bill and Elaine

When asked how it was possible that the value of LENGTH is 50 the first time and 100 the second, she came up with the surprising reply: "You said we can do it so it can *change*." Elaine's reply revealed an unexpected misconception about the notion of a variable in a procedure, namely, the idea that the variable name can be assigned different values *within* the procedure. This may have been reinforced because of her failure to *declare* the variable in the title line. Hence she could not conceptualize how an input is passed on to the commands within the procedure.

After she was reminded about the need to declare the variable LENGTH, and it was explained to her that the turtle will take for LENGTH whatever value it is given initially, she modified the procedure by letting LENGTH signify the shorter displacement *AB* (see figure 12). Interestingly, instead of operating on the variable within the procedure and writing 2 * LENGTH for *CD* (a multiplicative strategy), she used an additive approach and wrote FD :LENGTH, FD :LENGTH.

Having realized that his previous attempt to use REPEAT would not work, Norm wrote, at home, a generalized procedure RECT for a rectangle with a variable named LONG. His procedure was complete, though by choosing the initial turtle state at a vertex, he did not have to deal with the problem of two varying lengths. Bill looked over the procedure with some puzzlement:

Bill: "Where is your size for the rectangle? . . . How long do you want it to be?

Norm: You can put different numbers.

Norm began planning the pyramid "in action." He started with RECT 100 which produced a 100 × 10 rectangle. It was not centered on the screen relative to the "default" home position. Norm then decided to start with a 240 × 10 rectangle and also to have it centered on the screen. To do the centering, he incorporated a *fixed* displacement RT 90 FD 120 LT 90 into the generalized procedure, so as to move the turtle from a vertex to the midbase (see figure 17). After executing RECT :LONG for several values of the variable LONG, he realized that the displacement *AB* is a covariant of LONG. He ended up, just

RT 90 FD 120 LT 90

Figure 17 Norm's incorporation of a *fixed* displacement into the generalized procedure RECT

Figure 18 Elaine's shape

like Elaine, using LONG to signify two unequal lengths. It took one more attempt for Norm, who obviously had an excellent grasp of the sense of a variable, before he got his procedure to work as a proper subprocedure in the pyramid production.

Indexes of Change

Between sessions 15 and 27 the children worked with different generalized procedures, including one for an equilateral triangle. Yet, left to do their own projects, they seemed to be content to define and use fixed procedures only. None of their self-initiated projects beckoned for the use of the variable concept.

In session 28 Elaine was engaged in some activity that was not goal oriented and ended up with the shape shown in figure 18. This led her to the idea of writing a procedure for a hexagon. In doing so, she became the first child who *spontaneously wrote a generalized procedure*. Her procedure was

```
TO STOPSIGN :LENGTH
        REPEAT 6 [FD :LENGTH RT 45]
END
```

Without trying out specific instances of STOPSIGN (which would have alerted her that it did not produce a hexagon), she was triggered by the idea that it might also be possible to vary the number of repetitions (presumably, to produce *N*-gons). She asked if it was possible "to change the number of times it repeats," and with a bit of help, she wrote

Figure 19 Robert's perceptual organization of a house in terms of primary contour structures

```
TO STOPSIGN :LENGTH :TIMES
        REPEAT :TIMES [FD :LENGTH RT 45]
END
```

Elaine then raised a legitimate concern that the variables appeared in the procedure in the reverse order from which they were declared. She decided on her own to switch their order in the title line. She was disappointed with her procedure, since STOPSIGN 6 30 did not even produced a closed figure. She had not yet become aware of the relation between the angle of rotation and the variable TIMES. Nevertheless, her procedure pointed to several breakthroughs. It was the first time that a quantity other than length was parameterized, it was the first extension to a two-variable procedure, and its spontaneous definition pointed to a growing awareness on her part of the potential usefulness of such a procedure.

In the subsequent session (session 29) Robert took up the suggestion of constructing a village with different-size houses, using the generalized procedures SQ for a square and TRIANGLE for an equilateral triangle. His initial program for a house indicated that, once more, the perceptual organization of the figure was in terms of primary contour structures, as shown in figure 19. However, once it was pointed out to him that he could have used the triangle procedure as well, he executed in direct mode the commands SQ 30 FD 30 RT 30 TRIANGLE 30 and then entered in the editor:

```
TO HOUSE :LENGTH :SIZE
        SQ :LENGTH
        FD 30
        RT 30
        TRIANGLE :SIZE
END
```

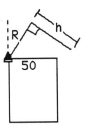

Figure 20 Norm and Bill's triangular roofs

The procedure HOUSE pointed to another conceptual leap, since it was the first instance of a two-variable procedure composed of generalized subprocedures (see figure 1). Even though he always assigned the same value to both variables, he kept it as a two-variable procedure, consistent with the "add on" variable strategy observed with other children. (It is interesting to note that in order to have two variables, Robert changed one of the variable names from LENGTH to SIZE.) The procedure also contained the recurring variable "bug"; part of the interface (FD 30) was left fixed rather than made a covariant.

In a much later session (about session 65) Norm and Bill were constructing a castle which also involved turrets with triangular roofs. The children were getting frustrated by trying to fit a triangle with a right angle at the top vertex on a fixed base. Having unsuccessfully tried several combinations of rotation R and length h (see figure 20), Norm simply defined a generalized utility procedure in two variables:

```
TO TRY :A :L
      RT :A
      FD :L RT 90 FD :L
END
```

This procedure clearly simplified their trial-and-adjustment strategy, and it pointed to the ease with which they defined generalized procedures, including the use of letters for variable names.

A generalized procedure for a regular N-gon, whether of fixed side length or not, is an example of a procedure in which a variable is operated on inside the procedure in a highly nontrivial way. Sessions 45 through 50 involved the construction of the polygon procedure. It was a difficult task for all the children, partly because they lacked some domain-specific knowledge including an oper-

Figure 21 Bill and Robert's parallellogram pattern

ational definition of a regular polygon (e.g., the invariance of the rotation at each vertex) and an understanding of the role of 360. Norm, for example, ended up eventually with a two-variable procedure:

```
TO SIDES :T :ANGLE
        REPEAT :T [LT :ANGLE FD 40]
END
```

One of the specific instances of the procedure that he tried was SIDES 18 360/18 which indicated that he was aware of the connection between the two variables. Nevertheless, like the other children, he seemed to believe that the relation exists "outside" the procedure, that the essence of polygons was the variation of both the number of sides *and* the angle, and that this had to be apparent in the procedure definition. Challenged to come up with a procedure without the variable ANGLE, he first wrote

```
TO SIDES :T :NO
        REPEAT :T [FD 360/:NO FD 40]
END
```

Norm was aware that the two variables had to take the same value, as he specialized to SIDES 7 7 and SIDES 8 8, and so on. However, he only gradually became convinced that he could actually eliminate one of the variables. His attempts also pointed to a growing tendency toward the use of letters to designate variables. His subsequent generalization to include a variable side length was by that time completely routine.

Bill and Robert experienced similar difficulties with their polygon procedure. Once they had completed the procedure POLY :N :L, they were not always clear about what the variable L signified when they specialized with fixed inputs. At times they interpreted L correctly as the length of the sides, though they also thought that L was the angle of turn. During session 50 they began a tesselation project with a basic parallelogram pattern (figure 21).

Their procedure for the figure was named BOX. After completing the fixed composed procedure (which called POLY 3 20 as a subprocedure), they immediately generalized it to BOX :L (which called POLY 3 :L as a subprocedure). This was a new level of specializing; a two-variable procedure was converted to a one-variable procedure by holding one variable fixed. As Uri Leron has pointed out, some first-year undergraduate mathematics students have trouble with this idea when they first meet it in a calculus course!

4   CONCLUDING REMARKS

In this analysis of the concept of variable in Logo, I have focused on only a part of its conceptual field. Even though I have restricted myself to the use of variable in nonrecursive procedures and to the graphics context, it is evident that the concept is rich and multilayered. Its appearance within a programming context means that it is a part of a network of associated concepts, such as procedurality, modularity, and interface, and that it has some computerlike aspects that need to be attended to in order to make it operational. It follows that when we speak of children's understanding of variable, we ought be clearer as to which aspects of variable use we are referring to.

One important conclusion that emerged out of this and others' research findings is that it takes quite a long time for children to begin to exploit the potential of variable as a programming tool. There is a general tendency for children to stick to the safe route of planning in action because they are not, in general, deterred by repeating a long sequence of instructions. Even when children show some fluency in using variables, they seem to lack a spontaneous sense of the *necessity* to define generalized procedures. Both my research and that of Sutherland's reported that children's projects often did not involve variables (nor procedures, for that matter), so their work with variable tended to be initiated by the teacher.

The role of the teacher in introducing and maintaining work with generalized procedures is therefore central to the concept of variable. The concept needs to be fostered by a selection of well-thought-out activities. The conceptual analysis of this chapter points to the necessity of delineating the different issues of variable use. A retrospective look at the choice of activities reveals that the variable work sometimes got bogged down by unintentionally complicated interfacing (as in the case of generalizing an inappropriate procedure for a task at hand). In other instances variable use was completely avoided by the children simply because a given figure was not easily perceived as being made up of components with a varying part. While such issues are part of the variable story, they need not be confronted at the outset of the process of making sense of a variable. For example, it seems that initial work with generalized procedures can be enhanced by projects in which the basic varying components were nonoverlapping (e.g., a pyramid made up of a stack of rectangles).

It is clear that length is the most natural component for children to parameterize. Since children tend to have more difficulty with rotation, and in particular with the relation between rotation and a constructed angle, they seldom use angle as a variable. Nevertheless, children ought to be introduced to a wider range of situations to generalize. For example, Sutherland reports work with the use of a variable scaling factor. Aside from providing another experience of variable work, the scaling factor also touches on issues relating to similarity of figures and the use of fractional numbers.

Children's conception of a variable such as LENGTH or TIMES is likely that of a generalized number. The observed tendency of children to add on variables reveals undeveloped functional thinking about variables. It would be a missed opportunity if no attempts were made to link children's work with variables to that of functions, by having them write an explicit expression of a covariant as a function. By helping children to make such linkage, Logo becomes a truly meaningful environment for algebraic thinking.

REFERENCES

Hillel, J. 1986. Procedural thinking by children aged 8–12 using turtle geometry. *Proceedings of the Tenth International Conference for the Psychology of Mathematics Education*, London, pp. 433–438.

Hillel, J. 1987. So they know about polygons? *Micromath* 3(2): 18–23.

Hoyles, C. 1987. Tools for learning: Insights for the mathematics educator from a Logo programming environment. *For the Learning of Mathematics* 7(2): 32–37.

Kieran, C., and Hillel, J. 1990. "It's tough when you want to make the triangles angle": Insights from a computer based geometry. *Journal of Mathematical Behaviour* 9(2): 99–127.

Leron, U. 1983. Some problems in children's logo learning. *Proceedings of the Seventh International Conference for the Psychology of Mathematics Education*, Israel, pp. 346–351.

Noss, R. and Hoyles, C. 1987. Structuring the mathematics environment: The dialectic of process and content. *Proceedings of the Third International Conference for Logo and Mathematics Education*. Montreal, pp. 27–39.

Papert, S. 1980. *Mindstorms*. New York: Basic Books.

Pea, R. 1984. Language-independent conceptual "bugs" in novice programming. Technical Report No. 31, Bank Street College of Education.

Sutherland, R. 1987. What are the links between variable in Logo and variable in algebra? *Recherches en Didactique des Mathématiques* 8(1.2): 103–129.

Vergnaud, G. 1982. Cognitive and developmental psychology research on mathematics education: Some theoretical and methodological issues. *For the Learning of Mathematics* 3(2): 31–41.

Vurpillot, E. 1972. *The Visual World of the Child.* New York: International Universities Press.

What Is Algebraic about Programming in Logo?

2

Rosamund Sutherland

1 INTRODUCTION

At the very heart of algebra practice is a paradox. Suspension of referential meaning is what gives algebra its power, but suspension of meaning with no awareness of the constraints of the system is what turns algebra into a meaningless activity for pupils. There are many challenges that face the algebra teacher, and assisting pupils to overcome this paradox is one of them. In turtle geometry pupils are able to keep in mind the constraints of the geometrical system while operating on the variables within the more abstract Logo procedure. Pupils can choose to manipulate the formal Logo procedure or to descend into the geometrical meaning behind the Logo formalism. The interactive nature of the Logo language allows for continual passages between formalism and meaning and this, I suggest, is the heart of the algebraic potential within Logo.

In this chapter I describe how certain experiences of Logo programming can help pupils begin to develop a more algebraic approach to problem solving. In particular I discuss how the Logo environment provides a structure that helps pupils discriminate between what is variable and what is invariant within a mathematical problem. The chapter derives predominantly from a three-year longitudinal study (Sutherland 1988) which was part of and an extension to the Logo Maths Project (Hoyles and Sutherland 1989). It is also influenced by subsequent work carried out with a class of twelve to thirteen-year-olds as part of the "Peer Group Discussion in a Computer Environment Project."[1]

2 BACKGROUND

There are essentially two polarized views about what constitutes school algebra. One gives priority to the manipulation of variables, usually in the context of

---

1. This project was carried out by the author in conjunction with Celia Hoyles and Lulu Healy and funded by the Leverhulme Trust. One of the aims of the project was to investigate the relationship between pupils' negotiation of a generalization in natural language and their formal representation of this method.

solving equations. The other prioritizes the expressing of generality, with abstract symbolism playing a minor role. Much of the existing research on pupils' difficulties within school algebra has focused on their use and understanding of variables, an emphasis that is reflected in the following statement: "When pressed to define algebra we might say that algebra has to do with the understanding of variables and their operations and we consider students to be solving algebra when they first encounter variables" (Usiskin 1988). Research suggests that many pupils have difficulty in understanding that a letter can represent a range of values (Booth 1984; Collis 1974; Küchemann 1981) and do not accept that different letters can represent the same value (Wagner 1981). They find it difficult to accept as an entity an "unclosed" expression in algebra (e.g., $a + 6$) that relates to their difficulty in operating on these expressions (Booth 1984; Collis 1974). They also find it difficult to understand that a systematic relationship exists between two variable-dependent expressions (Küchemann 1981). There appears to be an implicit assumption within this work that misconceptions associated with the use of variable are obstacles to developing an algebraic approach to problem solving.

Although the research within traditional algebra has highlighted pupils' difficulties with operating on variables, it appears that pupils can more readily accept these as objects within a Logo programming context. Studies have indicated that pupils can perceive a variable in Logo as representing a range of numbers (Noss 1986; Sutherland 1989). Within a Logo environment they do not have difficulty in accepting that any variable name can be used and that different names could represent the same value. They are also able to accept lack of closure in a variable-dependent expression (Sutherland 1989). However, these studies show clearly that understandings developed are closely related to the specific Logo experiences in which the pupils engage.

There is now substantial evidence that there is not a simple transition for pupils from an arithmetical to a more algebraic approach to problem solving. Filloy and Rojano point to the "existence of a didactic cut along the child's evolutionary line of thought from arithmetic to algebra." This cut corresponds to the major changes that took place in the history of symbolic algebra in connection with the conception of the "unknown" and the possibility of "operating on the unknown" (Filloy and Rojano 1989, p. 20). Others (Harper 1987; Herscovitz 1989) also relate pupils' difficulties to the historical development of algebra. When we turn to the computer programming context, we find that a similar barrier to using algebraic ideas seems to exist (Hillel 1990; Samurçay 1986;

Sutherland 1988). How these barriers can be overcome is the focus of the first part of this chapter.

3 MOVING FROM ARITHMETICAL TO ALGEBRAIC THINKING

At the beginning of the Logo Maths Project,[2] pupils were given the freedom to devise their own goals in order to build up self-confidence and autonomy, with an emphasis on pupils actively constructing their own knowledge. The aim was to make teaching interventions related to the idea of using variable within the pupils' own projects. After the first year of the project, it was found that the pupils (aged eleven to twelve at this stage) did not choose goals for which the idea of variable was an appropriate problem-solving tool. I am suggesting that these pupils, who at this point had had no previous experience of the interrelated ideas of formalizing and generalizing in either algebra or Logo, were not able to conceive of these ideas within a programming context. This was not necessarily the case for other mathematical ideas; for example, it would have been possible to introduce ideas of angle within the pupils' own chosen goals. Making mathematical generalizations was not a problem-solving strategy used by these pupils, and this supports the view that there is a gap between arithmetical and algebraic thinking (Filloy and Rojano 1989).

As a result of these findings teacher-devised tasks were developed that provoked pupils to use variables in Logo. One such task involved the pupils in scaling all the distance commands within a fixed turtle graphics procedure (figure 1). When pupils first engaged in this task, they necessarily did so in a rote manner, although this rote engagement confronted them with visual evidence that changing the value of a variable affects the overall size of the geometrical object produced. Progressively pupils began to develop their understanding of variable to the point where they became aware that a relationship exists between the component parts of a general geometrical object and that the way the variables are used affects this relationship. To illustrate this, I present an example taken from

---

2. Within the Logo Maths Project, one class of "mixed-ability" secondary school pupils (aged 11–14) worked on Logo during their "normal" mathematics lessons. Two computers were placed in the classroom, with pupils taking turns in pairs to work on the computer—each pair having approximately twenty hours of "hands on" Logo time during each of the three school years of the project. The data collected included video recordings of four case study pupils' interactions with the computer together with recordings of all their spoken interaction. These recordings were all transcribed.

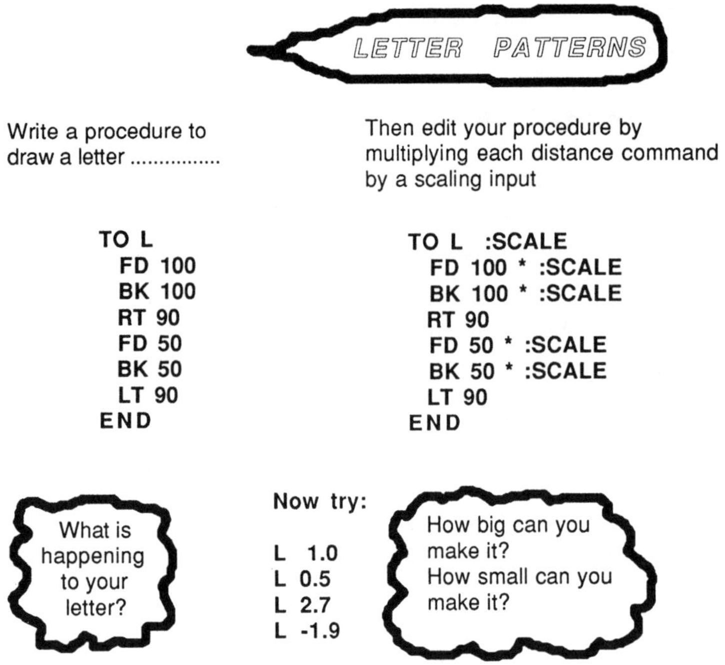

LETTER PATTERNS

Write a procedure to
draw a letter ....

Then edit your procedure by
multiplying each distance command
by a scaling input

```
TO L
    FD 100
    BK 100
    RT 90
    FD 50
    BK 50
    LT 90
END
```

```
TO L  :SCALE
    FD 100 * :SCALE
    BK 100 * :SCALE
    RT 90
    FD 50 * :SCALE
    BK 50 * :SCALE
    LT 90
END
```

What is
happening
to your
letter?

Now try:

L 1.0
L 0.5
L 2.7
L -1.9

How big can you
make it?
How small can you
make it?

Figure 1 General letter task: variable as scale factor

two case study pupils, Amanda and Shahidur (aged twelve to thirteen), who
were both poor achievers in school mathematics. They had never been introduced to algebraic ideas and were not likely to be introduced to algebra within
their secondary school mathematics curriculum.[3] This example is presented in
detail because it illustrates a number of important threads in the development of
an algebraic approach to problem solving.

Amanda and Shahidur were initially unable to accept the idea of a symbol
representing an unknown number. As they began to use symbols in Logo, they
came to accept these new objects, although one barrier was their restricted
understanding of decimal numbers. Initially they perceived a decimal as consisting of two fragmented parts; eventually, through their use of decimals in Logo,
they came to see a decimal as a "whole" object. They began to accept the idea of
using a variable to write a general procedure in Logo in order to produce

3. This curriculum was SMILE (Secondary Mathematics Independent Learning Experiment).

different-size images on the screen. We describe next some of the critical stages in Shahidur and Amanda's developing use and understanding of algebraic ideas.

Using the Unknown

Shahidur and Amanda were introduced to the idea of variable as scale factor in their eighth Logo session, when they were twelve years old. They were presented with the scaling letter task (figure 1), and Amanda's initial reaction to the task suggests that she was unable (at this point) to accept the idea of a variable as representing an unknown number.

Amanda: How can you do that if you don't know the number?

Teacher: Well when you run the program you put a number in and SCALE becomes the number you tell it.

The subsequent response from Amanda was an exclamation of surprise.

Amanda: You can pick any number you want!

Amanda and Shahidur were shown how to define a scaled *L* procedure (figure 1). They tried out their procedure with inputs of 5, 1.0 , 0.1, 0.01, and 9.9, having been specifically encouraged to draw the smallest and largest possible *L*. When Amanda suggested using an input of 8.8, Shahidur's response indicated that he interpreted the decimal input 8.8 to be a code in which the first 8 affected the size of the vertical part of the *L* and the second 8 affected the size of the horizontal part of the *L*.

Shahidur: You can't have 8.8 'cos it will be the same size . . . this way should be smaller.

They next tried an input of 4.2, and Amanda's comment indicated that she also had a fragmented view of decimals:

Amanda: Well we can make it bigger except it wouldn't look right . . . that's supposed to be shorter than that, and it would look too long.

Although they held this misunderstanding about decimals, they were beginning to accept the idea that changing the size of the variable somehow changes the size of the geometrical object, as illustrated within the following interchange:

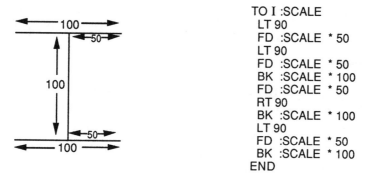

```
TO I :SCALE
LT 90
FD :SCALE * 50
LT 90
FD :SCALE * 50
BK :SCALE * 100
FD :SCALE * 50
RT 90
BK :SCALE * 100
LT 90
FD :SCALE * 50
BK :SCALE * 100
END
```

Figure 2 Shahidur and Amanda: general *I* procedure

Teacher: What does the scale do?

Amanda: It makes it go bigger or smaller.

Amanda and Shahidur then initiated the idea of writing a procedure for a variable-size letter *I*, asking the teacher for support.

Amanda: Miss you know on the *I* . . . will I put SCALE?

Within the Logo environment they were beginning to accept the idea of a variable representing an unknown number. They started by defining a fixed *I* procedure and then with help modified this to become a scaled *I* procedure (figure 2).

They negotiated the value of the input for their *I* procedure, still appearing to be confused about the effect of the decimal "code":

Shahidur: Now try 0.01

Amanda: No this side has to be bigger than that one . . . 1.0 . . . no . . . 0.10 . . . where would you say . . .

The height of the fixed *L* procedure had been 40, whereas the height of the fixed *I* procedure was 100 (figure 2). This turned out to be critical in provoking them to reflect on the processes within their scaled procedure because, when they tried an input of 4.2 to the general *I* procedure, the image drawn was much larger than they had expected (the height of their *I* was 4.2 timcs 100, and the height of their letter *L* was 4.2 times 40).

Amanda next reduced the input of 4.2 in their general *I* procedure to 1.1, and it seems that this relates approximately (even if inaccurately) to the relationship

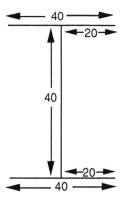

Figure 3 Shahidur and Amanda: modified figure for general *I*

between 100 and 40. She was beginning to reflect on the effect of the variable input within her scaled procedure, the first step in realizing that "any number you want" has some constraints.

At the beginning of their third session of using variable in Logo, Amanda and Shahidur used their scaled *L* and *I* procedures again. The most important aspects of this session were as follows:

1.   Discussion between Amanda and Shahidur indicating that they were still confused about decimal. "*No, it was 0.01 but that only made a line this way and it didn't make a line this way did it,*" and, "*Yeah, Miss, but it can't go that way because you know we haven't done a number for this way . . . we just done a number for this way.*"
2.   Teacher intervention, which used the visual computer feedback to confront Amanda and Shahidur with their misconception about decimals.
3.   Conflict, caused by the same input to the *I* and the *L* procedures producing different sized letters.

The critical intervention within this session was the suggestion by the teacher that they modify their *I* procedure (figure 2) so that identical input to the *I* procedure and the *L* procedure would produce letters of the same height. This encouraged them to reflect again on the processes within both of their procedures and to focus more precisely on the operations on the variable within these procedures. They successfully modified their *I* procedure by changing all the 50s to 20s and all the 100s to 40s (see figure 3).

Their view of a decimal being composed of two parts reappeared again in their fourth session of using variables in Logo. However, when they tried an input of 1.5 to their *I* procedure, the computer response provoked Shahidur into shifting his view.

Shahidur: Miss, you know 1.5 . . . is it 60 that way and that way?

They were beginning to understand that the input of 1.5 multiplied the 40 in both the vertical and horizontal components of the *I*. It was the feedback from the computer that provided important structure in this developing understanding.

By the end of these four sessions Shahidur and Amanda had begun to think of a decimal as a whole and had started to use a variable in Logo to represent a range of numbers (which included decimals). They had also written a general procedure to draw the letter E without any support from the teacher. The interaction with the computer was crucial in helping them come to this understanding of a decimal. Their emerging misunderstanding about decimals highlights the crucial link between the notion of variable and the numbers that the variable represents. Douady has suggested that mathematical concepts are first viewed as tools in order to make sense of new situations and then later as mathematical objects of further study (Douady 1985). Before pupils can use a variable as a tool for solving a specific problem, they need first to accept a decimal as a new mathematical object. I suggest that this process continues as a chain, so pupils need to accept the idea of a variable as an object before they can create for example $x + 5$ as a new mathematical tool.

Initially identical inputs to the general *I* and *L* procedures did not produce identical size letters on the screen. This feedback provided Shahidur and Amanda with considerable conflict and provoked them into reflecting on the processes within their two general procedures. They then began to realize that there was some relationship between the formal Logo commands (e.g., FD :SCALE ∗ 50) and the geometrical object produced on the screen. This problem evolved from the pupils' own work but would seem to offer potential if it were developed as a teacher-designed task.

The substantial support from the teacher, both in the form of providing an initial teacher-directed task (the *L* task) and in the form of interventions throughout the session, appears to have been critical. Without this support it is unlikely that Shahidur and Amanda would have reached the point where they could write a general E procedure on their own. It seems to be the use of variable in the programming context that is the critical factor in developing an acceptance and beginning understanding of the idea. In this respect the variable is used

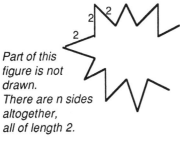

Part of this
figure is not
drawn.
There are n sides
altogether,
all of length 2.

Write down the perimeter

p = ...

Figure 4 Algebra interview question (from Küchmann 1981)

initially as a tool to solve a specific problem. Ultimately the aim is for this new tool to become an object of algebraic thinking.

Some further evidence that Shahidur had begun to understand that a variable in Logo represents a range of numbers was provided by the results of an algebra paper-and-pencil test that was given to the eight case study pupils at the end of the Logo Maths project[4] (there are no results for Amanda because she left the school in the middle of the project). In particular, when presented with a question (figure 4) that involved operating on a "letter as generalized number" (Küchemann 1981), Shahidur gave a correct response of $2 \times n$, and when asked to give a reason, he said "cos the size of them are 2 . . . and there are n of them . . . , so 2 times n will be the answer." This response seems remarkable considering that he had had no other experience of algebra than that which he obtained through his Logo work.

Of the eight case study pupils who were tested, six accepted the idea that a variable in algebra represents a range of numbers. It seems that this can be attributed to their Logo experiences if one takes into account the widely reported result that pupils normally have difficulty in accepting the idea that a variable represents a range of numbers in algebra (Küchemann 1981).

---

4. As part of a study focusing on the development of pupils' algebraic thinking in a Logo environment (Sutherland 1988) eight case study pupils were presented with items from the CSMS study (Küchemann 1981) in the form of a structured interview in order to probe whether or not they had made any links to a paper-and-pencil algebra context. Four of the eight case study pupils had never carried out any algebra work as part of their "normal" mathematics lessons.

Operating on the Unknown

Using a variable as a scale factor can provide an entry point into the use of algebraic ideas, but Filloy and Rojano maintain that it is only when pupils begin to operate on the unknown that they have made the break between arithmetic and algebraic thinking. Four out of the eight case study pupils who were part of the Logo Maths Project could confidently operate on an unknown variable within a Logo procedure (e.g., see figure 7). We had, however, been cautious about how and when we introduced the idea of variable to these pupils. We were considerably influenced by the fact that the teachers with whom we were working felt very strongly that algebra-related ideas were difficult. Subsequently a study with eight primary school pupils (aged ten to eleven) indicated that pupils with no experience of paper-and-pencil algebra could use the idea of operating on a variable within a procedure (Sutherland 1988). The realization that many of these ten to eleven-year-olds were using variable in a way that was more sophisticated than the thirteen to fourteen-year-olds of the Logo Maths Project provided evidence that being able to operate on a variable within a procedure is not inherently age related. This also influenced the way in which we introduced pupils to variable within the "Peer Group Discussion in a Computer Environment Project" (Healy, Hoyles, and Sutherland 1989). Working with twelve to thirteen-year-olds, we devised a task in which pupils were introduced to the idea of variable in the context of making a simple "multiplying by 2" relationship explicit (figure 5).

After working on this task, pupils were encouraged to extend the task to draw other letters involving other relationships. These pupils sometimes worked on teacher-devised tasks and sometimes chose their own goals. Within this group of twenty-four pupils, sixteen could confidently operate on a variable within a Logo procedure in order to make a geometrical relationship explicit. After working on the initial teacher-devised tasks, the majority of pupils initiated the idea of operating on a variable within their own project, as illustrated by the procedure PIPPY shown in figure 6.

The work on this project suggests that pupils' ability to operate confidently on variables within a procedure is more likely to be associated with the way in which they were introduced to variable than with any cognitive obstacles. In an experiment in which pupils were asked to construct a general procedure, Noss and Hoyles reported that some pupils, who were in many respects competent

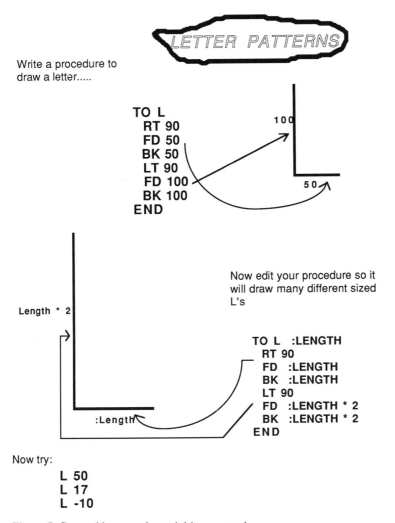

Write a procedure to
draw a letter.....

```
TO L
  RT 90
  FD 50
  BK 50
  LT 90
  FD 100
  BK 100
END
```

Now edit your procedure so it
will draw many different sized
L's

```
TO L  :LENGTH
  RT 90
  FD  :LENGTH
  BK  :LENGTH
  LT 90
  FD  :LENGTH * 2
  BK  :LENGTH * 2
END
```

Now try:

```
L 50
L 17
L -10
```

Figure 5 General letter task: variable operated on

PIPPY 2

PIPPY 1

PIPPY 1.5

```
TO PIPPY  :S
  FACE :S
  MIDDLE 1  :S * 45
  NOSE  :S/2
  MIDDLE  :S * 5
  MUSH  :S/2
  MIDDLE3  :S * 45
  GIJOE  :S/2
  MIDDLE4  :S * 25
  GOGEYES  :S/2
END


TO FACE :S
  REPEAT 180 [FD  :S  RT 2]
END


TO NOSE :S
  REPEAT 135 [FD  :S RT 2]
END


TO MUSH  :S
  REPEAT 30 [FD  :S RT 2]
END


TO GIJOE  :S
  LT 90
  REPEAT 36 [FD  :S RT 10]
END


TO GOGEYES  :S
  LT 90
  REPEAT 36 [FD  :S RT 10]
END
```

```
TO MIDDLE1  :S
  RT 90
  PU
  FD  :S
  PD
END


TO MIDDLE2  :S
  PU
  BK  :S
  PD
  LT 90
END


TO MIDDLE3  :S
  PU
  HOME
  RT 90
  FD  :S
  PD
END


TO MIDDLE3  :S
  PU
  HOME
  RT 90
  FD  :S
  PD
END


TO MIDDLE4  :S
  LT 90
  PU
  FD  :S
  PD
END
```

Figure 6 General procedure PIPPY

Logo programmers with many hours of Logo programming experience, kept adding on unrelated variables within their procedure definition (Noss and Hoyles 1988). If we look at these pupils' first experiences of using variable (Noss 1985), it seems that using variables to make certain relationships explicit was not a focus within their early experience of variable in Logo.

It appears that most pupils cannot begin to use algebraic ideas in the Logo environment without substantial support from the teacher. This support needs to be in the form of both teacher-devised tasks and specific interventions that provoke pupils to begin to discriminate between the variables and invariants within a problem. Ultimately we want pupils to operate on a variable within a procedure in order to make a relationship explicit, but for some pupils, being introduced to variable as scale factor may help them develop an understanding that a relationship exists between the component parts of a geometrical object. Critical stages in the development toward an algebraic approach to problem solving in Logo are

1.   understanding that a variable can be used to affect the overall size of the geometrical object produced,
2.   understanding that a variable can be used to represent a range of numbers,
3.   relating the effect of assigning different values of a variable to a change in the geometrical object produced,
4.   recognizing that a relationship exists between the component parts of a geometrical object and that the way the variables are used within a procedure affects this relationship,
5.   identifying the relationship between the component parts of a geometrical object and making this explicit within a Logo procedure.

Once pupils have accepted the idea of a variable as representing a range of numbers, accepting the idea of an unclosed variable-dependent expression is not such a difficult step. It is important for pupils to accept that expessions like $3x + 4$ are objects, and previous algebra research (Booth 1984; Collis 1974) has suggested that this often presents pupils with difficulties. Five of the eight longitudinal case study pupils for the Logo Maths Project (Sutherland 1988) accepted lack of closure within the algebra context of the structured interview administered to the pupils at the end of the project. This is more than would have been expected given their experience of paper-and-pencil algebra and suggests that certain Logo experiences can help pupils accept unclosed algebraic expressions.

Using Logo to Negotiate the General

In algebra pupils often use informal methods that cannot easily be generalized and formalized. "If children do not have that structure available in the arithmetic case, they are unlikely to produce (or understand) it in the algebra case" (Booth 1984, p. 102). The Logo environment enables pupils to interact with the computer and negotiate with their peers so that their intuitive understanding of pattern and structure is developed to the point where they can begin to discriminate between the variables and invariants within a problem. The algebraic process involves both identifying the mathematical relationships within a problem and making these relationships explicit with a formal language.

Importance of the Naming of the Variables to Be Used

There is evidence that naming and declaring the variables in the title line of a procedure helps pupils come to terms with what is variable and what is invariant within a problem: The naming of the variable seems to provide a structure to the generalizing process. In Logo pupils sometimes start by naming too many variables (Hoyles 1987; Sutherland 1988). As pupils proceed through the procedure definition process, and begin to make relationships between variables explicit within their procedure, they may decide to remove variables from the title line.

An example of this is provided by a situation in which two pupils, Sally and Janet, were presented with an arrowhead task (figure 7a) (reported in Hoyles and Sutherland 1989). After drawing the shape in direct mode, they began to define a general procedure. Janet immediately suggested that they use three inputs. She analyzed the shape into three varying parts and at this stage was not concerned with the interrelationship between the parts. Janet chose the variable names JACK, JOHN, and JILL and used them to signify the component parts of the arrowhead.

Janet: All right, now for this we need . . . we work it out 'cos that will have to be something called JACK . . . that JOHN and that JILL . . . if you get what I mean . . .

They typed the following Logo command into the computer:

TO HILL :JACK :JOHN :JILL

As they continued to define their Logo procedure, they realized that they wanted to make the relationships among JACK, JOHN, and JILL explicit. They ultia)

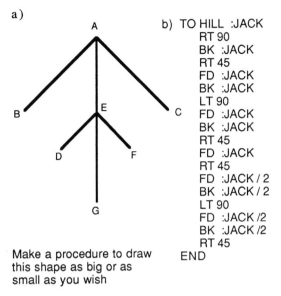

b) TO HILL :JACK
   RT 90
   BK :JACK
   RT 45
   FD :JACK
   BK :JACK
   LT 90
   FD :JACK
   BK :JACK
   RT 45
   FD :JACK
   RT 45
   FD :JACK / 2
   BK :JACK / 2
   LT 90
   FD :JACK /2
   BK :JACK /2
   RT 45
   END

Make a procedure to draw
this shape as big or as
small as you wish

Figure 7 Sally and Janet: the arrowhead task

mately removed JOHN and JILL from the title line of their procedure (figure 7b).

Another example of the importance of naming the variable is provided by Syreeta and Juliana while they worked on a general procedure to draw proportional heads:

Syreeta: OK, let's go, make this one be the size, all right . . . they're going to be called SIZE, aren't they . . . right, so we're going to work out the different sizes . . . what's SIZE divided by 2?

In using the Logo language to name the procedure as well as the variable inputs to the procedure, pupils structure the problem for themselves. Thus they are able to continue to discuss what is varying and what is invariant within their procedure. This is related to Hillel's discussion of the need for pupils to identify what is varying (Hillel, chapter 1 in this volume).

In Logo pupils have direct evidence, by changing the name within a general procedure, that the name of the variable does not affect the meaning associated with the name. This is another critical aspect of understanding the constraints on the variable name, and it relates to the development of a more substantial understanding of the idea of variable. It has been found that if pupils are encouraged to use a range of variable names, including nonsense names (which they know have no meaning), then they are more likely to accept single letter names for their paper-and-pencil algebra work.

Variable Names Play a Critical Role in the Negotiation Of the General

We now have enough evidence that for many pupils Logo formalism is not grafted on to an existing problem solution and that the discussion in natural language and intermediate interaction with the computer play crucially interacting roles in the evolution of a formal Logo procedure. Continuing analysis of this process was part of the Peer Group Discussion in a Computer Environment Project (Healy, Hoyles, and Sutherland 1990). The following discussion taken from a transcript of Sally and Janet working on the arrowhead task (figure 2.7) illustrates this point:

Janet: But I don't know how we're going to do it . . . we can get rid of JILL.

Sally: I don't know we never done it, did we . . . JACK divided by 2 . . . is it divided first . . . or what . . .

Janet: FD divide JACK . . . divide by JILL

Sally: No . . . right, so we want it to go forward by half of JACK . . . so would that be JILL . . .

Janet: Yeah I know . . . but just forget about JILL for the moment . . . how do we do it . . .

Pupils sometimes need to refer to the meaning behind their variable names (e.g., *"so we want it to go forward by half of JACK . . . so that would be JILL . . . "*) and sometimes operate on the variables without recourse to any referential meaning (*"JACK divided by 2 . . . is it divided first . . . or what . . . "*). As I have already implied, this possibility of using the variable name to allow slipage between multiple meanings is what I believe makes Logo an inherently algebraic activity.

4 CONCLUSION

Logo experiences cannot help pupils develop a more algebraic approach to problem solving until they begin to devise problems in Logo in which the idea of variable is an essential problem-solving tool. Not only does the Logo environment help pupils move toward this algebraic approach, but it also provides a structure for supporting pupils in identifying the constraints of a mathematical system. Here it seems that the naming and manipulating of the variable is important. Within the Logo environment it is possible to suspend referential meaning by manipulating the Logo procedure or give meaning to the manipulations by referring to the geometrical objects on the screen.

Perhaps the most important result from our work is that the algebraic understandings that pupils develop are closely related to the particular computer environment and the types of problem situations with which pupils have been engaging. This means that the role of the teacher is crucial in providing pupils with problems that develop their algebraic understanding and with information about the constraints on using these algebraic ideas within the relevant programming context. We are continuing to work in this area (Sutherland 1990), with the aim of integrating computer-based activities with paper-based activities.

Although Logo experiences do appear to enhance pupils' understanding of variable in an algebra context, it may be that these local understandings of variable are not as critical to developing algebraic thinking as mathematics educators have previously implied. In other words, algebraic thinking is not merely concerned with the understanding of variable but has more to do with accepting and using abstract algebraic symbols in the context of mathematical problem solving. I suggest that once the barrier to the use and understanding of algebraic symbols has been overcome through Logo activities, pupils will have transcended the most difficult obstacle to the use and understanding of algebraic ideas in a paper-and-pencil context.

REFERENCES

Booth, L. 1984. *Algebra: Children's Strategies and Errors*. Windsor: NFER-Nelson.

Collis, K. F. 1974. Cognitive development and mathematics learning. Paper prepared for *Psychology of Mathematics Education Workshop*, Centre for Science Education. Chelsea College, London, 28 June.

Douady, R. 1985. The interplay between different settings, tool object dialectic in the extension of mathematical ability. *Proceedings of the Ninth International Conference for the Psychology of Mathematics Education*. The Netherlands.

Filloy, E., and Rojano, T. 1989. Solving equations: The transition from arithmetic to algebra. *For the Learning of Mathematics* 9(2): 19–25.

Harper, E. 1987. Ghosts of Diophantus. *Educational Studies in Mathematics* 18: 75–90.

Healy, L., Hoyles, C., and Sutherland, R. 1990. Pupil discussion in a computer environment. Final Report to Leverhulme Trust. Institute of Education, University of London.

Herscovitz, N. 1989. Cognitive obstacles encountered in the learning of algebra. In S. Wagner and C. Kieran, *Research Issues in the Learning and Teaching of Algebra*, Erlbaum.

Hoyles, C. 1987. Tools for learning: Insights for the mathematics educator from a Logo programming environment. *For the Learning of Mathematics* 7(2): 32–37.

Hoyles, C., and Sutherland, R. 1989. *Logo Mathematics in the Classroom*. London: Routledge.

Küchemann, D. E., 1981. Algebra In K. Hart, ed., *Children's Understanding of Mathematics*. London: Murray, pp. 11–16.

Noss, R. 1985. *Creating a Mathematical Environment through Programming: A Study of Young Children Learning Logo*. Ph.D thesis. Published by Institute of Education, University of London.

Noss, R. 1986. Constructing a conceptual framework for elementary algebra through Logo programming. *Educational Studies in Mathematics* 17(4): 335–357.

Noss, R., and Hoyles, C. 1988. The computer as a mediating influence in the development of pupils' conception of variable. *European Journal of Psychology of Education* 3(3): 271–286.

Samurçay, R. 1986. Signification et fonctionnement du concept de variable informatique chez des éleves debutants. *Educational Studies in Mathematics* 16: 143–161.

Sutherland, R. 1988. A longitudinal study of the development of pupils' algebraic thinking in a Logo environment. Unpublished doctoral thesis. Institute of Education, University of London.

Sutherland, R. 1989. Providing a computer-based framework for algebraic thinking. *Educational Studies in Mathematics* 20(3): 317–344.

Sutherland, R. 1990. The gap between arithmetical and algebraic thinking: Computer effects. *Economic and Social Research Council*. Institute of Education University of London.

Usiskin, Z. 1988. Conceptions of school algebra and uses of variables. In: A. F. Coxford (ed.), *The Ideas of Algebra, K–12*. 1988 Yearbook.

Wagner, S. 1981. Conservation of equation and function under transformations of variable. *Journal for Research in Mathematics Education* 12 (2): 107–118.

Conceptually Defined Turtles   *3*

Herbert Loethe

1 INTRODUCTION

Having pupils work with turtle graphics can be done with very different aims in mind. In this chapter I concentrate only on work in geometrical contexts and pursue objectives that are related to geometry. This work becomes feasible by mapping geometrical concepts onto appropriately defined variations of the turtle. In section 2 I explain what I mean by the term *conceptually defined* and outline the consequences of this use of Logo for mathematics education. In the subsequent four sections I deal with four different turtles, or turtles with special equipment:

1. true turtles,
2. turtles with direction and distance finders,
3. space turtles,
4. space turtles with direction, dip, and distance finders.

Each concept is explained by using some examples. Then I report briefly on the work done with it in our Logo project. The project's basis was our experience with several isolated instances of Logo teaching, units of Logo work as part of regular school subjects and special interest groups of pupils (mainly aged ten years and older) over the past decade. These activities and materials have formed part of our teacher education courses on the "didactics of informatics" and have been reflected upon, enriched, and revised several times, resulting in a concise framework for teaching by manipulating learning environments. One of the characteristics of our project is the embedding of all experimental teaching in school in teacher education.

The following sections present this material in a didactically ordered way under the headings of the four different turtle concepts listed above. The related didactical models are described and examples are given, with the aim that the reader can easily make use of the presented material. In this top–down approach to presentation, it is very difficult to cite results on individual learning during the experimental work in a specific and precise way, since only parts of the whole development have been influenced by these results.

The term *didactical model* might need some comment. Teaching—at least in the German school tradition—always means developing concepts and insights by offering questions for discussion (never lecturing or reading a textbook together). This implies that teachers need to know how to introduce, intervene, or recap any part of the subject matter. Since there are usually several didactical approaches available, they have to decide and then guide the classroom work in a concise and systematic way according to the chosen model. In the case of practical work involving pupils at the computer, it is extremely important that the introduction and the recap are based on a well-developed didactical model. The learners only take advantage of their active and self-determined work at the computer if the teacher is able to help in defining higher levels of concepts and in allowing the possibility of starting the work again on these new levels.

It is not the task of this chapter to describe the implementation of the different turtles. In some cases it is reasonably obvious and trivial; for others, it is done elsewhere (see Abelson and diSessa 1980; Loethe, Woelpert, and Wolpert 1985; Reggini 1985; Loethe 1992).

2 BACKGROUND

The "classical" turtle, as defined by Seymour Papert, is a didactical simplification of a mathematical idea that grew out of the problem of the local description of curves using the kinematic image of a curve as a moving point. I trace the well-known metamorphosis of the idea of "localness" from physics to a didactical concept, in order to have a crystal clear example for further discussion. The roots of this mathematical idea may lie in Newton's mechanics. A geometrical mathematization was made in the nineteenth century by Frédéric Frenet and Gaston Darboux of the French school, and it is nowadays part of every differential geometry course. But in such courses the core idea is always there, often hidden by a mass of coordinate-related calculations.

The idea of localness suggests that the next step in a movement can be described in a natural way relative to the present state. A simplified version for learners that concretely conveys this idea involves an anthropomorphic model that can easily be grasped by using two fundamental actions in sequential order: "go straight on" and "turn around yourself."

The concretization as a drawing robot becomes productive for problem solving because of the accessibility of a body syntonic representation and the possibility of using computer graphics without thinking in terms of absolute coordinates (or computer functions). The Logo primitives for these actions are (usually) pairs of commands: FORWARD/BACK and RIGHT/LEFT. Using these pairs instead of only one command avoids the need for thinking in terms of angle and line orientation.

Logo systems usually extend the graphics vocabulary by adding (1) the heading commands HEADING, SETHEADING, (2) the coordinate commands POS (for position) and SETPOS, and (3) a combined heading–coordinate command TOWARDS. General experience shows that these commands are not accepted by children as part of their work as easily as FORWARD and RIGHT. For example, pupils solving problems by themselves very seldom use the TOWARDS command. The use of commands based on cartesian coordinates is more frequent since such commands are strongly motivated by school mathematical activities. Unfortunately, an unreflective use of turtle and coordinate commands usually ends up with an awful mixture of local and global geometrical descriptions that is nontransparent and usually cannot be used as building blocks for further work.

As a consequence of such experiences, I feel strongly that it is the teacher's task to restrict the repertoire of permitted commands: Teachers have to set "rules of the game" that comprise a clear model for thinking about the subject domain. Since a number of different geometrical "games" are available, the teacher has to determine for pupils which particular game is worthwhile and then assist them in making discoveries within that restricted context.

In the following list of rules, the rules of the geometrical games are represented by cybernetic turtles that are capable of different behavior with different equipment. What I mean by *equipment* can easily be explained by using the heading commands as examples.

Teachers often make the geometrical content of these commands concrete by equipping the turtle with a compass and a compass card for writing on. The following should illustrate this:

HEADING means "read the angle between NORTH and the current position of the turtle nose,"

MAKE "PHI HEADING means "mark the current heading on the compass card and name it PHI,"

SETHEADING :PHI means "turn the turtle's nose to the specified mark on the card," and so on. What we are doing by using these commands is making reference to the distant effect of an imaginery magnetic field. Or, in mathematical terms, we are partly changing the localness of geometrical description to a global (or absolute) polar coordinate system. Children who know nothing about the physics of a magnetic field have often experienced the usefulness of a compass. Therefore it makes sense to extend the syntonic representation of local geometrical description through the turtle with FORWARD and RIGHT by using such equipment.

Thus the hypothesis I consider here is not only whether the pupils' use of their own bodies constitutes knowledge and feeling about geometrical concepts but whether their manipulation of measuring instruments and tools can achieve the same result.

The question that naturally follows is: Is there a specific extension of the turtle concept that is well-suited for domains of geometrical problems or for a subdiscipline of geometry? The defining equipment of such a turtle environment are

1. a sublanguage of Logo with specific subject-domain-related extensions,
2. a subdiscipline of some parts of mathematics, physics, or other subjects,
3. a concise and clean model (e.g., a turtle with some equipment) that opens up the use of this sublanguage and the subdiscipline by simplifying the ideas of the subdiscipline and encouraging the imagination of the learner.

The domains of discourse for such a model should be broad. The richness of the environment, the expressive power of the sublanguage, and the simplicity of the model should give the learner a feeling of power over a wide variety of (e.g., mathematical) problems and the impression that there is a lot to discover. This feeling is necessary to convince the learner that working in this environment is general in some sense as well as far-reaching and widely applicable. Establishing such an environment is more on the level of clearing up the concepts of the discipline and redesigning it than on the level of arranging a set of problems for learning and hints for solution.

What about the example of the turtle with compass and compass card in this respect? Our experience suggests that this environment is comparatively limited in its domain of discourse, as will be shown in section 4. The presence of these commands in Logo systems seems to be a QWERTY-effect; up to now only LCN Logo has changed the semantics of TOWARDS to encompass a broader geometrical use (LCN 1988).

3   TRUE TURTLES

A wide variety of "mathland" learning activities can be undertaken by pupils experimenting with the turtle's FORWARD/BACK and RIGHT/LEFT commands. We will call this conception the *naive turtle*. It is not necessary to go into the obvious benefits of working with the naive turtle to learn geometrical concepts. Nevertheless, in some respects the geometrical domain is not very rich. The naive turtle is extremely self-centered and "knows" nothing about its surrounding world. The closest biological representation of a naive turtle would be an animal randomly pacing the ground. The term *geometry*, on the other hand, does mean "measuring the earth," and the naive turtle is not able to contribute anything toward describing its surroundings.

When it performs the well-known polygon procedure in which a circle is approximated by an inscribed polygon, the naive turtle gives no geometrical indication of "closing" the figure.

```
TO POLYGON :S :A
   RIGHT :A / 2
   FORWARD :S
   RIGHT :A / 2
   POLYGON :S :A
END
```

Teachers like to assign programming a stop rule for such a polygon procedure. Finding the underlying geometrical fact, and programming it (adding a variable for totaling the turns and inserting a stop rule), is not an easy task for younger children.

Since the need for totaling the turns of the turtle and also its forward steps regularly appears in turtle work, it is worth endowing the turtle with this ability. This is a didactical decision about the conceptual basis of the learning environment and related intuitions that allow learners to work in this environment.

We equip the turtle with two instruments for such bookkeeping: an odometer that sums the FORWARD steps, and a "rotameter" that sums the RIGHT turns of the turtle. We call this new conception the *true turtle*. The odometer is a common instrument present in every car, and the rotameter can be easily understood as an analogous instrument.

For an implementation the HOME and the CLEARSCREEN commands have to be rewritten so that they set the odometer and rotameter (as new state variables of the *true turtle*) to zero. FORWARD adds a step to the odometer, and RIGHT adds an angle (BACK and LEFT subtract, respectively). Two new functions ODO and ROTA output the odometer or rotameter reading. In the rest of this section the Logo primitives are changed to be understood in the *true turtle* sense. One mathematical justification for defining a concept like this is that the total turn (rotameter) and the total length of the path (odometer) are fundamental to the geometry of plane curves.

It is very impressive to have the odometer and rotameter displayed on the screen and observe the changes during the turtle run, especially during initial work with the *true turtle*. Pupils observing these instruments during their work with polygons find the "total turtle trip theorem" experimentally and can write the stop rule very easily. Nearly all well-known naive turtle activities can benefit from observing the odometer and rotameter readings. Here are two different examples.

Example 1
Graphical Simulation of the Archimedean Method of Calculating the Number π

This is a gamelike simulation in which we use the polygon procedure mentioned above with a stop rule (based on the rotameter) and a printout of the odometer reading.

```
TO POLYGON :S :A
  RIGHT :A / 2
  FORWARD :S
  RIGHT :A / 2
  IF 0 = REMAINDER ROTA 360 [PRINT ODO STOP]
  POLYGON :S :A
END
```

The circle is represented only by its diameter (e.g., 100), as shown in figure 1. It can be drawn by[1]

? CLEARSCREEN RT 90 FD 100 HOME

The true turtle can now be sent on a round-trip by commands like

? HOME POLYGON 30 60

---

1. Logo lines beginning with **?** are entered in direct mode with <return> or <enter> at the end.

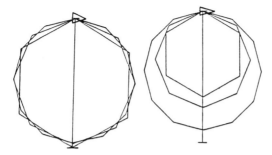

Figure 1 Two views of the π-game graphics

and it will run its course and print the path length at the end. By recalling the input line and changing the side length of the polygon, the pupil can try to hit the other end of the diameter in order to get a lower-bound approximation for π (see figure 1). By changing the angle, the guess can be improved. By using a circumscribed polygon, an upper-bound approximation can be gained. Though the accuracy of the approximation is limited to the resolution of the screen, the main idea and the potential of this method can be demonstrated very clearly without tedious calculations. We have used this game in two learning situations: in a turtle activity environment where it was an extension of work with turtle graphics and the pupil was programming and playing the game, and in the mathematics classroom where the software was developed as a group activity and the demonstration was performed by the teacher. Our experiences with this kind of transparent and unpretentious simulation as an introduction to π (in grade 8 or 9) have been very positive. Even if the turtle concept and the ideas of an odometer and rotameter have to be introduced to the pupils in order to explain the demonstration, the main aim of the lesson (the approximation of a circle) never gets lost.

Example 2
Teacher Education in the Setting of Turtle Geometry

A conceptually rich field for experimentation with the total turn is encountered through the "let-the-turtle-escape-from-a-maze" problem described in Abelson and diSessa (1980, p. 176). This problem is always employed as a basis for our teacher education work, for demonstrating that thinking in terms of total turns is more appropriate to topological problems than are compass deviations. The teachers have to deal with these different geometrical concepts and try to solve the maze problem. Trial runs with the true turtle in different mazes and the observation of the rotameter shows the underlying geometrical relations. One of the results is that the total turn function ROTA represents more geometrical information than the compass deviation since we easily can define the heading by REMAINDER ROTA 360 (if REMAINDER is properly implemented), which illustrates the loss of information in the case of using compass deviation.

The theoretical framework for the true turtle is the intrinsic geometry of plane curves. The arc length s (or ODO) is the fundamental coordinate for a plane curve. Mathematical theory tells us that a plane curve is completely described by only one function: the curvature as a function of the arc length. The curvature (:C) is a measure of the amount of turning (:DALPHA) relative to the chord length (:DS) for a small piece of the curve, or equivalently the rate of change of its tangent. That is,

:C = :DALPHA/:DS * (1/57.3)

so

:DALPHA = :C * :DS * 57.3

(:DALPHA/57.3 is the turn in radians.) Using :DS as a step variable for approximating the curve that is specified by the curvature function, we get the following procedure:

```
TO CURVE :DS :C
  RIGHT (RUN :C) * :DS * 57.3
  FORWARD :DS
  CURVE :DS :C
END
```

This procedure of course produces the correct curve only in the infinite case. In a finite approximation there would occur a systematic error. Usually we minimize the error factor by splitting the turn in half (as we did in the above polygon).

```
TO CURVE :DS :C
  RIGHT (RUN :C) * :DS * 57.3 / 2
  FORWARD :DS
```

```
    RIGHT (RUN :C) * :DS * 57.3 / 2
    CURVE :DS :C
END
```

A curve with constant curvature of course is a circle (with the radius as the reciprocal of the curvature). For example,

?CURVE 5 [1/100]

It is very instructive for teachers to experiment with curves and related finite approximations with different values of DS. Besides the constant curvature function the simplest curvature functions are the proportional and the reciprocal functions, which define infinitesimally the *clothoid* and the *logarithmic spiral*, respectively.

Clothoid	Logarithmic spiral
? CURVE a [b * ODO]	? CURVE c [d / ODO]
? CURVE 2 [0.001 * ODO]	? CURVE 2 [10 / ODO]

In these example *a*, *b*, *c*, and *d* are arbitrary constraints. In each case the odometer reading may have to be reset to accommodate it to the screen. We use these curves (and their finite approximations) in our teacher study for developing the basis for pupils' work with more familiar turtle folklore figures such as SPIRALs and INSPIs.

4   TURTLES WITH DIRECTION AND DISTANCE FINDERS

It often happens that descriptions of geometrical configurations that are simple in terms of euclidean geometry become very complicated when we use the turtle as a drawing robot. The reason for this is that in some cases the definition or the construction of a configuration is done by using points or lines. The ruler-and-compass constructions of euclidean geometry stress a thinking style involving points and lines that are fixed in an absolute plane. Unlike euclidean geometry, we define points and lines only relative to an initial geometrical setting specified by the initial state of the turtle (Loethe 1985); this means that the turtle itself sets these elements. Later on it can refer to them by using specific equipment. We call these elements *extrinsic*, as opposed to the intrinsic properties of geometrical configurations that can be formulated for a true turtle.

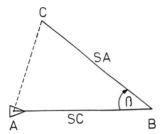

Figure 2 Triangle by given SC, BETA, and SA

These conceptions (together with an appropriate visualization) are illustrated by a simple example: the construction of a triangle given by two sides SA, SC, and the enclosed angle BETA (see figure 2). It is pretty clear that we can move the turtle from *A* to *B* and further on to *C* by using FORWARD and LEFT. But we are not able to close the figure by using these intrinsic commands since the turtle lacks the ability to refer to former positions.

Of course we can store the pair of coordinates of a position that the turtle has to use later on. But we want to do it by avoiding thinking in terms of an absolute cartesian coordinate system in the plane. The turtle starts at any position and orientation (initial state) for the construction of a figure. If it wants to mark a point for later use, it is able to set a signpost at its own momentary position:

POST <name>

Later on the turtle is able to measure the distance of such a signpost (from its present position)[2]

DISTANCE <thing of name>

and find the direction to a signpost relative to its (present) heading

DIRECTION <thing of name>

DIRECTION returns an angle that can be used to turn the turtle in the direction of the signpost by using the command RIGHT. Then the triangle can be drawn by the following procedure:

2. Editors' note: *Thing* is Logo-speak for "the value of."

```
TO TRIANGLE :SC :BETA :SA
  (LOCAL "A "B)
  POST "A
  FORWARD :SC
  POST "B
  LEFT 180 - :BETA
  FD :SA
  RIGHT DIRECTION :A
  FORWARD DISTANCE :A
  RIGHT DIRECTION :B
END
```

To help us think more concretely about the geometrical process of moving and drawing, we can imagine the turtle as being equipped with a spade and signposts, with direction and distance finders. Even if children do not know that distance finders are built into cameras and posts, that direction and distance finders are necessary for surveying, they can still get a clear feeling of the principal functions of these instruments.

The main point of using these new primitives is that we avoid coordinates by posting important points in advance. This makes these points elements of the geometric setting of a figure rather than elements of an absolute coordinate system of the plane. These posts are local to the related procedure, and posting in this way guarantees that the figure can be drawn in every position dependent only on the initial state of the turtle. Thinking in such geometric settings or configurations is in some sense *in-between* thinking in terms of local and global descriptions of geometrical figures.

Other useful extrinsic elements of configurations are ARROW (the vector in the direction of the turtle's current heading) and SPEAR (an oriented straight line consisting of the current position and heading of the turtle):

```
ARROW <name>
SPEAR <name>
```

Reference to these elements can be made by DIRECTION in both cases, and DISTANCE in the case of the spear.

In the above example it is not necessary to post the point *B*. The turtle has only to fix its initial orientation as an arrow and use it.

```
TO TRIANGLE :SC :BETA :SA
  (LOCAL "A "AB)
  POST "A
  ARROW "AB
  FORWARD :SC
  LEFT 180 - :BETA
  FD :SA
  RIGHT DIRECTION :A
  FORWARD DISTANCE :A
  RIGHT DIRECTION :AB
END
```

In chapter 4 of this volume is his study of different microworlds, Kynigos reports his observations of younger children working with POST, DISTANCE, and DIRECTION primitives (his PDD microworld). The psychological distinctions between working with the PDD primitives and coordinate-related ones are evidenced in the examples that follow.

Example 3
A Learning Environment for "Surveying Geometry"

Euclidean geometry with its dependence on the ruler and compass is the dominant activity that shapes the geometrical thinking of pupils in school. We tried the turtle concept with posting, distance, and direction finding with a group of eighth graders to see if they would discover "surveying geometry" in the learning environment. For these pupils it was like a game in which they explored the well-known classical euclidean constructions of the triangle by using the turtle with distance and direction finder.

After some introductory work with Logo and the naive turtle, the group was exposed to posting, distance, and direction finding and the surveying paradigm (Hoppe 1984, p. 163). Their task was to develop turtle procedures for the construction of triangles that were well known to them from regular classwork using ruler-and-compass methods. Almost no further help or hints were given. The tool-based, gamelike situation and the aim of making things work on the computer encouraged discovery. Their first finding was that known methods such as intersections of lines did not work. It was necessary to develop new methods, and there followed a long, fruitful path traversed between having the idea of an approximation method through a working procedure in the special case and a systematic method for enacting those procedures. The pupils designed solutions

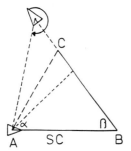

Figure 3 Triangle by given ALPHA, SC, and BETA

by nesting intervals and used different methods for improving their guesses. As an example, we cite a (final) version of a procedure for drawing a triangle specified by two angles and the enclosed side (see figure 3).

```
TO TRIANGLE :ALPHA :SC :BETA
  POST "A
  ARROW "AB
  FD :SC
  LT 180 - :BETA
  SEARCH 20
  RT DIRECTION :A
  FD DISTANCE :A
  RT DIRECTION :AB
END

TO SEARCH :S
  IF :S < 1 [STOP]
  TEST (DIRECTION :A) > 360 - :ALPHA - :BETA
  IFT [FD :S SEARCH :S]
  IFF [BK :S SEARCH :S / 2]
END
```

Here IFT and IFF (short for IF TRUE and IF FALSE) check the result of a TEST. On implementations without these primitives, the same effect can be achieved by the IF . . . THEN . . . ELSE construction.

As a part of our teacher education program, nearly all kinds of triangle constructions (altitudes, angle bisectors, medians, etc.) were assigned for developing such idealized surveying methods; the goal was again the demonstration of the tool dependence of geometrical work and the encouragement of discovery methods in a Logo environment.

Example 4
Definition of Plane Curves by Extrinsic Elements

Plane curves can be defined in very different geometrical contexts: using intrinsic properties like the clothoid or the logarithmic spiral, the simplicity of intersection with straight lines like the conic sections, and configurations as sets of points with certain properties with reference to fixed points, lines, or circles. In all cases the classical approach of cartesian-influenced geometry is to develop an equation in an appropriate coordinate representation.

These coordinate-related approaches to curves are well known to teachers. It is worth using the turtle concept to offer them an alternative and broader view of curves. The turtle approach encourages them to go back to the real geometrical definitions of the curves and to develop turtle representations that are often clearer and closer to the original definition.

In teacher education courses, strategies for defining curves in turtle geometry with extrinsic elements are introduced by drawing a circle in different ways. Afterward the teachers have to work on their own on conic sections and other curves by looking for the appropriate properties of these curves. An application of these activities is planetary orbits (without using coordinates). In this case the gravitation law is the defining property of the curves.

A first definition of the circle is as a curve with constant curvature. In intrinsic geometry this definition is the only possible one. But the center of a circle is an important extrinsic element of the circle, and definitions of the circle make use of it. Let us assume that we want the turtle to draw a circle with a given radius R starting at its present position and with its present heading. The first thing the turtle has to do is to post the midpoint in order to refer to it later:

```
TO CIRCLE :DS :R
  LOCAL "M
  RIGHT 90
  FORWARD :R
  POST "M
  BACK :R
  LEFT 90
  CIRCLE.STEPS :DS
END
```

Now we want to use the property of the perpendicularity of its tangent to the radius as the defining property for the circle. In CIRCLE.STEPS we approximate the circle by a circumscribed polygon:

```
TO CIRCLE.STEPS :DS
  FORWARD :DS/2
  RIGHT (DIRECTION :M) - 90
  FORWARD :DS / 2
  CIRCLE.STEPS :DS
END
```

There is always a systematic error in this approximation. We can reduce it when the turtle goes forward DS and measures the direction of the tangent at this point. Then it goes back DS/2 and turns right toward the specified direction, and again goes forward DS/2. This "broken" step and measuring example reduces the systematic error enormously (compare the POLYGON procedure in section 2).

```
TO CIRCLE.STEPS :DS
  LOCAL "A
  FORWARD :DS
  MAKE "A (DIRECTION :M) - 90
  BACK :DS / 2
  RIGHT :A
  FORWARD :DS / 2
  CIRCLE.STEPS :DS
END
```

As a third definition we can describe the circle as a locus of points with constant distance to the midpoint. The CIRCLE procedure is exactly the same as before, but CIRCLE.STEPS has to be rewritten.

```
TO CIRCLE.STEPS :DS
  FORWARD :DS
  RIGHT DIRECTION :M
  FORWARD (DISTANCE :M) - :R
  LEFT 90
  CIRCLE.STEPS :DS
END
```

In this case the turtle path has a shape like a saw blade that passes exactly through points lying on the circle.

The second definition of the circle corresponds to the following property of an ellipse: The tangent divides the outward angle between the focal rays in half. If we assume that the turtle has posted the foci F1 and F2, it can draw the ellipse by the following procedure which generalizes the corresponding CIRCLE.-STEPS procedure:

```
TO ELLIPSE.STEPS :DS
  LOCAL "ALPHA
  FORWARD :DS
  MAKE "ALPHA ((DIRECTION :F1) + (DIRECTION :F2)) / 2 - 90
  BACK :DS / 2
  RIGHT :ALPHA
  FORWARD :DS / 2
  ELLIPSE.STEPS :DS
END
```

We assume that the turtle starts at a point where the heading of the turtle is perpendicular to the axis of the ellipse. A is the distance to the midpoint, and E the linear eccentricity.

```
TO ELLIPSE :DS :A :E
  (LOCAL "F1 "F2)
  RIGHT 90
  FORWARD :A - :E
  POST "F1
  FORWARD 2 * :E
  POST "F2
  BACK :A + :E
  LEFT 90
  ELLIPSE.STEPS :DS
END
```

The generalization of the third definition of the circle to the ellipse results in a saw-blade approximation to this curve with exact points. For the correction of the distance of the turtle from the focus F1, we need the polar coordinate representation of a conic $r = f(\text{phi})$:

$$r = \frac{p}{(1 - \text{eps} * \cos \text{phi})},$$

where p is the parameter and eps the numerical eccentricity (epsilon) of the conic. Since phi is the angle between the focal ray and the axis of the ellipse, the turtle has to be able to refer to the direction of the axis at any time. The initial setting of the ellipse has to be enriched with p, eps, and the axis as extrinsic elements.

```
TO ELLIPSE :DS :A :E
  (LOCAL "F1 "F2 "AXIS "P "EPS)
  MAKE "EPS :E / :A
  MAKE "P :A * (1 - :EPS * :EPS)
  RIGHT 90
  ARROW "AXIS
  FORWARD :A - :E
  POST "F1
  FORWARD 2 * :E
  POST "F2
  BACK :A + :E
  LEFT 90
  ELLIPSE.STEPS :DS
END
```

For the step-by-step drawing of the ellipse, the turtle has to face the focus F1. Then it is able to measure the angle phi and use it to do the correction step in the direction of F1. Finally, it turns in the direction of the tangent by measuring the directions of the focal rays.

```
TO ELLIPSE.STEPS :DS
  (LOCAL "PHI "ALPHA)
  FORWARD :DS
  MAKE "ALPHA DIRECTION :F1
  RT :ALPHA
  MAKE "PHI (DIRECTION :AXIS) - 180
  FD (DISTANCE :F1) - :P/(1 - :EPS * COS :PHI)
  LT :ALPHA
  RT ((DIRECTION :F1) + (DIRECTION :F2)) / 2 - 90
  ELLIPSE.STEPS :DS
END
```

By using the corresponding properties of the other conics, we can get procedures that are very similar to the ellipse procedures.

Since for teachers conic sections are the most important illustrations of curves besides the circle, they are motivated to analyze the geometry of these curves with respect to a turtle representation. The definitions of these curves with extrinsic elements are geometrically quite natural and stress features that teachers have to find and experiment with. Later we use these activities to illustrate the difficulties of the approximation process and offer teachers the opportunity to think about methods to avoid them.

5 SPACE TURTLES

How to generalize the plane turtle to three dimensions should be obvious from looking at the differential geometry of curves in space. In this case the local description of a spatial curve is affected by using a moving triple of orthogonal unit vectors that describes the present tangent and osculating plane of the curve. As a first step we can think of the turtle as a robot that draws in space like an aeroplane producing condensation trails. The turtle only moves in the direction of its nose and is sitting on the osculating plane. Consequently the orientation of the turtle in space is described by the triple of perpendicular unit vectors, and the turtle can be steered by changing this orientation. This configuration of trails in space is represented on the computer screen by geometrical projections. The didactically important point in this context is that spatial thinking means thinking in movements of the turtle in space and not thinking in the two-dimensional mapping of a spatial configuration. The latter is the method used in descriptive or practical geometry. Several authors have generalized the turtle in this way and have described how the implementations of the necessary primitives for changing the orientation can be done on normal Logo systems (e.g., see Abelson and diSessa 1980, p. 144; Reggini 1985; Loethe, Woelpert, and Wolpert 1985); some of the 3-D primitives exist in professional Logo systems (Exper Logo, LCN Logo, etc.).

However, to be able to use the space turtle in a learning environment with pupils (and teachers), one has to develop didactical models of the space turtle itself, practical tasks involving it, as well as didactical models as conceptions for thinking and problem solving. The first task in arriving at such a didactical model is to simplify the notion of orientation in three dimensions that is described by the orthogonal triple of the longitudinal axis (unit vector $\mathbf{i}$), the transverse axis (unit vector **j**), and the upward axis (unit vector **k**). For the change of orientation of the "spaceship turtle," Abelson and diSessa (1980) propose three commands

YAW   \<degree\> : rotation around the upward axis
ROLL \<degree\> : rotation around the longitudinal axis
PITCH \<degree\> : rotation around the transverse axis

and the use of positive and negative angles. Movement is straight in the direction of the longitudinal axis by a certain number of turtle steps:

FORWARD \<steps\> : translation in direction of the axis.

Usually a turn in mathematics is considered to be positive if the turn is counterclockwise (looking from the top of the rotation vector of the turn). Getting the correct orientation of angles in a movement or configuration is very demanding on the spatial imagination of learners. A concrete model for working with this approach was proposed by Guido Bakema (1987)[3] for use in Dutch schools. He used three toothpicks in plasticine to represent the three turtle axes. To obtain the correct orientation of a specific action, the pupils were asked to take the model at the top of the appropriate toothpick with thumb and forefinger and to look from there at the turtle in order to try out the orientation of a rotation. By doing so, the pupils could always look at the model in a mathematically correct way. This model represents exactly the mathematical concept of angle orientation. But, in our experience, it has the disadvantage that the pupils have to change their position relative to the turtle. In general, it is not possible for them to mentally relate their own body to the turtle in some way. This connection can rather be done by seeing the turtle as acting like a bird or an aeroplane. The toothpick model forces the learner to think of being in a prone position which is quite unnatural. In our experience with learners of different age groups, the sitting position was preferred. The turtle was perceived as a flying vehicle that had to have the following geometrically relevant elements: (1) a plane with a perpendicular mast on it (an oriented plane that corresponds to the osculating plane of a curve) and (2) a nose (the turtle's nose) at the tip of the plane to indicate the direction of movement and drawing (this would correspond to the tangent to a curve).

---

3. Personal communication.

The learner has to imagine him or herself as a tiny person sitting on the turtle and commanding it. Thus the sitting position of the pupils has the advantage of simulating the basic experience of changing orientation and turning around the three orthogonal axes. When introducing the space turtle concept in the classroom, we encourage the pupils to try out turns by seesawing in their chairs so that they can get the feel for the basic turtle movements. Later this model avoids forcing the user to think in terms of the triple axes and the orientation of angles. The oriented axes are not necessary at all and negative angles can be avoided by defining pairs of turtle commands that are related to the tiny person sitting on the space turtle.

The commands YAW, ROLL, and PITCH reflect the movements of a ship or an aeroplane in a rather passive manner, under the influence of the moving water or air. It would be better if the tiny person on the turtle (representing the learner) were cast in a more active role so that geometrical objects could be created by steering a spaceship. Reggini (1985) introduced "veer" instead of "yaw," and I would like to add "tilt" and "pull" instead of "roll" and "pitch" for the English version. But ROLL and PITCH seem to have become a standard, so we will use them in the following abbreviations as basic commands.

The concrete model of the space turtle that would conform to this discussion would be the following: The drawing robot would be represented by a triangular platform on which a tiny person can sit and hold onto a mast (see figure 4). The steering would be done by this tiny person using the following commands. (The remarks in parentheses are for the implementer of the commands, not for the learner.)

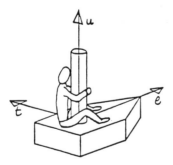

Figure 4 Space turtle with a tiny person steering it

VRT veer right (negative rotation on **i**)
VLT veer left (positive rotation on **i**)
RRT roll right (positive rotation on **j**)
RLT roll left (negative rotation on **j**)
PUP pitch up (negative rotation on **k**)
PDO pitch down (positive rotation on **k**)
GFD go forward (translation in direction **k**)
GBK go back (translation in direction −**k**)

The type of projection of the spatial configuration on the screen should always be chosen according to the projection that the pupils are familiar with from their own sketching and drawing activities in spatial geometry in school (e.g., a parallel projection that maps lines perpendicular to the screen onto lines at 45 degrees and distorts them by a factor of 0.5). Of course pupils should be able to change to other kinds of projections or views (Abelson and diSessa 1980, p. 145; Loethe, Woelpert, and Wolpert 1985). In any projection the screen will be the projection plane, and therefore turtle drawings will appear without distortion as long as the turtle moves only in this plane. (Some implementations that make use of this embed the usual two-dimensional commands into the three-dimensional ones [e.g., see LCN 1988]; in this case RT/LT and FD/BK is used instead of VRT/VLT and GFD/GBK.)

The space turtle idea is rather open-ended for instructional use; it reflects only the method of using orthogonal triples for working with geometrical objects. It is nearly impossible to let pupils—even after an introduction to the space turtle commands—work on their own by experimenting as they can in plane turtle graphics activities: They are usually *not* able to produce meaningful curves or shapes of solids. Consequently developing learning environments means designing specific models and strategies and putting them together with didactical models. These models correspond to habits of thinking, spatial imagination, and operations. In some cases they are connected to specific materials for concrete models of solids or ways of handling nets and solids. The development of such didactical models normally is too demanding for teachers; our experience suggests that preparation by researchers is necessary. This stands in marked contrast to the situation with the plane turtle where even the use of the naive turtle alone encourages a wide variety of meaningful activities.

Example 5
Three Fundamental Didactical Conceptions for Space Turtle Use

The first account offers the pedagogical essence of an approach we have used in an experimental learning setting with ninth graders (Loethe, Woelpert, and Wolpert 1987). We have put together the results of our observations in a didactical model and used it as a beginning activity with other age groups. After some experiences with the Logo system and plane turtle drawing of polygons, and so on, the problem of drawing squares in space was posed. As mentioned before, the basic commands for changing orientation were introduced by encouraging chair actions of the pupils and hands-on experience with a wooden model of the space turtle. But without giving an initial free play phase at the computer, the teacher posed the problem of drawing a square in space for discussion and the learners proposed solutions. The following three statements were selected by the teacher, and written on the blackboard:

REPEAT 4 [GFD 50 VLT 90]
REPEAT 4 [GFD 50 PDO 90]
REPEAT 4 [GFD 50 RRT 90]

These commands illustrate the main differences between the fundamental commands connected with specific spatial conceptions (Loethe 1987, p. 71):

1. The first line draws a square in the plane that the space turtle is "sitting" on, the turtle plane. Drawing within this plane is more familiar to the commander of the spaceship than changing it. The square can be imagined to be wire shaped but also filled as a plane face. In the latter case we can think of the turtle as "cutting" the square out of the turtle plane. Imagining cutting a paper face out of the plane helps in future actions and was encouraged by the teacher.
2. The second REPEAT command draws a square by changing the natural turtle plane several times. So it is better not to think in terms of a changing turtle plane, but instead in terms of a freely flying spaceship. By using the trail model, this square is primarily considered to be wire shaped and not filled by a paper face. The turtle is "tightrope walking" on the wire-shaped square.
3. The third REPEAT command does not draw a square at all but only a "twisted" line. This mathematical concept of a screwing motion is very important for spatial thinking.

The spatial conceptions of these commands become more apparent if we generalize the above statements by adding a square face that is considered to be

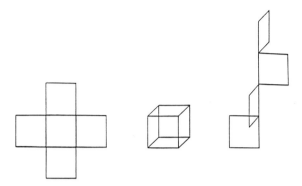

Figure 5 Three fundamental spatial conceptions

filled. Trying out these commands, varying and generalizing them, is a typical activity that can be done at the computer. In our experimental group this was the first activity of the pupils with the space turtle at the computer (see figure 5).

```
TO RT.SQUARE :S
  REPEAT 4 [GFD :S VRT 90]
END
?REPEAT 4 [RT.SQUARE 50 GFD 50 VLT 90]
?REPEAT 4 [RT.SQUARE 50 GFD 50 PDO 90]
?REPEAT 4 [RT.SQUARE 50 GFD 50 RRT 90]
```

The discussion of the results together with the teacher, and the use of paper models of the spatial configuration together with the wooden space turtle model, established the following intuitions:

1.   In the first case we get a plane figure which can be interpreted as the net of a cube (without the top face).
2.   In the second case we get a cube without the left and right lateral face, so it is like a tube.
3.   In the third case we get a configuration of "winding flags" or a kind of helix-shaped figure.

These figures served as prototypes for different kinds of spatial figures, and ways of programming the related procedures.

Nets of Solids and the Paper-Folding Strategy with a Base Plane
As an example of a wide variety of nets, we again use

REPEAT 4 [RT.SQUARE 50 GFD 50 VLT 90]

the above net of a cube. It is necessary to observe that the RT.SQUARE has a (mathematically) negative orientation (drawn by using VRT) and that the net is based on a square with positive orientation (drawn by VLT). The next step is representing the folding-up action by space turtle commands. There are different ways to do this (chaotic ones too). After a tryout phase at the computer, the teacher discussed the different results with the pupils. There was an agreement that the most elegant solution should be established as a strategy for folding with a base plane. Inserting RLT 90 before and RRT 90 after RT.SQUARE is a good rule for folding up the lateral face and returning the space turtle to the base plane:

REPEAT 4 [RLT 90 RT.SQUARE 50 RRT 90 GFD 50 VLT 90]

Here rolling is conceptually related to the paper-folding operation; the turtle is folding up its drawing paper along its longitudinal axis. There are of course alternatives using pitch commands. The most elegant version is

REPEAT 4 [PUP 90 LT.SQUARE 50 PDO 90 GFD 50 VLT 90]

The same spatial configuration is drawn, but it is not possible to start with a net and think of a folding-up operation.

Our experience shows that the teacher has to decide whether the use of an explicit strategy is forced or not. To proceed to more complex solids later on, it is absolutely necessary that at the beginning learners are guided in using a strategy that starts with procedures for the net and inserts roll commands for folding up. Other solutions of pupils have to be discussed and transformed to conceptually clear ones. In the above example of a cube, we can think in terms of one base and four lateral surfaces. The exercises that followed after establishing this folding-up strategy involved varied kinds of right prisms, pyramids, and other solids. As an example, we used a square-based pyramid. The net procedure is programmed by inserting a right-oriented triangle in the REPEAT loop of a left-oriented square.

```
TO S.PYRAMID.NET :S
  REPEAT 4 [RT.TRIANGLE :S GFD :S VLT 90]
END
```

Figure 6 A pyramid that is not closed

RT.TRIANGLE is an equilateral triangle.

TO RT.TRIANGLE :S
  REPEAT 3 [GFD :S VRT 120]
END

Now we fold up the net by using the folding angle *A* (see figure 6).

TO S.PYRAMID :S :A
  REPEAT 4 [RRT :A RT.TRIANGLE :S RLT :A GFD :S VRT 90]
END

   To develop their spatial sense, it is better to have pupils make systematic attempts at finding the value of *A* until the spatial figure is closed rather than calculate *A* at this stage even if they are able to. Another important activity for pupils is to generalize the S.PYRAMID to pyramids with regular pentagons, hexagons, heptagons, and so forth, as bases (always with equilateral triangles as faces). The pupils then experiment with trying to "close" these spatial figures.

The Tube Paradigm

Tubes are the generalization of the following cube which is "open" at both the left and right sides:

REPEAT 4 [RT.SQUARE GFD 50 PDO 90]

To get prisms, we have to start with a plane figure that is defined as a wire-shaped model using a pitch command, for example,

TO HEXAGON :S
  REPEAT 4 [GFD :S PDO 60]
END

Using a rectangle for the lateral faces, we get a prism by inserting the rectangle into the REPEAT-loop of the HEXAGON procedure.

```
TO RECTANGLE :A :B
  REPEAT 2 [GFD :A VRT 90 GFD :B VRT 90]
END
```

```
TO HEXAGON.PRISM :S :H
  REPEAT 6 [RECTANGLE :S :H GFD :S PDO 60]
END
```

Insertion is a very powerful technique in getting correct spatial configurations. The related effect on the turtle is that it interrupts its movement at a certain stage, performs a different figure, and then continues the original movement. In our experience this technique of producing figures is much more useful with the three-dimensional than with the two-dimensional turtle.

The Helix Paradigm
The helix pattern

REPEAT . . . [GFD . . . RRT . . .]

is a difficult spatial operation to perform mentally, but it is fundamental for movements in space. An illustrative example is a spiral staircase. A very simple one is the following (see figure 7):

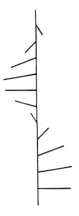

Figure 7 A helix-shaped staircase

```
TO HELIX.STAIRCASE
  REPEAT 12 [GFD 10 STEP RRT 30]
END

TO STEP
  VRT 90
  GFD 40 GBK 40
  VLT 90
END
```

To program more elaborate spiral staircases with nice steps is a very challenging task. Experiences with the experimental group showed us that the motivation of the work with the space turtle was extremely strong. The pupils had no difficulty in picking up the idea of the space turtle and the use of steering commands. Contrary to our expectations, they had almost no difficulties in decoding the displayed drawings on the screen—even complicated ones with several lines in different planes and no hidden lines. The reason was that they followed the construction of the figure as it was drawn on the screen, since we slowed down the turtle by our implementation. Mistakes were always corrected in terms of geometrical features related to the spatial configuration and to the projected image during the drawing process. Other problems arose for pupils because they tended to overestimate their abilities to produce and correct procedures mentally, instead of referring to real models of the solids and the wooden model of the turtle. This confirmed our hypothesis that the geometrical conceptions have to be very well formed at the beginning and have to be strongly related to real geometrical actions in space.

So far in this section we have reported the initial activities with our experimental groups only because they have become standard for our other teaching activities. On the basis of these fundamental conceptions, very different learning environments can be designed. For instance, combining different prisms and pyramids, architectural shapes like houses, churches, and castles, or programming a system that draws the usual school solids and performs the calculation of volume, surface area, and so on. Instead of giving examples for these activities, we want to concentrate on further conceptual steps we observed in another experimental group (for an alternative approach, see, e.g., Reggini 1985).

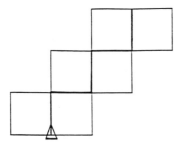

Figure 8 A net of cubes with the turtle path as folding lines

Example 6
Paper-Folding without a Base Plane—Platonic Solids

We have seen that folding-up the net is an important strategy for creating solids with the space turtle. This cannot be managed in all cases by using one face as a base and folding up the others relative to this fixed base. Folding-up without a base is more difficult to imagine. We developed the following strategy: As a first step, the procedures for the net have to be written and tested. By looking at the net and mentally moving the turtle around it, the appropriate roll commands can be inserted in such a way that every edge is folded exactly once. This strategy is more difficult to trace mentally in space, since the driver on the turtle is sitting on constantly changing planes. As an example of this method, we look at a special net of the cube. We have used this example several times during teacher courses on the didactics of computer use. These teachers had difficulties in producing the related procedures and found it very hard to grasp the process of 3-D turtle drawing. A short, elegant, and symmetrical version is constructed by alternating the folding with RRT and RLT (see figure 8).

```
TO CUBE
  REPEAT 3 [LT.SQUARE 50 RRT 90 GFD 50 VRT 90
              RT.SQUARE 50 RLT 90 GFD 50 VLT 90]
END
```

It is very difficult to trace the paper-folding process by rethinking the six spatial operations. But it is not necessary because the whole design process can be carried out by concentrating on the planar net and, by a second step, inserting the folding operations (RLT, RRT) corresponding to the paper folding actions

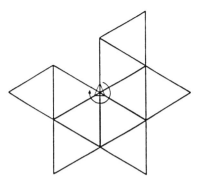

Figure 9 Half of an icosahedron net

by hand. This style of thinking in spatial operations, by watching the plane net and virtually folding it, is connected to spatial intuitions. The difficulties of the teachers originate, in our opinion, from refusing to accept this thinking style.

In a course of twelve tenth-graders (a special interest group on computers), we introduced the space turtle and the fundamental conceptions and paradigms in a similar way (Loethe and Wolpert 1990). Since the class was very able and motivated, we decided to work with them on the platonic solids, despite having had very bad earlier experiences with our teachers on this topic. The learning and teaching was organized in sessions of 90 minutes that usually started with a teacher-guided class lesson followed by work at the computers in pairs. During the preparatory phase of the course on plane turtle graphics, the class worked on figures that encouraged two thinking and working habits: analyzing figures into pairs of left- and right-oriented figures, and into figures that consist of polygons hanging on polygons. The pupils learned that these figures can be effectively produced by using polygons of different orientations. Let us use the net of half an icosahedron (drawn with right turns) which we will need later on as an example of this kind of plane figure. This net consists of five pairs of triangles, each defined as a right-oriented triangle with the insertion of a left-oriented triangle (see figure 9).

```
TO RT.ICOSAHEDRON.HALF.NET :S
  REPEAT 5 [RT.PAIR.NET :S VRT 60]
END
```

```
TO RT.PAIR.NET :S
  GFD :S VRT 120
  LT.TRIANGLE :S
  GFD :S VRT 120
  GFD :S VRT 120
END

TO LT.TRIANGLE :S
  REPEAT 3 [GFD :S VLT 120]
END
```

For the course on platonic solids, we decided to proceed as follows: Some parts of the activities were strictly planned and prepared (e.g., the nets for the solids), and others, especially the space-turtle-related ones, were left relatively free for self-determined work. This approach was necessary, in our opinion, to ensure that the pupils would not get lost in disparate activities. After an overview of the platonic solids, together with some plausible arguments that only five exist, the problem of representing the solids with the space turtle was posed. We made clear to the pupils that the challenge was to produce short and elegant solutions by finding the symmetries of the nets. The sequence of the solids was the following: cube, tetrahedron, dodecahedron, octahedron, and icosahedron.

In each of the five sessions, the nets were given by the teacher. She decided which of the possible nets (not always the easiest ones for space turtle representation) of the solids were used, and pattern sheets were prepared: one with hinges for producing a spatial model by pasting, and one without hinges for repeated folding actions during the problem-solving process. Both kinds of models turned out to be extremely helpful in certain phases of the work. The spatial model served as a mock-up of the model to be achieved, and the other model related the folding process to turtle actions. For work with both models, a small paper model of the space turtle was used throughout the sessions for moving over and around the paper models of the solids.

The class discussion with the teacher concentrated on the strategies of how to think with oriented figures in the net. To encourage helpful ways of thinking about spatial operations, specific solutions of the space turtle solids were encouraged by the teacher. But some groups of pupils solved the problems by using other strategies and alternative nets of the solids. We will discuss next both the teacher-recommended strategy and the different strategies of the pupils. We will,

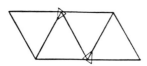

Figure 10 Tetrahedron and its net

however, limit our report to three typical examples involving the tetrahedron, the dodecahedron, and the icosahedron.

The class discussion on the tetrahedron focused on two pairs of triangles and the path between the two positions of the turtle (see figure 10).

```
TO TETRAHEDRON.NET :S
  REPEAT 2 [LT.TRIANGLE :S
  RT.TRIANGLE :S
  VLT 60 GFD :S VLT 120]
END
```

```
TO TETRAHEDRON :S
  REPEAT 2 [LT.TRIANGLE :S RRT 109.8
  RT.TRIANGLE :S RLT 109.8
  VLT 60 RLT 109.8 GFD :S VLT 120]
END
```

The folding angle of 109.8 degrees was calculated by some pupils and given to others. Some groups got the amount by systematic trials. The angles of the subsequent solids were given by the teacher.

The different strategies that the pupils used for the given net or even other nets showed us very early on that they usually accepted the class discussion as helpful for creating their own strategies for obtaining space turtle drawings. Afterward, during their practical work, they were motivated by the problems again and tended to rethink the solutions instead of just implementing them on the computer. This working style was observed throughout all sessions of the platonic solids.

By inserting a right pentagon in the REPEAT loop of a left pentagon, we easily get the net of a half of the dodecahedron (see figure 11).

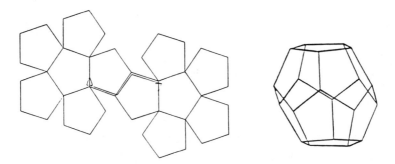

Figure 11 Dodecahedron and its net

```
TO DODECAHEDRON.HALF.NET :S
  REPEAT 5 [RT.PENTAGON :S GFD :S VLT 72]
END
```

The two halves are connected by a path along edges. A rule for such a path was discovered in a class discussion: The turtle has to walk in a way such that it uses an edge only once.

```
TO DODECAHEDRON.NET :S
  REPEAT 2 [DODECAHEDRON.HALF.NET :S DODECAHEDRON.PATH.NET
  :S]
END
```

```
TO DODECAHEDRON.PATH.NET :S
  VRT 108
  GFD :S VLT 72
  GFD :S VRT 72
  GFD :S VRT 72
END
```

The folding action is just as easy to understand as folding with a left pentagon: RRT has to be inserted before and RLT after each right pentagon.

```
TO DODECAHEDRON.HALF :S
  REPEAT 5 [RRT 63 RT.PENTAGON :S RLT 63 GFD :S VLT 72]
END
```

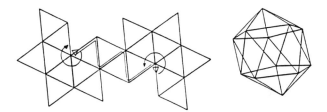

Figure 12 Icosahedron and its net

```
TO DODECAHEDRON :S
  REPEAT 2 [DODECAHEDRON.HALF :S DODECAHEDRON.PATH :S]
END
```

The path between the two turtle positions must be folded corresponding to the whole net. To set the correct roll commands, the pupils have to think intensively about the spatial situation; they found it helpful to repeatedly fold paper and sketch turtle traces. Compared with the later solids, the dodecahedron is relatively easy, and the pupils did not have any serious difficulties with it.

```
TO DODECAHEDRON.PATH :S
  RRT 63 VRT 108
  GFD :S VLT 72 RRT 63
  GFD :S VRT 72
  GFD :S VRT 72 RLT 63
END
```

In the class discussion the icosahedron net was structured as drawn (see figure 12). Again the main problem was the path between the opposite vertices.

```
TO ICOSAHEDRON.NET :S
  LT.ICOSAHEDRON.HALF.NET :S
  ICOSAHEDRON.PATH.NET :S
  RT.ICOSAHEDRON.HALF.NET :S
END
```

```
TO ICOSAHEDRON.PATH.NET :S
  GFD :S VRT 120
  GFD :S VLT 120
  GFD :S VRT 120
```

```
GFD :S VLT 120
GFD :S VRT 180
END
```

It is nearly impossible to achieve the right outcome by trial and error, for example, by trying roll commands and looking at the result on the screen. Only by clearly tracing the turtle actions on the net can the solution be achieved.

```
TO RT.PAIR :S
  GFD :S VRT 120
  RLT 42 LT.TRIANGLE :S RRT 42
  GFD :S VRT 120
  GFD :S VRT 120
END

TO RT.ICOSAHEDRON.HALF :S
  REPEAT 5 [RT.PAIR :S VRT 60 RRT 42]
END

TO ICOSAHEDRON.PATH :S
  RRT 42 GFD :S VRT 120
  RLT 42 GFD :S VLT 120
  RRT 42 GFD :S VRT 120
  RLT 42 GFD :S VLT 120
  GFD :S VRT 180
END

TO ICOSAHEDRON :S
  LT.ICOSAHEDRON.HALF :S
  ICOSAHEDRON.PATH :S
  RT.ICOSAHEDRON.HALF :S
END
```

The practical work of the pupils was driven by the challenge to solve these fascinating tasks, even more so by trying to do them with their own strategies and their own nets. The class discussions were only undertaken as exercises in space turtle strategy, not as a preparation for practical work. The procedures of all groups became more complicated than necessary, and the pupils had to struggle with several geometrical bugs in their procedures. Some pupils found that they

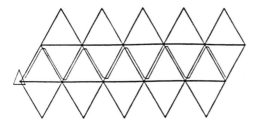

Figure 13 Alternative icosahedron net

had to modify the paper-folding strategy; they were forced to change existing veer commands of the net procedures as well. This situation allowed us to observe strategies on the part of the pupils.

There was a tendency away from acting in space (e.g., with the turtle on the paper model of the solid) to moving around the net entirely mentally. Unfortunately, the computer output as well as the misbehavior of the space turtle on the screen, hardly gave any useful hints for correction: Trial-and-error behavior at the keyboard was found to be totally ineffective and unsuccessful—the only way to debug was to repeatedly rethink the spatial operations. Facility in doing this grew with the difficulty of the solids despite the relative ineffectiveness of the teaching strategy: In fact the teacher clearly needed more time to come to terms with the pupils' own strategies.

The example we present next is an alternative solution for the icosahedron which we extracted from the work of one group. It suggests a completely different perception of the solution for an icosahedron. It starts with a zigzag path through the solid (the first line is simply for getting a better view of the configuration). Then the right and left triangles are inserted to get a ribbon (see figure 13).

```
TO ZIGZAG1 :S
   VRT 30 RRT 45
   REPEAT 5 [GFD :S VRT 120 RLT 42
             GFD :S VLT 120 RRT 42]
END


TO ZIGZAG2 :S
   VRT 30 PUP 10
   REPEAT 5 [RT.TRIANGLE :S GFD :S VRT 120 RLT 42
             LT.TRIANGLE :S GFD :S VLT 120 RRT 42]
END
```

The icosahedron is achieved by replacing the triangles by pairs of triangles.

```
TO ICOSAHEDRON :S
  VRT 30 PUP 10
  REPEAT 5 [RT.PAIR :S GFD :S VRT 120 RLT 42
            LT.PAIR :S GFD :S VLT 120 RRT 42]
END

TO RT.PAIR :S
  VRT 60
  RRT 42 RT.TRIANGLE :S RLT 42
  VLT 60
END

TO LT.PAIR :S
  VLT 60
  RLT 42 LT.TRIANGLE :S RRT 42
  VRT 60
END
```

Our experimental teaching and research on the use of the space turtle showed us that didactical work about spatial imagination and conception is at a very early stage. Past methods of working and teaching are closely connected to the classical drawing tools and on thinking in the two-dimensional projection of a spatial configuration. Space turtle activities offer a promising environment for future research.

6 SPACE TURTLES WITH DIRECTION, DIP, AND DISTANCE FINDERS

Solids and other spatial configurations can also be defined by using fixed extrinsic elements. For example, a pyramid is defined by a plane polygon and a point (not in the plane), the apex. Let us assume that we want to demonstrate the mathematical concept of a pyramid by drawing a wire-shaped model consisting of lines through the apex and the vertices of the polygon. In this case the setting has to consist of a "post in space" marking the apex that the turtle can refer to. Beside points other geometrical objects can be important in the setting. A prism is defined by a plane polygon and a vector (not parallel to the plane), a surface of rotation generated by a curve (under special conditions) and a line, the axis of rotation, and so on. All these elements have to be taken into account for the settings of spatial configurations.

Consequently the space turtle has to be able to set POSTs, ARROWs, and SPEARs in addition to the 2-D command SHIELD. SHIELD is a command for marking an (oriented) plane, the turtle plane at the point of definition (Loethe 1986).

POST   <name>   position of the turtle
ARROW   <name>   unit vector of the longitudinal
                          axis of the turtle triple
SPEAR   <name>   oriented straight line defined by
                          the position and the unit vector of
                          the longitudinal axis of the turtle
SHIELD   <name>   oriented plane defined by the position
                          and the unit vector of the upward axis

For referring to these elements, the space turtle is equipped with a distance finder that outputs the distance to a named object (a post, spear, or shield).

DISTANCE <thing of name>

For measuring the orientation relative to marked extrinsic elements, we equip the space turtle with two measuring instruments: a *dip* and a *direction* finder. The dip finder outputs an angle that can be used to roll the turtle to the right, so the point (or vector) belongs to the turtle plane, for example,

RRT DIP < thing of name >

After this turn the direction finder measures the angle for veering the turtle to the left so that it faces the point (or its longitudinal axis is parallel to the vector), for example,

VLT DIRECTION < thing of name >

It is often necessary to store dip or direction angles before rolling or veering the turtle (for remarks on the implementation and its problems, see Loethe 1986, p. 199).

As an example of work with these primitives, we define a particular square-based pyramid (height equals base side and the apex vertically above one vertex). We draw a wire-shaped model of the pyramid in a way that the turtle is drawing a triangle only by moving in the triangle plane. This means that the edges are drawn twice.

```
TO PYRAMID :S
  LOCAL "APEX
  POST "APEX
  GBK :S PDO 90
  REPEAT 4 [FACE GFD :S VLT 90]
  PUP 90 GFD :S
END
```

For drawing a FACE, the turtle measures the dip angle and rolls so that the apex is in the turtle plane. After drawing the triangle by using the distance and direction finder, the turtle rolls back to the base plane.

```
TO FACE
  (LOCAL "DIP.ANGLE "V1 "V2)
  MAKE "DIP.ANGLE DIP :APEX
  RRT :DIP.ANGLE
  POST "V1
  GFD :S
  POST "V2
  VLT DIRECTION :APEX
  GFD DISTANCE :APEX
  VLT DIRECTION :V1
  GFD DISTANCE :V1
  VLT DIRECTION :V2
  RLT :DIP.ANGLE
END
```

Since the PYRAMID only depends on the initial state of the turtle, it is straight-forward to draw three pyramids from different views (see figure 14).

```
TO PYRAMIDS
  PENUP
  GFD 60 VLT 90 GFD 75 VRT 90
  RLT 60 PENDOWN
  REPEAT 3 [RRT 45 PYRAMID 60
            . . . PENUP VRT 90 GFD 110 VLT 90 PENDOWN]
END
```

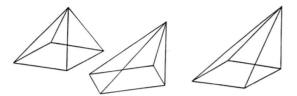

Figure 14 A nonright pyramid drawn from different starting positions of the space turtle

The work with extrinsic elements and the space turtle in the teacher courses was always the final element of our work with solids. When choosing architectural figures or certain solids on their own, the teachers often needed references to fixed elements. The usual behavior was that they first tried to use coordinates, both the 2-D coordinates of the screen and the absolute 3-D coordinates of space. Intervening, the course leader had to convince them that in both cases their solutions were geometrically unhelpful or at least not appropriate. In the first case the correctness of the solution is not invariant under projections of the space on the screen: This was reasonably acceptable. But in the second case the argument that the solution is not invariant under movements in space was not accepted so easily. It seems that the teachers had been influenced by their mathematical education where cartesian coordinate methods are predominant in geometry. The need for solids defined relative to an initial turtle state only becomes apparent when learners work on spatial configurations, which need to be formed by building blocks such as nonright pyramids and solids of revolution.

7 CONCLUSIONS

In this chapter I have demonstrated a method of designing turtles by including more general turtle abilities than the examples suggest at first sight. There is a large number of physical turtles to choose from. Very important, for instance, is the mechanical turtle with a distance and direction finder for simulating planetary orbits in a conceptually clear way. Pairs or packs of plane or space turtles with certain equipment allow us to define mathematical curves (e.g., curves of pursuit), mechanical principles (e.g., superimposing motions), and spatial operations (e.g., simultaneously moving space turtles for top, ground and side views) in a transparent way.

In our experience, designing conceptually defined turtles is more a method of computer-related didactical work in geometry than subject matter preparation for learning and teaching mathematics. We are quite sure about the turtle concepts themselves because they are well founded in mathematics. But the didactical work is only just beginning. The reported examples have been tried out only a few times, and the models of the didactical approach have changed considerably under the influence of our experiences. Thus the examples in this chapter should essentially be considered as no more than a progress report.

It might be that the reader would like to learn more about the specific thinking and working behavior of learners in the context of these turtle conceptions. We have tried several times to fix such observations. But almost every "result" was unstable in the following sense: Even small variations of the didactical introduction or methodological intervention of the teacher changes the results, sometimes totally. For instance, during the first experiments with the space turtle, we introduced the space turtle commands step by step: veer, pitch, and roll. We observed certain difficulties of pupils in using the roll commands, and we thought that roll commands were more alien to their spatial imagination than the others. By introducing the three commands at the same time, as reported in section 5, these difficulties completely vanished. In our opinion observations of learning behavior have to be used to improve the didactical models and make them stable. However, we can at least claim that the reported method of stressing the three fundamental conceptions for space turtle use (section 5) and the paper-folding strategy with a base plane have proven in our experience to be *nearly* stable didactical models.

ACKNOWLEDGMENTS

I would like to thank many colleagues who supported and commented on this chapter, especially Heinz Ulrich Hoppe, Werner Quehl, and Heinrich Woelpert. Beyond that, Sibylle Wolpert has made significant contributions to this work.

REFERENCES

Abelson, H., and diSessa, A. 1980. *Turtle Geometry*. Cambridge: MIT Press.

Hoppe, H. U. 1984. *Logo im Mathematikunterricht*. Vaterstetten: IWT-Verlag.

LCN. 1988. LCN *Logo Synopsis Version 2.0*. Nijmegen: Logo Centrum Nijmegen.

Loethe, H. 1985. Geometrical problems for a turtle with direction and distance finder. *Proceedings of the First International Conference for Logo and Mathematics Education*, London, pp. 123–129.

Loethe, H. 1986. Posting and direction finding for a space turtle. *Proceedings of the Second International Conference for Logo and Mathematics Education*, London, pp. 193–200.

Loethe, H. 1987. Didactical conceptions for the space turtle use. *Proceedings of the Third International Conference for Logo and Mathematics Education*, London, pp. 70–75.

Loethe, H. 1992. The implementation of different turtle concepts. Unpublished manuscript.

Loethe, H., Woelpert, H., and Wolpert, S. 1985. Raumigel—Einführung, Anwendungen, Implementation. *Informatik and Datenverarbeitung in der Schule*, vol. 7. Ludwigsburg: Paedagogische Hochschule.

Loethe, H., Woelpert, H., and Wolpert, S. 1987. Raumigel—Dokumentation einer Arbeitsgemeinschaft in Klasse 9 Realschule. *Informatik and Datenverarbeitung in der Schule*, vol. 14. Ludwigsburg: Paedagogische Hochschule.

Loethe, H., and Wolpert, S. 1990. Platonic solids in space turtle representations—experiences with a course of tenth graders. In G. Schuyten and M. Valcke (eds.), *Teaching and Learning in Logo-Based Environments*. Amsterdam-Springfield-Tokyo: IOS.

Reggini, H. C. 1985. *Ideas y Formas*. Buenos Aires: Ediciones Galapago.

The Turtle Metaphor as a Tool for Children's Geometry

Chronis Kynigos

4

1 THEORETICAL FRAMEWORK

Since the 1950s geometry has played a diminishing role in mathematics curricula, at least in the United Kingdom. A major factor has been that euclidean geometry, taught as a tight deductive system and considered a prestigious area of knowledge, came to be regarded as "inappropriate" for primary and secondary education, since children could only master its deductive structure by rote learning. Research into children's geometrical understandings, starting with the work of Piaget, has highlighted, on the one hand, the formal (in the Piagetian sense) nature of deductive thinking and, on the other, pupils' difficulties in achieving such thinking in the context of geometry (Freudenthal 1973; van Hiele 1959). Thus, inevitably the case for teaching geometry as a ready-made deductive system has become considerably weakened.

However, Freudenthal has put forward the case for reconsidering the pedagogical importance of geometry, arguing that it has a characteristic not so common in education, namely, that it is a field within which *both* inductive and deductive learning can take place. Regarding the former kind of learning, he argued: "Geometry can only be meaningful if it exploits the relation of geometry to the experienced space. If the educator shirks this duty, he throws away an irretrievable chance. Geometry is one of the best opportunities that exists to learn how to mathematize reality" (Freudenthal 1973, p. 407). Furthermore, it has been argued that understanding deduction is at least related to (if not dependent on) experience with inductive thinking. For instance, von Glasersfeld has argued that "the generation of deductive abilities in both logic and mathematics must be based on the practice of inductive inference" (von Glasersfeld 1985, p. 484).

Schooling seems to have been providing children with very little opportunity to engage in inductive thinking within the field of geometry. The substantial amount of research into children's learning of geometry inspired by the van Hiele attempts to model geometrical thinking (Hoffer 1983) has revealed that a very high proportion (85 to 90 percent according to Pyshkalo 1968) of children up to the age of twelve, both in the Soviet Union and in the United States, seldom actually engage in inductive thinking; they remain at a stage where, for instance, they recognize shapes by their global appearance (van Hiele's level 0), failing to consider their properties analytically. What is more, they are subsequently introduced to deductive geometry in secondary education, where they are required to engage in van Hiele's level-2 and level-3 thinking when their actual background is at level 0 (Paalz-Scally 1985). In other words—to use Douady's (1985) terminology—children are required to think of geometrical notions as *objects*, when they have had minimal experience in using these notions as *tools*.

Following the above arguments, a reappraisal of the importance of geometry in education would imply providing children with more opportunities to engage in inductive geometrical thinking, at least within their primary schooling. To what extent might we consider Logo, particularly turtle geometry, as an important tool by means of which children might engage in such thinking?

Research in the learning processes of children engaged in Logo programming activities has provided substantial evidence that Logo can be used to generate rich mathematical environments for children (Noss 1985; Hoyles and Sutherland 1989). Consequently one could be tempted to infer that in partaking in turtle geometric activities children have the opportunity to engage in inductive thinking, since they can explore and develop understandings from experience within mathematical situations. Recent research, however, has shown that children do not necessarily use geometrical ideas when working with turtle geometry (Hillel and Kieran 1987; Leron 1983), instead, they often restrict themselves to the use of perceptual cues in deciding how to change the turtle's state on the screen (Hillel 1986).

Furthermore little attention has been given to the nature of the geometrical content children can actually learn with the turtle metaphor. Analyses of the geometrical nature of turtle geometry have characterized it as intrinsic and differential (Abelson and diSessa 1980; Papert 1980; Harvey 1985), that is, as giving access to a geometry built on the idea of localness where a given geometrical state is fully defined by its relation to the immediately previous state (see also Loethe's analysis in chapter 3).

Although there has been a certain amount of recent research focusing on both the geometrical content learned by children working with turtle graphics and on the process of their learning (Hillel 1985; Kieran 1986b; Lawler 1985; Hoyles and Sutherland 1989; Kieran, Hillel, and Erlwanger 1986), there has been little explicit analysis of the conceptual framework of geometrical notions that children might use while engaged in such geometric activities. So, what is the geometrical nature of the notions children might use to control the turtle? Are these notions necessarily intrinsic only?

Within the above framework this chapter is about research carried out to investigate the potential for eleven- to twelve-year-old children to use the Logo turtle in forming inductively developed understandings of a wide span of geometrical ideas, from intrinsic geometry to other geometrical systems such as euclidean and coordinate systems. Before getting into the details of this research, I will review previous research on children's geometrical understandings in turtle-geometric environments to provide a background for contemplating children's thinking processes within the context of specific geometrical concepts.

2 CHILDREN'S LEARNING OF GEOMETRY WITH LOGO

After having carried out substantial work into children's learning of programming (Hillel 1985), researchers in Canada began to focus more on the geometrical content of turtle geometry (Kieran 1986a, b) and on the thinking schemas formed by children in relation to this content (Hillel 1986; Kieran, Hillel, and Erlwanger 1986). Hillel, for instance, carried out a study based on his longitudinal observations of Logo programming by eight- to twelve-year-olds. His aim was to investigate the links between children's thinking processes and the content of both programming and geometry.

On the process level Hillel provided evidence that the children's perception of working with turtle geometry was largely dependent on a "drawing-with-the-turtle" metaphor, namely, that they predominantly set themselves specific goals and chose inputs to commands based on perceptual cues rather than on inherent mathematical relations. Concerning the geometrical content, he perceived turtle geometry as embodying a particular type of geometry whose nature is independent from the use of computers but whose embedding within a computer language provides a new way to do mathematics and some interesting links between geometrical and programming concepts (Hillel 1986).

An illuminative example of how children form understandings of specific geometrical concepts in Logo is provided by substantial research concerning their understanding of the concept of angle. It is therefore worth reviewing this research in some detail.

Apart from well-established difficulties children have in understanding the notion of angle in general (Hart 1981; APU 1982), research has indicated that children find difficulties in understanding the concept of angle in Logo, in relating angles to turtle turns (Papert et al. 1979; Hoyles and Sutherland 1989; Hoyles and Noss 1987a; Paalz-Scally 1986; Zack 1986; Noss 1987; Kieran 1986a). For instance, while attempting to analyze children's understanding of the notion within a framework of the van Hiele model of geometrical thinking, Paalz-Scally unexpectedly found inconsistencies between students' understanding of static representations of angle and their ability to apply that knowledge to tasks that involve representations of angle using turtle notations (Paalz-Scally 1986).

Kieran's investigation of ten- to twelve-year-olds' developing understandings of angle in Logo corroborated this view (Kieran 1986a, b). She concluded that the children seemed to keep static and dynamic representations of angle in different "mental compartments" (Kieran 1986a) and that their experience with Logo seemed to encourage their understanding of exterior angles but not that of interior ones. Even when the twelve-year-olds were able to respond to questions about interior and exterior turns with similar facility, they had major difficulties in coming to understand the supplementary relation between the two.

Finally, Hoyles and Sutherland (1989) investigated the same issue within a wider research project involving a close observation of a group of children's learning of mathematics with Logo through their first three years of secondary schooling. Supported by background data from other pupils participating in the study, these researchers analyzed in detail and highlighted the work of Janet, a member of a collaborative working pair. In part, through the experiences of Janet, who carried her uncertainties with amount of turn and turtle orientation throughout the three years, the researchers concluded that "pupils may not perceive inputs to RT and LT as rotations in circumstances where the nature of these inputs is determined by the context . . . in such situations children compute inputs to RT and LT, add and subtract them or compose them at the level of action but do not necessarily synthesize their resulting input to a total amount of turn; put another way children might be adding and subtracting numbers or adding and subtracting actions but not angles!" (See section 3.)

In general, process-oriented studies have indicated that using an idea in different contexts—such as the static and dynamic view of angle—is by no means an easy task for children, either in Logo environments (e.g., Hoyles and Noss 1987b) or in an even more general sense (e.g., diSessa 1983; Lawler 1985). This could well be affecting children's limited use of the geometry embedded in Logo; Hoyles and Sutherland agree with Leron (1983) that children engaged in Logo activities will not necessarily use the mathematics that is there, adding that this happens especially when the projécts are chosen by the children themselves and are aimed at goals consisting of real-world figures.

The issue of children's limited use of geometrical notions within turtle geometric environments was also addressed by researchers in Canada who collaboratively analyzed how six eleven- to twelve-years-olds used geometrical concepts in trying to solve structured tasks (Kieran, Hillel, and Erlwanger 1986; Hillel and Kieran 1987). The main outcome from these analyses was the researchers' synthesis of the children's solution processes across tasks into two general schemas. First, there is the perceptual schema, where the children chose inputs on the basis of perceptual cues, namely, without using geometrical relationships or properties and without relating the turtle's state to the previous state. Second, they specify the analytical schema where they chose inputs on the basis of geometrical relationships inherent in the given information or "from mathematical knowledge", or both. The researchers concluded that most children tend to use the perceptual schema spontaneously, not perceiving the need for a different approach unless the task at hand is unsuccessfully solved (according to the child's own view). In such cases eleven to twelve-year-olds were more ready to shift to an analytical schema than younger children (Hillel 1986; Kieran 1986a). Moreover they concluded that the children's perception of the precision of a task influences the strategies they use to solve it. This finding is supported by Hoyles and Sutherland.

Little research has been carried out concerning the nature of the process by which children identify with the turtle to drive it on the screen, and in particular, the nature of "body-syntonic" learning (Papert 1980). Papert argued that identifying with the turtle enables children "to bring their knowledge about their bodies and how they move into the work of learning formal geometry" (p. 56), stating that the turtle metaphor enables children to make sense of an idea. As the above research suggests, however, although children employ the turtle metaphor, they do not seem to be using a lot of geometry to do so; they rely rather on their visual perception to control the turtle. We equally know very little about children's understandings of the differences among and the relations involved in constructing geometrical figures by means of turtle geometry (and its intrinsic nature) and by methods requiring nonintrinsic points of reference such as the center of a circle or the origin of the coordinate plane.

The research that comes closest to addressing the issues of the nature of learning arising from identifying with the turtle and children's perception of geometry within Logo in relation to other geometries was carried out by Lawler (1985). The research involved an in-depth investigation of six-year-old Miriam's thinking during her activities with Logo, which included activities with the turtle, and within nonturtle environments involving, for instance, use of cartesian coordinates. Two aspects of Lawler's conclusions are relevant here. First, Miriam's understanding of turtle geometry and coordinate geometry depended on disparate fragments of knowledge which, as Lawler argues, have their roots in a child's very early locomotion and visual experiences, respectively. Second, forming connections between such fragments (termed *microviews* by Lawler) is by no means a trivial task for the child. In my view, Lawler's in-depth probing of Miriam's thinking offers limited (in the sense of generalizable) but very precise evidence of a very close correspondence between the content differences separating two distinct geometrical systems and the respective fragments of knowledge the child applied to understand them. Lawler regards these fragments as descendants of intuitive ideas, deriving from early experiences with motion for turtle geometry and with vision for coordinate geometry. Freudenthal has also supported the idea that geometrical knowledge has deep intuitive roots: "Many geometrical objects and concepts have been formed early, most of them at the primary school age and some of them even earlier, though they do not yet bear verbal labels, or at least those labels that we have learned to attach to them in our geometry lessons" (Freudenthal 1983, p. 226).

To summarize, research has shown that children do not always use the geometrical ideas embedded in turtle geometry. Rather, they often employ perceptual cues, perceiving the turtle as an extension of their hand while drawing. Papert and Lawler suggest that the ideas the children do use in identifying with the turtle to drive it on the screen are based on deeply rooted intuitions concerning bodily motion and that this is why turtle geometry makes sense to them. Recent studies, however, have indicated that children find it hard to relate geometrical ideas understood with the turtle metaphor to the same ideas in "static" environments.

Thus the question raised earlier as to how far we might consider using Logo to encourage children to learn geometry in an inductive way seems to give rise to two problematic issues. First, children engaging in turtle geometric activities do not seem to make much use of analytical cues, thus ignoring a lot of the embedded geometry. Second, the geometry they do learn seems limited to the intrinsic geometry embedded in the conventional turtle microworld.

3 A RESEARCH STUDY: AIMS AND METHOD

To what extent can we therefore consider turtle geometric environments as a useful means with which to fill a well-established gap in children's geometrical experiences? In particular, to what extent can children use the turtle metaphor to develop geometrical understandings in an inductive way, and what kind of geometry can they learn by causing changes in the turtle's state on the screen? The latter two questions led me to investigate the process and content of children's geometrical understandings by closely observing pairs of children working collaboratively within three turtle-geometric microworlds especially designed to embed not only intrinsic but also euclidean and coordinate geometric ideas (Kynigos 1989).

A few words about how these geometrical systems were defined in the context of the three microworlds are needed here. Embedding geometrical ideas in a microworld involved the careful design of the microworld's "conceptual field" (in the sense of Vergnaud 1982). The prevailing characteristic of the conceptual field of all three microworlds of the research was that they retained the turtle and its state of position and heading as their mathematical entity while embedding either intrinsic and coordinate or intrinsic and euclidean geometric ideas.

The way in which ideas were incorporated in each of the three microworlds was by certain additional primitives (described below), providing the children with a choice of means by which to change the turtle's state. Changing the turtle's state would thus involve using an intrinsic or a nonintrinsic (euclidean or coordinate) idea. For instance, deciding on an input to a procedure to change the turtle's state, without referring to places outside the turtle's immediate vicinity, involved the use of intrinsic ideas. Making such a decision by referring to a distant point in the plane by means of an absolute system of reference involved the use of coordinate ideas. Deciding on an input by referring to a point of a geometrical figure away from the turtle's position (but not using an absolute reference system) involved the use of euclidean ideas.

By observing children working within the three microworlds, my objective was to investigate the potential for them to use their turtle metaphor to develop understandings of intrinsic, euclidean, and coordinate notions. Four issues were investigated: first, the nature of the "schema" (or set of theorems formed while acting on the environment) that children form when they identify with the turtle in order to change its state on the screen; second, whether it is possible for children to use the schema to gain insights into certain basic geometrical principles of coordinate geometry; third, how children might use the schema to form understandings of euclidean geometric notions developed inductively from specific experiences; and finally, fourth, the criteria children develop for choosing between intrinsic and euclidean representations of certain geometrical ideas.

Ten children aged eleven to twelve-years old from a Greek primary school in Athens participated in the research. They had previously had forty to fifty hours of experience with turtle geometry, working among a total of twenty children in groups of two or three in an informal situation with their normal teacher. The same group of twenty children continued to work in the same way during the period in which the research took place but independently of research sessions and activities. The research involved three case studies of pairs of children engaging in cooperative activities, each case study within one of the three geometrical Logo microworlds. The collected data included hard copies of everything that was said, typed, and written (verbatim transcriptions from audiotape, dribble files, and written notes were used).

Each case study involved a design balance between open-ended and task-oriented activities for the children, with the researcher intervening accordingly. The latter activities were designed to allow the pupils to choose the strategy used to achieve the set goal. The researcher's interest was focused on the process by which the children solved a task rather than on the actual goal that was set.

4   A SUMMARY OF THE THREE CASE STUDIES

Rather than present in detail the design and the specific results from each of the three case studies, I will synthesize certain features of the geometrical environments generated by the children that bear upon the main question of the research: What is the potential for children to use the turtle metaphor to form inductively developed understandings of a wide range of geometrical ideas?

I will begin by outlining a very brief sketch of the three case studies so that the relationship of the research to the subsequent synthesis will be made clearer. (A detailed account of the research can be found in Kynigos 1989).

The TCP Microworld Case Study

The first case study was used to probe the nature of the children's turtle schema and to investigate if, and how, they might use the schema to form understandings of coordinate notions. Three pairs of children were involved, each pair working for six hours in total. Each pair engaged in a sequence of preliminary activities leading to a final structured task within a rather complex microworld embedding intrinsic and coordinate ideas, the "turtle-in-the-coordinate-plane" (TCP) microworld. The complexity of the TCP microworld lay in the relatively large number of primitives among which the children could choose in order to change the turtle's state. The final task involved the children using the turtle to join points and to measure length and angle quantities on the cartesian plane. The microworld's primitives were the following:

1. FD, BK, RT, LT to cause turtle actions.
2. SETH, SETPOS, SETH TOWARDS to change the turtle's state by describing an absolute direction or location.
3. DIRECTION, DISTANCE to measure a right turn or a distance from the turtle's state to some point on the cartesian plane.

These commands were adapted from Loethe (1985). Since they play a more central role in the design of the microworld in the second study, they are described more analytically in the corresponding subsection below.

A prevailing characteristic of the TCP microworld was that no change of position, nor length measurement, was possible unless the turtle was facing the target location. Although mathematically superfluous, the restriction was built into the microworld to validate the existence of the turtle as the mathematical entity with position and heading. For instance, using the SETPOS command would first require changing the turtle's heading to face toward the target location (unless the turtle was already facing there).

Analysis of the data revealed that the predominant "theorems" the children had previously formed to control the turtle in conventional Logo involved two main ideas: that of a turtle action and its quantity, and that of sequentiality.[1] During the study, however, the children began to form theorems involving the use of coordinate ideas, such as changing a state solely by describing how the turtle would end up after the change (the end state). The findings suggest that the conflict created between former (intrinsic) and latter (coordinate) ideas acted as a catalyst for the children's forming of their coordinate schemas. Such conflict, for example, arose when the children mistook the input to a coordinate command to be the quantity of an action and, as a consequence of the computer feedback, realized that the input signified an absolute position or direction.

---

1. The linear sequencing of Logo commands.

Finally, although the children found it hard to relate one type of idea to the other, using the turtle metaphor helped rather than hindered them in making such relations. For instance, to discriminate a coordinate from an intrinsic turtle change of heading, they adopted and used the notion of the turtle "putting its nose to look at . . . " some direction instead of "turning this much. . . ."

The PDD Microworld Case Study

The second case study focused on the investigation of how children might use their intrinsic schema to form inductively developed understandings of euclidean geometry. The investigation was carried out in the context of a pair of children's activities within a microworld (adapted from Loethe 1985) which enabled angle and distance measurements between turtle states to be made. The POST–DISTANCE–DIRECTION (PDD) microworld consisted of the conventional action-quantity turtle commands plus the following additional primitives:

1. POST "name. Puts the turtle's current location into memory under the input name and "labels" the corresponding position on the screen by means of a cross sign on the respective point and the input name at close proximity.
2. DISTANCE :name. Outputs the distance between the turtle's current position and some other position (specified by the input) already labeled by the POST command.
3. DIRECTION :name. Outputs the degrees required for the turtle to make a right turn from its current heading to face the input location: Here too the position is already labeled by the POST command.

As implied from the outline of the conceptual fields of the three microworlds of the research (given in section 3), the geometry embedded in the PDD microworld is not intrinsic because the turtle can refer to "posted" points outside its immediate vicinity. Nevertheless, references to points in the plane can only be related to the turtle's trajectory; there is no absolute locating system available, as there is in the TCP microworld. This difference in the way points are referred to in the PDD and TCP microworlds is reflected, for instance, in the significance of the inputs to the DISTANCE and DIRECTION commands in each microworld.

The two children participating in the case study worked with the PDD microworld for fifteen hours, at a rate of two ninety-minute sessions per week. They engaged in three types of activities, each with the following emphasis:

1. Using the microworld's primitives in changing the turtle's state and measuring quantities between states.

2.   Constructing an isosceles triangle and investigating its geometrical properties by measuring angle and length quantities (e.g., quantities related to the bisector).
3.   Carrying out projects of personal choice where the children could decide the extent and the way in which they would use the PDD primitives or their experience with properties of the isosceles triangle.

The analysis of the data throughout the PDD microworld study indicated that inductive thinking was a predominant characteristic of the children's activities and that the geometrical content used by the children within this environment was extended from intrinsic ideas alone to both intrinsic and euclidean geometrical ones. In constructing isosceles triangles, for instance, the children formed theorems about turtle turnings on the triangles' vertices and about relations among the internal angles of the triangles.

The Circle Microworld Case Study

The third case study focused on the investigation of the children's criteria in choosing between the use of intrinsic and euclidean ideas. The study involved a pair of children working for twenty-four hours in total at a rate of two ninety-minute sessions per week and consisted of two phases. In phase 1 the children participated in a learning sequence involving the construction and use of four circle procedures, each of which embedded specific intrinsic and/or euclidean notions. In phase 2 these procedures were treated as the primitives of a Circle microworld, in addition to the conventional turtle action commands (FD, BK, RT, LT). The children were given structured tasks involving the construction of figures consisting of compositions of circles. They had the choice of which of the four circle procedures (primitives) to use in constructing the figures. Figure 1a illustrates the four circle procedures written by the children as a result of phase 1 of the case study and figure 1b gives some examples of the structured tasks subsequently given to the children.

   The analysis of the data suggests that the children did not seem to consider one type of notion (either intrinsic or euclidean) easier to understand than the other and that their use of the two types was balanced throughout the study. What is more, what mattered to the children in their choices between the two types of notions was related to other factors of the generated mathematical situations—such as whether using a notion had been part of their personal experience rather than whether a notion was intrinsic or euclidean.

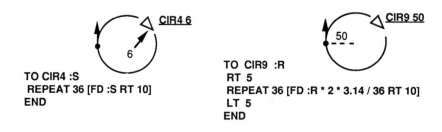

TO CIR4 :S
 REPEAT 36 [FD :S RT 10]
 END

TO CIR9 :R
 RT 5
 REPEAT 36 [FD :R * 2 * 3.14 / 36 RT 10]
 LT 5
 END

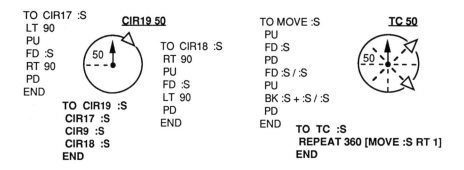

TO CIR17 :S
 LT 90
 PU
 FD :S
 RT 90
 PD
 END

TO CIR18 :S
 RT 90
 PU
 FD :S
 LT 90
 PD
 END

TO CIR19 :S
 CIR17 :S
 CIR9 :S
 CIR18 :S
 END

TO MOVE :S
 PU
 FD :S
 PD
 FD :S / :S
 PU
 BK :S + :S / :S
 PD
 END

TO TC :S
 REPEAT 360 [MOVE :S RT 1]
 END

◁ Denotes a turtle state during the execution of the procedure

↑ Denotes the turtle's start/finish

Figure 1a The children's constructions of the Circle microworld's primitives

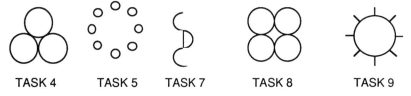

TASK 4   TASK 5   TASK 7   TASK 8   TASK 9

Figure 1b Examples of the structured tasks in phase 2 of the study

To sum up, the findings in the context of each specific microworld environment were that in the TCP microworld the children had formed an action-quantity and a sequentiality turtle schema that was useful in forming theorems about coordinate geometry during the study, in the PDD microworld the children engaged mainly in inductive thinking and used both intrinsic and euclidean ideas, and in the Circle microworld the distinction between intrinsic and euclidean ideas was not an important factor in children's use of geometrical ideas with the help of their turtle schema.

5 A SYNTHESIS OF THE FINDINGS

Synthesizing the findings across case studies enabled me to focus more on the question posed earlier: Can Logo be a useful tool for children to do geometry in an inductive way? The consequent reanalyzing of the data pointed to three process-related aspects of the environments generated by the children that threw light on the extent to which children might use the turtle metaphor to develop inductive understandings of geometrical ideas: first, the balance between using analytical and perceptual cues in deciding on inputs to turtle actions; second, the nature of the children's intrinsic schemas; and third, the extent to and the way in which their thinking was inductive.

In addressing the question of what kind of geometry children learned, two issues were studied: how the children employed their intrinsic schemas to form understandings of geometrical ideas belonging to all three geometrical systems, and how their employment of the intrinsic schema in using the above wide variety of geometrical ideas was related to their understanding of programming.

The Children's Use of Analytical and Perceptual Cues

Throughout the three case studies there is strong evidence that the children considered the use of perceptual cues at least an acceptable and valid method to make decisions about turtle commands and their inputs. This finding corroborates the results from previous research (Hillel and Kieran 1987). A key finding in the present research, however, was that influenced by the microworld environments (i.e., embedded ideas, activities, and researcher interventions), the children progressively incorporated the use of analytical cues. What is more, there is evidence that the children in the PDD and Circle microworld studies (which were of longer duration than the first) developed their own reasons for using analytical cues instead of their perceptions, such as an appreciation of the accuracy of their constructions.

It is consequently argued that making analytical decisions on inputs to turtle commands did not involve some higher-order quality in the children's thinking. Instead, it is suggested that there were two important factors influencing the children's use of analytical cues. The first one is related to the nature of the microworlds: It could be argued that compared with conventional Logo, the embedded geometrical ideas were dense (i.e., a greater number of geometrical ideas were embedded within a specific turtle activity) and more specific because of both the geometrical nature of the new primitives and the way the activities were designed for the children within the microworlds. The second factor was that the microworlds incorporated a wider range of geometrical notions than just those belonging to intrinsic geometry; these were made available to the children via the use of the new tools (primitives).

To illustrate how each of these two factors acted as a catalyst for the children's use of analytical cues, two episodes from the PDD microworld study are described below. The first episode illustrates how the microworld's primitives and the designed activities for the children related to their use of analytical cues. In the initial phases of the study, in deciding on input to turtle actions, Nikos and Philip started to use the DIRECTION and DISTANCE commands to measure angles and lengths within a triangle. The following activity is part of a sequence of similar structured tasks that involved the children being asked to use the turtle to join three labeled points on the screen with line segments and to measure the sides and internal angles of the formed triangle (the setup for each task was initialized by the researcher).

Nikos seemed to be in the process of developing a strategy for measuring the internal angles of the triangle. As shown in figure 2, he measured an external

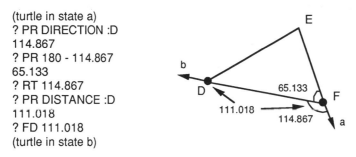

(turtle in state a)
? PR DIRECTION :D
114.867
? PR 180 - 114.867
65.133
? RT 114.867
? PR DISTANCE :D
111.018
? FD 111.018
(turtle in state b)

Figure 2 Using angle and length measuring instruments

```
POST "A
FD 70
POST "B
RT 135
FD 70
POST "C
RT DIRECTION :A
FD DISTANCE :A
```

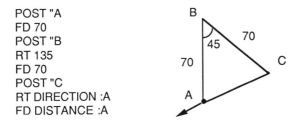

Figure 3 Constructing an isosceles triangle

(rotation) angle (turtle in state *a*) and then used the computer to subtract the outcome from 180 in order to find out the size of the internal angle. He then used the outcome of the measurement again to cause a turtle action. He therefore seemed to be using an angular measurement outcome for both dynamic and static interpretations of angular notions. Figure 2 illustrates the children's use of the outcomes of length and angle measurements, both for collecting information on the triangle's elements and for moving the turtle from one point of the triangle to the other.[1]

The second episode illustrates how the wide range of geometrical ideas embedded in the microworld (compared with conventional Logo) was conducive to the children's use of analytical cues. In a subsequent task Nikos and Philip were asked to construct a triangle with two equal sides, this time deciding on when and where to use the POST command for themselves. As shown in figure 3, their initial commands to change the turtle's state involved the use of intrinsic ideas: FD 70, RT 135, and FD 70 did not require any reference to points away from the turtle's state. At point *C*, however, in order to turn the turtle to face point *A* and then to move it from *C* to *A*, the children used the two measuring instruments in "action mode," that is, directly as inputs to turtle-action commands. Consequently, for both the turtle actions of rotation and motion, the children used a reference to point *A* (i.e., a point away from the turtle's state). The children's subsequent measuring of the remaining internal angles of the triangle was followed by their first conjecture regarding a euclidean property of the isosceles triangle (i.e., that it has two equal angles). Had the children not had the PDD instruments, it would have been impossible to use the turtle to construct an isosceles triangle and collect information on its elements unless the children already had knowledge of its properties.

---

1. Although it would be interesting to analyze the children's understanding of decimals, it did not have an important influence on and was not part of the research issues of the study.

In view of the two points made above, it is suggested, on the one hand, that the conceptual field of conventional Logo may lack in density of embedded geometrical notions and, on the other, that the available intrinsic notions are rather restrictive. It may be the case therefore that finding it difficult to synthesize the required geometrical knowledge from their schooling and also finding the process of using geometrical properties to make shapes on the screen not functional, children prefer to use direct perceptions. It could be argued that these impediments enhance the use of perception and could act as a catalyst for their use of a "drawing schema," observed by Hillel (1986). The children from the study had had considerable experience with conventional Logo, and not surprisingly, this influenced their use of perceptual cues, especially during the initial phases of the three studies.

Their progressive use of analytical cues during the study would consequently suggest that employing an analytical schema was not conceptually beyond the children's thinking but rather involved the use of a different framework of knowledge from the one that they had developed in using Logo. The argument that children's "naive" thinking is often a matter of the framework of knowledge that they use (Booth 1981) is therefore corroborated by the present study. The children's increasing use of analytical cues within the three geometrically rich microworlds of the study would corroborate Vergnaud's claim that there is a need to design conceptual fields where the children would find it inviting to formulate and refine "theorems in action" (Vergnaud 1987a).

The Children's Intrinsic Schema

Previous research has tended to perceive children's schemas for controlling the turtle as integrated with the use of geometrical notions (Papert 1980; Lawler 1985).The indications from the present research, however, support the argument that although children often identify with the turtle to drive it on the screen, it is far from axiomatic that they are necessarily engaging in geometrical activity. This section is about the theorems the children did form and use to control the turtle and discusses their perception of the nature of these theorems.

The findings from the three case studies indicate that the children saw sense in identifying with the turtle and using experience based on bodily motion in order to change its state. Identifying the theorems the children seemed to have formed for controlling the turtle was one of the research issues in focus during their activities with the TCP microworld. In addition the analysis of the data

REPEAT 4 [CIR19 20 PU FD 40 PD RT 90]

Figure 4 The children's solution of a structured task with circles

revealed episodes where the six children taking part in the case study implicitly used one or both of the following notions:

1.   An action-quantity notion, which involved a "turn degrees" notion for heading changes and a "move steps" notion for position changes.
2.   A sequentiality notion, which involved the notions of "one change after another" and "a change depends on the immediately previous state."

There is evidence of all six children readily using action-quantity and sequentiality notions during these activities. This, however, does not imply that they did not have difficulties with these ideas, such as problems with discriminating between the two states and between an action and its quantity, or with concentrating on one state change at a time.

What is more, the data from all three case studies suggested that using the above notions was not perceived by the children as using geometry but as using experience that they had acquired independently of the microworlds. This argument would be further supported by specific findings in the Circle microworld study where, for example, the children themselves (Alexandros and Valentini) expressed the view that no knowledge is required in order to understand the total turtle turn theorem, as illustrated by the following episode:

Within the context of discussing their solution of a task figure involving circles placed in a square formation (figure 4), both children said that they preferred explaining the turtle's turn of 90 degrees by means of the partitioning of a total turn rather than adding up the internal angles of the formed square. What is interesting is not their preference as such (after all, they were using the turtle to construct the figure) but the reasons they gave for and against the two methods:

Valentini: . . . they tell us, that definitely it's 360 (*she means that the sum of the internal angles is 360 degrees*) and that's it, you can't say anything, it's definitely 360, I know and you can't ask, you can't do a thing.

Alexandros: It's like I told you the other time. Geometry forces us, we can't ask about . . . this, since it's been discovered that this is that much, that much we'll write it. We can't ask why is it like that and why is it like this because they'll tell us because that's what it wants to be.

(Their reasons on why they preferred the total turn method.)

Valentini: Because it's more natural . . . yes, it's more natural, now I thought of that . . . anybody can understand it . . .

Alexandros: Even if he doesn't know about the turtle at all.

Researcher: Tell me something. What does someone have to know to understand this thing?

Valentini: Nothing.

So the children's perception of the "internal angles" rule as part of the geometry learned at school, portrayed geometry as a set of facts they were told of and not given the chance to question, let alone discover for themselves. Such ideas about school geometry are seldom made explicit by children in Greece, at least in the school where the research took place. On the contrary, their perception of the "turtle turn" rule seemed to be that they understood it even though they were not given any information about it. Thus, in contrast with school geometry, the children's view of the nature of a turtle-geometric rule corroborates Papert and Lawler's contention that children base their understandings of turtle geometry on intuitive knowledge.

Employing the Intrinsic Schema to Work on Geometry Inductively

The analysis from all three case studies supported the argument that under certain circumstances—such as widening the span of geometrical notions embedded in turtle geometry and creating microworld environments inviting children to use geometry in a functional way—Logo may have an important role to play in providing children with tools to engage in inductive geometrical thinking. The investigation of this potential in the PDD microworld case study provided evidence of the children's incorporation of euclidean notions into their developing use of geometry during their activities with the microworld. The children predominantly engaged in inductive thinking by using geometrical notions that they had generalized through specific observations made while measuring distances and angles on the plane and by using the information to decide on quantities of turtle actions.

```
TO LASER :N :P
  POST "I
  RT 90 - :P
  FD :N
  POST "H
  RT 180 - (180 - (2 *:P))
  FD :N
  POST "M
  RT DIRECTION :I
  FD DISTANCE :I
  RT 90
END
```

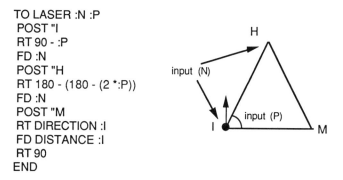

Figure 5 An outcome of an inductive process: the children's LASER procedure

Let us take an example of the process of the children's inductive reasoning by discussing a rather sophisticated generalized procedure for an isosceles triangle that the children wrote midway through the case study; it is shown in figure 5.

The first input to the procedure, signifying the length of the equal sides of the triangle, is not very important in this case. The second input signified the size of the internal equal angles. It is apparent from the structure of the procedure, that the children used the angle properties of the triangle in a sophisticated way on two occasions: (1) in deciding on the input to the first right turn of the turtle in order to construct the triangle in an upright orientation (RT 90 - :P), and (2) in deciding on the input to the turtle's right turn at the H vertex, which involved combining turtle turn and internal angle, the sum of the angles of a triangle, and the equal-angles property of an isosceles triangle.

The point here is that the generalizations required to use the above angle properties were made by the children as a result of specific experiences—that is, by measuring specific internal angles in relation to turtle turns (as in figure 1), by adding up the angles of specific triangles and conjecturing that their sum must always be 180 degrees, and by comparing their measurements of the angles of isosceles triangles and conjecturing that two of them are always equal. As is apparent from the LASER procedure, the children were only in the process of making inductively derived generalizations. Although one could infer that they would be able to work out the quantity of the turtle's turn at point M, they used the DIRECTION command to turn the turtle to face point I. Nevertheless, they worked out the quantity of such a turn (see figure 5) later in their "striped triangle" project, as shown in figure 7.

N: "It should look upwards this..."
(she types SETH TOWARDS -20 90)
  "Now we'll tell the protractor..."
I: "We'll find the angle now..."
(they type PR DIRECTION 70 -70)

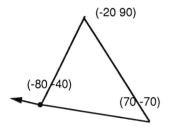

(-20 90)

(-80 -40)

(70 -70)

Figure 6 Measuring an internal angle in the TCP microworld

The Employment of the Intrinsic Schema and the Use of Geometrical Notions

As mentioned above, the research indicates that the children's use of the intrinsic schema did not necessarily entail the use of geometrical notions, that is, the ideas embedded in the microworlds. This argument, however, does not in turn imply that the children did not use geometrical ideas before and during the research. Furthermore the analysis indicates that their increasing use of analytical cues was accompanied by an increasing use of the embedded geometrical notions. The main aim of this section is to describe how the children employed the turtle metaphor in using geometrical ideas from the three systems.

Let us first take the case of the children's use of intrinsic and coordinate notions. In the later stages of the TCP microworld study, all three pairs of children were given the task to use the turtle to join three unlabeled points on the coordinate grid and measure the lengths and angles of the triangle that is formed. The following example will illustrate different ways in which the children used intrinsic and/or coordinate ideas on a particular occasion during the task. On that occasion all three pairs coincidentally found themselves having to measure the internal angle at point $(-80 -40)$ while the turtle was in the state shown in figure 6.

Natassa and Ioanna used coordinate notions in changing the turtle's heading to face point $(-20\ 90)$. Natassa used a coordinate notion when she changed the turtle's heading with reference to a location described by means of the cartesian coordinates, that is, by typing in

SETH TOWARDS $-20\ 90$

She therefore changed the heading with a non-action-quantity method: What causes a heading change with the SETH TOWARDS command is a description of a location on the cartesian plane. The children then performed a measurement without seeming to relate it to the quantity of a turtle action (*"now we'll tell the protractor"*). Ioanna's comment indicates that the children perceived the measurement independently of their action-quantity schema.

Anna and Loukia's strategy also consisted of two parts: changing the heading and then measuring the angle. To change the turtle's heading, however, they seemed to combine an intrinsic and a cartesian idea; by typing in RT DIREC-TION [−20 90], Anna seemed to perceive the change of heading as a turtle turn. On the other hand, what determined the quantity of that turn (i.e., the input to RT) was a reference to a plane location by means of the cartesian coordinates. Anna's verbal explanation to her peer supports this argument.

Anna: We'll turn this way . . . [*she means toward −20 90*], and then from here we'll ask it . . . we'll say PR DIRECTION . . . 70 −70, and it'll tell us.

Instead of saying something like, "We'll turn this much . . . " (i.e., action quantity), she said, *"We'll turn this way . . . "* (i.e., action direction); furthermore the latter part of the strategy, was expressed as a nonaction measurement (*"we'll ask it . . . and it'll tell us"*). In general, although the children used both types of geometrical ideas, they found it hard to relate one type to the other. This would support Lawler's view that intrinsic and cartesian ideas are based on different types of intuitions.

The schema the children formed in order to use euclidean notions did not involve such drastic changes to their intrinsic schemas, such as abandoning the notions of action-quantity and sequentiality. The euclidean notions were used in deciding on quantities and in referring to parts of a figure away from the turtle's position. Here too, however, the common basis for using intrinsic and euclidean notions was the ability to use the turtle schema, that is, to think in terms of the turtle changing its state on the screen. An example of an episode illustrating children's use of their turtle schema and euclidean ideas will be taken from the PDD microworld study where this issue was in focus.

The episode in question took place during the final stages of the case study, where the children were asked to carry out a project of their own choosing. They decided to make a "triangle with a stripe" and used the general procedure for an isosceles triangle which they had written earlier (the LASER procedure; see figure 5). Relevant here is not so much the procedure itself but the fact that the children knew that the triangle they made was isosceles and that the input they

(turtle in state a, Nikos addressing Philip)
N: "RT... 230. You know why I'm putting 230?
Because 230... look... from here to here it's
180 isn't it? (P. agrees) *This angle, isn't
it 50?* (P. agrees again) *O.K., 180 and 50
doesn't it make us... for the turtle to go
woop, woop and it does us 230?"*

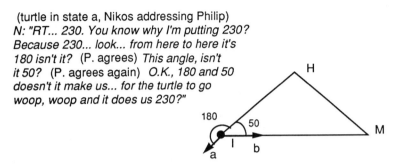

Figure 7 Adding two components of an angle to turn the turtle

gave to the procedure signified the internal angle HIM (see figure 7). In attempting to make the stripe, the children took the turtle somewhere on the segment IH and then realized that there was no accurate way to take the turtle to segment IM. They consequently decided to take the turtle back, make a POST half-way along IM, and then refer to the POST from a point on IH. The episode in question refers to the process by which Nikos decided to turn the turtle from state *a* to state *b*, as shown in figure 7; this is illustrated by the way he explained it to his peer, Philip. Rather than using the DIRECTION command (i.e., RT DIRECTION :M), he added the two angular components of the respective right turn, thus using euclidean angle properties to perform an intrinsically oriented action and its quantity in degrees by typing RT 230. Notice how Nikos made an angle calculation (*"180 and 50, doesn't it make. . . "*), seemed to pause to think, and finally seemed to change to talking about the outcome of the calculation as if it was the quantity of a turtle turn (*"for the turtle to go . . . and it does 230."*).

In this context of employing the intrinsic schema to use ideas from the three geometrical systems, the analysis of the data from all three studies showed that it is possible for children to generate learning environments akin to the ones generated in studies of children using conventional Logo. This issue, which was in research focus during the PDD microworld study in the context of euclidean geometry, supports the argument that turtle-geometric environments need not be restricted to intrinsic geometric notions if they are to preserve their dynamic characteristics. This conclusion is reinforced by the Circle microworld study, which indicated that the children did not find inherent qualitative differences between euclidean and intrinsic notions used while employing their turtle schema. That is, they did not find one type of notion harder to understand than the other.

```
TO TR :S
 RT 30
  REPEAT 3 [CIR19 :S FD 50 RT 120]
 END
```

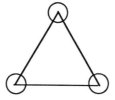

Figure 8 Using intrinsic and euclidean ideas while solving a structured task

To illustrate this point, an example will be given from the late stages of the case study, discussing Valentini's and Alexandros' final solution of a structured task consisting of a figure of three circles whose centers were placed at the vertices of an equilateral triangle (as shown in figure 8). The children's solution indicates a coherent use of a combination of intrinsic and euclidean ideas; the latter involve the use of the CIR19 circle procedure (see figure 1a), where both the input and the commands necessary for state transparency refer to the length of the circle's radius and to its center (both notions "unknown" to an intrinsic turtle); they also involve the use of the notion of a circle's center to explain the connection among the positions of the three circles. Valentini's written explanation of why she used that particular circle procedure (CIR19) illustrates the above point:

Valentini: I used the CIR19 because at the place where one of the lines of the triangle ends and the other one starts is the point that is in the middle of the circle.

In explaining to her peer the turtle's turn of 120 degrees in the TRI procedure shown in figure 8, however, Valentini used the intrinsic notion of partitioning a total turn of the turtle into three equal turns (the structuring of the procedure was achieved through her initiative); referring to the turtle, she said that "*there were three turns which were. . . 360, and therefore dividing 360 by 3 gives 120 degrees for each turn. . . .* " Furthermore, in explaining why the total turn was 360 in this case, she coherently used the turtle's total turn in the children's TC procedure (figure 1a) as an example, that is, the procedure embodying the euclidean definition of the circle as the set of points equidistant from the center point!

So, as in Valentini's use of both euclidean and intrinsic ideas in the same task, the children alternately employed ideas from the two systems without seeming to find one type harder to understand than the other. The Circle microworld study thus indicates that children may find the intrinsic schema equally useful for learning intrinsic and euclidean ideas.

In general, the research has elaborated that the children did not seem to find qualitative differences in understanding intrinsic, euclidean, or coordinate notions to control the turtle in the respective microworld environments. Employing the intrinsic schema did not necessarily imply that the children were aware of using geometrical notions. Furthermore, when geometrical notions were used, they were not necessarily intrinsic. This finding would suggest that the turtle metaphor need not invite children to learn only intrinsic geometrical ideas, as implied by Papert.

Relationships among the Intrinsic Schema, Programming, and Geometrical Content

In the present research the geometrical aspect of the children's activities was analyzed separately from the programming aspect. Earlier studies of children engaged in Logo activities have varied in the degree to which they have perceived those two aspects separately. I do not enter here into a discussion of the relationship between programming and mathematics: Papert et al. (1979) and Noss (1985) have argued that activities with Logo can generate integrated programming–mathematical environments and that programming is an essentially mathematical activity. While I do not disagree with this view, I argue here that there is still a need for the illumination of subtle features concerning the programming and the mathematical aspects of children's Logo activities, with emphasis on the latter. Recent research seems to support this view (Hillel 1986; Kieren 1987).

In the present study the distinction between the children's use of geometrical and programming notions served as a means by which to focus on geometrical issues arising from the children's activities. The children's programming strategies were analyzed through the perspective of how they related to the children's use of geometrical notions.

During the PDD and Circle microworld studies the children, not surprisingly (considering the structure of their activities), showed an increasing fluency in using procedures, subprocedures, and variables. However, the relationship between their increasing mastery of structured programming and their use of geometry was not always positive. For instance, Nikos' and Philip's use of geometry and programming during their own projects in the later stages of the PDD microworld study seem, at least in some cases, to contrast with each other. For example, the striped triangle project, while not involving the use of modular programming, did involve a relatively sophisticated use of the geometrical notions embedded within the given triangle. In another project, however, although they used the LASER procedure with fixed inputs as a building block in order to make a superprocedure of nested triangles, their use of geometrical properties was minimal. Furthermore Valentini and Alexandros' fluent superprocedure-building strategies during their projects in the Circle microworld study often involved very little use of the geometry embedded in the circle procedures. In contrast, their project involving the most use of geometrical notions did not involve structured programming.

A factor that might have influenced contrasting uses of geometry and programming for Nikos and Philip could be the nature of the PDD microworld tools. Measurements in the plane in order to decide on inputs to specific direct-drive action commands may initially have encouraged direct- drive programming. A further factor may have been the relationship between structured programming and regular figures, such as a square or an equilateral triangle. In mathematical terms regular figures can be constructed via consistent intrinsic rules (e.g., REPEAT 4 [FD 50 RT 90]) that do not require reference to the plane. The children's use of euclidean notions enabled them to write procedures for a wider class of geometrical figures (e.g., the LASER procedure, figure 8), which, however, did not involve programming the details of the procedures to generate them.

In general, the research highlights the complexities involved in the relationship between the programming and geometrical aspects of children's Logo activities; consequently it supports the view that we need to know more about ways in which children can be helped to make links between the two aspects and to use them in a complementary way for the development of their mathematical thinking.

6 CONCLUSIONS

Rather than attempting to generalize from a few cases, the role of this study was to act as a probe in investigating if, and how, we could use Logo for something that we know is actually missing in children's mathematical experiences, at least in geometrical education. This is the opportunity to form inductively developed understandings of geometrical ideas before they are required to use these ideas in the deductive geometries of conventional curricula.

Taking into account the nontrivial problems in children's learning geometry with Logo that have emerged from previous research, the above issue was investigated by closely observing children working with specially designed geometrical Logo microworlds in order to see (1) how densely they might use geometrical ideas in an inductive way among their activities and (2) whether the learned content could be broadened from an intrinsic geometry to non-intrinsic geometries such as the euclidean and coordinate.

In addressing issue (1), the extent to which the children used the turtle metaphor to inductively develop understandings of geometrical ideas was analyzed as a threefold, process-related issue. First of all, studying the balance between the children's use of perceptual and analytical cues revealed a distinct progress in the use of the latter—a finding not in line with previous research. This was attributed to the microworld environments' incorporation of a wide variety of specific and densely embedded geometrical ideas in relation to conventional Logo. More important, however, the analysis suggested that using analytical cues did not require some higher-order thinking on the part of the children but was rather a matter of learning the rules of a new game, that is, a new framework of knowledge.

Second, analyzing the way in which the children used the turtle metaphor revealed that to drive the turtle on the screen, they had developed two types of theorems involving the ideas of action-quantity and sequentiality. Not surprisingly, they did not seem to perceive these ideas as geometrical. They did, however, perceive them as simply making sense, not really requiring any special knowledge. It is argued that this finding supports Papert and Lawler's view that the turtle schema is based on intuitive knowledge.

Third, the children's thinking was predominantly of an inductive nature. That is, they often used geometrical ideas that they had generalized from specific observations. Again, rather than finding it a difficult task, the children progressively engaged in inductive thinking as a meaningful method by which to use the microworlds' tools in their activities.

The analysis thus indicates that the extent to which children might engage in the practice of inductive inference with the use of Logo is not tightly restricted by boundaries related to the quality of their thinking processes or inherent to Logo-generated environments. Given environments such as were used in the present study where, with the help of careful pedagogical intervention, the children were encouraged to employ an intuitive thinking vehicle (the turtle) and to use analytical cues densely in making decisions to control it, the way in which they developed geometrical understandings was predominantly inductive.

Issue (2) was related to learning content. In order to probe the possibility of broadening the geometrical content of Logo environments, the investigation focused on the children's use of the geometrical ideas embedded in the three microworlds. The analysis showed that the children employed their turtle metaphor to use ideas from all three geometrical systems impartially and with equal ease. Furthermore, although the sophistication of their programming in a given activity was not necessarily related to the complexity of the geometrical ideas employed, they showed overall progress in their programming skills.

The analysis therefore indicates that with the use of specific Logo microworlds, a substantial broadening of the learned geometrical content is possible without making important concessions on what Logo has to offer vis-à-vis children's learning process. Observing how and what the children learned during the study has therefore been revealing. It has shown that by carefully constructing geometrical microworld environments within Logo, we may be able to provide children with opportunities to enrich their experiences of inductive inference, at least within an important part of the field of geometry.

It is suggested that the microworlds of the study were crucial in providing the children with the opportunities to learn in the way described above. Most important here was the equal emphasis on designing conceptual fields rich with geometrical ideas, embedding them in a powerful programming language, and providing the children with an intuitive vehicle with which to explore them. The last was the turtle metaphor, which seemed to mesh with the way in which they themselves come to grips with physical action through space.

In conventional Logo the turtle metaphor seems designed to invite children to employ experiences of bodily motion to understand intrinsic ideas. In the microworlds of the present study, however, there were indications that the children drew upon their own experiences of *movement in the real world* in their use of the metaphor of a turtle equipped with the means to refer to distant points on the plane. What is more, it is suggested that this turtle metaphor invited the children to use a wider span of geometrical ideas (as shown in the specific findings of the three case studies), and it made equal, if not more, sense than the strictly intrinsic turtle. After all, children acting out a turtle path would not stumble over a chair that was in their way!

It is therefore argued that Logo microworld environments such as the above can provide the opportunity for children to do geometry in an inductive way and for mathematics educators and teachers to reappraise the role and the importance of geometry in education by perceiving it as a field where children can engage in inductive and deductive thinking.

Further research needs to be carried out, however, in order to map out specific content areas that can act as catalysts for the creation of microworld environments such as the ones described above. At the same time there are grounds for more work on designing generalized microworlds that offer a wide range of geometrical ideas for children to explore. Finally, there is a need to investigate the potential for generating such environments among children of an extended age group; it is suggested, for instance, that an area for further investigation would be to find ways in which children with considerable experience in using geometry in an inductive way might use the same geometrical ideas in environments requiring deductive thinking.

REFERENCES

Abelson, H., and diSessa A. 1980. *Turtle Geometry: The Computer as a Medium for Exploring Mathematics*. Cambridge: MIT Press.

APU. 1982. *Mathematical Development Primary and Secondary Survey Reports*. London: HMSO.

Booth, L. 1981. Child-methods in secondary mathematics. *Educational Studies in Mathematics* 12: 29–41.

diSessa, A. 1983. Phenomenology and the Evolution of Intuition. In D. Gentner and A. Stevens (eds.), *Mental Models*. Hillsdale, NJ: Lawrence Erlbaum Associates.

Douady, R. 1985. The interplay between the different settings, tool-object dialectic in the extension of mathematical ability. *Proceedings of the Ninth International Conference for the Psychology of Mathematics Education*, vol. 2, pp. 33–52. Montreal.

Freudenthal, H. 1973. *Mathematics as an Educational Task*. Dordrecht: Reidel.

Freudenthal, H. 1983. *Didactical Phenomenology of Mathematical Structures*. Dordrecht: Reidel.

Hart, K. 1981. *Children's Understanding of Mathematics:* 11–16. K. M. Hart and John Murray (eds).

Harvey, B. 1985. *Computer Science Logo Style, vols. 1–3*. Cambridge: MIT Press.

Hillel, J., and Kieran, C. 1987. Schemas used by 12-year-olds in solving selected turtle geometry tasks. *Recherches en Didactique des Mathématiques* 8(12): 61–103.

Hillel, J. 1985. Mathematical and programming concepts acquired by children aged 8–9 in a restricted Logo environment. *Recherches en Didactique des Mathématiques* 6: 215–168.

Hillel, J. 1986. Procedural thinking by children aged 8–12 using turtle geometry. *Proceedings of the Tenth International Conference for the Psychology of Mathematics Education*: 433–438.

Hoffer, A. 1983. Van Hiele based research. In R. Lesh, and M. Landau (eds.), *Acquisition of Mathematical Concepts and Processes*. New York: Academic Press.

Hoyles, C., and Noss, R. 1987a. Seeing what matters: Developing an understanding of the concept of parallelograms through a Logo microworld. *Proceedings of the Eleventh International Conference for the Psychology of Mathematics Education*, pp. 17–23.

Hoyles, C., and Noss, R. 1987b Children working in a structured Logo environment: From doing to understanding. *Recherches en Didactiques de Mathématiques* 8(12): 131–174.

Hoyles, C., and Sutherland, R. 1989. *Logo Mathematics in the Classroom*. London: Routledge, and Kegan Paul.

Kieran, C. 1986a. Turns and angles—What develops in Logo? *Proceedings of the Eighth International Conference for the Psychology of Mathematics Education North American Group*, pp. 169–177.

Kieran, C. 1986b. Logo and the notion of angle among fourth and sixth grade children. *Proceedings of the Tenth International Conference for the Psychology of Mathematics Education*, pp. 99–104.

Kieran, C., Hillel, J., and Erlwanger, S. 1986. Perceptual and analytical schemas in solving structural turtle geometry tasks. *Proceedings of the Second Logo and Mathematics Education Conference*, pp. 154–161.

Kieren, T. 1987. Logo, language and intuitive mathematical knowledge building. *Proceedings of the Third International Conference for Logo and Mathematics Education*, Montreal, pp. 1–10.

Kynigos, C. 1989. From Intrinsic to Non-intrinsic geometry: A study of children's understandings in Logo-based microworlds. Unpublished doctoral thesis. Institute of Education University of London.

Lawler, R. W. 1985. *Computer Experience and Cognitive Development. A Child's Learning in a Computer Culture*. Chicester, UK: Horwood.

Leron, U. 1983. Some problems in children's Logo learning. *Proceedings of the Seventh International Conference for the Psychology of Mathematics Education*.

Loethe, H. 1985. Geometrical problems for a turtle with direction and distance finder. *Proceedings of the First International Conference for Logo and Mathematics Education*, London, pp. 123–129.

Noss, R. 1985. *Creating a Mathematical Environment through Programming: A Study of Young Children Learning Logo*. Doctoral thesis. Published by University of London Institute of Education.

Noss, R. 1987. Children's learning of geometrical concepts through Logo. *Journal for Research in Mathematics Education* 18(5): 343–362.

Paalz-Scally, S. 1986. A clinical investigation of the impact of a Logo learning environment on students; van Hiele levels of geometric understanding. *Proceedings of the Tenth International Conference for the Psychology of Mathematics Education*, pp. 123–128.

Papert, S. 1980. *Mindstorms. Children, Computers and Powerful Ideas*. Hassocks, UK: Harvester.

Papert, S., Watt, D., diSessa, A., and Weir, S. 1979. Final report of the Brookline Logo project. Part 2. MIT Artificial Intelligence Laboratory. Cambridge, MA.

Pyshkalo, A. M. 1968. *Geometry in Grades 1–4, Problems in the Formation of Geometric Conceptions in Pupils in the Primary Grades*. Moscow: Prosresticheuive Publishing House.

van Hiele, P. M. 1959: La Pensée de l'enfant et la geometrie. *Bulletin de l'Association des Professeurs Mathematiques de l'Enseignement Public*: 198–205.

Vergnaud, G. 1987a. About constructivism. *Proceedings of the Eleventh International Conference for the Psychology of Mathematics Education*, pp. 42–55.

Vergnaud, G. 1987b. Conclusion. In C. Janvier (ed.), *Problems of Representation in the Teaching and Learning of Mathematics*. Hillsdale, NJ: Lawrence Erlbaum Associates.

von Glasersfeld, E. 1985a. Representation and deduction. *Proceedings of the Ninth International Conference for the Psychology of Mathematics Education*, pp. 484–489.

Zack, V. 1986. A study of ten-to-eleven-year-old students' notion of right angle in Logo geometry. *Proceedings of the Second International Conference for Logo and Mathematics Education*, University of London, Institute of Education, pp. 96–103.

A Logo Microworld for Transformation Geometry

5

Laurie D. Edwards

> ... the Turtle defines a self-contained world in which certain questions are relevant and others are not . . . this idea can be developed by constructing many such "microworlds," each with its own set of assumptions and constraints. Children get to know what it is like to explore the properties of a chosen microworld undisturbed by extraneous questions. In doing so, they learn to transfer habits of exploration from their personal lives to the formal domain of scientific theory construction.—Papert (1980, p. 117)

1 INTRODUCTION

A growing number of researchers and educators have taken up the idea of constructing microworlds for exploring mathematics and science, and a new body of data and theory is accumulating on how such environments can support children's learning. The Logo programming language has been the medium for many such environments (Hoyles and Noss 1987a, 1987b; Thompson 1985, 1987; Hillel 1985; diSessa 1982, 1985; White 1981); others are not based on Logo but also embody the objectives of encouraging exploration and mathematical or scientific reasoning (e.g., Dugdale 1981; Schwartz and Yerushalmy 1987).

This chapter describes a particular Logo-based microworld that instantiates the central objects and relations in a corner of mathematics known as *transformation* or *motion* geometry. Transformation geometry is concerned with mappings of the plane to itself, including, but not limited to, the rigid motions such as translation, rotation, and reflection. As part of a project on the principled design of computer-based learning environments, the microworld and an introductory curriculum in transformation geometry were presented to a group of twelve middle-school students over a period of five weeks.

The aim of the curriculum was twofold: first, to give the students the opportunity to construct a working understanding of the transformations by using them in functional and gamelike contexts and, second, to encourage "habits of exploration," in Papert's phrase, in which the children attempt to discover and express mathematical patterns in the domain. The students participating in the study had all been exposed to at least one semester of Logo programming prior to meeting the microworld. A central focus of the research was on how prior conceptual structures, which are built up in various school and nonschool contexts, may have supported and/or interfered with the students' understanding of the new domain. In particular, it is proposed here that the children's experience with Logo provided a context for both positive and negative partial understandings of a range of concepts in transformation geometry.

In the following sections I will describe transformation geometry and justify its choice as a domain for children's mathematical exploration. The literature that provides the context for the current research will be examined, followed by a detailed description of the microworld, which is called TGEO. The aims and methodology of the project will be given, along with an overview of the major results of the research. The focus of the remainder of the chapter will be on the relationship between Logo and transformation geometry. First, a number of specific findings will be presented concerning the implicit role played by the children's prior experience in how they conceptualize transformations. A general discussion will follow, addressing the explicit curricular connections that can be made between Logo and transformation geometry.

2   TRANSFORMATION GEOMETRY

Transformation geometry is an approach to the study of the plane that has been part of European and British secondary school curricula for some time (e.g., in the School Mathematics Project [SMP] curriculum; Willson 1977) but that has only recently begun to make its appearance in American textbooks (Graening 1980; DeVault, Frehmeyer, Greenberg, and Bezuska 1978; Bumby and Klutch 1982). Geometry instruction in the United States has traditionally been based on teaching the implications of Euclid's postulates for plane figures and has focused on deductive proof. Although the domain of interest in high school geometry classes is nominally the euclidean plane, the plane has been used primarily as a source of easily visualized problems to which the techniques of deductive reasoning are then applied. This style of geometry curriculum is entirely consistent with the historical viewpoint concerning what constituted "geometry" up until the end of the nineteenth century. At that time geometry was seen as a deductive system, comprising the investigation and formal proof of the logical consequences that follow from a set of axioms concerning points, lines, planes, and so on. In 1872, however, Felix Klein proposed using the notions of transformations, groups, and invariance to classify and lend order to the growing number and type of "geometries" that were emerging in the wake of the discovery of noneuclidean geometries. In what has come to be known as the *Erlangen Programme*, Klein redefined a "geometry" to be "a study of properties (expressed by postulates, definitions, and theorems) that are left invariant (unchanged) under a group of transformations" (Meserve 1955, p. 21).

Informally stated, transformation geometry focuses on mappings of the plane as the objects of study. These mappings or transformations may change some properties of figures of the plane and preserve others, and the defining properties of each kind of geometry are precisely those that are left unchanged by a particular set of transformations. For example, the euclidean transformations, which make up the core of the operations in the TGEO microworld, preserve the properties of distance, angle measure, area, shape, perpendicularity, parallelism, and incidence. The four euclidean transformations, also known as "rigid motions," are *translation* (informally, "sliding"), *rotation*, *reflection*, and *glide reflection* (the combination of a reflection over any mirror line and a translation parallel to that line). These four transformations make up a group under composition; they are illustrated in figure 1.

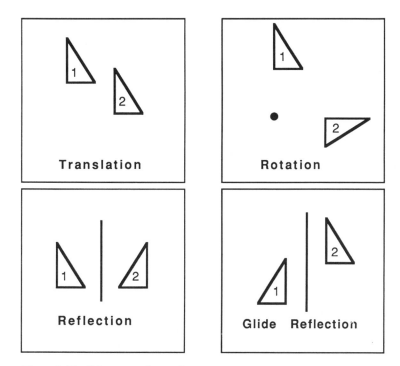

Figure 1 Euclidean transformations

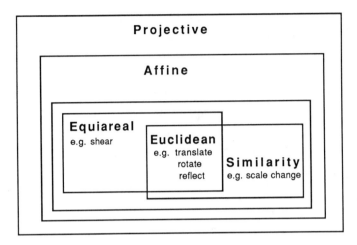

Figure 2 Groups of transformations

By relaxing various of the requirement for invariance, more general geometries are generated. If area alone, for instance, is allowed to vary, we obtain the group of similarity transformations, including scaling operations. Alternatively, we find the equiareal transformations, such as shears, when the requirements for invariance in angle measure and perpendicularity are removed. Further relaxations of required invariances lead to the groups of affine and projective transformations (for details, see Meserve 1955). Figure 2 illustrates the hierarchy of families of geometries generated by various groups of transformations.

In most textbooks and curricula for precollege mathematics, transformation, or motion geometry consists of an introduction to the euclidean transformations and, sometimes, change of scale. Depending on the grade level and depth of treatment, texts may also address sequences of transformations, results on invariance, congruence, and similarity, or alternative representations such as matrices (Bumby and Klutch 1982; DeVault et al. 1978; SMP 1972).

Transformation geometry was chosen as an arena for children's exploration because it is mathematically rich and yet connects with children's everyday experience with motions, shapes, and actions. In this sense it shares with Logo a concern for the learner's "personal geometry"; in Papert's term (1980), it is "body syntonic." Children bring to the learning situation a wide range of knowledge and strategies about how to move themselves around in space, and about rules and regularities in moving other objects (e.g., the rules of checkers or other board games). Students can make use of their existing skills of visualization and spatial reasoning, as well as apply thinking tools acquired in the context of school mathematics (e.g., the use of the coordinate system to name points on the plane). The microworld has the potential of allowing the learner to actively encounter both a formal and a visual/concrete embodiment of the entities in a mathematical domain. It is one of a class of interactive computer environments in which "the learner is both engaged in the construction of executable symbolic representations and is provided with informative feedback" (Hoyles and Noss 1987a, p. 133).

Although the curriculum presented in the current research was at an introductory level, transformation geometry can be the basis of instruction and exploration in more advanced areas of mathematics. An obvious direction for more sophisticated mathematical exploration would be to examine simple groups, comprised of subsets of transformations (e.g., rotations) and to investigate the "algebra" of composing transformations. First steps in this direction were made in a portion of the introductory curriculum that asked the students to find inverses for each transformation, as well as to combine pairs of transformations to find simple equivalent operations.

The TGEO microworld itself is neutral; it is a tool that automates hand plotting of mappings of the plane, and it is adaptable to a wide range of tasks and topics. Transformation geometry utilizes and reinforces such fundamental mathematical ideas as mappings (functions), invariance, and group structure. There are ties between this approach and traditional deductive euclidean geometry in that transformational methods can be used to prove a range of standard geometric results, including congruence and similarity (cf. Maxwell 1975). Matrix representations for transformations can be introduced, forging links to linear algebra and finite mathematics. The idea of spatial transformation itself, as well as the related concept of symmetry, plays an important role in numerous scientific domains, from molecular biology to crystallography, in which the language of geometry is used to describe structure in space. One of the benefits of a computer-based microworld such as TGEO (as compared with computer-based tutorials) is that this tool can be used with learners at many levels, and in investigating a wide range of related mathematical topics.

3 SOME RELEVANT LITERATURE

One can view a microworld as a conceptual tool with which a learner encounters multiple representations of new mathematical entities and through manipulation of these objects constructs a new understanding of a domain. Typically a programming language or a simple symbolic system is used as one representation, and a dynamic visual or graphical presentation is linked in "real time" to the symbolic inputs. The research literature related to learning with this kind of artifact ranges from theoretical work on the nature of conceptual change to empirical studies of learning or performance in specific mathematical domains. The project described in this chapter attempts to build upon this research base by examining in depth the course of short-term conceptual development in a small number of students who interacted with the TGEO microworld.

As has been noted, the theoretical context for the research is constructivist, focusing on the interaction between a learner's prior conceptual structures and the new experiences he or she encounters. The idea that previous knowledge contributes to and shapes new understandings goes back at least to the Piagetian notions of assimilation and accommodation (Piaget 1937). In another vein Greeno (1983) has hypothesized that the acquisition (or construction) of "conceptual entities" plays an important part in the solution of problems and in the ontology of a domain (where "ontology" refers to "the entities that are available for representing problem situations" [p. 227]). According to Greeno, conceptual entities are "cognitive objects that the system can reason about in a relatively direct way, and that are included continuously in the representation" of a problem. In the TGEO project the "system" in question is the child as he or she engages in learning, and one way to formulate the research is to ask how the microworld and the activities built around it can help the learner to abstract new conceptual entities (e.g., the transformations themselves) and use them in problem solving. It is proposed that although some version of the conceptual entities corresponding to the transformations are present "continuously" throughout the learning situation, there are significant changes in the nature of these entities as the child progresses through the microworld-based curriculum. Delineating the nature of the changes in the learner's ontology and in the conceptual objects he or she constructs is one of the goals of the research on TGEO.

A recent investigation and theoretical reformulation of the idea of "conceptual structures" is found in Bob Lawler's work (1985). Lawler observed the intellectual development of his young daughter over a period of several years, particularly noting the clusters of expectations and actions that emerged as she acted within everyday and Logo contexts. Lawler referred to such clusters as "microviews" and asserted that they play a major role in children's learning. Microviews are aggregations of domain-specific knowledge and procedures that compete in the child's mind to interpret and act on new situations. They are also the elements of cognitive restructuring when multiple views merge at points of insight or surprise. An example of a way in which previous Logo experience can structure learning in arithmetic is found in Lawler's daughter's selective knowledge of certain sums: "Miriam knew 90 plus 90 equals 180 because this sum (whose quantity and representation are cultural accidents) embodied a significant action (turning around) in worlds of experience" (Lawler 1985, pp. 61–62). The idea of a "Logo microview" helps to make sense of a number of episodes in the students' learning of transformation geometry; examples will be presented in later sections.

Genetic or constructivist analyses have begun to clarify the nature of students' learning in various specific domains, for example, in newtonian physics (diSessa 1982) and in children's understanding of the balance beam (Kliman 1987). These studies are more limited in duration than Lawler's, but they share the goal of tracing the course of conceptual change in students as they interact with their environment. In discussing his analysis of children's learning with an interactive dynaturtle, diSessa describes the goal of tracing children's learning through what he terms a *genetic* analysis: "A genetic task analysis is intended to be a fundamentally different slicing of a domain than that achieved with an abstract task or conceptual analysis; genetically antecedent, partial understandings replace logical prerequisites as elements" (diSessa 1982, p. 63). In the TGEO research a genetic analysis is carried out for the children's learning in the transformation geometry microworld. In addition to demonstrating that the environment is effective in helping students to learn about and use the transformations, the goal is to describe in detail the sequence of partial understandings that go into this improvement in performance.

Previous empirical studies of children's abilities to use transformations have for the most part focused on performance at a single point in time; detailed attention to conceptual change has been minimal. For example, Moyer (1978) and Schultz and Austin (1983) presented transformational tasks to students of various ages and drew conclusions about the relative difficulty of each type of motion (e.g., slides are the "easiest"; motions involving diagonals more difficult). Grenier's (1985) work with reflections examined in more depth the factors that seem to influence students' ability to make freehand drawings of transformations. Her work, which took place in the context of actual classroom instruction, is valuable in highlighting cognitive and perceptual factors that can affect how students think about and carry out reflections. Another valuable classroom-based study was that done by Ludwig (1986), in which a middle-school class was followed over a period of eleven weeks as students worked through a Logo-based curriculum for transformation geometry.

The study of Logo and transformation geometry also takes place within the context of a growing number of studies relating Logo and a range of mathematical topics, from angles and proportions to the use of algebraic variables (e.g., Hillel, chapter 1 in this volume; Hoyles and Noss 1989; Sutherland, chapter 2 in this volume; Leron and Zazkis 1989b).

On the purely mathematical side a detailed consideration of the formal relationship between turtle motions in Logo and transformations is addressed in chapter 11 by Leron and Zazkis (and in Leron and Zazkis 1989a). Briefly, the TGEO microworld can be seen as a practical implementation, through programming, of the relationship between the Logo primitives RT and FD and the set of euclidean transformations (translation, rotation, and reflection). In using TGEO, students are not expected to consider the mathematical foundations that make this implementation possible, nor need they be aware of this mapping. Instead, they can use the transformations as primitives in a new microworld built on top of Logo itself. Nevertheless, the mathematical work by Leron and Zazkis clarifies why the programming of TGEO works, as well as points toward intriguing issues concerning informal versus formal thinking about transformations.

A final source of ideas relevant to the current research is found in work on the nature of instruction with interactive learning environments. The pedagogy underlying microworlds and similar didactical situations holds that knowledge arises from children's active use of and reflection about new entities rather than from "being told" about them. As Vergnaud states, "knowledge emerges from problems to be solved and situations to be mastered" (1982, p. 31). In TGEO and in other Logo microworlds, students actively employ new procedures in a variety of contexts so that they can construct a meaning for these new conceptual objects by *using* them rather than from formal definitions (cf. the UDGS framework, Hoyles and Noss 1987a). Furthermore, through the use of a symbolic representation, the learner's "theorems in action"—as Vergnaud terms the implicit expectations that organize children's understanding about a domain—can be made more explicit. In addition to building a model of *what* children learn by interacting with the TGEO microworld, a further aim of the study is to add to our understanding of *how* interactive microworlds can work to support learning in a new domain.

4 THE TGEO MICROWORLD

Since transformations involve a set of points (e.g., the plane), an operation, and an image resulting from the operation, a microworld for transformation geometry must selectively represent these components in some way. This section describes the embodiment of the transformations chosen for inclusion in the Logo-based TGEO microworld. The TGEO microworld instantiates three euclidean transformations of the plane (SLIDE, ROTATE, REFLECT), one similarity transformation (SCALE), and simple local versions of three of the transformations (PIVOT, FLIP, SIZE). Figure 3 illustrates the euclidean transformations; it is the help sheet given to the students when they first encounter TGEO. Figure 4 shows the change-of-scale transformations, which are introduced later in the curriculum.

In the microworld the plane is represented by the turtle window in Logo, with a grid of dots spaced ten turtle steps apart, which is used to specify locations and distances. The conventions used in Logo for angles and headings are carried over into the TGEO world, with north given the heading 0 degrees, and clockwise angles represented by positive values (see the bottom of figure 3). A block letter-L shape starts out in the center of the grid; this demarcates a portion of the plane so that the effects of each transformation can be seen by comparing the "before" and "after" state of the screen. The before state, or pre-image, is shown as a gray shadow of the L shape in the original location; the after or image state is represented by the L shape in its new location.

The user executes the transformations by typing in a predefined Logo procedure for each, choosing appropriate values for the inputs. For example, the SLIDE transformation takes two inputs, the first for the horizontal displacement and the second for the vertical displacement. This representation for slide was chosen in preference to using distance and direction because, when combining slides (one of the tasks in the curriculum), it was felt that it would be easier to add displacements (vectors in rectangular component form) rather than operate on vectors in polar form.

The procedure for the most general form of a rotation, ROTATE, takes three inputs, the first two naming a center point anywhere on the plane and the third specifying the amount to rotate the plane as measured from its current heading. REFLECT, the third euclidean transformation, also takes three inputs, all of which are used to specify a mirror line anywhere on the plane. A slightly redundant scheme was used so that the notation for lines would depend only on

SLIDE 10 -20
slides the shape 10 *across* and 20 *down*

ROTATE 25 25 45
places a center point at 25 across, 25 up
and then rotates the plane 45 degrees
clockwise around that point

REFLECT 20 0 45
places a mirror line which goes through
the point 20 across, 0 up with the
heading 45, then flips the plane
over that line.

PIVOT 45
pivots the shape 45 degrees *clockwise*
around the bottom corner.
PIVOT -45 would turn *counterclockwise.*

FLIP
flips the shape over its long side

Lengths and Angles (Headings)

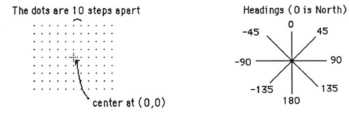

Figure 3 Help sheet: euclidean transformations

SIZE 2
enlarges shape by a factor of 2,
starting from the bottom corner

SCALE -20 -20 3
enlarges shape by a factor of 3,
from a fixed point at (-20, -20)

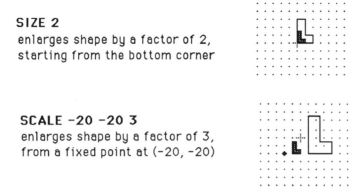

Figure 4 Size and scale

the children's previous Logo experience (e.g., not on algebraic formalisms). To specify a line in TGEO, the user first selects a point somewhere on the plane, using two inputs, and then "pins down" a particular line through that point by choosing a heading. So, for example, the horizontal line that is 20 turtle steps above the origin is specified by the inputs "0 20 90," for 0 steps across, 20 steps up, at a heading of 90 degrees. However this line could equally well be specified by "10 20 90" or "any-number-across 20 90." Although this is certainly a non-standard representation for lines, it turns out to be useful in the kind of tasks the students encounter in the microworld. For example, in this representation it is easy to read off the "slopes" of lines, since all parallel lines have the same absolute heading.

An underlying objective in choosing the representations of the transformations was to take advantage of the children's prior conceptual structures, both their intuitive understanding of motion in space and their existing knowledge about the conventions of Logo and turtle motion. Evidence for the effectiveness of this aspect of the microworld design will be presented in later sections when the effects of Logo knowledge and children's "personal geometry" on learning of the transformations are discussed.

The symbolic interface for the transformations was easy to create, since the commands are simply Logo procedures. This representation of the commands has the additional advantage that combining transformations is equivalent to calling both procedures, either on the same line or on two consecutive lines. Thus the Logo conventions make it easy to work with more than one transformation at a time. A further advantage of using Logo commands for the transformations is that they can be taken out of the context of the computer and used in paper-and-pencil or oral exercises. In contrast to, for example, a menu-based interface, a microworld based in Logo is not limited to the interactive computer context but can be used in symbol-based reasoning in noncomputer media. Both spontaneously and when asked to do so, students in the study were able to create symbolic "sentences" (e.g., SLIDE 10 20 SLIDE 30–10 = SLIDE 40 10) to represent combinations of transformations. Thus the microworld supported both a visual and a more formal symbolic understanding of the transformations.

In general, the TGEO microworld shares the advantages of other Logo-based microworlds, most clearly seen in the opportunity for learners to engage in interactive, personally meaningful problem solving exercising new forms of symbolic representation. For instance, in TGEO one of the first activities in the microworld is a *Match game* in which the user is challenged to superimpose two congruent shapes by executing a sequence of transformations. To succeed at the game, the students must learn and use a new formalism for the transformations, as well as take note of the features of each particular motion. The visual feedback from the microworld helps them to make sense of the symbolic commands, and the commands are the only tool they have to implement the transformations and to make progress in the game. This combination of the functional and the formal is typical of good Logo learning environments and has been remarked upon in previous work by Noss and Hoyles: "We wish to emphasise that it is a unique attribute of the Logo environment that functional activity and formalisation take place *simultaneously*. This is no small claim given that the gap between pupils' activity and its symbolisation has been an outstanding problem facing mathematics education" (Noss and Hoyles 1988). Microworlds based in Logo, such as TGEO which call on the learner to make use of multiple modes of representation, can help in creating this link between action and formalization.

5   AIMS AND METHODOLOGY OF THE RESEARCH

The aim of the research reported here was to engage in the principled design and evaluation of a microworld for learning in transformation geometry. The dual goals of the study were to build a fine-grained model of students' learning in the domain and to use empirical data about their interactions with the microworld in order to improve the environment and to better understand how children learn with microworlds.

To address these goals, the microworld was designed, programmed, and refined over a period of two years, during which time it was field-tested with sixty-five middle-school students and piloted in depth with four additional children. A set of activities comprising an introductory curriculum was created, and the main study took place with twelve middle-school students, aged eleven to fourteen. The curriculum and microworld were used over a period of five weeks with these students (nine boys and three girls from a small private school in California). The children were given a set of pretests, then were introduced to the transformations in two initial classroom sessions, and thereafter met once a week with the investigator. At these weekly sessions, which lasted an hour or an hour and a half, one pair of students at a time would work with the microworld on a Macintosh computer. The pedagogical model was that of guided discovery rather than direct instruction. The students were presented with a series of worksheets and were asked to find the answers by using the microworld. For example, one of the first worksheets asked the students to find the inverses for particular and general forms of the transformations, to find the move that "undoes" SLIDE 50 30 or ROTATE A B X. The students would try out their guesses on the computer by first typing in the problem and then their candidate solutions. The microworld thus provided the necessary feedback for the children to determine for themselves whether they were right or wrong. The role of the investigator was to clarify the initial instructions, to give assistance when the students had exhausted their ideas on how to proceed on a particular task, and to probe for details on students' thinking and solutions. So, for example, students might be asked why they thought a particular solution worked or whether they noticed a pattern in their solutions. The purpose of such questioning was both to gather verbal data on how the students thought about the transformations and to promote reflection about the activities. In this sense the research was a kind of teaching experiment, although the role of the investigator was intended to be minimally interventionist, with most of the activity occurring between the students and the microworld. At the end of the five weeks, the students were given a series of post-tests and a final off-computer written examination on the transformations

The curriculum based on TGEO had the objectives of assisting the students to build a working understanding of the transformations, and to learn to use the transformations and the microworld in problem solving and mathematical generalization. These objectives were addressed in the following sequence of activities:

1.   The investigator introduced the transformations to the whole group, representing them as the concrete motions of two sheets of paper sliding, rotating, or reflecting (folding). She then elicited from the students a description of invariances: What changes and what stays the same in each transformation?

2.   In the second class session the students were introduced to the TGEO computer microworld and were given about twenty minutes for open-ended exploration of the euclidean transformations (shown in figure 3).

3.   Following the unguided exploration, the students were shown the Match game: The object of the game is to superimpose two shapes by applying a sequence of transformations. Students worked together in pairs playing the game; the investigator questioned students about their strategies and encouraged certain students to find more efficient solutions.

4.   To make theorems-in-action explicit, students were given worksheets on finding inverses and combining transformations. On these worksheets they were asked to execute several specific examples and then to express the mathematical pattern in a semialgebraic notation (e.g., SLIDE A B followed by SLIDE X Y is SLIDE A + X B + Y).

5.   To find symmetry, students were presented with worksheets showing seventeen different figures and were asked to use the microworld to find the list of transformations that would leave each figure in place (i.e., the list of symmetries). Students also sorted the figures based on their symmetries.

6.   To make sense of two new transformations, students were asked to use the microworld in any way they wanted so that they could find out how the two new transformations, SIZE and SCALE, worked. After they verbally described each transformation, they were given worksheets for finding inverses and combinations of these new transformations.

7.   For the evaluation, students were given a set of evaluation tasks, including a written final exam (the final exam was based on materials from the British CSMS study [Hart 1981]).

6   OVERVIEW OF RESULTS

The results of the study, in brief, showed that the students were successful in using the microworld and the curriculum to build an initial and generally correct understanding of the euclidean transformations and in applying this new understanding to problems in the domain. In the final exam, which consisted of twelve tasks identical to those used in the CSMS study (Hart 1981) and twelve additional tasks, the students performed above the average for Hart's population on ten of the twelve items. Thus this group of students, who had a total of about seven hours of experience with the microworld, performed at a level comparable to the students in Hart's study, who were taught the topics of transformation geometry as part of their mathematics curriculum over a period of several years. The students in the TGEO study also had the benefit of individual attention from the investigator, but I believe the opportunity to work interactively with the microworld in a concentrated way contributed most to their learning.

In addition to their performance on the final pencil-and-paper measure, all of the students were able to complete worksheets in which they were asked to generalize patterns for combining transformations; some went beyond the given tasks to generate and test novel examples of their own. Finally, the students were able to make sense of two new transformations, SIZE and SCALE, indicating that their knowledge of how to use the microworld was not specific to the initial set of transformations but could be generalized. Details on the students' performance in the microworld will be presented in the following section, which focuses on the relationships among Logo, the TGEO microworld, and the children's conceptualization of the domain.

7 SPECIFIC FINDINGS: THE CONCEPTUAL LEVEL

The thesis of this chapter is that the students' knowledge of Logo, building as it did on their "personal geometry," contributed in both positive and negative ways to their learning in transformation geometry. The argument is that Logo knowledge, as well as more general experiences with the physical world, helped to build antecedent conceptual structures that shaped the ways in which the students assimilated the new mathematical entities and operations encountered in the microworld. Although it was but one of a number of prior conceptual structures derived in both school and nonschool contexts (see figure 5), an understanding of Logo appeared to be a significant influence on a number of the children as they progressed through the new domain.

In this section I will describe several episodes in the children's learning that support the claim that Logo acted as an organizing conceptual structure or microview. The effect of the children's personal geometry and previous Logo knowledge was seen in the ease or difficulty in learning particular transformations, in familiarity with angles and motions, and in characteristic misinterpretations of the ROTATE command. Finally, I will describe two mental models of the plane, one based on turtle motions in Logo, and one based on whole-plane transformations, that must be reconciled in order to build an accurate understanding of transformation geometry.

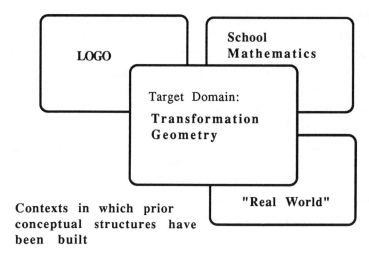

Figure 5 Prior contexts affecting learning

Turtle Motions and Transformations

To the child encountering transformations for the first time in the TGEO micro-world, the context may look very much like that of the turtle in Logo. Although in introducing the transformations, the instructor took care to use concrete ma-nipulations of sheets of paper in order to emphasize that it is the *plane* that is being transformed and not an isolated figure, when the students move to the computer context, it is natural to assume that their previous experience with Logo in this same context will come into play. Thus one would expect that stu-dents might "map" their understanding of transformations onto their previous experience with moving the turtle in Logo. This implicit mapping or association should make certain transformations easier to learn and remember than others. In addition the students' previous experience with inputs to turtle commands might act as a model for the inputs to the transformations.

In discussing the relationship between turtle moves and transformations, we must distinguish "local" from "global" actions. Technically all transformations map the entire plane, leaving certain sets of points invariant. For instance, in a rotation the center point stays where it is, while the remainder of the plane moves around it. Similarly, for a reflection the mirror line remains invariant, with the rest of the plane mapped across it. However, in the TGEO microworld there are simpler, "local" versions of these transformations called PIVOT and FLIP. For the "global" ROTATE the center point can be any location on the plane. But for PIVOT the center point is always the starting point for the figure shown on the screen, for example, the lower left corner of the block letter L (see figure 3). The center point for PIVOT is "local" because its location varies with the location of the figure.

The local transformation PIVOT is very close in appearance to the turtle commands for turning, RT and LT, and thus the children's knowledge of turning in Logo may assist them in learning PIVOT. The center point for PIVOT does not need to be explicitly named when it is executed; instead, only the angle amount of rotation is input. Thus a "PIVOT 45" and a "RT 45" have virtually the same visual effect on the TGEO shape and the Logo turtle. The students found PIVOT easier to use and to remember than the more general, global form ROTATE. One student, Mik, commented explicitly, "I think pivot and slide are easy," and later, "Rotate is hard." Additionally, when the students played the Match game, in which they can choose which transformations to use in superimposing two congruent shapes, they selected PIVOT more often than ROTATE. This was particularly evident in the first game when PIVOT was used three times as often as ROTATE. As the students progressed in the game, they increasingly tried to make use of the more powerful ROTATE command, and in the end the relative occurrence of PIVOT and ROTATE effectively evened up.

It should be noted that since only students with Logo experience were involved, the data available in the main study do not allow us to attribute the ease of learning the local transformation PIVOT solely to previous knowledge of Logo. It is quite likely that even for students without Logo experience, PIVOT would be easier to learn and to use than ROTATE. This is because, like the Logo commands FD and RT, PIVOT is body syntonic; that is, it is "firmly related to children's sense and knowledge about their own bodies" (Papert 1980, p. 63). However, it is also plausible that additional experience with formalizing such body syntonic commands, through the use of Logo, would strengthen the conceptual structures that support an understanding of PIVOT.

Although the local command FLIP has no counterpart in Logo, it seemed to be more easily learned and more readily used by the students. In FLIP the mirror line is local to the figure; the shape always reflects over a line that has the starting heading and location of the turtle. Similarly the simple, local version of change of scale, called SIZE, acts directly on the figure, increasing its size while keeping the same location. In contrast, in the global version SCALE, a fixed point (which can be separate from the figure) is held invariant while the rest of the plane is expanded or contracted from that point. After experimenting on their own, all of the pairs of students were able to describe quickly and accurately how SIZE works. But most of the students were less articulate about how SCALE functioned, and many required hints from the investigator to understand the fixed point.

The transformation SLIDE shares some characteristics of the turtle motion FD and yet differs from it in ways that are reflected in errors made by the children. Both SLIDE and FD change the location of the shape; however, SLIDE takes a horizontal and a vertical input, while FD takes only a single input and moves in the direction the turtle is facing. A quarter of the students at some point attempted to give SLIDE a single input; for instance, Sha tried to execute a SLIDE -60. These students were either corrected by their partners, or they self-corrected their errors after finding that the microworld would not execute the command as typed. The expectation that straight-line motion can be described using a single input is attributable to the students' previous experience with Logo, since in Logo, the command for straight-line motion, FD, does take a single input.

Thus Logo turns and straight-line motions (RT and FD, respectively) seemed to constitute a kind of mental model for the similar transformations PIVOT and SLIDE. More generally, "local" versions of the transformations, which act directly on the figure and do not call upon the students to consider points of the plane separate from the figure, were more easily comprehended and more readily used. This is evidence that, at least initially, the children's familiarity with the simple, local motions of the Logo turtle, and the correspondence of such motions with their "intuitive" personal geometry, influenced their learning of the transformations.

Knowledge about Angles and Motions

The students brought to the TGEO learning situation not only a qualitative understanding of turns and motions in the Logo plane but also a store of facts and familiar quantitative values for angles, headings, and distances. Although the students' Logo instruction had taken place the previous semester, and some had to be reminded about the conventions for representing headings, most of the students were quick to remember how to represent angles and distances. They recognized standard or prototypical values for angles, such as 180 and 90 degrees; one student stated "180 was, like, one of the standard turns." They utilized general strategies of adding to or interpolating between such values in order to find less-familiar headings. And they were able to find the inverses of transformations by negating the appropriate inputs and to combine transformations like PIVOT and REFLECT by adding angles. Though these kinds of tasks undoubtedly drew upon general skills of computation and reasoning that may have been learned prior to encountering Logo, these skills, as well as familiarity with angle sizes and headings, were likely to have been further developed by the children's experience with Logo.

The students also seemed to carry over from Logo (or from more general experience with physical motions) an ease in describing linear motion using relative terms. To specify a SLIDE, they needed to state how far across and how far up or down the plane or shape must move, relative to its current location. This is similar to the FD command in Logo, in which forward motion is always measured in turtle steps from the turtle's current position. The students had no difficulty in measuring or executing the motion of a SLIDE relative to the current position. For ROTATE and REFLECT, however, the first two inputs specify an absolute location on the plane (the center point, or a point on the mirror line). Two students had some initial confusion about these inputs, as they tried to count out a location relative to the shape, rather than from an absolute origin. In this case the emphasis in Logo on relative motion was counterproductive, but the students were able to overcome their confusion after one or two examples of the new transformations.

An Initial Faulty Model for ROTATE

An example of how a Logo-based model for motions can give rise to misconceptions about the transformations is found in a common "bug" about the ROTATE command. This conceptual (as opposed to procedural) bug was found in three out of four of the pilot subjects, in the work of at least two of the twelve students in the main study, and in the work of several adults who used the microworld at various stages of its development.

As noted above, in executing ROTATE, one specifies a center point anywhere on the plane around which the entire plane turns, carrying the figure with it. The students with the ROTATE "bug" had an interesting initial misinterpretation of this transformation. Instead of imagining the entire plane rotating around the center point, or even an object connected to the center by a string, these students thought that the shape would first slide over to the specified point and then turn around it in place. For example, Suz asked, "But don't we have to

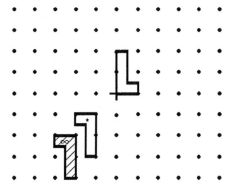

ROTATE -10 -10 180

* Lee's answer
∞ correct answer

Figure 6 Example of rotate "bug"

slide that one over to it to rotate it, or do we?" and later, "It won't move it to, like, down to that point?" Ser drew his own example of a rotate in which the shape first moved to a particular point and then pivoted.

One of the pilot students, Lee, drew the shape marked with an asterisk in figure 6 when she was asked to execute the transformation ROTATE −10 −10 180. This would be the location of the image if the shape were to move to the point (−10, −10) and then pivot 180 degrees. The correct image, shown shaded, results from holding the point (−10, −10) invariant and rotating the entire plane around it.

This interpretation of ROTATE is consistent with the kinds of motions students are accustomed to making in Logo: The turtle is moved forward to a desired location and then turned, using RT or LT. In the Logo experience one almost never applies an action to a shape "at a distance." Furthermore it seems reasonable to conjecture that in the everyday experience of most children, rotating or turning things (records, the hands of a clock) have the center point located within the bounds of the object. However, in order to conceptualize a global ROTATE, the children must think about the plane as a whole object that is mapped or moved to a new location. This requires the construction of the plane itself as a conceptual object (cf. Greeno 1983), which may not be an easy thing for a young child to accomplish.

The rotate bug was more prevalent and more persistent among the pilot students who were introduced to the transformations only through the computer microworld than among the main study group. The main group was introduced to the transformations by means of concrete manipulations of sheets of paper. These sheets of paper were meant to serve as physical representations of the plane for the children. The concrete manipulations of the sheets, which did behave the way a whole plane would, may have helped to provide an accurate mental model of whole-plane rotation for most of the students in the main study.

Mental Models of the Plane

I would like to propose that many of the misconceptions described above are due to an implicit mental model of the plane which the children derived from their experience with Logo. This model, in contrast to explicit knowledge about angles and headings, is not likely to be part of children's verbalizable awareness, yet it is both appropriate and adequate for dealing with most Logo tasks. However, it has serious limitations as a model for transformations of the plane, and in fact a new mental model of the plane must be constructed in order to think about transformations correctly.

The model of the plane for Logo, depicted in figure 7a, can be described as follows: The turtle is an independent, mobile agent who exists *within* a single plane and who moves about this plane via commands given relative to its current location and heading. This is the intended mental model of the turtle plane, abstracted from the action of a robot turtle on a real physical floor. Its motion is always local, and reference is never made (at least in the early stages of Logo instruction) to absolute locations on the plane. In fact the plane itself (as an abstraction consisting of an infinite span of locations in two-dimensional space) can never be constructed as a conceptual entity, since it is not necessary to think of the plane in this global sense in order to solve the problem of moving the turtle around the screen with local commands.

In contrast, a mental model that can be used correctly to conceptualize transformations consists of two planes: an infinite "moving" plane to which any transformation is applied, and a stationary reference plane "behind" it (see figure 7b). This reference plane is used to specify the mapping precisely, for example, by the use of a grid of dots and standard headings. Instead of a single plane with a turtle moving inside of it, the transformations can be thought of as occurring in a dual-plane system in which motions or mappings are applied to the "top" plane as a

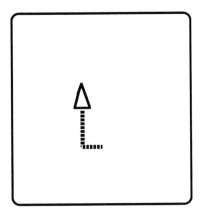
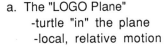
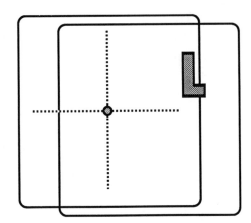

a. The "LOGO Plane"
-turtle "in" the plane
-local, relative motion

b. The "Transformation
Geometry Plane"
-dual planes
-whole plane motion

Figure 7 Two models of the plane

whole and described with reference to the "bottom" plane. The "top" plane may contain embedded figures; however, these figures do not move *in* the plane but instead are simply marked subsets of points that move along with the entire plane.

The students' relative ease of learning the local transformations, which more closely conform to motions in the Logo plane, is one piece of evidence in support of this view about alternative mental models. Another example is found in some students' initial tendencies to focus on attributes of the figure alone when describing a global transformation. For instance, figure 8 shows a reflection that the students were asked to identify. Although all of the students recognised the transformation as a reflection, and even drew in the correct mirror line, when they named the mirror line, many students gave the heading as 45 or −45 degrees. This is the heading of the letter-L shape; apparently the salience of the heading of this shape was greater than that of the mirror line. Perhaps the students were thinking of the L shape as a turtle and, when they needed to come up with a heading, simply responded with the apparent "heading" of the initial shape. Similarly the ROTATE bug, in which the shape was expected to move to a location and then turn, is more consistent with an independent turtle moving within a single plane than with a whole plane rotating around an invariant point.

Identify the transformation:

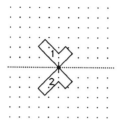

a correct answer: REFLECT 0 0 90
a common answer: REFLECT 0 0 45

Figure 8 Salience of shape's heading

One of the features of a microworld environment for learning is that students can confront their misconceptions by seeing the difference between what they expect to happen and what actually takes place. For the students who showed conceptual bugs about the transformations based on an inappropriate mental model of the plane, the visual feedback from the TGEO microworld was sufficient to help them to overcome these misconceptions. One possible modification to the microworld that might further assist the students to construct a more appropriate mental model for transformations of the whole plane is to show more than one figure at a time. When a transformation is executed, each object will undergo the same change; thus the students may be able to more easily visualize the "invisible" plane in which the multiple objects are embedded.

Visual and Symbolic Representations

Stepping back from the children's specific understanding of transformations, it is intriguing to consider the pattern of student use of the different representational modes provided in the microworld. Although it is difficult to quantify a description of this pattern, it seemed that in using the TGEO microworld, the students showed a tendency to alternate in a characteristic way between their use of the visual and symbolic information available to them. The visual information on the screen was used, quite naturally, in carrying out the first examples of a new task. However, as soon as the students perceived a symbolic pattern, they would extend this pattern, predicting results verbally *before* typing them into the microworld to check them visually. The visual information was often ignored unless it contradicted a pattern they had abstracted symbolically.

For example, when asked to determine inverses and combinations of transformations, most students initially used screen information to find the results, either counting distances or estimating headings. But as they recorded their results, they would notice patterns in the symbolic representations (e.g., SLIDE A SLIDE B results in SLIDE A + B). The students often would then extend such symbolic patterns to calculate and predict the results for new pairs of transformations. (Some students were so confident in the correctness of these patterns that they asked whether they had to try out their answers on the computer!) This led to cases of incorrect overgeneralization; for example, after adding distances to combine SLIDES, and angles to combine PIVOTS, one student proceeded to add the inputs for the center points when combining two ROTATES. If such an overgeneralization resulted in an error when executed in the microworld, it would show up when the students tested their solutions. On finding that the pattern was incorrect, the students would often turn back to the visual output in order to give meaning to and debug their symbolic patterns.

This interplay of the symbolic and the visual seems to be characteristic of children's behavior in other microworlds, for example, in Dugdale's green globs (Dugdale 1981) and in the Parallelogram microworld described by Hoyles and Noss (1987a). For example, Hoyles and Noss note that "pupils tend to focus either on the visual image/figure or on the symbolic representation and . . . sometimes 'lose' their understandings of relationships built up in one context when transferring them to another" (p. 166). In the case of the TGEO microworld, it was more common that students would overgeneralize when they focused only on the symbolic context and would use the visual mode to check and reestablish a basis for the patterns they found. Again, the power of microworlds as learning environments, particularly those in which symbolic representations are linked to other modalities, is in the potential for students to synthesize across multiple representations. In TGEO and in other microworlds, it is encouraging to observe students who call on both visual information and generalizations of symbolic patterns in order to construct a plausible conceptual model of the target domain.

8 GENERAL DISCUSSION: THE PEDAGOGICAL LEVEL

The findings presented thus far have discussed the implicit cognitive constraints and supports that arise from children's previous experience and that can affect new learning in transformation geometry. In this section an additional issue relating Logo and transformation geometry will be addressed: the possibility of making explicit connections between the Logo language and transformation geometry.

The students who took part in the TGEO project had all had at least one semester of Logo programming, but they were not asked to use this programming knowledge during the experiment. Since the focus of the research was on the development of new mathematical knowledge, it was preferable that the data on this process not be confounded with any individual differences in the students' programming skills. However, from time to time in the study, students spontaneously used Logo (e.g., one student wanted to see what would happen when he typed REPEAT 1000 [FLIP]). During the piloting of TGEO, one student used Logo to create his own set of new shapes and then played the Match game using these shapes. Another bright student spontaneously speculated about how the transformations were programmed in Logo, stating, "And then it has a turtle, and what it does is draws it and turns it." Thus in some cases students brought forth their previous Logo knowledge, without prompting, while interacting with the microworld.

In other studies, Logo has been used explicitly and intentionally as part of the pedagogy, often as a way for the learner to represent transformations. For example, in Ludwig (1986) an entire seventh grade curriculum in transformation geometry is implemented by having the students write Logo procedures for simple transformations. In the Motions microworld by Thompson (1985) the basic transformations were preprogrammed in Logo, but student teachers who used the microworld were asked to write Logo procedures to create new combinations of transformations. In this kind of activity, as in other microworlds based transparently in Logo, the programming language itself is a tool for "dissecting" mathematical entities and formalizing one's knowledge about how they work.

There is another potential use of Logo in the learning of transformation geometry that stops short of programming transformations from scratch. Students can use Logo to make explicit the connections among the various transformations. That is, students can be challenged to write a Logo procedure for one transformation in terms of another. For example, a number of the TGEO students spontaneously noted that FLIP was like REFLECT or that PIVOT was a kind of ROTATE. To bring this qualitative knowledge into a precise form, the students could be asked to implement FLIP using REFLECT, and PIVOT using ROTATE. A stronger challenge would be to find the single transformation that can be used to generate all of the euclidean motions. This kind of activity

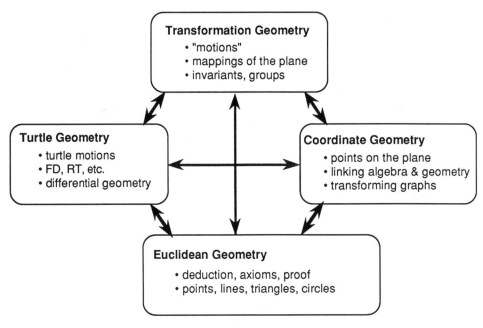

Figure 9   Exploring connections among geometries

calls both on the learner's deep understanding of the mathematical system of transformations and on his or her facility with Logo programming. Finally, an advanced curriculum in geometry (or geometries) could explore the formal connections and relationships among turtle geometry, transformation geometry, coordinate or vector representations, and euclidean geometry. Each of these views of the plane brings different characteristics to the forefront; students comfortable with Logo programming could use it as a medium for discovering and testing patterns within and among alternative geometries (see figure 9).

9 CONCLUSIONS

The development of the TGEO microworld, and the research on children's learning, can be seen as a case study in the principled design of a Logo-based environment for mathematical exploration. The aim of the research reported here was to design and investigate an interactive computer environment in which students could explore geometric transformations. On completing the initial design of the microworld and curriculum, empirical data were collected about the students' interactions with the microworld. These data were used to build a qualitative model of the learning path through the domain as well as to feed back into an improved pedagogical design. A particular focus of the research was on the ways in which the children's prior experiences, such as with learning Logo, contributed to their new understanding of transformation geometry.

The relationship between Logo and transformation geometry was considered both on the implicit, conceptual level and in terms of explicit pedagogical connections. Pedagogically Logo can be used as a way for students to create, extend, or adapt the TGEO microworld by programming transformations and new shapes. Logo can also be used as a medium for expressing explicitly the relationships among the transformations and for making connections to other kinds of geometries (turtle geometry, coordinate geometry, euclidean geometry).

At the conceptual level, there are many ways in which prior knowledge of Logo, as well as each learner's personal geometry, can act to guide and structure the students' developing understanding in transformation geometry. An underlying source of both misconceptions and some positive conceptions in the domain is an implicit mental model of the plane reinforced by and appropriate to turtle motions in Logo. Since the students encounter the transformation geometry microworld in a context previously used for such turtle motions, it is natural that they should initially interpret the transformations in the light of a model of the Logo plane. This model seems to support the students' understanding of the simple, local versions of the transformations but leads to conceptual bugs in some students' models of global transformations. One of the most important features of microworld environments is that such misconceptions can be corrected by students themselves through a process of conceptual "debugging." The microworld provides meaningful, interpretable feedback that the learners can use to refine their understanding of the structure of the new mathematical entities they encounter.

Research on children's use of microworlds is starting to build a more complete picture of how such environments can support new learning in mathematics, science, and other domains. Yet students come to these new technologies not as blank slates but with a background of skills and knowledge gained in a variety of prior contexts. One important focus of analysis of children's learning is in how prior conceptual "microviews" structure initial interpretations of new experiences and are eventually themselves modified and incorporated into a richer understanding of a domain.

ACKNOWLEDGMENTS

This work was partially supported by the Sloan Foundation, the Dorothea Constance Weinman Foundation, and the National Science Foundation under grants MDR-85-96025 and MDR-86- 42177.

REFERENCES

Bumby, D. and Klutch, R. 1982. *Mathematics: A Topical Approach.* Columbus, OH: Merrill.

DeVault, M., Frehmeyer, H., Greenberg, H., and Bezuska, S. 1978. *SRA Mathematics.* Chicago: SRA.

diSessa, A. 1982. Unlearning Aristotelian physics: A study of knowledge-based learning. *Cognitive Science* 6: 37–75.

diSessa, A. 1985. A principled design for an integrated computational environment. *Human-Computer Interaction* 1: 1–47.

Dugdale, S. 1981. Green globs: A microcomputer application for graphing of equations. *CERL Report E-21.* Urbana: University of Illinois.

Graening, J. 1980. *Geometry: A blended approach.* Columbus, OH: Merrill.

Greeno, J. 1983. Conceptual entities. In D. Gentner and A. Stevens (eds.), *Mental Models.* Hillsdale, NJ: Lawrence Earlbaum Associates.

Hart, K. 1981. *Children's Understanding of Mathematics: 11–16.* London: CSMS, University of London.

Hillel, J. 1985. Mathematical and programming concepts acquired by children, aged 8–9, in a restricted Logo environment. *Recherches en Didactique des Mathématiques* 6 (2, 3): 215–263.

Hoyles, C., and Noss R. 1987a. Children working in a structured Logo environment: from doing to understanding. *Recherches en Didactique des Mathématiques* 2 (12): 131–174.

Hoyles, C. and Noss, R. 1987b. Synthesizing mathematical conceptions and their formalization through the construction of a Logo-based school mathematics curriculum. *International Journal of Mathematics Education in Science and Technology* 18 (4): 581–594.

Hoyles, C., and Noss, R. 1989. The computer as a catalyst in children's proportion strategies. *Journal of Mathematical Behaviour* 7: 53– 75.

Lawler, R. 1985. *Computer Experience and Cognitive Development: A Child's Learning in a Computer Culture.* Chichester, UK: Ellis Horwood Ld.

Leron, U., and Zazkis, R. 1989a. A turtle view on geometrical transformations (and vice versa). *Logo Exchange* 7 (4): 20– 22.

Leron, U., and Zazkis, R. (eds). 1989b. *Proceedings of the Fourth International Conference on Logo and Mathematics Education*. Haifa, Israel: The Logo Centre, Technion.

Ludwig, S. 1986. Indicators of growth within a Logo/motion geometry curriculum environment. Unpublished master's thesis. University of Alberta.

Maxwell, E. 1975. *Geometry by Transformations*. Cambridge: Cambridge University Press.

Meserve, B. 1955. *Fundamental Concepts of Geometry*. New York: Dover.

Noss, R., and Hoyles, C. 1988. The computer as a mediating influence in the development of pupils' conception of variable. *European Journal of Psychology of Education 3*, (3): 273–288.

Papert, S. 1980. *Mindstorms: Children, Computers, and Powerful Ideas*. New York: Basic Books.

Piaget, J. 1937. Principal factors determining intellectual evolution from childhood to adult life. In E. Adrian et al. (eds.), *Factors Determining Human Behavior*. Cambridge: Harvard University Press.

School Mathematics Project. 1972. Cambridge: Cambridge University Press.

Schwartz, J., and Yerushalmy, M. 1987. The geometric supposer: An intellectual prosthesis for making conjectures. *The College Mathematics Journal* 18 (1): 58–65.

Thompson, P. 1985. Experience, problem solving, and learning mathematics: Considerations in developing mathematics curricula. In E. Silver (ed.), *Teaching and Learning Mathematical Problem Solving: Multiple Research Perspectives*. Hillsdale, NJ: Lawrence Earlbaum Associates.

Thompson, P. 1987. Mathematical microworlds and intelligent computer-assisted instruction. In G. Kearsley (ed.), *Artificial Intelligence and Instruction: Applications and Methods*. Reading, MA: Addison-Wesley.

Vergnaud, G. 1982: Cognitive and developmental psychology and research in mathematics education: Some theoretical and methodological issues. *For the Learning of Mathematics* 3 (2): 31–41.

White, B. 1981. Designing computer games to facilitate learning. *AI-TR-619*. Artificial Intelligence Laboratory. Cambridge: Massachusetts Institute of Technology.

Willson, W. 1977. *The Mathematics Curriculum: Geometry*. Glasgow, Scotland: Blackie & Sons Ltd.

Styles and Strategies

II

Chapters 6 through 9 consider the interaction between pupils and teachers in a Logo setting and how the nature of this interaction crucially affects pupils' learning. Thus the authors begin the task of discussing the question of pedagogy in a more explicit form, as well as the role and nature of teacher intervention. There are some deep social, epistemological, and psychological issues here, and the contributions reflect this in the diversity of their focus: Curiously, despite their obvious importance, noncognitive issues tend not to be addressed by researchers. These four chapters do not present a single or cohesive view but, in raising these ideas explicitly, go some way toward redressing the balance.

Sylvia Weir (chapter 6) looks at LEGO-Logo activity from a sociocultural point of view, drawing on her many years of experience at MIT, and specifically on her observations of primary school children working within Project Headlight at the Hennigan School in Boston. Tamara Lemerise (chapter 7) brings to the issue of learning styles a psychologist's perspective and extracts data concerned with the variability and malleability of learning styles from one of her research projects in Quebec with pupils aged between ten and twelve years. A theoretical model of the growth of mathematical understanding is offered by Canadian mathematics educator Thomas Kieren (chapter 8). The Logo mathematics environment has provided him with fertile ground for validating and developing his model. Finally, Swiss psychologist Jean-Luc Gurtner (chapter 9) focuses on the linkage between Logo and mathematics and suggests pedagogical strategies for elaborating these connections, using his metaphor of tunnels and bridges.

The thrust of Weir's argument is that learning cannot be separated from the social interaction in which pupils are engaged. She draws on Vygotsky's concept of the *zone of proximal development* as a way of "providing the framework for understanding cognitive change in terms of a complex social, interactional setting." Weir believes that computer-based tools can serve as cultural symbols and "can act as vehicles to mediate the knowledge to be appropriated by the learner." Thus for Weir the cultural associations of LEGO are paramount (it is said that over 90 percent of U.S. homes with children contain LEGO), and she emphasises the natural playfulness and plasticity that this adds to the Logo setting. Weir clearly points up the gap between teacher and pupils' goals and the need to reassess pupil actions in the light of their goals rather than the teacher's. She is also concerned to address the issue of *individual* differences and argues that the LEGO-Logo environment provides external representations that are particularly suitable and appropriate for certain pupils. She gives examples of how different facets of the LEGO-Logo environment can catalyze superior performance, a point taken up in the following chapter by Lemerise.

Weir stresses the importance of Vygotsky's notion of the role of play as a means of detaching meaning from the object. Therefore it is crucial for her that play is not underestimated. It provides a synergism of the manipulation of objects and of symbols, it provides "a pivot for detaching meaning from the concrete object, by creating imaginary situations that emancipate the learner from situational constraints": She sees that children working with LEGO-Logo are sharing pragmatic knowledge of both mathematics and physics. (It is interesting that she sees these two knowledge bases as essentially the same, and this identification does not impinge on her argument: We point to what we see as important differences between the two domains in our concluding chapter.)

Naturally her emphasis on the social and cultural dimensions of learning has implications for her pedagogical strategy. Weir maintains that classroom situations ought to assist teachers in a recognition of their pupils' goals and suggests that the LEGO-Logo environment is exactly one such set of situations where there are "negotiations between teacher and learner during which there is a mutual appropriation of goals." The emphasis of her argument is that the companionship between teacher and pupil is one of uncertainty and negotiation. Yet despite (we might say *because*) of the natural playfulness with which most children approach LEGO, Weir stresses the need for teacher intervention—for example, by encouraging pupils to test out their ideas and see the consequences, to approach a question systematically, and to provide a language for problem solving.

There is no contradiction here: It is rare for initiation into the formal codes of school-based knowledge to be grounded in objects and relationships that are familiar to children through their home experiences. Or, to be more precise, where such attempts to link school and "everyday" knowledge are attempted, they are often problematic (as Martin Hughes 1986 has pointed out in relation to early number work) and even counterproductive (e.g., see Valerie Walkerdine's 1989 critique of primary mathematics practice). Weir's contribution can be seen as an attempt to draw the two practices—home and school—together, but there is no sense in which there is a symmetry between them: Culturally embedded activities such as LEGO can provide the hook on which to hang pedagogical intervention, but they do not obviate the need for such intervention.

Returning to the theme of learning styles, Lemerise puts forward a strong case for appreciating the multitude of styles available to each individual and the need to design learning experiences that allow each individual to make use of these many different learning styles. She begins by posing the suggestion that there is a link between school success and learning style, particularly in the dominance or the supremacy of the "rational analytic" style. Lemerise argues that the Logo environment is well suited for favoring a variety of both interindividual and intraindividual behaviors. In her analysis of pupils' learning, she poses a series of dichotomous styles of interaction with Logo: *data* driven or *concept* driven, *process oriented* or *product oriented*, or *linear* versus *procedural*. The key point in her argument is that intraindividual variety appears to be a function of the amount of experience with Logo and the activities undertaken. Thus the Logo setting needs to value variety rather than one style more than another. It is of course the case that the Logo mathematics community has been one arena in which the question of learning styles has been taken seriously, and some attempts at accommodating a variety of styles has been undertaken. But, at least in some of the literature, there has been an implication that individuals *have* styles, that a learning style is a more or less unique attribute of a learner. Lemerise argues the reverse: "A context that values variety and sees it as an important developmental quality is more facilitative than a context that values one style more than others, or that views styles as being mutually exclusive."

Taken together, both Lemerise and Weir state a strong case for an open and playful Logo setting deriving from the pragmatic knowledge mobilized by the learner. In the absence of such variety and openness, they would, however, draw slightly different implications. Lemerise would suggest that an unfavorable setting would result in the dominance of a particular learning style over others, whereas Weir would be more concerned in the resulting dominance of teacher goals.

In his contribution Kieren is similarly concerned to stress the importance of pragmatic knowledge, and he attempts to build a theoretical model of child-Logo interaction that might at once make sense of the ways in which this knowledge can act as a basis for or as an obstacle to mathematical understandings. Without such a model Kieren warns that Logo mathematics can simply be seen as involving behaviors of writing and debugging procedures. The purpose of his contribution is to look beneath this perception of activity and pull out the essence of Logo mathematical knowing as a whole. In so doing, Kieren uncovers many embedded levels of knowing within children's effective Logo mathematical activity. These levels are perceived to be self-similar, that is, *recursive* in that each exhibits complementary facets of form and process, language and action. The basis of his argument is that Logo mathematical knowing at any level entails the coordinated use of language and action in the process of decontextualization.

Kieren argues that the virtue of conceptualizing Logo mathematics in this way is that Logo mathematical knowledge of any topic *can be seen to exist at many levels at once for a child*. Thus in some ways his argument supports that of the existence of intraindividual variety of styles proposed by Lemerise. Kieren argues that in building higher-order ideas or using more sophisticated procedures, a child can "fold back" to simple ideas and actions as *part of* or as a precursor to higher-order activity. Furthermore a child can always validate more sophisticated, abstract Logo use against knowing at a simpler more action-oriented level. Here Kieren complements Weir's argument for the importance of playful activity with objects.

Kieren's view also suggests ways in which teachers can provoke this higher-order activity. In the absence of such provoking, a child may stay at an "unsophisticated" but perfectly successful level of knowing—a phenomenon reported in much of the Logo literature. However, if the teacher gives pupils tasks that promote distinctions within his or her current level of activity, Kieren suggests that the knowing can become deep and sophisticated as well as more complex.

That Kieren's view is somewhat at odds with Weir's is evidenced by his use of language: Labeling pragmatic activity as "unsophisticated" is not uncontroversial. Yet Kieren makes it clear that he values such activity as a basis for further reflection, a view not explicitly shared by Gurtner whose contribution differs in a number of fundamental respects from the preceding three.

First, Gurtner essentially rejects the notion put forward by Weir of the centrality of pragmatic knowledge, arguing that there is "no mathematics without noticing it." He proposes that a greater degree of explicit connection should be made between Logo and mathematics. Thus he argues for a more structured approach to Logo activity that involves intervention rather than negotiation, where the teacher has the task of building bridges. Gurtner claims that Logo is mathematical, but *only* if there is an explicit link with mathematics—a bridge; in the absence of such bridges, children are unlikely to appreciate the mathematics they are doing and will use, for example, perceptual rather than analytic strategies or will generate misunderstandings particularly arising from differences in formalism between Logo and mathematics. Gurtner offers some practical suggestions about the construction of bridges between Logo and mathematics in terms of task selection, microworld development, verbal interventions, and explicit teaching. He also advocates that students be encouraged to search for these bridges and links themselves. Gurtner contrasts such an approach with one that allows students to opt for tunnels between Logo and mathematics rather than bridges. Avoiding the scenic route can lead to students avoiding the interesting connections between Logo and mathematics, and—continuing his metaphor further—he argues that teachers need to "open windows" for pupils to gain a better view of the mathematics from within their activity.

One feature of Gurtner's argument is that he talks about Logo classes and mathematics classes as distinct entities (we are aware that, unfortunately, this represents curricular reality in many school cultures). He clearly presents ways of promoting links between the two domains but is less concerned than, for example, Weir, to see what might be lost in this structured approach. Gurtner's strategy consists of a mediational teaching program following on higher levels of mastery and metacognitive prompts: He emphasizes the importance of reflective and metacognitive activity (here he echoes some of the arguments of Weir and Kieren). It is interesting to contrast Gurtner's designation of strategies that best fit a task with the argument for promotion of variety in individual styles suggested by Lemerise.

Thus the four chapters in part II raise important questions of style and strategy from both theoretical and practical standpoints. We see a need to synthesize these issues with the cognitive questions discussed in part I, and we attempt such a synthesis in our afterword.

REFERENCES

Hughes, M. 1986. *Children and Number*. Oxford: Blackwell.

Walkerdine, V. 1988. *The Mastery of Reason*. London: Routledge.

LEGO-Logo: A Vehicle for Learning   6

Sylvia Weir

Human learning presupposes a specific social nature and a process by which children grow into the intellectual life of those around them.—Vygotsky (1978, p. 88)

1 INTRODUCTION

In this chapter I look at LEGO-Logo activity from a sociocultural point of view. I have previously described the connection I see between the educational use of computers and the sociocultural approach to learning of Vygotsky and his colleagues (Weir 1989). Learning cannot be separated from the social interactions in which individuals are engaged. During such interactions, individuals internalize pieces of shared culture, making that knowledge part of their own understanding.[1] I use the context of LEGO-Logo learning to examine a number of issues. What forms does culturally located knowledge take? What are the external representations of knowledge that an individual needs to internalize? How would classroom teachers benefit from a deeper understanding of culturally mediated interactions? What circumstances, what classroom activities, will facilitate this appropriation of knowledge?

From the point of view of the individual learner, social representations of knowledge are external to his or her cognitive system. They serve as receptacles of the culture, their meaning can be appropriated during social interactions, and they mediate the culture. Language dominates as *the* mediating symbol system, augmented by other systems such as the symbols of mathematics or visual representations such as graphs, maps, or architectural/electronic circuit diagrams. Here I am concerned to identify the role in classroom learning of a new set of cultural, knowledge-mediating symbols generated by the computer. The graphics screen turtle is one example. Especially important for our purposes here are mathematics- related computer "objects" such as Logo procedures and variables. I am talking about the significance of the computer not just as an external

---

1. Cognitive change comes from the transformation of knowledge among persons, interpsychological understanding, into knowledge within a person, intrapsychological understanding (Vygotsky 1978, editor's preface and ch. 4).

tool like a hammer, when using the computer as a fancy typewriter to generate printed copy, although that in itself can be a powerful stimulus to learning. The importance of computer-based activity such as Logo lies in its potential for enabling the student to appropriate the computer as an inward-directed tool with the semiotic power of language or mathematical formulas—a tool that amplifies thinking.

Internalizing the shared culture occurs during the myriad social interactions among individuals as the different generations do things together. Informal learning takes place in the home and in the streets. The goal of that learning has a pragmatic character. One learns what is useful, whatever allows one to get done the things one wants done. "In everyday situations, thought is in the service of action" (Rogoff 1984, p. 7). The mathematics underlying grocery shopping, for example, takes the form of finding opportunistic solutions rather than taking a formal approach. At a certain point when the calculation gets complex, shoppers will choose an option other than calculation as a basis for deciding between two varieties of the same food product (Lave 1984). It is clear that for many students in today's classrooms, the kind of learning expected of them in the classroom bears little resemblance to their street learning. They do not share the academic goal structure that deems certain concepts important and worth learning.

A setting that has fostered interestingly different social relationships for learning is the MIT-based Project Headlight at the Hennigan School, an innercity elementary school in Boston, Massachussetts. Here computers are a freely available resource being integrated into the learning environment of some three hundred schoolchildren. The LEGO-Logo activities I will describe took place as part of this project. Underpinning the educational interactions observed is the geographical layout of computers arranged in four networks in a large central space into which individual classrooms open. As one walks through that space, the constructions of persons working at the computers are visible on their graphics screens in a very public sort of way. Individuals of all ages and abilities can see these productions, can ask how they are done, and can attempt to imitate them.

That central space becomes a kind of culture cauldron in which children learn from each other how to do things that excite them. In this space the informal cultural transmission—child centered, child invented—that occurs out in a community now starts to occur in a school setting. Computer objects such as Logo procedures and graphics objects can act as external representations, easily picked up by the students in a pragmatic way. Students do not need to understand them deeply before they can use them to create interesting effects to show to their friends. Combining LEGO with Logo enhances this accessibility. Students can connect together motors and gears, lights and sensors, to create effects whose mechanisms are not deeply understood.

In the Hennigan setting we get a more extreme version of what has sometimes been observed during Logo activity, namely, a culture of result-producing rituals passed along the grapevine, elaborated, and refined. Effects are achieved by the use of oft- repeated frames. An example that will be familiar to all Logo teachers is the use of REPEAT n [something]. Another is the procedure frame: TO < procedurename > . . . END. Frames like these have an obvious relation to concepts in mathematics, as pointed out by many Logo researchers (Hillel and Samurçay 1985; Hoyles 1986; Hoyles and Noss 1987, 1989; Leron and Zazkis 1986; Hoyles and Sutherland 1989; Noss 1986; Papert 1980; see other chapters in this book). LEGO-Logo activity forms a rich extension of Logo in the way it continually presents examples of mathematical themes like reversibility, symmetry, fractional parts, ratios, and measurement of extent. LEGO bricks are like Cuisenaire rods in that they can be classified by the number of nodes—it is easy to count nodes and holes, and this provides an intrinsic measure. Whereas Cuisenaire rods do not appear to connect to a real-world purpose, LEGO bricks obviously do. Gears provide a scaffolding, a mediating object, a physical representation of the physical concept of mechanical advantage and of mathematical concepts such as ratio.[2]

However, as has been pointed out (Leron 1985a,b; Noss and Hoyles, chapter 14 in this volume), these examples of mathematical concepts are not seen *as such* by many of the students who use them. Indeed, the whole enterprise has been attacked on the basis of a demonstrated lack of any deep understanding of constructs like procedures and variables (Pea and Kurland 1984). This kind of complaint shows a misunderstanding of the nature of pragmatic knowledge. Having a pragmatic understanding of how to achieve certain effects does not ensure an automatic grasp of the concepts underlying the production of those

---

2. In addition to examples of math concepts, LEGO-Logo constructions embody physical themes, such as the notion of using machines to enhance power and the trade-off between speed and power, focusing on the relation between moving parts, notions of friction and efficient connections or linkages, center of gravity and balance; the relation between motion and the passage of time; the use of gear boxes to change speed, direction, and turning force. LEGO-Logo introduces engineering notions not usually encountered in the school curriculum, such as the state of a machine.

effects. What it provides is the basis upon which such an understanding can be built, an incipient understanding of that real mathematics content.

The Zone of Proximal Development

Consider the Hennigan learning context in terms of Vygotsky's concept of the *zone of proximal development*, defined as the "distance between the actual developmental level as determined by independent problem solving and the level of potential development as determined through problem solving under adult guidance or in collaboration with more capable peers" (Vygotsky 1978, p. 86). The concept is to be understood not as a function of the individual learner's cognitive system—the collection of schemes and operations and understandings in an individual's head—but as providing the framework for understanding cognitive change in terms of a complex social, interactional setting. Components of the setting include the following:

1.   A collaborative effort among persons working on a problem that some of them could not work on alone in any effective way—for Hennigan, this includes extensive peer-peer interaction and a growing pool of shared pragmatic knowledge.
2.   Access to a set of cultural symbols that can act as vehicles to mediate the knowledge to be appropriated by the learner. Computer-based symbols can play an important role in this regard. Their use can catalyze the maturation of an understanding of abstract concepts (Weir 1987; Hoyles and Noss 1989). This will be a central theme in the data to be presented here. A second theme concerns the special significance of computer-generated symbols for individuals who have trouble with the heavily language-based traditional curriculum (Weir 1987). Such individuals can become transformed from struggling special-needs students into computer experts who make significant academic progress.
3.   A level of development in the individual learner appropriate to the activity to be undertaken; "the zone of proximal development defines those functions that have not yet matured but are in the process of maturation" (Vygotsky 1978, p. 86). For Hennigan students working with LEGO-Logo, this would refer to the existence of pragmatic mathematics and physics knowledge that is on its way to becoming an understanding of abstract mathematics and physics concepts.
4.   The presence among the more experienced members of the group of some sense of what is to be learned—*a goal structure*. Typically teachers and students do not share goals. The Hennigan setting brings out the differences between student goals and teacher goals in a particularly clear fashion. Logo and LEGO-Logo activity serves the utilitarian aims of students and is its own reward. Teachers' goals are academic. From their point of view, the activity is directed toward (is undertaken for the purpose of catalyzing) the

acquisition of certain important concepts. The educator can use the richness of the pragmatic knowledge to articulate a more formal understanding of the (mathematical) concepts involved only if steps are taken to ensure that what is being internalized is *both the rich raw experience of manipulating cultural objects and an appreciation of their significance.*

The LEGO-Logo Setting

Successful classroom interactions require that there be a *mutual* appropriation of goals. Teachers need to get better at recognizing and taking account of student goals. LEGO-Logo provides an academic milieu in which students can develop their own goals: They can choose a goal, work to realize that goal, and convey their goal to the teacher. The "play" nature of LEGO can enhance learning by building on the emotional engagement of children. Good emotional relationships facilitate the mutual recognition of each other's goals. Success in the LEGO-Logo setting leads to an improved self-image. If a student has a good self-image, he or she will be less inclined to defend against the goals of others.

The degree of definition of goal varies from ritualistic rebuilding of the same motorized vehicle to less defined explorations of the properties of the materials out of which goals emerge. This process is aided by the clarity with which function is related to the form of the material—the skeletal nature exposes the principles of the structure. For example, a child might pick up some girders in order to build a square frame. As she explores this deformable shape further, she may experience the forces of tension and compression in a way that in time could become the basis for a more formal analysis. Out of seemingly mindless acts of repetition, like snapping links of tractor tread or gear chain together, the creative idea emerges. Some children use less obvious combinations, put things together in ways others do not. For example, a hinge is a defined device, but these children will look at a hinge and see a new purpose to it. They tend to avoid preconceptions and use analogy to make connections between things that are not usually connected. LEGO-Logo invites creativity.

After working with LEGO materials for a while, one comes to admire the economy of parts, with some pieces having several uses quite unrelated to one another but all working together to make an evocative learning environment.

Learning That Drives Development

Combining the physical properties of LEGO with the symbol-generating properties of the computer, combining the manipulating of concrete structures with the manipulating of symbols, produces a synergism that can lead to functional maturation. Important issues arise concerning the development of abstract thinking and the decontextualization of meaning. One can think of LEGO-Logo as capable of supporting all Piagetian stages and of making growth possible between stages. The LEGO-Logo combination supports two kinds of constructive activity—building LEGO structures and building Logo programs. During each experience the knowledge generated is first embedded in the context of the particular construction. *Learning happens first in context* (Brown 1978). The goal of the educator is to decontextualize that understanding. I believe the computer can play a crucial role in this transition.

First, computer-generated external representations are half-way between concrete and abstract in nature—they are objects that can be acted upon in much the same way concrete real-world objects can; on the other hand, they serve as visible versions of ideas—they conceptualize the domain. They serve a mediating role. Mediation of knowledge occurs, too, during LEGO-Logo. LEGO materials are real world and concrete enough, yet LEGO objects can act as visualizations of physical concepts.

Second, to the extent that the activity of programming makes the intermediate steps of problem solving more transparent than they would otherwise be, the similarity of related experiences can emerge—"the same step occurs here as occurs there." Both Logo and LEGO are incremental and modular, and provide powerful images ready for appropriation by the child. The same Logo programming construction keeps coming up. To the extent that a particular LEGO construction, a particular module that performs a particular task, is required over and over again in whatever the student builds, this experience can facilitate what Vygotsky called the "decontextualizing of mediational means," an essential attribute of higher mental functioning (Wertsch 1985).

LEGO-Logo can become both a medium for expressing and formalizing ideas and a medium for generating the embryo of an idea. I turn to a consideration of these themes as they manifested themselves in a series of LEGO-Logo sessions at the Hennigan School.

2 THE PRESENT STUDY

LEGO-Logo was developed at MIT in cooperation with the Danish toy company (Ocko, Papert, and Resnick 1988). In LEGO-Logo students connect their LEGO constructions to the computer using a special interface box, and they write programs to control these devices. For example, if students plug LEGO motors into the interface box, they can then type commands to make the motors turn on, turn off, or reverse direction. Similarly students can get readings from LEGO sensors (touch sensors, light sensors) plugged into the interface box.

Participating in the activity was a group of six students in the special-needs classroom, working with Steve Ocko, one of the main developers of LEGO-Logo, and myself. Two of these students form the main focus. Sam (ten years old) and Peter (nine years old) present a nice contrast. They had spent some time constructing LEGO machines of various sorts but had not yet written programs to drive their constructions. In this short study our focus was on the LEGO-Logo combination, so we decided to finesse the LEGO construction phase by building the vehicle we needed to introduce the LEGO-Logo primitives we were interested in exploring.[3] Our vehicle had two motors: One drove the back wheels (motor *A*); the other motor was connected to a rack and pinion to turn the front wheels (motor *B*). We worked with this vehicle on and off for four sessions of approximately one hour each. We also refer to the work of Karl, an eight-year-old learning-disabled student who built a LEGO crane.

LEGO-Logo as Language

Session one (June 1) began with Peter seated at the keyboard, Sam seated on his right, and Steve Ocko on his left. Sylvia Weir was seated on the other side of a low table. We were in one corner of the resource room. Other students were occupied at other tables with worksheets and books, supervised by a teaching aide.

Ocko introduces TALKTO by making an analogy with TELL in LogoWriter. He demonstrates the effect of the commands ON, OFF, and RD on the motor.

Peter: How do you tell it to go forward? FD?

Ocko: Try it and see.

Peter tries FD 30, and the screen turtle appears and moves.

Ocko: So we need a different set of words to talk to the motors.

---

3. TALKTO "A   tells the computer to get ready to talk to port A on the interface box.
        ON   turns on the motor.
      OFF   turns off the motor.
       RD   reverses the direction of the motor.
  SETEVEN   sets the motor in the even (forward) direction.

The interaction took the form of a conversation. We see turntaking: First Ocko initiated activity, and then Peter asked a question. Ocko used the metaphor of communication with the motors: "We need a different set of words to talk to LEGO motors"; and he used Logo itself as a metaphor: TALKTO was introduced by analogy with TELL in LogoWriter.[4] Note also how Ocko explicitly introduced a try-it-and-see way of working, which would be adopted later by Peter. The context is suggestive, and Ocko takes full advantage of it. The session continues.

Peter (having done a series of RD's):   Let me try to control it

Ocko (responding to this overture):   Let's write a procedure. Do you know about procedures? What's a procedure?

Peter: A procedure is a lot of words and you try to make . . .

Ocko: Never mind. We'll come back to that.

They write a procedure to control motor *A*. Peter and Sam are unable to spell WIGGLE, and settle for the shorter WIG as the name of the procedure.

Ocko: What will happen when you type WIG?

Peter: It will do what you told it to.

Ocko: So now, why do we want procedures?

Peter: Because otherwise you would have to do too much writing.

They continue to define procedures, concentrating now on motor *B*, which will control turning. At first Peter suggests WIG1 as the name of the right-turning procedure. When he comes to define the left-turning one, he goes back and changes WIG1 to WIGRT, and calls the other one WIGLT. Under Ocko's guidance they try both of them out. The new procedures involve a new LEGO-Logo command—SETEVEN—to distinguish slot 0 from slot 1.

Mathematical Thinking

The first session ended with an unexpected display of mathematical virtuosity from Peter. He saw an interesting issue connected with odd and even, and almost played with us as he explored its possibilities.

---

4. In LogoWriter, TELL 3, for example, directs all future commands to turtle number 3.

Peter is playing with WIGRT and WIGLT. He types REPEAT 9, pauses, looks up with a smile.

Peter: Oh! I am going to have an even number.

He changes 9 to 10, and now has REPEAT 10 [WIGRT WIGLT]

Ocko: So where does it end up?

Peter (triumphantly):   Right back where it started! That's because I chose an even number.

Peter then tries an odd number, and lo and behold, it still lands up right where it started.

Ocko: How can you get it so that repeating it odd and even number of times makes a difference?

Peter thinks for a very brief moment and types REPEAT 9 [WIGRT WIGLT WIGRT]

Great delight all round!

Peter's delight is expressed in his smile, in the timbre of his voice, and in the reasons he gives for doing what he does as he tackles the problem of breaking the symmetry. My sense of what Peter understood goes as follows:

His train of thought seems to have been started by the SETEVEN command. That prompted the intuition that one can use programming to achieve alternating events, that the way to do this is through the odd-even distinction, and that one can systematically change the components in a program statement to try to achieve the desired effect. The first step he took was to change the number of repeats. He began with an even number (10) to show that the process lands up where it was at the start. Then he tried an odd number—whoops! His hypothesis was not confirmed. So he looked for another place in the program statement that could affect alternation. He noticed that there were an even number of turns within the REPEAT bracket, so he changed that to an odd number of turns. In fact, to achieve his alternation goal, he needed to have a variable to toggle. Since he had not been introduced to variables yet, he did not succeed in breaking the symmetry.

What I find impressive was Peter's display of mathematical intuition. He treated the problem as a parity one. He made a prediction, checked it out, and found his prediction correct; he checked the limits by trying the remaining case, saw the problem, and tried to correct it. For such a child, then, one would want to say that his zone of proximal development at that time included the readiness, indeed the need for, the introduction of variables. This sequence is particularly remarkable in the light of his status as a child with learning disability. I return to this later.

A more traditional elementary school topic in mathematics came up in a later session (session three, June 5), as we worked with Karl.

Karl had finished building his crane. He demonstrated the power of his construction using an assortment of heavy objects. Karl explained to admiring onlookers how gears trade speed for power: "When it goes slower, it is stronger." His machine became the basis for a discussion on division and proportion. He had coupled an eight-tooth gear with a forty-tooth gear. He had "not done dividing by" in class but knew that $40/10 = 4$. Would $40/8$ be bigger or smaller? There followed a discussion about "dividing by" in terms of "How much would each one get?"

Karl's LEGO-Logo work was beginning to provide a bridge between his informal mathematical understanding and the formal algorithms he would be learning in class. Gears provide a scaffolding, a mediating object, an external representation. As it turns out, Karl was reluctant to pursue the question of whether $40/8$ would be bigger or smaller. He frequently showed this kind of resistance to this kind of question (see section 3).

Problem-Solving Strategies

The LEGO-Logo setting provides concrete physical embodiments of problem-solving strategies: finding the bug, seeing cause and effect, breaking the problem into parts. Frequently the problems are mechanical or electrical: check the connections of this motor, loosen that gear drive. Since each procedure involves one particular event—a starting or a stopping of a movement, the activation or deactivation of a sensor—testing out the procedures one at a time allows the student to develop a systematic approach to problem solving. However, it is not enough simply to provide the opportunity. We saw, above, how Ocko *explicitly* introduced a try-it-and-see way of working. All the way through the first session, Ocko had repeatedly articulated the need for systematic testing of each physical connection and checking the effect of each Logo procedure. The beginning of the second session (June 3) saw Peter and Sam adopting this advice to find the missing TALKTO that gets the motors going. The debugging process was a social, collaborative process, without intervention from the adults.

The session began without Ocko, who was talking to the teacher at the other end of the room. Peter was seated at the computer; Sam was standing at the table working with the car. They were having trouble getting the motors to respond to commands. Sam checked mechanical connections, and Peter tried various commands unsuccessfully. Then,

Peter: Oh, I know why it doesn't work, Sam.

Sam: What?

Peter: Watch!—(types and says) T–A–L.

Sam: TALKTO! *B*! No wonder it didn't work!

Ocko returned and the second session continued with an explicit introduction of the term "bug." Part of the activity is to *acquire the language of problem solving*, and for Sam that was not straightforward. We had posed a problem for him at the end of the previous session, namely, to figure out how to drive the car round the side of an obstacle.

Sam tries WIGRT and the car moves back.

Sam: Look at that!

Ocko: OK Let's look at the procedures. There's has to be a reason for that. Show me which procedure. What does BACK talk to?

Sam: *A*.

Ocko: Now what is *A* plugged into?

Sam: Black . . . so right here.

(Follows the wire from the *A* slot to the vehicle.)

Ocko: So which motor is it actually . . .

Sam (interrupts):   It gotta be in this motor.

Ocko: That's the bug.

Sam: That's the bug?

Ocko: Do you know what bug is? Did you ever hear that story when they first had a bug?

Ocko tells story of bugs getting into the parts of the early machines, and how they found the bug in the switch.

Ocko: And so they still talk about finding the bug to fix it. And what bug did we just find?

Sam does not respond directly, and it is not clear just what he has taken in. He moves on to demonstrate that things are working now.

Ocko (assuming that Sam has understood):   So we fixed it.

Sam (pointing to the obstacle—returning to the goal set up before):   Do you want me to try to get round this?

Ocko: Without touching it?

Sam (thinks, and while giving the WIGRT command, says):   Right.

The result is unexpected.

Ocko: It seems like there's a bug.

Sam (takes the car in his hand and turns it over):   A BUG? . . . Where's the bug?

Ocko: Well that's what we got to find out.

Sam: I don't see no bug.

Ocko: Why isn't it working? A bug is a . . . we use the word bug to mean the reason the thing isn't working. Well look, try and turn it. Oh, it's working. But that's because it's working in this position. See what's happening? This is turning, but that's not working because it's too loose . . .

Sam: So we gotta tighten it?

Ocko: Yes. There you are. So when something doesn't work, the first thing you have to do is figure out where the problem is. If things don't work, there is always a reason. Right, let's go back to the job.

Sam took the bug story very literally. We were struck repeatedly by his need for concrete explanations. Sometimes he would echo what we said to him, as a question, as though the words were not meaningful to him. But then he would surprise us by what he had taken in. It is as though the process of appropriation was going on, but at a slow pace. So in this case we found ourselves wondering just how much he had understood about "bug?" The subject came up again in the third session (June 5), and we were pleasantly surprised.

At this point the car stops responding.

Sam (looking puzzled):   A bug?"

Ocko locates a mechanical looseness.

Sam (with satisfaction):   It was a bug!

Varieties of Fulfillment

The reactions of the two students Peter and Sam made a nice contrast. Each was achieving at his own level, and each at a higher level than either did in the regular class. I have already described Peter's sense of achievement when he invented and explored the odd-even problem. For another view of the intense satisfaction LEGO-Logo activity generated, we continue with Sam's behavior during the second session. In his own way Sam felt very good about his obstacle-maneuvering procedure. Using the set of WIG operations, he successfully sent the vehicle round the side of an obstacle in what amounted to direct drive. The task then was to teach the computer how to do this. Ocko was called away at this point, and Sam and Weir continued to write that procedure.

Weir: OK, then. Let's work out the steps. What's step one?

Sam starts typing and needs persuading.

Weir: Let's work it out first. Before we type. What was your first step when you we did that? What did you do first?

Sam (goes back and looks at the commands on the screen):   Went forward.

Weir (writing on notepad):   Went forward first . . . so . . . step 1 is go forward. And step 2?

Sam: Left.

Weir: Step 2 is left. OK. Step 3?

Sam: Back.

Weir: Step 3 was back. You went forward, left, back.

Sam: Then right.

Weir: All right, and then . . .

Sam (continues to check screen):   Five is . . . there's only four.

Weir: Only four. So step 5 would be do 1 again, go back to step 1. Shall we say that?

Sam: mmmuh.

Weir: Go back.

Sam: To 1.

Weir: OK, so now let's write the procedure. Do you want to have this near you so that you can copy it? Or I'll read it out to you, and you type it.

Sam (types TO):   What about a name?

Weir: You choose a name.

Sam: WIG1 (types in WIG1, thinks, types REPEAT). Shall I put REPEAT?

Weir: Well think about that. What was the first step?

Sam (reading from pad):   Go forward.

Weir: What did you use to go forward down there?

Sam (goes down to command center):   WIG.

Weir: Now what next?

Sam: WIGLT . . . now back . . . now right.

Weir: OK, shall we try it out?

Sam (types and says): WIG1. Whew! It did it! (almost disbelief in his voice) OKayyy! Watch this! WIG1!

Weir: OK . . . and now . . .

Sam: I'm going to do it all over together! Now, watch this!

He uses arrows to repeat WIG1 over and over again. Ocko returns.

Sam: Steve, we did it! (demonstrates the movement) That's the procedure (pointing).

Sam savored his achievement and refused to let Weir go on with whatever it was she had in mind with her "OK . . . and now . . ." He had made this happen, and he was going to enjoy it, to see it again and again. Note how, during the interaction, Weir tried to give only as much help as Sam needed. He took over just as soon as he knew how, and she gradually retreated.

Context-Dependent Learning

Looking at the feedback on the computer screen had helped Sam during the many hours he had spent working in the central computer area, using REPEAT to make his squares and circles. Within that context he knew all he needed to know about REPEAT. When he first came to the LEGO-Logo setting, he brought an understanding of procedure writing that was totally context bound. For him, writing a procedure meant retrieving a procedure frame with a RE-PEAT statement in it:

To < name of procedure > REPEAT . . . END

and, as we saw, that is what he offered when asked to write a procedure: "Shall I put REPEAT?" During the next period of activity, we see evidence to suggest that his understanding of the concept of a procedure was in the process of being decontextualized.

Session three began with Sam in the driver's seat. Following on his success at the task of writing a procedure for maneuvering the vehicle round an object, he continued with the more complicated task suggested at the end of session two, namely, that he write a procedure to park the vehicle. He arrived at the session all excited and announced that he had a parking procedure.

At first the car to be parked did not respond to computer commands. Ocko murmurs "a bug," as he checks out the system. He finds that wires have been plugged in incorrectly. Together Sam and Ocko correct this. It seems Sam has arrived at the session with a planned procedure to park his car. He is very proud of this. What he had done basically was to string together the procedures that had been written the previous session. He types in

```
TO WIG2
  WIGLT
  WIGRT
  WIGBK
  WIG1
  WIG2
END
```

When asked what that WIG2 at the end was for, he quickly removed it (he evidently did not intend recursion!). Ocko proceeded to step through the WIG2 procedure with him, but Sam looked blank/dull when it was explained to him that WIGRT followed by WIGLT does not change anything—"It's just canceling out."

Ocko (abandoning the procedure):   Let's step through what we would need to park it.

Sam was able to describe verbally the steps needed for the parking procedure.

One description of what had happened emphasized what Sam did not do. What he needed to see was the alternation between turning and moving that was involved both in navigating forward and in reversing. He had carried out this alternation when navigating forward round the obstacle in direct drive. When he wrote a procedure to navigate forward, he had included the alternating actions because he was copying the list of commands from the command center on to a piece of paper and then into a procedure. It seems that during that copying process he had not registered the *significance of the alternation*. Again, in direct drive, he had carried out the alternation (of moving and turning) when he parked the car (the reverse of the first task). However, when he came to write the procedure to do this, the abstraction step—recognizing the alternation of moving and turning—was missing. We were disappointed at what felt like very little progress. Had we moved outside his zone of proximal development?

Upon reflection, an alternative description suggested itself; it takes a more optimistic view. Let us review Sam's progress up to this point. Recall that first he had used the set of WIG operations to function in what amounted to direct drive, with immediate feedback (a one-one correspondence between each command typed and a visible effect on the vehicle), to generate a sequence of commands to maneuver the vehicle around an obstacle. He had then used that command sequence, displayed in the command center (an external representation acting as a memory aide), as the basis for writing the procedure to do this. All this had been accompanied by ample help. It seems that the concrete steps in the LEGO-vehicle maneuvering process had indeed made a difference as to how he thought about a procedure—not enough of a difference to write a correct procedure but enough to have moved him away from the idea of *procedure as something with REPEAT in it*. I would suggest that as a result of this LEGO-Logo activity, Sam took home the message at the end of session two: "If you want to write a procedure, string together the names of procedures that move the vehicle." So he arrived with this procedure, WIG2, that simply strings the basic WIG procedures together.

He had not yet learned to get the order of those procedures correct on his own, but he had learned something. I have talked of LEGO-Logo as a series of negotiations between teacher and learner during which there is a mutual appropriation of goals. Ocko's goal at this point was to "get that car parked." Sam's goal was to show his recently acquired understanding of how to write a new kind of procedure that didn't have REPEAT in it but that strung WIG commands together. To do so was his own idea, a self-initiated gesture, announced with pride. Unfortunately, his new achievement met with a distinct lack of appreciation, and he withdrew in disappointment.

I think both of these descriptions are true. The first tells us what we—Sam, Ocko, and Weir—had yet to achieve. The second tells us what we had already achieved. In Vygotskian terms we could still be within Sam's zone of proximal development, provided we revised the level of our support structure. In these terms we do not say: "Here is an individual who cannot engage in the process of abstraction." Rather we say, on the basis of the bug experience, and in the light of his success in working in the semiabstract LEGO-Logo mode: "Here is someone who takes slow, small steps in the direction of the abstract, who can make it there with appropriate help." Over the period of our interaction with him (and this applies to many of the children we have worked with), we noticed that the difficulty he had in appropriating verbal descriptions tended to disappear when we adopted a participatory do-it-with-LEGO-Logo approach.

In summary, I would say that there is evidence that, during the process of LEGO-Logo activity, there had been some restructuring of Sam's understanding of the concept of procedure. Restructuring can be a slow process, and we need to learn to understand better the features of different LEGO-Logo situations so that we can continue to trigger this kind of restructuring. In Sam's case the hypothesis is that the semiabstract nature of the tools in this new setting had begun to, and would continue to, facilitate the transition from concrete to abstract. Indeed, this has been borne out by his subsequent progress in school. Four months after the events described here, Sam was observed in his homeroom doing a project that involved concentric squares and circles. At that time he was described by his regular mathematics teacher as "doing very well at computers." Nine months later I came across Sam in a group doing extra computer work: The teacher taking this group described him as making amazing progress. Several months after that Sam participated in the Boston-wide computer competition as a member of a four-student group who achieved second place in the contest. At about this time Sam was retested by the school psychologist and scored twenty points more on the WISC than previously.[5]

The Last Session: This Was Peter's Day

Recall that we met Peter in the special needs classroom. It is clear that Peter's problem was not an inability to work in the abstract. Everybody realized that he was bright. The problem was that all the work he was required to do was heavily dependent on being able to read the instructions telling him what to do and that is just what he had difficulty with. He was classified as a bright learning-disabled student. His past experience with the traditional language-based curriculum had been bad. When we met him, he introduced himself to us this way: "Hello, I'm Peter, and I don't read."

---

5. Wechster Intelligence Scale for Children.

The notion of external representations facilitating knowledge appropriation needs to be refined to include the important fact that representations vary in the extent to which they suit different individuals. In Peter's case it is the procedural, primarily nonverbal nature of the new tools that has been the main catalyst in the emergence of his superior performance. He was seen as reasonably good in mathematics, but his real brilliance did not emerge until he moved into this computer/LEGO-Logo environment. Furthermore LEGO-Logo provided an environment in which his sharp intelligence could be stretched, in which his strong mathematical intuitions could be triggered.

During the fourth and last session (June 7), Peter took over a double conveyor belt which he had watched Karl build and used a labeled photograph (wiring diagram) to connect this construction to the computer. He was very clear about what each motor and each sensor did, checking them out systematically and adjusting appropriately. Ocko and Peter intended to use the conveyor belt to build an object sorter. The computer they were using did not have a built-in counter, and they proceeded to write a counter procedure. Peter interrupted programming periodically to insist on trying out each completed step as part of his systematic approach: Build a part; test it; if it works, go on to the next step. At one point a wire became caught in a worm gear. Ocko put his hand out to disentangle the wire physically. He was interrupted by Peter, who, quick as a flash, used the computer to reverse the direction of the motor and smiled as the wire unwound gracefully from its entanglement.

The counter procedure required Peter to learn several new Logo facilities. He learned for the first time about inputs, MAKE, and the use of variables. Then came an explanation of recursion, and even Peter had had enough. He picked up another model and began playing with it, his signal that that was enough new material. This is a common signal that the student has changed goals: He will pick up something lying around and start asking questions about it, or begin building a small construction of his own. This was what Peter moved on to do. He plugged this hastily-put-together object with no wheels into an outlet on the interface box. It moved in a shaky kind of vibration. Peter explained: "It's the shaking that makes it move."

3 DISCUSSION

I have used the cultural setting of LEGO-Logo at the Hennigan School to describe the performance of two students, Sam and Peter. Their speed of anticipation and ability to operate in an abstract mode differed significantly (measured IQs differed markedly: IQ 80 versus IQ 140 using the WISC). Despite the contrast between their behavior, both had difficulties related to language processing. To each, the LEGO-Logo materials and the Hennigan setting offered opportunities to explore, to flourish, and to grow. The setting in which our students were operating involved a change in the relationships that support the internalization of interpersonal knowledge, both with respect to the control of the learning process and the kind of things that are learned. I recapitulate the important features of this learning.

Previous Experience

A significant element in the events we encountered was that both Sam and Peter had worked with LogoWriter since the beginning of the school year. This meant that the specific LEGO activity was undertaken in the context of a body of knowledge acquired as part of that computer experience. They were both adept at the mechanics of moving around the system. Both were skilled typists and had used most of the simple facilities: They were completely at home with the turtle-driving commands and used facilities like REPEAT, the cut-and-paste functions, and the page-handling routines. They were eager to take the typist's seat and readily volunteered suggestions about the next programming step. They had a series of well-established moves that they made when in control of the typing. An example that came up frequently was Peter's use of a previous line of typing as a "frame," changing only the specific things he needed to, and his use of the cut-and-paste functions to reverse two instructions. Sam took a much less sophisticated approach but was nevertheless impressively speedy and pragmatically efficient.

Fashioning Tools to Aid Internalization of Socially Embedded Knowledge

Certain materials that are good for manipulating in their own right can also be good representations of crucial concepts in the subject domain. When this is the case, these material representations can facilitate the internalization of those concepts. For example, a combination of powerful mediating symbols from the two systems, LEGO and Logo, form the framework within which the mathematical thinking described in the parity incident occurs. The Logo procedure captures (encapsulates) a piece of knowledge and, as such, adds to the repertoire of available representations such as words and diagrams. Naming is a central activity in Logo. At first Peter called his procedure WIG1. Then he changed it to WIGRT and introduced WIGLT and WIGBK. Creating and naming the WIG series produced a set of basic operations, each one with a single effect, providing the students with a set of high-level primitives whose effect was observed on the concrete LEGO structure. It seemed to me that the LEGO primitive SETEVEN triggered the sequence, which was then played out in terms of the REPEAT primitive, a programming counterpart of the TIMES operation corresponding to repeated addition.

Sam used the commands displayed in the command center section of the computer screen as a memory aide—here the screen functioned as a scrapbook, a vehicle for external representations. The structure of LEGO-Logo facilitates the acquisition of good problem-solving strategies. Breaking a problem into parts is helped by the modular nature of both Logo and LEGO. Finding the bug is helped by the physical nature of the functioning parts. Repairing the bug is facilitated by the structure of the LEGO units. It is easy to see cause and effect. Peter's use of a wiring diagram to connect up a double conveyor belt was a case in point. Indeed, he took surefooted control of the external representation and revealed a systematicity in his thinking that impressed us.

Individual Differences

The LEGO-Logo combination provides external representations that are particularly fruitful and apt for some students. I have described the felicitous consequences of a happy match between mental representation and medium (Weir 1987, 1989). For non-verbal students LEGO-Logo is often the first opportunity they have to demonstrate just how good they are at visual-manipulatory activities and, indeed, to get academic credit for this skill. Often the students' mastery of computer commands contrasts sharply with a low level of operation in other academic contexts. Sam and Peter provide particular examples of how the activity can mobilize skills otherwise dormant and unused in a classroom context. As they work with LEGO materials, students show a variety of spatial and manipulatory skills: an economy of movement, a sense of scale, an appreciation of the need to stabilize moving parts and to provide space for moving parts, and an understanding of the concept of mechanical advantage. They display smart heuristics; for example, they see a whole sequence of movements in a look-ahead mode.

All skills are a matter of recognizing patterns, finding repeating units embedded in a specific context. Just as some people have a good sense of repeating visual patterns, so do some have a good sense of repeating operations. To incorporate LEGO design principles as Logo procedures requires that the learner articulate these repeating patterns of operations. Reversibility is a constantly recurring theme: FD-BK and RT-LT of turtle geometry; go-forward-round-vehicle versus go-back-and-park; trading power-for-speed versus speed-for-power in LEGO. A facility for recognizing repeated operations may emerge in the concrete LEGO setting and then become translated into abstract programming terms that capture those patterns (i.e., the REVERSE DIRECTION operation in LEGO-Logo). In several cases students doing LEGO-Logo can be identified as belonging to the category of the gifted learning disabled.

LEGO-Logo as an Environment Both for Revealing Existing Student Goals and for Generating Genuinely Academic Goals

There is a clear sense of ownership that characterized the kind of knowledge our students had acquired. This ownership had led to an emotional identification with the activity that was a crucial ingredient of the personal growth in understanding we saw. Each of our students found his own level of fulfillment and was able to express his goals readily. I assign a central knowledge-mobilizing role to emotions (Weir 1987). Signs mediate meaning, not simply meaning as the referent of the sign but meaning within the goal structure of an individual, within the emotional framework of what makes sense, what fulfills, what drives the learner. Often a teacher's task is not so much finding out what the student's goal is as contriving circumstances in which the student can begin to entertain any academic goals at all and see them as relevant to his or her situation. The LEGO-Logo medium generates and supports students' goals, and facilitates the teacher's task of recognizing those goals.

Peer–Peer Teaching and Learning

It is the pragmatic, utilitarian flavor to the LEGO-Logo activity that some of the Hennigan students have found so attractive. The pieces of utilitarian, often un-analyzed, knowledge can become the fragments out of which larger conceptual structures are built (diSessa 1988). Frames such as: REPEAT n [something], or TO < procedurename > . . . END act as representations of concepts that function as pragmatic rituals used, typically, without being fully understood. We saw how the LEGO-Logo procedures WIGBK, WIGLT, and WIGRT became such a set of external representations that could be used without unpacking. Computers, suitably programmed, can provide good ways to mediate child inventions to be internalized by other children. To the extent that the computer supports peer– peer teaching and learning, it can bring new forms of classroom relationships. The traditional vertical flow of information, from knowledgeable teacher down to naive student, is augmented by an strong horizontal flow of expertise among the student users.

The emergence of "student experts" during computer-based activity is a very real phenomenon and can lighten some of the burden when the teacher is the only source of knowledge in the classroom. Clearly this requires a change in teacher attitude. She needs to feel comfortable with the thought that she does not need to know everything. She needs to be prepared to learn from her students, to learn with her students. This change is helped by the nature of the activity, which can take the form of a joint exploration. As both teacher and child sit and wait for the effect of what has been typed in, neither being sure of exactly what will happen, the joint experience of uncertainty can lead to a certain kind of companionship.

Tenacity of Ownership of Pragmatic Knowledge

Sometimes the pride of ownership can handicap the process of learning. A frequently observed phenomenon is the way students hold on to their pragmatic rituals.[6] What we see is that once a satisfactory solution has been found, there is a reluctance to change it. The pieces were acquired for utilitarian purposes and will be dislodged from their association with those student purposes only in the service of new student purposes. The student may very well feel there is no need to change. His goal has been satisfied. It may not concern him that the adult in the situation has other, more academic goals.

Example
Having invented his own path through a problem space, Karl was reluctant to give it up, as in this extract from a Logo session I observed during the same

---

6. Students invent their own stereotypical behaviors. Observers of Logo, ourselves included, have remarked on how students often develop favorite numbers as inputs to turtle commands and stick to these despite the feedback which to us adults would indicate that these are not "good" numbers. It seems to me now that this behavior fits into the same pattern I have been calling "pragmatic ritual."

period we observed the LEGO-Logo activity. He was carefully constructing the beaker in a screen diagram intended to illustrate the experiment on air in water that he and Peter had just completed. In fact he had carefully studied Peter's screen diagram and was now reproducing it, more or less.[7] He went up one side of the beaker in FD 4 steps: FD 4 FD 4 FD 4 . . . then went to the other side of the rectangle and began to carefully repeat FD 4 FD 4. . . . I intervened to press the mathematics question: "How many fours did you go forward on the other side?" He continued to type, not looking away from the screen, saying politely but firmly: "I'd rather do it my way."

The FD 4 functioned as a unit step that Karl had created for himself, that worked for him, that he trusted. His approach had a characteristic pragmatic, utilitarian flavor to it. Why should he multiply 4 by 3, subtract 9 from 90, and so forth, when he could do it the straightforward "empirical" way? Some problems are easiest solved by finessing them, witness the grocery shoppers referred to above. It was characteristic of Karl to resist adopting a teacher goal that he perceived as having to do with "math" while he was engaged in *his* LEGO-Logo work (see section 6.2). Years of academic failure made this very bright, strong-willed youngster guard ownership of his self-acquired skills jealously. We need to respect this position. We need to develop ways of encouraging progress that do not usurp the sense of ownership. In fact at this juncture Karl was making excellent progress in the regular mathematics classroom.

Decontextualizing the Means of Mediation

Sam too had experienced academic failure. The LEGO-Logo setting we provided seemed to suit his developmental needs to a striking degree. Abstract notions were being explored in the context of the immediate feedback generated by

---

7. Notice how Karl used his neighbor's diagram as a handle into the representation problem. The copying phenomenon is frequent in Logo and in LEGO-Logo circles, and its significance should not be dismissed with an "Oh, it's just copying." For the period of the copying, the other child's picture or LEGO construction acts as an external representation for the copier, facilitating appropriation. In the same spirit we see waves of fashion pass through a group of LEGO users: For a day or two, everyone in the LEGO-Logo corner will be making twirly rotating objects all based on the same principle—a small configuration of bricks and rods attached to the axle of the motor—each with its own character, each acting as a minimodel for a fellow inventor. Then the fashion will change. Someone in the group will tackle a LEGO-supplied diagram, and soon there are several students helping each other to master the visual language of LEGO units that these diagrams rely on.

the manipulation of concrete LEGO structures, all occurring within a complex social, interactional setting. A significant feature of the LEGO-Logo combination is that the student moves backward and forward between alternative representations, and this alternation can provide the nudge to decontextualize. Sam's understanding of the use of the procedure was entirely in the context of turtle graphics and the use of the REPEAT command to achieve polygon drawings on the screen. He then met procedures in the context of moving a LEGO-Logo vehicle around. That began the process of decontextualization of the concept, which in turn led to an efficiency in programming that surprised us. We were led to a decontextualization of our view of his ability to understand abstract notions, a view generated in the context of the traditional curriculum.

Other aspects of the LEGO-Logo setting might have played a role in this process. Vygotsky (1978) pointed out the role of play as a pivot for detaching meaning from the concrete object, by creating imaginary situations that emancipate the learner from situational constraints. Play represents a transitional stage between the situational constraints of early childhood and adult thought, free of real situations. Presumably this effect is enhanced when the objects played with are quasi abstract, as in the case of the WIG procedures. Our function was to exploit this transitional stage by making it the object of self-reflection.

Thinking about Thinking

In this setting problem-solving steps were taken as a series of "turn-taking" acts accompanied by talk about that problem solving. In effect the students were acquiring small pieces of the language of problem solving, as well as of the language of computing. For Sam the concrete experience of LEGO-Logo debugging helped him to understand the abstract use of a physical object—a juxtaposition of mediational means. An essential part of this coming to understand lay in the *explicit* reference to debugging, necessary for the conscious realization of what is going on. Hands-on activity alone is not enough. The student needs to think about that doing. LEGO-Logo provides a good context for talking about what is going on. The ease of use of both LEGO and Logo can provide the framework for interactive experience between learner and computer and, most important, between one learner and his or her neighbor—a potentially fruitful soil upon which academic structures can be built. The crucial requirement is that steps are taken to ensure that some metacognitive reflection occurs. Without this the ease of entry can become a disadvantage.

From the Vygotskian point of view, then, I could say that for the students I have been describing, making a change both in the cultural tools available and in the kind of collaborative setting provided has led to an improvement in academic performance. I have talked in detail about ways in which the computer can extend the range of external representations of knowledge available in a classroom. Such representations vary in the extent to which they facilitate knowledge appropriation, and this has an obvious importance for curriculum planners. The challenge for us as educators is to develop a large repertoire of learning situations from which to choose activity that fits a given learner's next step, the zone of proximal development.

REFERENCES

Brown, A. 1978. Knowing when, where, and how to remember: A problem of metacognition. In R. Glaser (ed.), *Advances in Instructional Psychology*, vol. 1. Hillsdale, NJ: Lawrence Erlbaum Associates.

Davydov, V. V. 1975. The psychological characteristics of the "prenumerical" period of mathematics instruction. In L. P. Steffe (ed.), *Soviet Studies in the Psychology of Learning and Teaching Mathematics*, vol. 7. Chicago: University of Chicago.

diSessa, A. 1988. Knowledge in pieces. In G. Forman and P. Pufall (eds.), *Constructivism in the Computer Age*. Hillsdale, NJ: Lawrence Erlbaum Associates.

Hillel, J., and Samurçay, R. 1985. The definition and use of general procedures by 9-year-olds. In *Proceedings of the First International Conference for Logo and Mathematics Education*, 1985. Department of Mathematics, Statistics and Computing, University of London Institute of Education, London.

Hoyles, C. 1986. Scaling a mountain—a study of the use, discrimination and generalization of some mathematical concepts in a Logo environment. *European Journal of Psychology of Education* 2: 111–126.

Hoyles, C., and Sutherland, R. 1989. *Logo Mathematics in the Classroom*. London: Routledge.

Hoyles, C., and Noss, R. 1987. Children working in a structured Logo environment: From doing to understanding. *Recherches en Didactique des Mathématiques* 8(12): 131–174.

Hoyles, C., and Noss, R. 1989. The computer as a catalyst in children's proportion strategies. *Journal of Mathematical Behavior* 8: 53–75.

Lave, J. 1984. The dialectics of arithmetic in grocery shopping. In B. Rogoff and S. Lave (eds.), *Everyday Cognition: Its Development in Social Context*. 1984. Cambridge: Harvard University Press.

Leron, U. 1985a. Logo today: Vision and reality. *The Computing Teacher* 12: 26–32.

Leron, U. 1985b. Some thoughts on Logo 85. In *Logo 85: Theoretical Papers*. Massachusetts Institute of Technology, Cambridge.

Leron, U., and Zazkis, R. 1986. Functions and variables: A case study of learning mathematics through Logo. *Proceedings of the Second International Conference for Logo and Mathematics Education*, July 1986. Department of Mathematics, Statistics and Computing, University of London Institute of Education, London.

Noss, R. 1986. Constructing a conceptual framework for elementary algebra through Logo programming. *Educational Studies in Mathematics* 17: 335–357.

Ocko, S., Papert, S., and Resnick, M. 1988. LEGO, Logo, and Science. *Technology and Learning* 2(1): 1–3.

Papert, S. 1980. *Mindstorms*. New York: Basic Books.

Pea, R., and Kurland, M. 1984. Logo programming and the development of planning skills. Technical Report #16. Center for Children and Technology, Bank Street College of Education, New York.

Rogoff, B. 1984. Introduction. In B. Rogoff and J. Lave (eds.), *Everyday Cognition: Its Development in Social Context*. Cambridge: Harvard University Press.

Vygotsky, L. S. 1978. *Mind in Society: The Development of Higher Psychological Functions*. Edited by M. Cole, V. John-Steiner, S. Scribner and E. Souberman. Cambridge: Harvard University Press.

Weir, S. 1987. *Cultivating Minds: A Logo Casebook*. New York: Harper & Row.

Weir, S. 1989. The computer in schools: Machine as humanizer. *Harvard Educational Review* 59(1): 61–73.

Wertsch, J. V. 1985. *Vygotsky and the Social Formation of Mind*. Cambridge: Harvard University Press.

On Intra- and Interindividual Differences in Children's Learning Styles

Tamara Lemerise

7

1 THE QUESTION OF LEARNING STYLES IN EDUCATION

In today's educational milieu the question of individual differences between children is again topical. It is a pervasive question that has confronted education for decades, especially since the onset of compulsory education, but with the increasing variety of school populations it has become a priority. The hypothesis, whether implicit or explicit, that individual differences between children are linked to differences in learning and school success, makes the question practically unavoidable for many researchers and practitioners in the field today. The problem of learning- style differences appears to be but the tip of the iceberg of the larger problem of individual differences.

The analysis of the impact of individual differences on school learning is obviously a highly complex process given the number and variety of dimensions along which children can vary: intellectual skills, psychomotor abilities, interest and motivation, past experience, subculture, to name but a few. While it is easy to understand the positive correlation between school success and high motivation or superior intellectual and psychomotor development, it is less easy to understand the exact nature of the link that many researchers and practitioners make, implicitly or explicitly, between school success and specific learning styles. Simply stated, the link implies that some children appear more predisposed than others to profit from schooling (see Snow 1986; Schmeck 1988). In other words, the learning style with which a child arrives at the beginning of school may have a strong influence on that child's subsequent performance at school. For example, a child demonstrating a reflective, rational, analytic, and field-independent style has, generally speaking, a better chance of succeeding in school than another one showing signs of an intuitive, visual, holistic, and field-dependent style. So it seems that the observed disparity in school success among children is linked to an inequality of chances for success related in part to the type of preferential learning style each child assumes during infancy and early childhood.

Historically solutions have been envisaged to resolve this inequality of opportunity for school success. Basically the solutions proposed belong to one of three categories: (1) change the learning style of the child who is in need to a more adaptive style so that he or she will "fit" better into the educational system; (2) change the educational system, its teaching and evaluative methods, so that it can match the variety of observed learning styles; and (3) change both the child and the system so that every child can master more than one work style and the system offers more than one teaching and evaluative approach. The simple fact that these three options run parallel to each other, each carrying its own system of interpretation, in large part explains the difficulties encountered in solving the problem posed by individual differences. Each set of alternative actions is indeed based on a specific and fixed interpretation of the very nature of learning-style differences. A brief description of each of the three schools of thought guiding each course of action will help to clarify their relative incompatibility—at least at the level of educational goals—and help to explain the apparent paralysis in the field.

Learning Styles: Three Schools of Thought

The Hierarchical View of Learning Styles

The first school of thought tends to define differences in learning style in hierarchical terms, some styles being judged better than others. Indeed, despite the fact that the literature tries to put different learning styles on an equal footing, there is still a strong belief in the educational milieu that one style is "richer" than another (see Corno and Snow 1984; Bradley 1985). For example, the style that is actually linked to school success—a reflective, rational, analytic, field-independent style—is often evaluated, perhaps implicitly, as the winning style; or, given equal success on a given task, a style that maximizes efficiency will be valued more highly than one that is judged more time-consuming. At other times certain styles—for example, an intuitive, visual, holistic, field-dependent style—are associated, perhaps implicitly, with a school performance of lesser quality.

One consequence is that this perceived hierarchy of styles, shared by many practitioners, tends to orient educational objectives more toward changing the child who is "lacking something" than toward changing the learning environment in order to offer equal opportunities to each style. Thus the educational settings that have been proposed here to "solve the problem of different learning styles" focus on promoting the style that is linked to school success to help the child who is "lacking something" to learn the ABCs of the winning style. Other styles are at best valued for extracurricular activities or for school activities that do not really "count" (art, physical education, etc.). The fundamental role and value of different learning styles is subtly replaced by the familiar ideology of hierarchy, not only a hierarchy of knowledge but also of cognitive tools, some cognitive tools being judged more efficient and more valuable than others.

The Egalitarian View of Learning Styles

The second school of thought argues for changes in the instructional system that would offer equal opportunities to every style. This approach really puts the different learning styles observed in children on an equal footing and asks for equally rich educational settings supporting the development of each particular style. The implicit assumption that styles are mutually exclusive (e.g., visual/auditory, field dependent/field independent, internal/external locus of control) justifies the creation of equally rich educational settings in order to respect the principle of equal developmental chances for everyone. This approach is based on a pluralistic view of education that assumes and takes account of interindividual variety in school populations. The burden of change is put on the educational system rather than on the child so that, for example, different teaching styles have often been proposed to meet the needs of the different learning styles (Joyce and Weil 1972; Bennett 1977). The role and value of different learning styles is fully respected. Conversely, this approach claims respect for different teaching styles.

The Integrationist View of Learning Styles

The third school of thought aims at facilitating the development of more than one "style" within each individual. This approach is based on the concepts of malleability and plasticity of learning styles: Through time and experience, differences in learning styles tend to shift ground from interindividual to intraindividual differences. It is postulated that given adequate educational contexts, children can learn to apply more than one work and learning style. Educational settings are envisioned that focus not only on the variety of knowledge but also on the variety of tools: The goal is to give as complete a set of tools as possible to all children in order to facilitate and support their success in and out of school. The burden of change rests on both the child and the environment. The latter should be rich and varied enough to facilitate the acquisition and mastery of multiple learning styles by every child, and every child should, in addition to his or her preferential style, develop a variety of skills so as to have real choice when confronted with a range of problem situations. The concept of learning style is subtly redefined here as a pattern of styles employed by a single child across time and space. Now differences in styles among individuals stem (1) from differences in the opportunities encountered for the development of more than one work style and (2) from differences in each child's organization of already-mastered styles.

Educational Contexts Supporting Learning-Style Differences Are in Danger

There are important nuances between the three interpretations sketched above. Although all three agree that it is time to take learning-style differences in education into account, they frame remedial action quite differently. The first option proposes action on the basis of an observed lack of competence in a so-called disadvantaged population (*curative approach*). The second option proposes action that could prevent the inequality of opportunities for different learning styles from fully developing (*preventitive approach*). The third option proposes action that favors the development of multifaceted competence for every child in order to allow each to profit from more than one type of learning environment (*promotional approach*). Educational curricula committed to differential learning styles could be based on any one of the three conceptions and could be interpreted from any one of the three points of view. This creates quite an ambiguous state of affairs since each conception is seen, for historical reasons, as incompatible with the other two. Each time a new and exciting educational setting is implemented in the educational milieu, it runs the risk of being gobbled up by more than one school of thought and of being used in quite contrasting frameworks. The original philosophy of the founder is then in danger of being lost to other ideologies and the original goals unmet. In the following section I will briefly illustrate the nature of the impasse that the Logo community finds itself in because of the omnipresence of these three schools of thought, which actually live parallel lives in the educational world.

Learning Styles in Logo: How Are They Interpreted?

One of the major goals of Logo has always been to offer children a versatile work environment, an environment full of opportunities for constructive and positive experiences embracing a variety of children's work styles. The original Logo community tried to be undogmatic toward learning-style differences. It adopted an open but nevertheless partial position: an egalitarian point of view open to the integrationist interpretation. In other words, it kept the frontier open between inter- and intraindividual differences in learning styles. The original Logo community was also fully aware of the need for observational data. What follows is a brief description of how the Logo community, as well as the larger educational community interested or intrigued by the Logo phenomenon, interpreted the data collected in the past decade. Three sources of data are described.

First, in the early Logo literature Papert, Watt, diSessa, and Weir (1979), Watt (1979), Solomon (1982), Rampy (1984), and others, set out to illustrate the variety of approaches that children could adopt when placed in a Logo environment. All observed different work styles in children. Some children were identified as planners, others as explorers; some were seen as product oriented, others as more process oriented; some as analysts, others as "impressionists." Although the investigators were very careful to mention the nonexclusivity of styles—that the same child could hypothetically be called process oriented in one problem situation and product oriented in another—nonetheless the accent was usually placed on the interindividual differences in work styles. It should be mentioned that researchers at the time were mainly interested in identifying the variety and the nature of each observable work style in a Logo environment: just how rich an environment Logo was in its possibilities for allowing different approaches.

But interpretations soon appeared. On the one hand, it was tempting for some practitioners, as well as for some researchers, to conclude that planners were the heroes of the new microworld. Studies of programming styles reinforced this temptation. Despite the fact that different programming styles could lead to success in their own way, "top-down" programmers came to be seen as higher in the hierarchy than "bottom-up" programmers, and procedural programming as more valuable than a linear approach. Some practitioners perceived longitudinal studies (Hoyles and Sutherland 1989; Lemerise and Kayler 1986) as tending to support such conclusions: Despite the fact that children of all styles were obviously progressing, some were readily identified as progressing "better" than others.

On the other hand, it was easy for others to see Logo as the ideal environment for supporting styles often neglected or rejected in usual school curricula (Weir 1987). In a Logo environment one child could explore, follow personal intuitions, and create high-quality, nonanticipated products, while a neighbor on another microcomputer could proceed in an organized and structured way and realize a highly specific project. From such a point of view Logo appeared perfectly suited to support interindividual parallel processing.

Finally, it did not go unnoticed by a number of others in the field of education that the same child could, across situations, be either process oriented or product oriented, could write either procedural or linear programs, and so forth. This phenomenon led those practitioners to intuit that under certain conditions children could vary their work styles: Cohabitation of different work styles within the same subject was then a highly plausible hypothesis. Moreover the longitudinal studies mentioned above (Hoyles and Sutherland 1989; Lemerise and Kayler 1988) provided data on the potential variety of styles within a single child and, most important, underscored the role of context and experience on the quantity and quality of tools possessed and mastered by each individual.

Second, the more theoretical developmental studies within the Logo literature tended to stay above the debate on different learning styles. They looked at the "meta" abilities each child should possess in order to become more and more competent in Logo (see Mendelsohn 1985 on general programming abilities; Hillel and Samurçay 1985 and Lemerise 1988 on procedural abilities; Hoyles 1987 and Hoyles and Noss 1987 on general mathematical abilities; Carver and Klahr 1986 and Klahr and Carver 1988 on debugging skills). By focusing on the general tools each child *should* possess, the developmental approach attenuated the phenomenon of interindividual differences. Hierarchy, when mentioned in these studies, was seen in terms of knowledge and abilities acquired through time and experience much more than in terms of work styles of different strength and value. These studies underlined, even more than those cited above, the potential role of experience in determining preferential styles in children, for it is hard to adopt a style when one has never been introduced to it or familiarized with the component abilities required by that style.

Finally, a third group of researchers, the investigators of problem-solving styles in Logo (McAllister 1985; Bradley 1985), tended to slant their research toward the problem-solving paths that children traced while solving different types of problems. Of course dichotomous classification of the main problem-solving styles—concept driven versus data driven, goal oriented versus stimulus bound—here again favored a certain hierarchization: The concept-driven strategy was usually seen as more sophisticated than the data-driven one, and so on. On the other hand, here again there is a place in the Logo world for the expression of different strategies by different children, strengthening ipso facto the egalitarian point of view. However, there is evidence that both strategies can be observed in the same subject. Coté and Kayler's (1987) notion of "construction schema" translates well the idea that multiple processes are available to the child: How a child uses what she or he knows is not fixed but varies from situation to situation. Different construction schemas are elaborated for different kinds of problems. Indeed, problem-solving strategies are seen as a malleable construct: Strategies are learnable and changeable in time and space.

A New State of the Question: An Opening up of Perspective

The brief summary presented above shows that it is relatively easy to interpret Logo data by means of all three of the interpretive models available but that, in so doing, the nature of the goals changes each time. This brief review clearly shows too that rigidity in interpretation is not at all founded given the variety of facts actually observed: For example, hierarchy does sometimes show up, and interindividual differences do coexist with intraindividual ones.

Indeed, hierarchy exists not only in the teacher's head but in reality too. Some styles might actually be more "effective than others," but it is important to clarify why this is so. Recall that the educational setting in which children are placed before their Logo experience typically favors the expression and development of some styles, while ignoring or disparaging the expression and development of others. Thus one main cause of the observed hierarchy resides in the type of educational environment offered to the child (and in the kind of educational values supporting it). Of course the next question that arises is why all children could not equally benefit from such a unique educational environment offered to *all* in the first years of schooling. The answer becomes obvious when one realizes that a style is something acquired, in large part at least, through experience with the abilities it embodies: through familiarization with those abilities, practice with them, and challenges brought about through their frequent deployment, and so on. The type of ecological and developmental environments young children are provided with before schooling—social milieu, family context, cognitive and affective needs called upon by specific life context, for example—determines how well each child will thrive in the monolithic educational setting. The "*engrenage* phenomenon" (Garbarino and Asp 1981) usually takes care of the rest: Initial failure in school, for example, leads to difficulties or "disconnection" that brings about more difficulties that become hard to overcome or escape from, and that provoke the maintenance and escalation of the difficulties initially encountered.

Interindividual differences obviously exist too. At times they can be linked to different developmental rhythms, some children going through developmental steps faster than others. Here again, although it is not possible to rule out genetic factors, it is obvious that the amount of experience offered to the child—possibilities for initiating or participating in various activities—is an important determinant in their developmental rhythm. At other times the interindividual differences can be linked to such global factors as cultural background, sex, motivation, and affective state, which can influence not only the rhythm of development but primarily its orientation. Thus preferential styles manifested by children can be caused as much by lack of experience and support in certain kinds of abilities as by a specific response to particular individual needs in the particular life contexts in which the children evolved (micro contexts as much as macro contexts; see Bronfenbrenner 1979). Preferential style is obviously a reality but not necessarily an immutable one. The power of a preferential style could become very limited if it were the only possible option available to a child living in an already varied and complex world.

Finally, intraindividual differences exist too. The detailed protocol analyses found in Papert et al. (1979), Hoyles and Sutherland (1989), Lemerise and Kayler (1986), and Côté and Kayler (1987) demonstrated the existence of intra-individual differences in some subjects despite the strong influence of preferential styles. McAllister (1985) and Bradley (1985) also pinpointed intraindividual variety across problem situations. Some children can and do exhibit more than one work style. Some children call on different schemas for analyzing and solving problems across time as well as across situations. They can analyze the organization of parts to arrive at the comprehension of the whole. They can start from a comprehension of the whole and later come to see links between parts. They can sometimes make detailed plans, but they can also plan in a general way. They can anticipate a plan, or it can emerge after a series of concrete actions. Logo obviously helped at uncovering and supporting different preferential learning styles; some data led us to believe that it helped too in the development and mastery of more than one learning style within each individual.

In summary, it is by now difficult to deny that the Logo environment is particularly well suited for favoring the emergence of a variety of interindividual as well as intraindividual behaviors. The cold war of interpretation between schools of thought should obviously stop and give way to an integrated approach that really looks at the conditions under which hierarchical, interindividual, and intraindividual differences could peacefully coexist. The first step toward such a noble goal would be to better document evidence of intraindividual differences and to spell out their relationship with interindividual differences. What appears to be most needed in the field is an identification of the conditions under which interindividual differences are transmuted into intraindividual ones.

2 IN SEARCH OF THE GATEWAY BETWEEN INTRA- AND INTERINDIVIDUAL DIFFERENCES: SOME DATA

First, I will present from one of my research projects some data that tend to support the malleability of learning styles.[1] Next, after analyzing the environmental conditions under which these data were collected, I will discuss the potential role of the Logo environment in fostering the passage from inter- to intraindividual differences in learning styles.

The data summarized below come from the observation and protocol analyses of ten target subjects (five fifth graders and sixth graders) ranging from ten to twelve years of age. They came to the Logo laboratorary once a week. Half of the group were relative beginners who had had five to six hours of initiation to Logo, while the other half were "old timers" who had had about twenty-five hours of previous experience with Logo. Thus what is under analysis here are the learning styles of children varying in their amount of Logo experience. Most data in the field come from protocol analyses of beginners who are familiarizing themselves with the Logo environment (Rampy 1984; Solomon 1982; Watt 1979).

Two work settings were provided: a setting based on individual projects and another one centered on assigned tasks. Most prior data have been collected from educational settings based primarily on individual projects. My comparison of the overall performance of children across many work situations is based, as is usually the case in Logo studies, on exhaustive case studies of each individual subject; my emphasis, however, is put on the presentation of the overall performance of each child *across* tasks rather than on the detailed presentation of each individual protocol for each analyzed task.

Finally, for purposes of finer analysis, I have categorized learning styles into three types: work style (the type of project worked on), programming style (the type of program produced), and problem-solving style (the nature of the information guiding the path to solution).

---

1. My research has been supported by grants from FCAR, Ministère de l'Education du Québec, during 1985–89.

Defining the Categories of Learning Styles Adopted

I have adopted the three style categories for analyzing the children's behavior in each of the two types of proposed settings (individual projects and assigned tasks). Each style can be manifested in two different ways, briefly described below.

Children's Work Styles: Process Oriented or Product Oriented?

Based on an overview of all the children's projects, the categorization that appeared the most appropriate for my analysis was one differentiating process-oriented from product-oriented projects (categories adapted from Rampy 1984). Contrary to Rampy, I do not categorize the child but instead the type of project worked on. Also the category definitions, though generally similar, differ significantly in detail from Rampy's.

A *process-oriented project* can be defined as one *primarily* centered on the "how to do": how to connect or organize specific procedures or a series of elements. It is as though the main goal were to work on the relationships between general types of commands or different kinds of procedures. Even though there is a construction of parts or procedures, what is first anticipated by the student and focused on is the way parts or series of elements are going to be connected to each other. Different kinds of projects enter into this category: for example, making a tunnel with squares of decreasing size where what matters the most is how the squares are going to be related to each other, creating objects by organizing different shapes (a flower with rotating squares or a spider's web with right and left, large and small, octagons) where the emphasis is on how the shapes are going to be connected to each other, generating movement for a car or for a wheel, representing something in three-dimensional perspective (letters, shapes), creating a bank of REPEAT projects (with systematic variation in the number of repetitions, of FDs, or of angles), and combining REPEAT formulas in order to create specific effects (a sun, flashes). The main feature here is that the child focuses first on the problem of "how to": how to transform and/or organize an initial procedure or series of commands in order to create a specific output. Such projects can be planned in advance though they sometimes emerge from the subject's actions with the turtle (cf. the discussion below on problem-solving styles).

A *product-oriented project* can be defined as one that is mainly centered on the reproduction of an object or a scene. The identification and construction of the parts are the main focus. The "how to do" is secondary. For example, such projects as constructing houses, boats, rockets, robots, faces, landscapes, and writing names or messages out of letters belong to this category. This type of project usually calls on defining, either procedurally or linearly, the successive parts of the sought-after product (base, roof, door, windows; head, eyes, nose, ears; letters A, L, and O; etc.). So the main feature here is that the child first focuses on the problem of the parts (and their figural relationship) that will be the building blocks of the project: What parts should be reproduced, linearly or procedurally, in order to realize the sought-after product? Subjects engaging in a product-oriented project usually have a specific image, often a drawing, of what is to be reproduced, but this image can be a vague inspiration, a guiding idea, or a highly detailed plan. As will be seen in the next category, the subject's initial choice with respect to these "images" can strongly influence the nature of the problem-solving path adopted.

Such a dichotomy that opposes process-oriented and product-oriented types of projects is not completely watertight, of course, but out of the forty or so projects I examined, no serious classification problems arose. Both the general climate of working on projects that would be presented to the class and the fact that I only classified the projects declared "finished" by children helped to eliminate ambiguities in the analysis of the data. Sometimes, however, I had to divide certain types of projects in two: for example, in a village project the first part of the project (construction of houses, street, and car) was classified as product oriented, but the second part, the spontaneous idea of moving the car along the street, was associated with a process-oriented project. Such a division occurred in only two cases; most of the time children divided up their own projects.

Children's Programming Styles: Linear or Procedural?

Programming styles were defined as *linear* or *procedural*. I chose a relatively simple and traditional way of analyzing programming styles, differentiating between children who use procedures and the ones who do not.
The *linear type* can be of three kinds:

1. Type L describes the classical case of a string of commands (where, on occasion, a procedure is used just like any other command) and is usually regrouped as a procedure at the end of the session in order to be saved.
2. Type L_e means that the list of commands is typed directly in the editor.

3. Type L_r refers to the use of REPEAT formulas having more or less the status of procedures (i.e., defined independently, transformable, exportable, and organizable with other procedures or other REPEAT formulas).

The *procedural type* of programming refers to the elaboration of new procedures and subprocedures beforehand or in the course of a project. P_2 indicates that there were only two types of procedural abilities observed: define and organize; P_3, three types: define, transform, and organize; and P_4, four types: define, transform, export, and organize.

Children's Problem-Solving Styles: Concept Driven or Data Driven?

Since all of the ten target children were observed throughout their Logo work, it was possible, through the analysis of children's verbalizations (before and during the execution of each task) and through the observational notes taken by each participant-observer, to identify what was guiding the problem-solving path of each problem solver: a specific concept or the visual data following the turtle moves? Generally speaking, all children had a goal (an objective) at the outset of their project. What is at issue here is to what extent each child used that goal to guide the choice and organization of turtle actions.

The problem-solving path was called *concept driven* when a specific idea, a guiding concept or a plan was observed to determine the choice of actions throughout the execution of the task. The process was called *data driven* when the child proceeded more or less by trial and error, so "what to do next" was largely and mainly determined by the result of previous actions.

For example, the child who first identified the general actions that have to be done in order to move a car along a street—namely, put the pen up, place the turtle in the right position, move the turtle ahead, replace the turtle in the needed position, and then put the pen down—was described as concept driven. The pattern of actions identified is assumed to guide the child's work, even though at times he or she also had to use trial and error to determine the exact length of the FD, or the exact size of the RT or LT turns. Similarly a child who identified all the parts of his or her project and their order of production—the base of the house, then the roof, then the door, and finally the windows—and who effectively used that general plan was also identified as employing the concept-driven approach.

Conversely, another child who also had a house project in mind would be associated more with a data-driven approach, if the output of his or her figural analysis was not used at all to guide the actions in the Logo mode. In such a case the whole decision process about the turtle move or about the next part is usually a function of the impact of the last turtle move. Typically a data-driven subject constructs, step by step, a path not previously identified and often not even recognized afterward. The concept-driven child, reproduces a path, step by step, already identified and eventually confirmed as "good" or "not so good."

Analysis of Children's Learning Styles in a Setting Based on Individual Projects

The main goal of the analysis is to identify to what extent children vary intra- and interindividually in their work styles, their programming styles, and their problem-solving styles when working on individual projects. As a secondary goal it is interesting to look for possible interrelations among the variety of styles actually observed: Is the programming style of a child, for example, related to his or her choice of work style? Is problem-solving style linked to the child's work approach?

This phase of individual projects covered an average of twenty sessions of forty-five minutes each. All children, at any point in time, worked either alone or in pairs. The five participant-observers assured a rich environmental support, helping with debugging once children had tried to solve the problems by themselves. The only formal demand put on the children was to present their project(s) to their classmates after each block of five or six weeks. The purpose of the presentation was to allow a group discussion on the good ideas of each child, the difficulties encountered, and the means used to cope with them. The total time covered by this part of the project was five months during the academic year.

Table 1 summarizes the data obtained for each child on two of the main dimensions studied: work style and programming style. At the level of general data, it first shows that the more experienced, older children completed more projects than the less experienced, younger ones (27 compared with 16). As to variety, the more experienced children chose process-oriented and product-oriented projects about equally often, whereas the children with less experience in Logo tended to choose more product-oriented projects than those more familiar with Logo.

As far as programming style is concerned, beginners more frequently displayed a linear rather than procedural style; moreover intraindividual variety was infrequent for those subjects. Among the older, more experienced children, however, a certain variety of programming styles was observed. This variety is

Table 1 Number of individual projects categorized by children's work and programming styles

Subjects	Process-oriented programming style		Product-oriented programming style	
Grade 6				
S1	4	L_e/P_4	3	L_e/P_4
S2	3	L_r/P_3	3	P_3
S3	3	P_4	3	P_4
S4	2	L_r	2	L
S5	2	L	2	L/P_2
Total	14		13	
Grade 5				
S6	2	L_r/P_3	2	P_3
S7	0	—	3	L/P_2
S8	1	L_r	2	L
S9	1	L_r	2	L
S10	0	—	3	L
Total	4		12	

Note: L = linear, L_e = linear in the editor, and L_r = linear with "repeat" formula. P refers to a procedural programming style: specifically, P_2 = define/organize, P_3 = define/transform/organize, and P_4 = define/transform/export/organize.

not necessarily linked to the type of project. One child, S1, used both styles for both types of projects; S2 and S5 also mixed styles, though less frequently. On the other hand, two of the sixth graders maintained constant styles across projects: S3 loved to work procedurally and defined all his projects in a modular way; S4 hated it and despite suggestions and offers of help refused to use procedures. S8 and S9 are qualitatively different from S4: their use of a linear type of programming was more due to a lack of experience with procedural abilities (defining, transforming, organizing, and exporting procedures) than S4 who had been initiated into them the year before.

Table 2 compares the data on children's work styles with data related to their problem-solving styles. A mixed problem-solving style was identified during the protocol analysis, which we called *data/concept driven*. Children would start with a data-driven approach, but through their actions they would discover a guiding concept that would determine their subsequent behavior. Symmetry was often what set off a concept-driven path: For example, when constructing a face, a

Table 2 Number of individual projects categorized by children's work and problem-solving styles

Subjects	Process-oriented problem-solving style				Product-oriented problem-solving style			
	Number of projects completed	C	D/C	D	Number of projects completed	C	D/C	D
Grade 6								
S1	4	4	—	—	3	3	—	—
S2	3	2	1	—	3	2	1	—
S3	3	3	—	—	3	3	—	—
S4	2	—	2	—	2	—	2	—
S5	2	—	—	2	2	—	—	2
Total	14	9	3	2	13	8	3	2
Grade 5								
S6	2	1	1	—	2	2	—	—
S7	0	—	—	—	3	—	1	2
S8	1	—	1	—	2	—	—	2
S9	1	—	1	—	2	—	—	2
S10	0	—	—	—	3	—	—	3
Total	4	1	3	0	12	2	1	9

Note: C = concept-driven, D = data-driven, and D/C = data/concept-driven.

child proceeded by trial and error for one ear or one eye and discovered afterward that the same general pattern of actions—sometimes with a reversal of angle direction—could be used for the other ear or the other eye. At other times a step-by-step construction of the first part of a particular design gave birth to specific links that guided the subsequent actions—the construction of the base of a house would trigger the planning of the size, location, and relationship between windows and doors. Here again the more experienced children definitely showed more concept-driven projects than the less experienced ones: seventeen as opposed to three. There were two exceptions: S5 of the older group always functioned in a data-driven style, while S6 in the younger group tended to pursue a concept-driven problem-solving path.

No particular links could be made for the majority of our subjects between work style and problem-solving style. In general, the children's performance was pretty stable, independent of the type of projects worked on. However, we could discern among the beginners a small tendency to follow a data/concept approach in process-oriented projects and a data- driven approach in the more product-oriented types of projects. Most of the older children, however, functioned at a direct or indirect conceptual level. S4 was particularly interesting because he always followed the same pattern of starting without guidelines and then discovered them in the course of action. There was one exception: S5 behaved as though it were his first Logo project, not using any other problem-solving strategy than following the turtle moves step by step.

In summary, in this phase of individual projects, most subjects displayed a certain variety in their work styles and in their programming styles. Where low variety was observed, either insufficient exposure to Logo or very strong preferences (S3 and S4) appear to be the main explanatory factors. Interestingly, variety in problem-solving style is mainly found in the less experienced subjects, the oldest confining themselves to a single problem-solving path.

Analysis of Children's Learning Styles on Two Assigned Tasks

Specific tasks were introduced for two main reasons. First, children were in need of a change and of a new challenge as they got tired of generating new projects all the time. Second, the presentation and discussion of projects ended up by being perceived mainly as a nice way of getting feedback but not necessarily as an easy way of learning from one another. So to the great delight of the group, I proposed some specific tasks and announced a discussion based on the identification of the different ways of doing the same task. The real purpose of the second phase was (1) to sensitize the children to the question of interindividual variety *within the same task* and (2) to underline intraindividual variety, when it could be found, within the two assigned tasks.

In this phase the same ten target children worked alone on their computer; privacy was assured by means of a reorganization of the work space. All children had their own observer whose role here was to observe but not to intervene. The chosen tasks were purposely ill-defined to maximize the range of different processes (see Greeno 1978). Task 1 was to construct a checkerboard, with no model presented. Task 2 was the construction of a bicolored snowflake, with a few examples briefly presented. In both tasks two steps were required. The first step was the construction of the basic element: the dark square in task 1 and the branch in task 2 (see figure 1). The second step was the execution of the task itself, using the previously defined element.

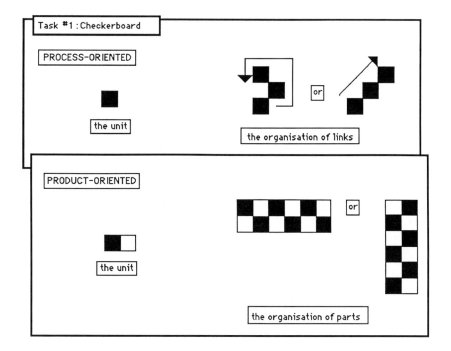

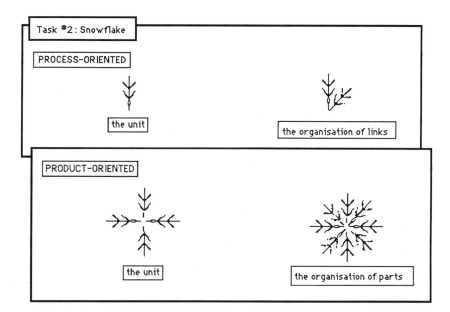

Figure 1 Process- and product-oriented approaches on the two assigned tasks

Table 3 Stylistic patterns of the ten subjects in two assigned tasks

	Task 1			Task 2		
Subject	Work style	Problem-solving style	Programming style	Work style	Problem-solving style	Programming style
Grade 6						
S1	Process	Concept	L_e	Product	Concept	P_3
S2	Product	Concept	P_3	Process	Concept	L_e
S3	Product	Concept	P_3	Product	Concept	P_3
S4	Process	Data/concept	L_r	Process	Data/concept	L_r
S5	Product	Data	P_2	Process	Data	L
Grade 5						
S6	Process	Data/concept	L	Process	Concept	P_3
S7	Process /product	Data/concept	L/P_3	Process /product	Data/concept	L_r
S8	Product	Data	L	Process	Data	L
S9	Process	Data	L	Product	Data	L_r
S10	Process	Data	L	Product	Data/concept	L_r

Note: L = linear, L_e = linear in the editor, and L_r = linear with "repeat" formula. P refers to a procedural programming style: specifically, P_2 = define/organize, P_3 = define/transform/organize, and P_4 = define/transform/export/organize.

To identify and classify the stylistic patterns observed, the same general categories are again used here, that is, those bearing on the nature of the project (process versus product), the style of programming (linear versus procedural), and the type of problem-solving path adopted (concept driven versus data driven). Table 3 presents a breakdown of the ten subjects' performance on the two tasks according to these three categories. These data will be discussed category by category.

Process-Oriented Versus Product-Oriented Project Work

Recall that this category refers to the way the subject defines the task: A subject who initially focuses on the identification and organization of links that relate the parts of the task is process oriented, whereas a subject who first concentrates on the identification and construction of the parts is product oriented. Six children were process oriented in their approach to task 1, which means that they linked one dark square to another dark square, and so on, until a checkerboard of a given size was obtained (a 3 × 3, 4 × 4, or 8 × 8 board). In this approach the unit of work was the dark square, and two ways of linking the squares were devised: circular or diagonal, as illustrated in figure 1. Four subjects were identified as product oriented. The unit of construction was a pair of light and dark squares, and the parts were the ranks and files (or lines and columns) of the checkerboard. One child, S7, started with a process-oriented approach but in the course of solution changed his point of view and adopted a product-oriented approach; he did a similar about-face on task 2.

On task 2 five subjects (counting S7) were identified as product oriented: The basic unit was a complex part that could be rotated in different ways—at a 45-degree angle or a 22.5-degree angle—and painted any color. The other five subjects conceived the task in a more process-oriented way: They saw the solution as a process of moving the basic element (the branch) around a central point and changing its color alternately.

What is most interesting about these data, however, is the observed stylistic mobility across tasks by seven of the ten subjects. Seven children were sometimes process oriented (primarily oriented toward the construction of links), sometimes product oriented (primarily oriented toward the construction of parts). Thus many children do have more than one perspective, more than one work style. Three of the children, however, remained faithful to one approach. As on the individual projects, S3 and S4 again expressed a preference for a single style.

Concept-Driven versus Data-Driven Problem Solving

Table 3 shows there is practically no variety in the problem-solving styles of our children. Three subjects chose a concept-driven path for both tasks, three others adopted a data-driven approach, and two used a data/concept approach for both tasks. Only two subjects showed minimal variation going in one case from a data/concept to a concept-driven approach (S6) and from a data-driven to a data/concept approach (S10). It is difficult here, however, to differentiate normal mobility from stylistic variety!

A few typical examples of each type of problem-solving approach will help make the nature of our data more concrete. The concept-driven path is well illustrated by the behavior of S1 who, right from the beginning realized that after each dark square the turtle would only have to do a RT 90 to produce a sequence of attached squares in a circular manner. He even anticipated that at one point in time a FD of the size of the square would be needed in order to go on ith a new layer of circular squares. So he started his checkerboard with that pattern of action in mind and adjusted it as needed. S3, for his part, analyzed that he first needed a pair of squares in order to construct a line, then a pair of lines to construct his sought-after 8 × 8 board.

S6 illustrates the data/concept-driven path. In task 1, for example, she started with a dark square, played with the turtle, and then made another dark square. By chance the new dark square was corner to corner with the first one, so she then got the idea of linking the dark squares in a circular fashion, first from the left, then from the right. From then on, she knew what she wanted to do; she knew that what was needed were actions of the type RT 90 or LT 90 and some FD related to the size of the square. The subject had developed a general path of actions that guided her work until task completion.

Subjects following a data-driven approach start their projects with their basic element—the dark square or the colored branch—and command by command, through trial and error, construct a product corresponding to the suggested task. The main characteristic of these subjects is that no guiding concept seems to emerge from their long string of successive actions. If they were given the same task again, they would probably reproduce the same work approach, though maybe a little bit faster!

In summary, I found relative consistency in the type of problem-solving style adopted in the two assigned tasks. Even more so, no major differences could be observed in the subjects' behavior across the two types of settings (individual projects versus assigned tasks). It is worth mentioning, however, that unlike their behavior in the first phase of the research, S8 and S9 did not follow a data/concept-driven path in their process-oriented task. S10, for his part, showed slightly more variety in the second setting than he did in the first one.

Linear versus Procedural Programming

The analysis of programming styles makes use of the same terminology employed in the analysis of individual projects. What emerges from table 3 is an apparent connection between programming style and the perceived nature of the task: That is, a process-oriented task is generally carried out by a linear approach, while a product-oriented task is often accompanied by procedural programming. This may explain why children are not always procedural despite the fact that they have the requisite abilities in their repertoire. For those who have a rich repertoire, programming style may depend on the nature of the work chosen for each task. In task 1, for example, S1 mentioned beforehand that he would not organize his program in procedures and subprocedures because he believed that the checkerboard could be built through an organization of simple commands: TURNS (90 degrees) and FD (related to the length of the dark square). S6 came to the same conclusion, once she had come to grips with the pattern of actions that guided the construction of her checkerboard. But for children who have not yet developed the abilities underlying procedural programming, it is not quite fair to talk about a preferred style; indeed, no choice is yet available to them. Subjects S8, S9, and S10 run the risk of having no choice other than linear programming, since they have had very little opportunity to exercise the abilities required for procedural programming (see table 1).

The data thus are quite clear with respect to the diversity of programming styles within the same child and the futility of trying to place those styles into a hierarchy. Linear programming can be accompanied by a highly conceptual approach as easily as by a step-by-step, data-driven approach. Obviously linear programming that is carried out directly in the editor or by means of REPEAT formulas, which are often as powerful as procedures, provides interesting variations that should be considered. Taking account of all these nuances, eight out of ten children varied their programming style across tasks.

Analysis of Some Additional Individual Projects

Only a few sessions remained after the assigned tasks, so children were asked to finish up their school year with individual projects. It was suggested that they use colored shapes, which many children had been longing to do all year. Most of them had time to complete only two projects. Interestingly all children started with a process-oriented project, defining one specific element that they used over and over again in the same or a slightly modified version in their project: Ranks of inverted triangles of alternating colors, a pyramid of pentagons of decreasing size and alternating colors, a four-leaf clover constructed out of a basic colored shape (e.g., an inverted triangle), an abstract painting made out of partial or complete colored circles, a Japanese flag, a French flag, and so on.

Also of interest was how children darkened a new shape, for example, a rectangle: Either they adapted their own coloring techniques, which they had used for the checkerboard, or, even more often, they borrowed a new technique that had been presented by another child during the discussion on the similarities and differences among techniques. Thus, to color triangles, pentagons, and so forth, children used the technique of the embedded growing shapes: For example, a colored triangle was defined by a procedure of cumulative triangles that grow by two or three turtle units each time. Others borrowed the simple coloring technique of going forward, then backward, before slightly changing the position of the turtle to generate a formula to color a circle or part of a circle: For example, REPEAT X [FD X BK X RT 90 LT 90] in a REPEAT Y [FD Z BK Z RT 1]. All but three projects corresponded to the P_2, P_3, or P_4 program types because all children had to define or export, to organize and at times transform procedures, in order to accomplish the tasks they had set themselves. The other three consisted of the two flags and the abstract painting projects, which called for programs of the L_r type where diverse repeat formulas were combined to produce the desired effect.

Finally, it was quite surprising that all of the second projects were product oriented! They varied from a house consisting of colored shapes to a wizard with colored pants and shirt, from a San Francisco street with colored houses and street lights to a face with colored eyes, nose, mouth, and so on. One project was difficult to classify as it consisted of regrouping and completing a series of European flags (of France, Belgium, Italy, Germany, and Russia) and a series of African flags (of Mali, Chad, Guinea, and Gabon). All but one child integrated colored parts in their projects. All children who used colored parts in their product-oriented projects had programs of the P_2, P_3, or P_4 type; the child who excluded colored shapes (S10) produced a linear type program (L).

Since all children's projects, except one at the very end, were oriented toward the use of colored forms, the children found themselves conceptually guided in each task. A few of course, started with a data-driven approach but soon found the guiding "formula" needed by their project. To bring their project to completion, children had to identify the kind of repeat formula needed (the choice of a coloring technique, the approximate size of the desired shape, etc.); they had to establish relationships between colored forms and other parts of their projects (the parts where just the outline was traced; the interfaces between parts; etc.).

In this third phase of working with Logo, there was obviously an implicit group phenomenon at work in the choice of project. Still, what this phase revealed was the ability of every child to learn from different perspectives (process oriented versus product oriented) with different frameworks of problem analysis: The use of colored shapes facilitated the recourse to procedural programming or to a sophisticated form of linear programming and really helped in adopting a problem-solving path guided by a concept and not only by data. It should be mentioned here that the children did not spontaneously become geniuses. On the one hand, the five participant-observers were present to help children work out local difficulties during the execution of the individual projects—their role was different during the assigned tasks, however, where they were noninterventionist observers. On the other hand, children were in fact more daring and more confident in their abilities to learn and, with encouragement, applied more new approaches at the end of the Logo project than at the beginning. Their use of all the various abilities mentioned above should not, by any means, be interpreted as a definitive measure of their abilities but much more as a measure of their level of familiarization with certain tools. These tools must be used again and again in exciting contexts before they can be fully mastered and become an important element in the child's tool box.

Sex Differences

Given the fact that sex differences are often observed in contexts involving computers (Turkle 1984; Hoyles and Sutherland 1989), one may wonder whether these differences had any effect on our results. Obviously the small sample size here—six boys and four girls—precludes any systematic study of the question, but some general observations may help in planning future research or in interpreting others' results.

Among the sixth graders S2 is the only girl, and her attitudes and behaviors do not differ in any significant way from two (of the four) sixth grade boys, S1 and S3, who were judged to have an equivalent range of abilities and experience. Among the fifth graders S6, a girl, and S7, a boy, presented quite similar behaviors and competence, and the other boy, S10, showed the same general behavior pattern as the two other girls, S8 and S9.

Proportionally intraindividual variety in styles was observed as often in girls as in boys. As to general attitudes toward the computer, the observers' notes showed that two girls, S2 and S6, and three boys, S1, S3, and S7, were fully at ease with the kind of learning called upon by Logo and the "machine": They showed good control of their computer despite the fact that they did not master it completely. The other two girls, S8 and S9, and three boys, S4, S5, and S10, were somewhat shyer, and at times overwhelmed by the precision required by the programming language.

3 DISCUSSION

Summary of the Data

My data demonstrate intraindividual variety in the work and programming styles of children observed in two different Logo contexts. Variety within a child, however, appears to be a function of the amount of experience with Logo: The less experienced children tended to be more attached to a single approach. To enjoy a range of tools, it is as if the child must have had time to become familiar with each tool and with the different abilities called upon by the components of each style.

Programming styles were not related to work styles in the first phase of individual projects, but they appeared to be so in the second phase of assigned tasks: Linear programming accompanied a process-oriented work style, and conversely, procedural programming accompanied a product-oriented style. It is also worth mentioning that all children who displayed a concept or a data/concept problem-solving path produced sophisticated programs, whether linear (L_e or L_r) or procedural (P_3, or P_4).

Finally, my data on problem-solving styles seems to support the finding of interindividual variety more than intraindividual variety. Children tended to take up one problem-solving style and stick to it across tasks and settings. On occasion there was a certain mobility, with a few children passing either from a data/concept approach to a concept approach, or from a data approach to a data/concept one. I now turn to some other Logo data, as well as my own, seen first from the standpoint of interindividual variety and then in terms of intraindividual differences.

Logo and Interindividual Variety in Learning Styles

Throughout its brief history, Logo has been shown to provide a potentially rich setting for uncovering and supporting interindividual differences in learning styles. Indeed, interindividual differences were observed and upheld in all sorts of Logo contexts: in open contexts that were focused on individual projects carried out either by beginners (Rampy 1984; Solomon 1982; Watt 1979) or by well-initiated subjects (Papert et al. 1979; Hoyles et al. 1984; Lemerise and Kayler 1986); in more structured contexts where specific tasks were proposed to subjects as an important part of their Logo work experience (Lemerise 1986; Marcotte 1989; Grenier 1989); in new and expanded contexts such as the LEGO-Logo activities described in chapter 6 by Weir. Thus by now it has been clearly demonstrated that Logo environments can favor the externalization and the development of many equally rich work approaches. The observed interindividual variety, however, could be a function of the type of problem worked on. Marcotte (1989), for example, who set her subjects well-defined figurative tasks (sailboats on the sea, rows of identical houses, etc.), observed less interindividual variety than Grenier (1989) who gave much more abstract and ill-defined tasks (a piano keyboard, a Vasarely painting, etc.). Interindividual variety thus appears to diminish with well-defined tasks, which produce a reduction of variability in task perception and mode of execution.

Different developmental levels and/or preferred styles are also possible sources of interindividual differences. My data on interindividual differences appear to be related to the former: The observed upward mobility is the first important indication of a developmental trend. The older and more experienced subjects were largely concept driven, yet there was no giant step from a data-driven approach to a concept-driven one without passing through the intermediate data/concept approach.

The second indication has to do with the nature of the children's problem-solving ability. My data tend to support the notion that problem-solving ability, as described here, is a "meta-ability" that ought to be fully mastered by all subjects independently of their work approach or programming style. Indeed, all children who were able not only to set a goal but also to create and maintain links with that goal and their organization of Logo actions produced elegant project solutions, whether process or product oriented. Thus the ability to trace a conceptually-driven problem-solving path appears to be a necessary condition for children to make progress and develop mastery in Logo, independent of their preferred style. The interindividual differences observed here could also be interpreted as developmental differences in the rhythm of acquisition of a general ability.

Obviously my data also show the interindividual differences that are related to preferred work style or programming style. It would be shortsighted, however, to interpret those differences solely in terms of interindividual differences and to ignore the intraindividual differences also observed.

Logo and Intraindividual Variety in Learning Styles

Very few researchers have evinced much concern for the analysis of intraindividual differences, as though the establishment of interindividual differences were the end point of the research. I rather see the establishment of interindividual differences as an interesting first step that serves to clear the way for a major second step—namely, the promotion of intraindividual differences in children's learning styles. In other words, the very first mission of Logo is to uncover and support interindividual variety, but once that is done, it is then to foster the acquisition of intraindividual variety stemming from the tremendously rich variation observed in people. It is from this point of view that I will discuss and interpret my data.

Interpretation of Intraindividual Data

Implicit in the intraindividual perspective adopted here is the assumption that every child should be exposed, at some point in time, to educational settings that allow the development and mastery of a vast repertoire of abilities. *Children cannot use tools until they possess them, nor can they make deliberate choices until they are conscious of alternative tools* that can be used for solving different problems of the same general category.

It is interesting in this respect to note the differences between the first and second phases of my research: In the first phase, that of individual projects, there was a great variety of projects, but the children behaved like observers to that variety. They admired each other's productions but rarely realized that they could learn anything for themselves—though the most experienced children did borrow ideas, but rarely processes. (They were sufficiently advanced in Logo to be able to generate their own processes once they got a new idea.) Nor was there any evidence that children were conscious of their own variety of learning processes. In general, the individual projects were relatively complex and demanding of those who produced them, so, once they had mastered all the details, it was pretty hard to go back afterward and analyze how they had proceeded. The presentation and discussion of the projects had a certain effect, though a rather minimal one largely confined to the more advanced children. Listening to and really understanding the description of another child's process is very hard for a child-observer who does not see the other child at work or who does not work on a similar project.

Matters changed dramatically in the second phase during the assigned tasks. It was easier for children to talk about tasks that had been done by all of them. There was discussion about specific anchor points: the construction of the basic element, the dark square or the colored branch; the execution of the main task, the checkerboard or the snowflake. Discussion directed toward the similarities and differences among children triggered interest and curiosity. The children were amazed, for example, at the number of different techniques that the group had invented for darkening a square (see Lemerise 1988 for a description of the different techniques observed). They were fascinated by the possibility of different perspectives for the same task: to construct a checkerboard by hooking dark squares together was seen as an ingenious idea by those who had adopted a more classic strategy. They were surprised to realize that individuals of different levels of competence could have the same ingenious idea in common: Constructing a checkerboard out of ranks and files, or out of a single dark square, were ideas found in children at all levels of competence. Moreover, in the discussion following the assigned tasks, children who manifested stylistic variety within tasks were aware of that variety and of what led them to change approaches—namely, their perception of the task or the specificity of their goals.

It seems that the observation and discussion of these interindividual differences favors the emergence of a variety of styles within a child. This would appear to be an example of the internalization process so well described by Vygotsky (1978) (see also Wertsch 1984). In fact Vygotsky describes development, at least in part, as a process of progressive appropriation or internalization of what is first done or experienced with other people, mainly the people in the learner's zone of proximal development, that is, the learner's next accessible zone given his or her developmental level.

It thus appears that the second phase created an educational setting that allowed children to appropriate a variety of approaches; moreover the behavior observed in the third phase of the research lends support to this hypothesis. In the additional individual projects, first the choice to work with colored shapes strongly influenced the children's programming styles. Most children were readily drawn to use the P_2, P_3, or P_4 procedural type of programming, even those who had not made much use of it before, which underscores the fact that when a tool is needed and when children have previously been introduced to it, directly or indirectly, they can easily call upon it. Second, an obvious group effect brought children to work on their projects first from a process-oriented perspective and then from a product-oriented one. The first step in familiarizing someone to something new—in our case the colored shapes that all children were eager to work with—is often to "manipulate" it, which means working at a more process-oriented level. Later on it needs to be integrated as one part among others, which means working at a more product-oriented level.

In summary, I see the data in this study as illustrative of the existence of intraindividual differences in learning styles, with experience playing an important factor in building up the repertoire of intraindividual variety. I also propose that intraindividual differences stem, at least in part, from interindividual variety. However, for a transfer to take place, some educational conditions appear to help more than others. Conditions that appear particularly helpful are, first, those that allow an easy and meaningful contact with other children while they are at work and, second, those that facilitate an easy and active taking stock of the variety in one's own processes when such variety arises and lends itself to observation. Finally, the environmental context is important: A context that values variety and sees it as an important developmental quality is more facilitative than a context that values one style more than others or that views styles as being mutually exclusive. More research is obviously needed to verify these hypotheses and to consolidate this point of view.

Intraindividual Data in Perspective

The data in the Logo literature does not yet confirm the reality of intraindividual differences, but it does not deny it either. As has already been mentioned, because of lack of relevant data, some researchers limited themselves to postulate the nonexclusivity of styles, while others who were involved in longitudinal studies noticed intraindividual variety, though minimal at times. In the actual cultural and educational context, these data suggest that children do not spontaneously develop versatility in their work styles. In the absence of outside intervention that encourages the development of intraindividual variety, children seem more inclined to stick to their preferred styles than to develop alternative work styles that can be called upon when problems are presented from another angle.

In this regard the analysis done by Hoyles and Sutherland (1989) on the types of goals underlying their subjects' projects is quite revealing. They analyzed the three-year productions of pairs of subjects in terms of loosely defined versus well-defined goals and abstract versus real-world goals. Although half of the observed pairs experimented with the four types of goals across the years, there was a strong bias each time for specific types.

At first glance these and comparable results would appear at variance with my own. On the one hand, they illustrate the phenomenon of preferred styles in children, but, on the other hand, they do not deny the hypothesis of intraindividual variety: Many children displayed a variety of goals, although rarely in equal proportions. It appears to me that the main factor explaining the disparity in results is related to work settings and the research goals underlying the choice of settings.

The main objective of my research was to expose children to variety and to bring them to notice that variety—by having them, for example, present their projects, discuss them, and observe and compare processes. In a way what my research has primarily illustrated is that styles are malleable under certain environmental and educational conditions. Hoyles and Sutherland (1989) had a different objective, yet they did demonstrate that children spontaneously have a tendency to opt for the status quo, to develop what is clearly established as their own strength. Preferred styles are obviously not a bad thing per se, but I believe that it is a developmentally positive achievement (see Garbarino 1982) to be able to work with more than one kind of cognitive tool and that this opportunity should be made available to all children. If preferences do appear for one reason or the other, let them be based on the experience of real choice rather than on the experience of no other choice!

REFERENCES

Bennett, N. 1977. *Teaching Styles and Pupil Progress*. Cambridge: Harvard University Press.

Bradley, C. A. 1985. The relationship between students' information-processing styles and Logo programming. *Journal of Educational Computing Research* 1: 427–433.

Bronfenbrenner, U. 1979. *The Ecology of Human Development: Experiments by Nature and Design*. Cambridge: Harvard University Press.

Carver, S. M., and Klahr, D. 1986. Assessing children's Logo debugging skills with a formal model. *Journal of Educational Computing Research* 22: 487–525.

Corno, L., and Snow, R. E. 1984. Adapting teaching to individual differences among students. In M. Wittrock (ed.), *Third Handbook of Research on Teaching*. New York: Macmillan, pp. 605–629.

Coté, B., and Kayler, H. 1987. Geometric constructions with a turtle and on paper by 5th and 6th grade children. *Proceedings of the Third International Conference for Logo and Mathematics Education*. Montreal: Concordia University, pp. 76–85.

Garbarino, J. 1982. *Children and Families in the Social Environment*. New York: Aldine.

Garbarino, J., and Asp, C. E. 1981. *Successful Schools and Competent Students*. Lexington, MA: Lexington Books.

Greeno, J. G. 1978. A study of problem solving. In R. Glaser (ed.), *Advances in Instructional Psychology*, vol. 1. Hillsdale, NJ: Lawrence Erlbaum Associates, pp. 3–75.

Grenier, C. 1989. La Pensée procédurale chez l'enfant de 5ième et 6ième année. *Mémoire de maîftrise inédit.* Montreal: Université du Québec.

Hillel, J., and Samurçay, R. 1985. Analysis of a Logo environment for learning the concept of procedures with variables. Research Report. Québec Ministry of Education. Concordia University, Montreal.

Hoyles, C. 1987. Tools for learning: Insight for the mathematics educators from a Logo programming environment. *For the Learning of Mathematics* 7: 32–37.

Hoyles, C., and Noss, R. 1987. Synthesising mathematical conceptions and their formalisation through the construction of a Logo-based school mathematics curriculum. *International Journal of Mathematics Education in Science and Technology* 18(5): 343–362.

Hoyles, C., and Sutherland, R. 1989. *Logo Mathematics in the Classroom.* London: Routledge.

Joyce, B., and Weil, M. 1972. *Models of Teaching.* Englewood Cliffs, NJ: Prentice Hall.

Klahr, D., and Carver, S. M. 1988. Cognitive objectives in a Logo debugging curriculum: Instruction, learning and transfer. *Cognitive Psychology* 20: 362–404.

Lemerise, T. 1986. Mathematical learning and the repeat command: An analysis of the different levels of competence observed in children working on three specific tasks. *Proceedings of the Second International Conference for Logo and Mathematics Education.* London: University of London, pp. 25–29.

Lemerise, T. 1988. Developmental factors for attaining a first level of competence in procedural thinking in Logo. *Proceedings of the Twelfth International Conference for the Psychology of Mathematics Education*, vol. 2. Hungary: OOK Printing House, pp. 463–471.

Lemerise, T., and Kayler, H. 1986. The epistemology of learning: A longitudinal analysis of the progressive growth of competence in children doing Logo. *Proceedings of the Tenth International Conference for the Psychology of Mathematics Education.* London: University of London, pp. 171–176.

McAllister, A. 1985. Problem solving and beginning programming. Paper presented at the Annual Meeting of the American Education Research Association. Chicago, IL.

Marcotte, L. 1989. Elaboration de mises en situation pour le développement et l'apprentissage d'habiletés de la pensée procédurale en Logo chez les enfants de 2ième cycle primaire. *Mémoire de maîtrise inédit.* Montreal: Université du Québec.

Mendelsohn, P. 1985. L'Enfant et les activités de programmation. *Grand N* 35: 47–60.

Papert, S., Watt, D., diSessa, A., and Weir, S. 1979. Final report of the Logo project in the Brookline public schools. Logo memo 53. Cambridge: Massachusetts Institute of Technology.

Rampy, L. M. 1984. The problem-solving style of fifth graders using Logo. Paper presented at the American Educational Research Association Annual Meeting. New Orleans, LA.

Schmeck, R. R. 1988. *Learning Strategies and Learning Styles*. New York: Plenum.

Snow, R. E. 1986. Individual differences and the design of educational programs. *American Psychologist* 41: 1029–1039.

Solomon, C. 1982. Introducing Logo to children: Teaching Logo requires an awareness of different learning styles. *Byte* (August): 196–208.

Turkle, S. 1984. *The Second Self: Computers and the Human Spirit*. New York: Simon and Schuster.

Vygotsky, L. S. 1978. *Mind in Society: The Development of Higher Psychological Processes*. Cambridge: Harvard University Press.

Watt, D. 1979. A comparison of the problem-solving styles of two students learning Logo. *Creative Computing* 5: 12–15.

Weir, S. 1987. *Cultivating Minds: A Logo Case Book*. New York: Harper and Row.

Wertsch, J. V. 1984. The zone of proximal development: some conceptual issues. In B. Rogoff and J. V. Wertsch (eds.), *Children's Learning in the "Zone of Proximal Development."* New Directions for Child Development, vol. 23. San Francisco: Jossey-Bass.

Mathematics in a Logo Environment: A Recursive Look at a Complex Phenomenon

8

Thomas E. Kieren

1 BACKGROUND

From his technical and theoretical inclinations, as well as from his observations of young children over a great number of years, Papert (1980) concluded that turtle geometry is both body and ego syntonic. In other words, he saw turtle geometry as being "in sync" with natural ways of mathematical growth and knowing. Papert viewed computer use as essentially a visit to "mathland" allowing a child to confront in a natural way significant mathematical ideas such as procedure, structure, recursion, and debugging. By the early 1980s there had already been significant work done developing Logo environments and microworlds within them that reflected the optimistic philosophy of Papert.

Independent of the original extensive work at MIT and elsewhere, there have been a number of projects over the last six years that sought to understand in detail what Papert might have meant by ego-syntonic mathematics. The researchers involved in these studies also tried to see if students actually built mathematical knowledge in Logo environments and to observe the qualities of this knowledge and its relationship to qualities of the learning environment.

It is the purpose of this chapter briefly to support the claim that mathematics can be learned in a Logo environment. Both teachers and researchers can look at Logo mathematical knowledge in terms of the effective actions we see children and young adults using. These actions might entail directly using primitives that have certain mathematical effects: An example of this is using a translation primitive that exhibits the pre-image and image under a translation. Effective Logo mathematical actions might be writing procedures that accomplish a certain mathematical task as exemplified by the flag-making tasks in Hillel and Kieran (1988) or the "increase the size of the N" task in Hoyles and Noss (1989). I will argue that these *explicit* visible mathematical actions are themselves leveled and complex in nature. It has been suggested that such complex, leveled phenomena can be viewed as recursive in nature (Vitale 1988). I use the idea of recursion in a number of ways to look at Logo mathematical knowing. Bohm and Peat (1987) see knowing and understanding as implicit and generative in nature.

I attempt to use various ideas of recursion to look at this implicit side of Logo mathematical knowing. I use the theoretical ideas developed here to contrast student performances with a study of geometry learned in a Logo environment, as well as to reflect on instructional practices in Logo mathematics.

Of course there are many ways to look at the whole enterprise of knowing mathematics in a Logo environment. Hillel (chapter 1 in this volume) uses a path structure to illustrate the conceptual field of Logo mathematics, showing growth links from primitive use to the building of composed generalized procedures and beyond. His essay focuses in detail on the growth in use of variables both in given and constructed procedures. In particular, he considers what it means to generalize a fixed procedure and identifies factors in the growth to composite generalized procedures. This chapter, however, tries to consider Logo mathematical knowing as a whole and to highlight the embedded nature of the levels of such knowing.

2 LEARNING MATHEMATICS IN A LOGO ENVIRONMENT

Some of the most extensive, independent research on Logo mathematics has been conducted under the direction of Hoyles and Noss at the London Institute of Education. They have argued both theoretically and from the results of a number of long-term studies with children that "Logo derives its power as a mathematical learning environment by allowing functional experimental activity to take place simultaneously with the act of formalization" (Noss and Hoyles 1987, p. 27). To describe growth in such an environment and to highlight the ways and areas of contribution of the teacher and deliberate instruction in effective open Logo mathematics environments, Noss and Hoyles have developed the UDGS model (use, discriminate, generalize, synthesize). They suggest that children move (and can be "nudged" and supported in doing so) from a level *of use* to one of *making discriminations* among visual/symbolic actions to *generalizing* such actions and finally to *synthesizing* new ideas/actions based on such discrimination and generalization. They have gathered extensive case evidence of children's activity producing Logo mathematics knowing, which is usefully described by their theory.

In another long-term series of projects in Montreal, Hillel and Kieran, working over extended time periods with small groups of children, have been trying to identify visually oriented, mathematical strategies and analytical (quantitative) strategies used by children in working on geometric tasks and trying to understand growth and change from one to the other. In one such study over the course of a year, they observed children developing visually oriented strategies for doing geometric tasks. Children with such strategies also used visual verification for testing the correctness of a solution. However, later in the year children appeared to come to a new level of mathematical awareness and seemed to be able to predetermine and calculate measures of various geometric features in tasks. In this more sophisticated activity the test for validity seemed to reside in the procedure itself and not in the visual screen output (Kieran, Hillel, and Gurtner 1987).

There have been other studies of growth in particular geometric knowledge in a Logo environment. For example, Ludwig (1986) used van Hiele's theories of levels of geometric activity and curriculum, to develop Logo motion geometry tasks for seventh-grade (twelve-year-old) students working in pairs. Her research indicates that children do learn geometry in such an environment and that they gain sophistication in talking about geometric objects and processes through such activity. Like Noss and Hoyles, and Hillel and Kieran above, Ludwig found her students working at many levels of mathematical sophistication with only a few using sophisticated procedures independent of actions. Nevertheless, in a sequence of twenty-two different geometric task environments, students completed the tasks at some satisfactory level over 80 percent of the time. Further there was distinct growth in the use of procedures to describe and control geometric activity paralleled by increased use of geometric properties as they discussed, built, and used the Logo procedures. One conclusion that can be drawn from the above literature, as well as from many other studies of children using Logo in learning mathematics, is that children can and do learn mathematics in such environments.

3 LOGO MATHEMATICS AS A COMPLEX, LEVELED PHENOMENON

What is the character of Logo mathematics as done by a young person? In work over the last half dozen years at the University of Alberta, Kieren and Olson (Kieren 1987; Olson, Kieren, and Ludwig 1987) have tried to understand and interpret Papert's view of turtle geometry as ego-syntonic mathematics. To do this, they attempted to see how doing geometry using Logo would square with the van Hiele theory of geometric thinking (Hoffer 1983). This led to the consideration of mathematics done in a Logo environment as leveled but complex in nature. In part this characterization derived from the mathematics itself. The van

Hieles argued that personal, geometric knowledge (and a like argument could be extended to other mathematics) exists as complex effective actions at many levels. At the lowest level this knowing entails using geometric objects (or processes) as wholes. At the next level the knower of geometry again uses the objects but this time as a bearer of properties. The third level knowledge is of local logical relationships, and the final level(s) entails embedding and synthesizing one's earlier knowledge in a structure. From this point of view personal mathematics is leveled.

The claim for leveled complexity in Logo mathematics also derives from observations of Logo use. One of the virtues of Logo is that it is an action-oriented, not just an action-possible, language. Thus Logo knowing is *word* oriented; that is, given a primitive either from Logo or defined for a particular mathematical situation, a child can use the procedure word to drive action directly. In doing mathematics using Logo, a child is encouraged to make and use procedures. But this kind of knowing exists at several levels. At its most primitive level a procedure simply serves as a *list of word-driven actions* or a collection of actions done. There is no analysis of the particular commands nor of the sequence. The child observes that a particular set of actions has a result worth repeating easily and that coding this list as a procedure allows one to replace the list with a single word.

A step above such list-collecting behavior would be a *procedure as a generated set of actions*. At this point a list of word-generated actions is created before or in anticipation of related actions and a prepictured result. Children can plan ahead by playing turtle or using more formal means, and then use this plan to accomplish a Logo mathematical task. Still at this level the procedure does not seem to have existence independent of action. Nevertheless, it can be created prior to actions and not simply reflect actions already done. (A word is a "put" for a sequence of actions.)

Another level of Logo use occurs when the procedure can itself be observed for its features. For example, consider the following:

```
TO DIAMOND.CORNER
  HT
  PU
  RT 45
  FD 50
  PD DOT
```

```
PU
RT 90
FD 50
PD DOT
PU
RT 90
FD 50
PD DOT
PU
RT 90
FD 50
PD DOT
RT 45
END
```

A child, rather than simply making a list of imagined actions, now starts to consider whole features *of the procedure itself*. (Each feature of course has a parallel in actions on the screen.) At this point the child could consider using REPEAT or uses variables to generate the "diamond" as a whole family of different-sized "diamonds."

One might call such a procedure a *distinguished* procedure. The child has made distinctions in the previous level of functioning and now uses them. Geometrically such a child is ready to see that a diamond (of this form) is a square and hence may also now use SQUARE.CORNER as a subprocedure.

```
TO DIAMOND.CORNER.2        TO SQUARE.CORNER
  HT                           REPEAT 4[FD 50 PD DOT PU RT 90]
  PU                         END
  RT 45
  SQUARE
  LT 45
  PD
END
```

In all of the above uses of Logo in doing mathematical tasks, the use of the language has been highly regulated by the actions and objects on the screen. A study of distinguished procedures one has made—perhaps using REPEAT, variables, and simple subprocedures—can bring one to a new level of awareness that *procedures are a class of things that have structures*. At this point one might be ready for and might start making what could be considered *structured proce-dures*. Procedures themselves can be taken as elements of one's thinking. One might ask "What would a procedure for a geometric translation (have to) have in it?" While such a question is still tied to action, now the action is very much an analogue of the language of the procedure. One could use the language without actually executing the procedure. At this level, structured or driver procedures seem possible as does a knowing use of recursion.

As in the use of any language, there are higher levels of Logo use to which a child or an adult might aspire. One needs only to think of those procedures that generate classes of complex, recursive, geometric objects or that allow a computer to act as an artificial intelligence with geometric objects (Weston 1985). Like other languages Logo contains the potential for (and indeed has primitives for) controlling sophisticated constructs, logics, and grammars; like mathematics Logo can be thought of as leveled.

In using Logo to learn mathematics, a child is using language in a deliberate way that brings with it levels as well. The language scholar Northrop Frye (1982) has described four levels of language use, moving from experience-tied to experience-independent uses. The first level he calls *hieroglyphic*; here a person uses language only in association with actions or objects. At the next level, termed *hieratic* or *metaphoric*, a person "puts" language for actions. But this also is an immanent use—that is, language is used to tell the story of, to recall imagi-natively, or to anticipate action. At a third level language is used apart from actions and objects—Frye terms it an *analogic* use. Here language use can be thought of as an independent analogue to a corresponding scenario involving action and objects. At a final level language is used *demotically* or *analytically*. Here using the language itself generates its own meaning—it is independent of the logic of actions and objects. Because through Logo there is always a man-ifestation of the mathematics as patterns on the screen or patterns of sets of numbers, it is easy for an observer to see at least the first three of these levels in children's or young adults' Logo use. And if one thinks of a procedure to de-scribe a fractionally dimensioned object such a von Koch curve, one realizes that such a procedure must have a recursive logic that is evident in the whole of the resulting shape but not in the step-by-step execution. Thus one can envision demotic (experience-independent) use of Logo as a language. While at a less analytic level, Logo language use is driven by or is at least an analogue of action, at an analytic level it might be thought that language use might "invent" new forms of mathematical actions not previously anticipated.

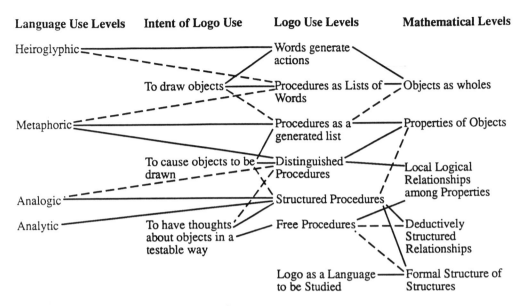

Figure 1 The elements of Logo mathematics

Thus in terms of mathematics, language use, and Logo use, it has been argued that Logo mathematics is a leveled phenomenon. Figure 1 shows Logo mathematics as a *complex* involving language, the computer, and mathematics. It could have been expanded to show the fact that Logo mathematics grows in an interactive social environment. The complexity of the enterprise as seen here seems to fit with the features of Hoyles and Noss' UDGS model, and especially with the complexities of the student actions they have described. In a way this complex overlaps the leveled analysis of Olive (1986) who used the SOLO taxonomy (psychological) and van Hiele levels to analyze Logo mathematics instruction. The complex in the figure situates the learner as a person constructing mathematics who is influenced by language, technology, and culture. This squares with a modern view of mathematics as a dynamic system of knowing influenced by science, technology, art, culture, and language (Davis and Hersh 1986).

4 VIEWS OF RECURSION

If, as argued above, Logo mathematics is a complex leveled phenomenon, then, as suggested by Vitale (1989), it could be considered from the point of view of recursion. In popular terms, something is recursive if it somehow turns back on itself. In trying to go beyond this view and distinguish recursion from such ideas as iteration, Vitale (1988) suggests the following psychologically useful definition:

A phenomenon A is *recursive* if

$$A = (. . . , A, . . .).$$

That is, A is used in its own definitions. The A on the right- and left-hand sides are somehow the same (self-similarity). However, the A on the left is distinct or in some way different from the A on the right (level stepping).

Vitale uses this definition to examine evidence for children's use of recursion in problem situations, and particularly in Logo, in contrast with other kinds of repetitive or multiplicative thinking and procedures. Of course this definition and the related idea of recursion are more general and less procedural than the ideas of recursion in Logo, in computing in general, or in recursion theory in mathematics. However, this definition (and the other ideas of recursion below) can be used, as it is used here, to help look at the complex, leveled phenomenon of learning mathematics in a Logo environment.

Philosophers Maturana and Varela (1987) think of knowing as the ability to take effective action (in the eye of an observer). This notion of knowing is useful in thinking about Logo mathematics. One of the virtues of a Logo environment is that the teacher can pose a mathematical problem as a Logo task. For example, Hoyles and Noss (1989) ask students to make Ns that are proportional to one another, while Hillel and Kieran (1989) ask students to build structures using a particular isosceles triangle-making primitive. A teacher can then observe the effective action that the young person takes and can say something about the child's knowledge. How does such knowing or personal knowledge grow? Maturana and Varela would see the young person as self-referencing and self-maintaining in an environment. Because a person is self-referencing, growth in knowledge is a recursive activity. That is, the young person uses the product(s) of previous processes as an "input" into these processes. Of course this phenomenon could be iterative and not recursive. For example, a child could continue to do all presented mathematical problems at a "visual" level using Logo in direct mode. Because children can and do accomplish quite complicated mathematical tasks in this way, a teacher could observe their knowledge as complex. But it would not be deep, and its growth would be limited by the restrictions of visual imagery, the tedium of direct mode activity, and the lack of sophisticated language use. How does one step up the level of one's knowing? Maturana and Varela see *making distinctions* as critical to such growth. In particular, young persons are capable of distinguishing the apparent source of their thinking as external (in our case the words, procedures, and images on the screen) or internal (a personal invention).

Tomm (1989) describes a multileveled, recursive system of knowing which he and Maturana have developed. It seems applicable to the analysis of Logo mathematics because it envisions knowing as involving interaction (with another or with oneself) and in fact considers *knowledge to be in that interaction*. Tomm and Maturana see knowing as starting with action. The first "growth" takes place when two persons working together (or a person observing his own action) use language to coordinate their actions. This *linguistic action* allows them, in a particular setting and under particular conditions, to act together. In Logo this might mean coordinating one's next direct mode step with what one has so far developed on the screen to accomplish some mathematical task. It might also mean a child realizing that a list of actions accomplishes a particular end. That is, not only does the child accomplish something mathematical on the screen, he or she is cognizant of the fact that a set of actions lead to it. Still, this set or list of actions is local to the setting. It involves what Hillel (chapter 1 in this volume) calls "planning in action" rather than "action planning."

Tomm and Maturana call the next level of growth *languaging*. It is making distinctions in one's linguistic actions. This is a critical kind of knowing because it makes things for a person. For a person or group working in Logo, this means the realization that a list of actions producing a particular result is no longer local. Such children can now see a procedure as a thing and not just as a convenient coordination of actions in direct mode. In a sense the image and the mathematical idea represented continue to exist for a child away from the computer environment.

The next level of growth involves making distinctions in one's languaging. For children in a Logo mathematics environment, such distinctions are still very much related to actions on the screen or to particular "physical" results. But now a group of children can see *features* in procedures *that are regular or that are properties*.

Just as languaging allows a person to create things that are "independent" of action by making distinctions among distinctions in *action*, Tomm and Maturana see the next distinctions as allowing a person to reach a level of *self-conscious reflection or thought*. This level involves making distinctions among distinctions in *languaging*. Hence they would argue that self-conscious thought has the power to be independent of things. In Logo mathematics this might mean that a child can produce a procedure with a new character. The procedure is not simply used to carry out a mathematical task or to represent one's idea on a screen. It might be thought of as a definition of such a task or mathematical idea.

Maturana and Tomm see several levels of knowing beyond self-conscious thought. The first of these they call *observing*. Persons make distinctions in their self-conscious thinking. In Logo this might enable a child to compare qualities of two procedures as ways to show a mathematical idea rather than simply comparing their execution. It also allows for use of Logo to develop mathematical ideas independent of their execution on the computers. The final two kinds of knowing represent distinctions in the levels of knowing presented above. The first kind of knowing is *explaining* and involves logically evaluating how the learning of others works. The last kind of knowing is called *free agency*. This means being able to choose an alternative sequence of thought or a different logic for one's work.

To apply this structure to Logo mathematical knowing of children or adults, it is critical to understand certain features of the model. First, although it describes eight kinds of knowing, these are recursive in that knowing at any one level entails making distinctions at a previous level. There is self-similarity in the process used at any level of knowing. Using the language of Kieren and Pirie (1992) one level *transcends* the previous ones (level stepping) in that this process of distinction is applied to qualitatively different kinds of Logo activity. This frees one from the specifics of the prior level but also leads to a kind of recursive blindness (Tomm 1989) to those actions at a lower level that bring forth the higher-level knowing. For example, having a simple procedure for a particular geometric figure allows one to invoke it and study it without the tedium of repeatedly making the list of direct-mode actions. But it might blind one to all of the characteristic moves that went into the original sequence of actions. Thus children who are asked to discuss how to make a rectangle using Logo may simply execute the procedure RECT :S1 :S2 (developed by the child) several times. A task of embedding a square in a rectangle may draw from these children a procedure using RECT :S1 :S2 and SQUARE :S as subprocedures. A challenge by the teacher to build the new procedure only using RECT might be necessary to have the children recover the basic actions and language used in building RECT. This "blindness" to lower-level action may have to be "lifted" in order for children to "see" mathematical relationships in this case between squares and rectangles. The virtue of Logo is that their previous thought/action is available in the contents of the procedure and can be reenacted in direct mode if necessary.

Figure 1 gave us a view of the elements of a structure for Logo mathematics. This was a static catalog of behaviors that has proved useful in identifying levels of Logo mathematics performance (Olson, Kieren, and Ludwig 1987). Any of the descriptions of recursion above allow us to consider Logo mathematics knowing as a dynamic whole. This is particularly true of the dynamic, embedded, leveled structure of knowing taken from the work of Maturana and Tomm. Suppose that one considers a child working with another child and a given set of primitives in Logo in direct mode. The children are faced with some mathematical task and are trying to show their knowledge of that mathematics by taking effective Logo action. Such action can entail just that—using Logo in direct mode to do something. The children will likely be aware of one another's work and locally coordinate their use of primitives to achieve a particular effect. They might go so far as to distinguish among actions by looking at a text screen *list* of such actions, which might for them constitute a solution to a mathematical problem. They might agree to use a particular list, perhaps now stored as a procedure under a name to represent or accomplish that particular mathematical action. It is difficult to call such a procedure a procedure, except nominally, but it does represent linguistic action in Logo. A group of children has distinguished a set of steps as constituting an action and has signaled this action to themselves or others in the learning context by saving this action as a procedure.

After seeing others do sequences of language/actions or make such lists, children now might move to a new level of effective Logo mathematics action. They can see procedures and their results as things, without first having executed the action sequence. They can *consensually coordinate a list of actions as a thing in itself*. For example, they can generate a simple procedure for some mathematical action. This would be *languaging* in Logo mathematics, and as Maturana and Varela (1980) suggest, it is this languaging that characterizes a *thing* in Logo mathematics. Of course such early generated procedures are not any more sophisticated than previous lists of actions, but now a child can contemplate a procedure *without* having to have or reenact the action. Ludwig (1986) gives testament *to the freedom of this new level*; she observed that persons working at the direct mode or list level cannot take a pre-planned Logo activity and successfully use it on the machine. The pre-planning was an act in itself; the execution at the machine was a new act. But at a procedure level, since a procedure is a thing in itself, one can sketch out a procedure and then use it. Of course such procedures are what Hillel (chapter 1 in this volume) calls simple, fixed procedures and may still involve long strings of standard or teacher-given Logo primitives. The mathematical analysis represented will have a visual character. Still, such procedures represent a first step in freeing one's mathematical thinking from direct action.

One important feature of Logo is that the procedure exists in two forms. It can be executed as a form of mathematical action (e.g., show a geometric transformation, show two proportional figures, give a solution to a particular level of the "handshake" problem). Through the edit mode it can be observed as a list. This seems critical for the next level of recursion. Now the child makes distinctions (coordinated with self or others) in procedures themselves. Because, as Noss and Hoyles (1987) pointed out, a procedure exists both as a process on the screen and a form or language set, such distinctions can be made on either the procedure or its result on the screen or by some combination of the two. It is this experience of distinguishing features of procedures that leads to and in fact constitutes the next level of effective actions, making what have been described above as *distinguished procedures*. What are the features of effective Logo mathematics action at this level? In trying to look at previous simple procedures and their results as things, children are now looking for features or properties. For example, procedures that generate particular examples of translations on the screen might be seen to have a part that generates the figure, a part that "produces" the motion, and a part that generates the figure in the transformed position. If given a task, or the opportunity to generate tasks where it is useful, a group of children might be prompted to write a procedure that replaces the parts of a previous simple procedure with a procedure that at least looks more general:

```
TO SHOW.TRANS.1
  FIGURE.1
  TRANS
  NEW.FIGURE.1
END
```

Ludwig (1986) in her study of twelve-year-olds noted that such procedures did not have a top-down structured character. But in writing them, children saw a procedure as being made up from other procedures and observed translations as having certain mathematical properties. Children were observed to talk about such properties as they constructed procedures to do geometric tasks. Thus procedures (and related mathematical ideas) changed from being simple things to things that themselves are made up of other identifiable things with properties. A procedure now has the character of a procedure of procedures, or a superprocedure.

Such thinking can also manifest itself in seeing replicates in a mathematical process or thing and in the use of replicates (REPEAT) in procedures. This use of REPEAT represents such replicative thinking, whereas previous uninformed use of REPEAT might just have been another primitive of action—it generated a complex or beautiful object but did not bring a thing or a subprocedure into existence.

Finally, a child might make distinctions among procedures that are many variations of a single procedure using different numerical values. This allows for the potential development of a family of objects or a generalized figure. In such a figure there are parameters (e.g., length, vertical move, and angle) and such properties manifest themselves as procedures that contain variables. The reader is alerted to the detailed examples of growth from simple fixed procedures to procedures that involve single variables or to composed procedures that involve more than one variable and use them in a coordinated way in subprocedures, as shown by Hillel (chapter 1 in this volume). Hillel highlights the fact that a child using variables in a procedure shows an awareness of features or properties in geometric objects and procedures that can vary, as well as an awareness of the relationship of variables to other aspects of the procedure. It should be noted that the more formal use of variables occurs in generalized procedures not directly oriented to action. In such procedures variables can be considered as algebraic entities rather than as parameters for specific physical properties. Such procedures are beyond the level of distinguished procedures.

The distinguished procedures and related mathematical properties still seem very related to screen action or results. To observe growth to another level of effective Logo mathematics action, we consider again the process-action/form-list complementarity observable in Logo mathematics. If one has used many Logo procedures, subprocedures, repeat clauses, and variables to describe mathematical properties metaphorically, one now can look at such procedures and become aware of *the idea of a procedure* as an act of one's self-conscious thought. Now when faced with a mathematical task, a child could envision this task *as a whole* with parts that correspond to properties and logical interrelationships, either in formal logical terms or in sequence. A child would think of creating a procedure to describe the mathematical object or process, and in the domain of the observer it would be seen as a *structured procedure*. This use of the Logo language is analogical in nature—it is independent from but testable in action. Children at this level appear aware of the definitional power of a procedure. In a study of eleven-year-olds a number of years ago, when Logo first became available on microcomputers, two boys realized (after several days play with a spiral-generating procedure) that if they wished to have the spiral family members spiraling inward instead of outward, they would have to make interrelated logical changes to the procedure. Thus they saw the procedure SPIRAL :ANGLE :SIDE :INC as a definition, and before ever physically making inward spirals, they realized that a new procedure with a different but related logic, INSPIRAL :ANGLE :SIDE :INC, would make a whole related class of such spirals. Another example of work at this level comes from two students in Ludwig's (1986) study. These two students wrote a general procedure for translation that used variables for the angle and distance and correctly coordinated the value of the :ANGLE variable with the orientation of the object and the image:

```
TO TRANS.2 :ANGLE :DISTANCE
  OBJECT
  TRANS :ANGLE :DISTANCE
  OBJECT
END

TO TRANS :ANGLE :DISTANCE
  RT :ANGLE
  FD :DISTANCE
  LT :ANGLE
END
```

These students also observed the invariance of the object under translation. Ludwig found that this pair was the only one to write any procedures with coordinated use of variables and in fact was the only one to write many procedures with subprocedures.

As inferred from Tomm (1989), this level, which features structured procedures, would have numerous recursive levels, much as one might envision a child looking at a piece of mathematics as a series of interrelated procedures. Further at this level the nature of a recursive object and particularly the nature of the recursive procedure in operation become usable. Because Logo is a fully recursive language, it can enable a student to study recursive mathematical objects such as fractals or view other mathematical ideas or problems (compound interest, various series, the "handshake" problem, etc.) in an explicitly recursive manner. However one views recursion in Logo, using recursion does go *beyond* the level of making distinctions in simple procedures. It represents self-conscious thought in two senses. For example, consider the "squiral" procedure below that when executed draws triangular, square, star . . . "spirals":

```
TO SQUIRAL :ANG :SIDE :INC
   IF :SIDE > 100 [STOP]
   FD :SIDE
   RT :ANGLE
   SQUIRAL :ANG :SIDE + :INC :INC
END
```

Children making such a procedure not only have to see that SQUIRAL is made up of repeated chunks (FD :SIDE RT :ANGLE) but must see these chunks as changing in a controlled way (:SIDE + :INC). Finally, even this simple tail-recursive procedure requires explicit logical relationships and not simply sequential, positional relationships among the chunks. Writing a recursive procedure requires that procedures be objects of thought for the writer. At the lower level of distinguished procedures, one can think of an action as made up of other distinguished actions and that these subactions can be coded in a procedure that uses subprocedures explicitly. With recursion a subaction must be a copy or "clone" of the action. If one is at the level of conscious thought about procedures or can write structured procedures, then one can envision a procedure calling itself or copies of itself. Thus both conceptually and linguistically even using tail recursion to represent mathematical ideas requires observing a procedure as an idea and not simply as a code for action. Obviously using embedded recursion requires even more sophisticated thinking at the level of observing features of procedures as ideas or of observing properties of structured procedures. It is interesting to note that Harvey (1987) shows these levels of "recursion" as distinct for instructional purposes as well.

   Of course a teacher can give a child recursive procedures to execute and use in reaching the level of having a procedure as an idea. This allows the children to observe mathematical objects that are complex, leveled phenomena and Logo mathematical language used in ways of which they themselves might not yet be capable independently. But a teacher should not mistake such use of recursion by a child for a high level of mathematical thinking or of Logo use (Vitale 1989).

It is beyond the scope of this chapter to detail Logo mathematics as a recursive structure beyond the level of self-conscious thought. Nevertheless, such levels exist in answering questions such as "What is true of all Logo procedures?" and "What is Logo's structure?" These levels of explanation are exemplified by the logical description of Logo that accompanied the original Apple Logo. However, practical applications of making distinctions on structured procedures (action at the level of "observing") exist as well. Procedures that make multiple and hence multileveled recursive calls are one illustration of such action. Such procedures enable a person to describe recursive, mathematical objects such as the von Koch curve. They also allow one to use the mathematical idea of a function to build an "artificial intelligence" such as a "blocks world" or a binary-tree intelligent tutor (Weston 1985). Finally, there have been numerous alternative "Logos" created by persons working at the *free agent level*. These systems are Logo-like but involve different physical, informative or logical structures. These creations, like the creation of noneuclidean geometry for mathematicians, provide new scenes of mathematical action for children.

It has been the purpose of the above discussion to characterize Logo mathematical knowing as a dynamic leveled phenomenon. For children it is apparently a fluid, nonlinear phenomenon characterized by using and making procedures of various kinds. But beneath this one can perceive a growing organic whole. This whole is characterized by self-similarity or symmetry across levels in that there is action/word complementarity at any level and in that any new level of effective action comes about through making distinctions in the lists or procedures and their consequences at a previous level. Level stepping or transcendence is clearly evident because the grounds for this process of making distinctions changes from *coordinated action* to *simple procedures*, then to *distinguished procedures*, and finally to *the idea of procedure*. This knowledge as a whole is seen also in the work of children at different levels so well described in the research cited at the outset of this chapter (Kieran, Hillel, and Gurtner 1987; Noss and Hoyles 1987; Ludwig 1986). Thus knowing in a Logo mathematics environment can be seen as a leveled, embedded, recursive phenomenon.

5 SOME APPLICATIONS

The view of Logo mathematics as a recursive phenomenon should have consequences for theory, research, and particularly for educational practice. A recursive view should be a useful tool. What follows are some ways in which one might

Table 1 Comparison of activities that could involve procedure

Categories	Proportion of episodes involving category		Fisher Z
	Group 1 (number of episodes = 27)	Group 2 (number of episodes = 22)	
Started as a procedure	0.93	0.55	3.10**
Successfully completed task	0.85	0.82	0.28
Discussed properties	0.33	0.18	1.19
Trial-and-error construction	0.30	0.68	2.65**
Assistance needed	0.09	0.32	2.03*
Debugging done visually error by error	0.52	0.68	1.13

Note: *significant at 0.05 level; **significant at 0.005 level.

use or apply this view in analyzing or creating Logo mathematics environments. In Ludwig's (1986) research cited above, forty-five children studied geometry using specially designed primitives and course materials working in pairs at the computer for at least twenty hours spread over six weeks. Prior to this Logo geometry study these children worked on Logo, wrote procedures, and were exposed to most features of Logo through a once-a-week, one-hour Logo session over six months. Five pairs in the geometry study had their screen work recorded. Audio records of the pair interactions were kept as well. Over one hundred working-session tapes were analyzed in detail for markers of growth in this environment. As part of her study, Ludwig contrasted the records of pairs of students from group 1, who appeared to be the most sophisticated mathematically and in their use of Logo, with those from group 2. It should be noted that all five pairs, as well as the other thirty-five children in the study, learned geometry as measured by post-test and long-term retention tests not related to Logo geometry. Further they all made progress toward more sophistication in Logo, although the children in group 1 were the only ones to write with any level of consistency what have been typified as distinguished procedures and were the only ones to produce a structured procedure.

There were predictable differences between groups 1 and 2 (see table 1). Group 1's children might be firmly classified as being at the level of making distinguished procedures as a means of "describing" geometry. They were procedurally oriented from the beginning of the twenty-two lessons on geometry and continued to use procedures more than the children of group 2. They also made much less use of trial-and-error construction than did the children of group 2, and this was usually done by executing a piece of a procedure at a time. For group 2 trial and error, especially at the beginning of the set of geometry lessons, involved direct-mode, "clear-screen-and-start-over" activity. In its working styles group 1 was more independent in its approach than group 2, particularly in the amount of help and suggested activities from the teacher.

Since group 1 saw geometry in terms of procedures, the geometric objects (in this case transformations) were things in their own right; group 1 could make distinctions in screen displays and write procedures to reflect them. Actual study of the video and audio tapes of the Logo geometry work of group 1 suggests that the children were making distinctions among simple procedures as well. For example, they constructed procedures with subprocedures and used variables in a simple way. They constructed one structured procedure described previously. Perhaps it is a criticism of this Logo mathematics environment, and potentially of Logo mathematics environments, that these children did not see the "need" to do this consistently and were content to work on other transformations by writing simple procedures that did not always reflect distinguished mathematical properties. This might have been a critical place for teacher "nudging." As suggested by Hillel (chapter 1 in this volume), students have to see the utility in using more sophisticated Logo levels and more sophisticated and general mathematical ideas. The teacher can stimulate higher-level behavior by posing tasks that "need it" and by having students reflect on previously constructed procedures.

The children in group 1 were making distinctions among procedures and could see at least some procedures in terms of chunks. This might indicate that they saw some connections between properties of transformations. They did articulate these properties more than did those of group 2, but not significantly so. Again it might be that the geometric primitives and Logo itself prompted group 1 to focus on mathematics as coordination of language and action rather than on mathematics as properties expressed in language. These children may have been making what Hoyles and Noss call *discriminations* in actions but not making the generalizations on those discriminations. It should be noted that both groups (and in fact all children in the study) completed most of the geometric tasks successfully, at least at a visual level. Logo enabled geometric performance by the children (and a high level of achievement as measured by non-Logo-related geometry tests) at different levels or in different ways. Viewed as a complex whole, one might say that the capability of doing the geometry was embedded at each of the levels reached by the children in this Logo geometry environment, another kind of level self-similarity.

From the point of view of a recursive analysis, it is interesting to note that in both groups most debugging was visual and entailed direct-mode activity. It would seem that when stuck, both groups dropped to lower-level activity. Was this direct-mode activity really lowlevel? It would seem that the return to direct-mode activity after previous work on the same or related tasks at procedure or distinguished-procedure levels *is not the same as initial direct-mode* experience. This was particularly true for group 1; the children in that group used direct-mode debugging to create "test pieces" for use in a repaired procedure. For example, after constructing an initial version of TRANS.2 described above and finding that the orientation of the image was not right, they returned to direct mode and made several trials at that level *before* rewriting the procedure using information and language sequences in direct mode. It would seem that this and other direct-mode or visual debugging moves of group 1 were recursive *in the sense of folding back in order to reconstruct part of or to make an extension of a Logo mathematical idea.* This new direct-mode experience is now based on, and is in fact part of, procedural-level Logo mathematical thought. Such direct-mode activity is informed by and uses language sequences similar to those in distinguished procedures. Thus a recursive view of knowing allows us to cast a different light on changes in level within a person's Logo mathematics performance. It allows a researcher or a teacher to contrast *the recursive folding back to move ahead* in which a child not only tests a move at direct-mode level but returns the corresponding word to a higher-level procedural activity, with a *dropping back to direct-mode activity with no return.* For example, group 2 devised a task that used mirror images. These children wrote a simple procedure that failed. They then returned to direct mode. After several attempts they got the screen image they wanted and then went on to other tasks. They did not "return" the ideas or language they generated to the level of writing a procedure. They were satisfied with the specific, local action result. It might be said that a child who has done this is still at the level of linguistic action with respect to a particular Logo mathematical idea. The idea is not yet a thing for a child. On the other hand, folding back to move ahead suggests that a child who does so is making a distinction in a Logo mathematical idea held at a procedural level or perhaps even at the level of conscious, independent thought. It is a virtue of Logo mathematics that one always has in one's repertoire direct-mode linguistic actions that one can "call" or fold back to in building more linguistically sophisticated and generalized mathematical ideas.

What lessons does this recursive view of Logo mathematics have for teachers in such situations? Tomm (1989) suggests that there are positive and negative ways of "going together in language." This phrase seems highly pertinent to student-teacher relationships in Logo mathematics. Since Logo mathematics takes place in an environment where student and teacher have some mathematical action to talk about and the potential for a coordinated use of language, it is an environment that can lead to growth. But since higher-level mathematical action is a recursion on lower-level effective action, the teacher should not think of giving students higher-level attainment. As seen in much Logo research, when a teacher simply gives a student a higher-level approach, the student might be able to mimic it in the teacher's presence. But since such action is only linguistic action between student and teacher, it does not represent or create a new process or object *for the student*. Thus, when the teacher leaves, the process or object does not exist for the student, or does so only as a primitive for action. Typically such a child appears to ignore what the teacher has done, or the child might make the procedure and related mathematics his or her own through trials, making distinctions based on such trials.

The movement from level to level, from preprocedural to procedural activity or from procedural to structural Logo mathematics activity requires energy. Since new levels arise from distinctions in actions at lower levels, a teacher must allow for sufficient activities at any level. The students may need to have significant and successful direct-mode activity; the students may write many simple procedures before making real property distinctions. But through suggestions of "next activities," the teacher can point to higher-level Logo mathematics behavior. For example, this may mean suggesting building a geometric object that contains a large number of different-size objects of a particular type in order to prompt for variables. One could also have students make hard-copy displays that contain all the steps in procedures used to accomplish a task. Taking ten such displays and having children study them might provoke a focus on subpatterns of commands (or subpatterns in mathematical objects or processes). The key point is that in maintaining a higher-level point of view, the teacher *stands with the child* in what he or she is doing and simply points to alternatives.

Noss and Hoyles (1987) have used the term "nudge" to suggest ways in which teachers might move students to higher levels of effective action in Logo mathematics. If one sees such action as containing within it "copies" of that action at lower levels, then a child who has been given evidence of higher-level behavior may later choose to stay at a related lower level of effective action. For that child a nudge may mean describing projects in a way that the higher-level approach will prove more effective. Thus a child might be challenged to write a procedure as a driver procedure (move to structural procedural level), might be challenged to generate a sequence before going to the computer (move to procedural level), or, as in Kieran, Hillel, and Gurtner (1987), might be introduced to ways of focusing on properties or structures of properties central to the resolution of a task (move to distinguished procedural level). The teacher might nudge students by reviewing a body of previous related work or procedures with students that have made them. The intent of this review is not to see "how we did it before" but to allow students to see language and mathematical patterns in procedures and output.

6   CONCLUDING REMARKS

Logo mathematics environments and student actions within them have been described as complex, leveled phenomena. As such, it was argued that recursion would be a useful way to look at Logo mathematics. Tomm and Maturana's theory of recursive levels of knowing was then applied to Logo mathematics. It was argued that each level contains the same basic complementarity of language and action, form and process, and that the act of distinction on prior levels creates new levels of effective behavior. Thus there is symmetry across levels of effective Logo mathematics actions. Children show what they know about mathematics but at differing levels that reflect distinctions made on direct-mode linguistic action, on simple procedures themselves, on distinguished procedures that use variables and subprocedures but flow from action in some way, and, finally, on structured procedures or procedures as reflections of more formal thought. Thus the Maturana-Tomm definition of recursion is at least sufficient for the Vitale definition of recursion involving self-similarity and level stepping. Since children often drop back to reconstruct knowledge recursively at a higher level, one can see that the turning-back-on-itself notion of recursion also applies in Logo mathematical thinking and knowing.

Viewing Logo mathematics as a constructive, personal phenomenon of a recursive nature has consequences for our theories of instruction, as well as how we as teachers view and sponsor growth in a Logo mathematics environment.

This view further highlights *procedures as the objects* (and object generators) of *Logo mathematics* and *structured procedures as the essence of Logo mathematics thought*. In this view structured procedures represent more formal mathematical thinking, which derives from making distinctions among distinguished procedures reflecting mathematical properties of a less formal nature. These distinguished procedures derive from distinctions made on simple procedures that help the child create mathematical objects, and they represent distinctions made on direct-mode activities. Thus both the objects and the thinking in Logo mathematics can be linked back to a level of actions. This means that persons working in a Logo mathematical environment at any level have available ways of knowing at less sophisticated, more action-oriented levels, which they can "call" in building up or extending higher-order ideas. Because of this Logo mathematical relationships constructed by children have a built-in validation mechanism and hence represent sound knowledge. Finally, since Logo environments involve interaction with others and self, there is a continuing opportunity for growth and transcendence.

ACKNOWLEDGMENT

Ideas on transcendence, complementarity, and folding back in this chapter come from lively and challenging discussions with Susan Pirie.

REFERENCES

Bohm, D., and F. D. Peat. 1987. *Science, Order and Creativity*. New York: Bantam.

Davis, P., and R. Hersh. 1986. *Descartes' Dream*. San Diego, CA: Harcourt Brace Jovanovich

Frye, N. 1982. *The Great Code*. San Diego, CA: Academic Press.

Harvey, B. 1987. *Computer Science Logo Style*. Vol. 1: *Intermediate Programming*. Cambridge: MIT Press.

Hoffer, A. 1983. van Hiele-based research. In R. Lesh and M. Landau (eds.), *Acquisition of Mathematics Concepts and Processes*. San Diego, CA: Academic Press.

Hoyles, C., and Noss, R. 1989. The computer as a catalyst in children's proportion strategies. *Journal of Mathematical Behaviour* 8: 53–75.

Kieran, C., J. Hillel, and J. -L. Gurtner. 1987. Qualitative strategies in logo centering tasks. In J. Hillel (ed.), *Proceedings of the Third International Conference for Logo and Mathematics Education*. Montreal: Concordia University, pp. 126–138.

Kieren, T. 1987. Levels, Logo, language and intuitive mathematical knowledge. In J. Hillel (ed.), *Proceedings of the Third International Conference for Logo and Mathematics Education*. Montreal: Concordia University, pp. 1–11.

Kieren, T., and S. Pirie. 1992. Recursion and the mathematical experience. In L. Steffe (ed.), *The Epistemology of the Mathematical Experience*. New York: Springer-Verlag Psychology Series.

Ludwig, S. 1986. Indicators of growth within a Logo/motion geometry curriculum environment. Masters thesis. Edmonton: University of Alberta.

Maturana, H., and F. Varela. 1980. *Autopoiesis and Cognition*. Vol 42. Boston University Philosophy of Science Series. Dordrecht: Reidel.

Noss, R., and C. Hoyles. 1987. Structuring the mathematical environment: The dialectic of process and content. In J. Hillel (ed.), *Proceedings of the Third International Conference for Logo and Mathematics Education*. Montreal: Concordia University, pp. 7–39.

Olive, J. 1986. The collection and analysis of qualitative data in a Logo learning environment using dribble files. In G. Lappan and G. Evan (eds.), *Proceedings of the Fifth Annual meeting of PME-NA*. East Lansing: Michigan State University, 315 pp.

Papert, S. 1980. *Mindstorms*. New York: Basic Books.

Tomm, K. 1989 Consciousness and intentionality in the work of Humberto Maturana. Presented before the Faculty of Education, University of Alberta.

Vitale, B. 1989. Elusive recursion: A trip in a recursive land. *New Ideas in Psychology* 7(3): 253–276.

Weston, D. 1985. *The Second Logo Book*. Glenview, IL: Scott Foresman.

Between Logo and Mathematics: A Road of Tunnels and Bridges

9

Jean-Luc Gurtner

1 INTRODUCTION

It has become a common metaphor in education to use the term *bridges* for the connections one tries to build for students (or would like students to build for themselves) between two different domains, two different topics inside a same domain, or different aspects of the "school world" and everyday life. This metaphor has already been applied to the connections between Logo and mathematics (Delclos, Littlefield, and Bransford 1984; Hoyles and Sutherland 1989; Leron 1982) and used to present one of the strengths of LEGO-Logo (Weir, chapter 6 in this volume). For someone traveling along a river bank, a bridge allows for crossing onto the other bank and for the possibility of a more comfortable journey. Similarly the existence of bridges between Logo and mathematics offers the same kind of opportunities. So, for example, switching to a geometrical approach might provide quick help in finding the size of a particular angle in a Logo drawing, while going back to a more perceptual approach might help in finding an approximate angle that would have been too difficult to calculate analytically.

However, the type of connections generally expected, and very seldom observed, between Logo practice and mathematics is *transfer*. In this perspective it is suggested that a rather long period of Logo practice (one that is rich in reflection) is necessary before transfer to mathematics can occur (Salomon and Perkins 1987). Transfer is not as obvious in the other direction, from mathematics to Logo. Research on the kind of mathematics students use (or don't use) in their Logo work shows that nonmathematical strategies are often chosen over mathematical strategies in determining turtle turns or the segment sizes of a figure, even when the correct mathematical relations have already been acknowledged (Hillel, Gurtner, and Kieran 1988). In contradistinction to the notion of transfer, the connections between Logo and mathematics, which may be evident to us, are often not so clear to students. The bridge metaphor, however, allows and even encourages connections to be stated as early as possible between the two domains. In using the bridge conception of how to connect Logo and mathematics, one must take appropriate care in selecting the stones out of which the bridges are to be built, as I will try to show here.

Extending the travel metaphor, I would like to suggest that some of the characteristics of Logo situations may even be seen as representing tunnels where bridges should have been built. Tunnels, at least in my country, are often built to allow a traveler to stay on the same bank of a river despite the difficult terrain. Nevertheless, although using a tunnel renders easy what would have otherwise been a difficult journey, it causes a temporary break of contact with external reality and with the charming landscape on both sides of the river. Thus, it is argued, students often miss interesting perspectives on mathematics and geometry while advancing along their Logo tracks. Tunnels of course are not bad things for the traveler, since they render a road more comfortable. The presence of a tunnel sometimes even attracts people to places that they would never have come to otherwise. In the same way working with Logo enables children to visit certain mathematically rich areas that they would not have ordinarily approached (Papert 1980). My concern is that in maintaining an easy progression on the Logo bank, some features of Logo designed to help students make their way through the mathematically difficult areas might also render them less likely to pass over to the mathematical bank.

In this chapter I will first try to show how some of the current implementations of Logo in relation to mathematics[1] are partly responsible for the lack of connection between mathematics and Logo, and vice versa, as evidenced in both students' Logo work and classroom mathematics. I will then try to examine how the connections between these two domains can be made more obvious for students.

2 THE LOGO TUNNELS

Detecting the Logo Tunnels

Among the characteristics of Logo situations that may serve as tunnels, that hide interesting connections between Logo and mathematics from the students, I place the "easy task" illusion often present in classroom tasks, the constant

---

1. In this chapter I will ignore evident variations due to the specifics of each Logo class, such as the student-teacher ratio, the structure and content of the lessons, or the particularities of the chosen dialect of Logo.

availability of immediate feedback, differences in formalism, and the popular "do-math-without-noticing-it" philosophy relating to the teaching of Logo.

The "Easy Task" Illusion

Teacher-directed classroom tasks lead to mastery of Logo (Delclos et al. 1984), broaden the scope of mathematical ideas used by students (Hoyles and Sutherland 1989), and elicit more curiosity and more productive discussion among students than do students' individual projects (Lemerise, chapter 7 in this volume). Classroom tasks often consist of figures with a small number of lines and angles organized into a geometric pattern (Hillel and Kieran 1987; Noss and Hoyles 1987). As "drawings," and as compared with the kind of pictures a child would like to be able to produce on the computer screen, such mathematically interesting tasks look simplistic. On the other hand, mathematical problems like those students are used to dealing with in mathematics class are generally seen as very difficult. Because of this discrepancy students tend to minimize the amount of mental effort that they should invest when addressing easy-looking Logo tasks.[2] This attitude toward Logo tasks further affects students' interpretation of their difficulties in the solution process. Unexpected problems in an easy-looking task tend to be seen as local execution difficulties (Gurtner 1987) rather than as a consequence of a lack of analysis of the geometrical properties of the target figure.

Immediate Feedback

Another important and often acclaimed feature of Logo is its immediate graphic feedback. Being able to see right away on the screen the effect of a modification in the code on the behavior of a language is a powerful, and often useful, feature of a highly interactive program like Logo. This advantage can, however, sometimes turn into a disadvantage. For instance, Hillel, Gurtner, and Kieran (1988) show how the availability of feedback can sometimes lead a student to abandon progressively all the mathematical relations he or she had correctly detected in a

---

2. This apparent easy task phenomenon is even trickier for those who try to use Logo to teach general problem-solving techniques. Easy-looking tasks—especially when they are part of the students' everyday real or fantasy life, like letters, triangles, houses, or castles—also look familiar. A well-known result of early information processing studies states that when facing familiar situations, people tend to rely on their domain-specific knowledge, while they tend to use more general methods in unfamiliar situations (Chase and Simon 1973). Drawing on the apparent ease of Logo to teach general problem-solving techniques may just be a psychological contradiction.

figure, while maintaining a false impression of a progressive approach to the solution. Hillel, Kieran, and Gurtner (1989) also show that the presence on the screen of an acceptable approximation to the target figure often curtails any real verification phase at the end of the work. In Logo the presentation of both the problem and the result often takes the same form—a computer printout of the target picture. Verification of the correctness of one's solution is reduced to a perceptual matching activity. Immediate feedback makes the checking of one's final result against the data—such an important but problematic objective of teaching problem solving in mathematics—appear an unnecessary task to perform at the end of the work and may leave students with the false impression that correct solutions simply "look right" that way.

Moreover availability of immediate feedback ensures that a trial-and-error approach remains attractive to the student. Such an approach may be appropriate at certain stages during the learning process (Hoyles and Sutherland 1989), but its simplicity of use, together with its economy in terms of geometrical reflection, can prevent the adoption of a more mathematically oriented approach. In direct mode the advantage of exclusively using a trial-and-error approach is counterbalanced by the tedium of multiple rewriting of the instructions. In the programming mode modification of programs becomes a less tiresome activity, once the basic editor commands are mastered. Paradoxically immediate feedback may therefore have an even more negative effect in programming than in direct mode. This paradox should not, however, lead to the conclusion that students should be discouraged from working in a programming mode. Procedures offer many benefits for students as well for teachers.

Differences in Formalism

Between the Logo and the mathematical approaches there are differences as well as similarities. Similarities can be used to form bridges. Differences can inspire creative attempts at synthesis. Consider, for example, differences due to underlying geometries. One must deal with this problem when trying to make the turtle draw a triangle; at a more sophisticated level a child encounters it when he or she tries to draw a circle. Turtle and coordinate geometries complement each other. A child's conception of a circle or an angle developed from one perspective is enriched by having to deal with it from another perspective. Other differences that do not have such potential for enrichment may function more like tunnels, concealing similarities and connections from students. Differences in formalism, I suggest, are of this latter kind.[3] As an example, note that while $y = 3x$ is used in functions to stress a relation between x and y, which stays true for any value of x or y, $:y = 3 * :x$ only appears in Logo for conditionals and is false for all but one value of x or y. Considering the difficulties children are known to have in giving appropriate meaning to the equal sign in algebra (Kieran 1984), the help Logo brings to the understanding of variables (Hillel 1984; Noss 1986; Sutherland 1987) is highly undermined by the ambiguity it raises at the level of relations.

The Do-Math-without-Noticing-It Philosophy of Logo

The early idea that Logo could be a good way to provide fun with mathematics to students whose poor results are due to a classroom-developed aversion to math (Papert 1980) has led the Logo community to avoid making explicit to students the mathematical objectives underlying Logo tasks. Of course connections are more likely to be made with a topic if students know what to expect in the course of their work. Revealing to students what they are really doing does not necessarily lower their motivation for the activity (consider Mr. Jourdain's happiness when Molière's well-known character learned that he was effectively using prose each time he spoke). This philosophy is no longer adequate now that research has shown that Logo is most effective when introduced in the early school grades at the same time as the teaching of mathematics is begun (Clements 1986, 1987; Lehrer and Randle 1987; Rieber 1987).

Opening Windows in the Logo Tunnels

Just as it would be silly to block the entrance of a tunnel on the road simply because it prevents the traveler from seeing part of the landscape, it would be equally wrong to deny students access to these Logo tunnels. What is needed is to try to put windows in the tunnels so that nobody going through them will be able to resist looking out! Here are three suggestions:

First, try to overcome the easy task illusion and elicit a more mindful and mathematically oriented attitude while working in Logo by embedding mathe-

---

3. Differences in formalism clearly have the "disconnecting" function of tunnels. They may not share their other function of making the travel locally easier on the Logo bank of the river because the Logo formalism may not always be easier to understand than the mathematical one. On the other hand, most nonmathematical formalisms seen in Logo may be more consistent with its globally programminglike syntax. This consistency certainly makes, at a more general level, the learning of Logo more comfortable.

matically interesting problems into tasks that *look* more challenging. The gain in apparent complexity of the tasks should not, however, be at the cost of requiring long sequences of mathematically uninteresting code nor of superimposing various mathematical topics on top of each other. Ideal tasks should provide so-called variations around a theme that allow the student to consolidate and generalize his or her earlier discoveries. In addition there should be several tasks that have the same basic pattern or that are related to the same geometry problem. The Logo productions of the tasks should be delayed until the common pattern has been extracted by the students and a general solution approach verbally described. Then more meaningful mathematical activity can be presented, with student time and effort spent in extracting the pattern for the whole set of tasks rather than in producing the code for each figure sequentially.

Second, allow the use of a trial-and-error approach when appropriate but discourage the use of exclusively visual strategies (Hillel and Kieran 1987) when a more reflective mathematical approach is within the reach of the student. A sensible option would seem to be to provide the teacher with the possibility of setting the immediate feedback on or off on the graphic screen without turning off the editor screen. Ultimately this possibility should be built into a still-to-be-designed intelligent Logo tutor.

Third, make the checking of the result against the data more active and meaningful by presenting tasks in ways other than the "classic" computer print-out. Written descriptions of the figure being constructed, for instance, could provoke more meaningful activities relating to understanding the problem and verifying the solution.

As an example of a way to open a window in the "formalism difference" tunnel, we are currently working on a microworld, called *EquaLogo*, in which the student can use algebraic notation to define a size or angle relation (Gurtner 1988). In this microworld the student receives a computer printout of the target figure with letters labeling each of its segments and angles and a computer print-out of the general procedure which has as many inputs as letters appearing on the printout. Ultimately the student's task is to find an appropriate value for each input. These values can either be typed in by the student when calling the procedure, or they can be supplemented by the program on the basis of equations specified by the student according to the geometrical relations he or she has noticed in the figure. For instance, in using the printout shown in figure 1 and the corresponding program, the student would try to find the appropriate

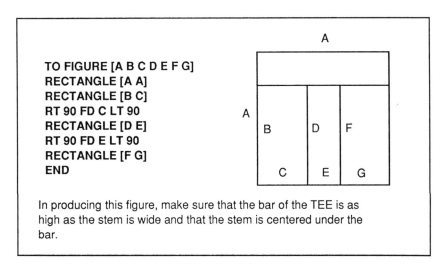

```
TO FIGURE [A B C D E F G]
RECTANGLE [A A]
RECTANGLE [B C]
RT 90 FD C LT 90
RECTANGLE [D E]
RT 90 FD E LT 90
RECTANGLE [F G]
END
```

In producing this figure, make sure that the bar of the TEE is as high as the stem is wide and that the stem is centered under the bar.

Figure 1 Example of task with the figure to draw and the corresponding program given to the student using EquaLogo

value for each of the inputs or reduce the number of inputs by equating one of the quantities to one or more of the others.

Figure 2 illustrates two main additional options that this microworld offers to students, besides the two classical direct and programming modes. By typing S, the student enters a substitution-mode dialogue where he or she can formulate relations among quantities in a format compatible with the description of functions learned in mathematics class. Pressing T allows the testing of the simplified procedure for which the unequated variables remain to be specified. Additional facilities allow the student to retrieve all the successive equations made so far for a given input or to display simultaneously all the currently specified relations. The command BACKTO <input> unbinds a variable, allowing the substitution process eventually to adopt a different direction.

Although equations can be edited and revised at any time, the possibility of using mathematical operation symbols can also help counteract the negative effect of the screen feedback on mathematical verification described earlier. The main benefit expected from this feature is that it makes the connection between Logo and algebra look clearer and more applicable to the student. Of course the do-math-without-noticing-it philosophy of Logo can be abandoned in favor of techniques that *explicitly* present looking for connections between Logo and mathematics as an objective of a task.

```
THE CURRENT FORM OF THE PROGRAM IS:
FIGURE [A B C D E F G]
? S
WHAT SUBSTITUTION WOULD YOU LIKE TO DO?
? A=C+E+G
THE CURRENT FORM OF THE PROGRAM IS:
FIGURE [B C D E F G]
? T
TO TEST IT TYPE IN THE NAME OF THE PROGRAM AND
YOUR VALUES FOR [B C D E F G]
? FIGURE   40 20 40 10 40 20
```

Figure 2 Excerpt of screen dialogue in EquaLogo. Lines starting with a ? are the pupil's entries; the others come from the program

3   BUILDING BRIDGES BETWEEN LOGO AND MATHEMATICS

As I have noted at the beginning of this chapter, mere practice of Logo is often not enough to lead students to connect Logo with their classroom mathematics. Help can be provided at different levels to render the construction of bridges between these two domains.

How to Help Students Build Bridges between Logo and Mathematics

Task Selection

To increase students' facility in making connections between Logo and mathematics, the tasks presented should be structured and focused on a particular mathematical topic. With structured tasks students' work can be directed toward areas that a teacher deems appropriate and relatively easy for the construction of bridges. However, to prevent students from entering the easy task illusion tunnel (mentioned earlier) instead of building a bridge, careful attention should be given to the design of each task's difficulty so that its mathematical aspect is not reduced.

Microworlds

Microworlds designed to help students bridge Logo and mathematics should focus student involvement in mathematical concepts (see Edwards, chapter 5 in this volume) or offer problem-solving tools similar to those used in geometry or other mathematics classes (Côté and Kayler 1987; Hillel 1988; Kynigos 1986).

Verbal Interventions

When a student is facing a problem that might best be solved mathematically, the teacher could intervene to orient the student toward the mathematical solution. Likewise the connection between Logo and mathematics might be introduced in the mathematics class when a new concept is being taught. Verbal interventions at a point when students are experiencing difficulties in one domain can provide a bridge that directs them toward the other domain and help students make the intended connection. What is described here is not a built-in necessary connection between two disciplines, rather a way of offering another perspective on the same problem, two viewpoints across a river.

Explicit teaching

A final way of helping students build bridges would be to instill in them an attitude of searching continually for possible connections, based on their knowing that the disciplines are similar. They would not only be taught the strategy of systematically looking for connections but also how to make these connections.

Mathematics educators interested in Logo have frequently used the first three techniques with some success. The fourth has rarely been considered in the context of Logo and mathematics. It is, however, important in other activities such as memorizing, reading, writing, and even learning mathematics. Various programs have been designed in each of these areas to teach students to look actively and systematically for connections as a powerful way to improve both comprehension and performance. Following a brief presentation of these programs and their results, we will try to draw out characteristics that contribute to their success. Finally, we will try to envision what Logo classes might be like if given these characteristics.

How to Teach Students to Look Systematically for Connections and to Build Bridges: Examples of Successful Programs in Other Domains

In Memory

Lines of prose are better remembered when they are accompanied by so-called elaborations aimed at making sense of the sentences. Pressley et al. (1987) have shown that when subjects are asked to make their own elaborations, they remember more sentences than when similar elaborations are made by the experimenter. Both the more active verbal involvement in the situation and the relation of sentences to chosen relevant elaborations are factors in the memorization process.

In Reading

Reading comprehension derives from connections one makes in learning to give meaning to a text just read by linking it to one's own knowledge about the subject. Different kinds of programs have been used to teach how to make connections that improve one's reading comprehension skills. For example, Davey and McBride (1986) showed that students who practice asking questions about the text just read understand it better than if they simply answer similar questions about it. Even better results were achieved when the students were taught how to generate good questions. The two main features of their teaching program were learning to "link information in one part of the passage with information in another part of the passage" (p. 258) and learning to use a self-evaluation checklist, addressing metacognitive questions like "How well did I identify important information?" "How well did I link information together?" or "Did I use good signal words?" With only five sessions of such training, sixth-grade students asked better questions, understood more accurately the texts they read, and demonstrated greater awareness of how well they had mastered the passages.

The so-called cloze strategy has been another successful technique used to improve reading comprehension (Dewitz, Carr, and Patberg 1987). It is also based on learning to link and to monitor one's understanding. The cloze strategy's aim is to teach students how to integrate the new information presented in a text with their prior knowledge. Students first learn to supply information blanked out of short texts by using contextual information and their own general knowledge. They are then taught to search intact texts in a similar manner to find the answers to inferential questions asked by the teacher at the end of the study. Both the validity of the answers and the way they were found are discussed before the entire class. The students also learn to use a self-monitoring checklist, to test their answers and to point out and evaluate the clues they used to formulate them. The teaching of this strategy to fifth-grade students brought gains in reading comprehension superior even to that obtained by students who were given (and trained to use) a chart presenting the structural organization of the information in the text they had to understand.

Salomon's (1988) computer-based "reading aid," designed to improve comprehension of text read on a screen, also incorporates metacognitive questions appearing in a separate screen window along with the text to be read. Examples of such questions are: "What kind of image have I created from the text?" "What thoughts occur to me on the basis of the title?" "What do I understand from the text so far?" Seventh-graders taught to answer such metacognitive questions showed even greater improvements in comprehension than did students trained to answer content-specific questions while reading. Practice of reading under metacognitive guidance even led to better writing.

Perhaps the most dramatic improvements in reading comprehension were obtained by Palincsar and Brown (1984) with their so-called reciprocal teaching technique. Based on the scaffolding model defined by Wood, Bruner, and Ross (1979), this technique involves modeling for the students four skills that expert readers use to make sense of text and coaching them on how to use them; these are (1) asking questions, (2) summarizing, (3) making predictions, and (4) looking for clarifications. The technique derives its name from another pedagogically interesting idea, the turn-taking of roles. Modeling and evaluation is not only done by the teacher, but each pupil gets his or her turn to practice or monitor the other pupils' use of the four skills mentioned above, as well as the general progression of the work undertaken by his or her group.

In Writing

Scardamalia, Bereiter, and Steinbach's program (1984) aims at improving students' writing skills by training them to adopt techniques used by skilled writers. Building on the observation that good writers don't write only to say something but also to be understood by their readers, Scardamalia, Bereiter, and Steinbach trained their students to think about the readability of their writing, that is, to connect the activity of writing with that of reading. To do so, they also taught the students to take advantage, while writing, of a preorganized list of self-questioning cues, prompting them to analyze and improve the structure and the understandability of their production. As a result of this training, the students made more reflective statements during the elaboration process and, in the final text, made more efforts to communicate to the reader as well as possible the field's interest or actual controversies within it.

In Mathematics

Learning how to make connections between one's knowledge and activity is often related in mathematics to the idea of learning to transfer, and more specifically to the question of the transferability of problem-solving skills. From this perspective the teaching of general processes along with (and sometimes over) that of domain-specific knowledge is recommended (Hayes 1981).

Logo also is sometimes presented as one possible way to foster general problem-solving skills and to promote higher thinking abilities. However, expert-novice comparisons in problem-solving strategies, as well as a lack of transfer in attempts to teach problem-solving techniques at an abstract and very general level, suggest the importance of knowledge organization and representation in specific domains. These have led to a questioning of the effectiveness of the teaching of general problem-solving techniques (Glaser 1984). Evaluations of Logo as a problem-solving and general thinking enhancer also suffered from lack of transfer (Horan 1985; Pea and Kurland 1984; Retschitzki 1987).[4]

In contrast to the study of memorizing, reading, or writing, where explicit teaching is given on how and why to make connections, how and why and what to transfer is never explicitly part of teaching programs. Bridges are expected, but their construction is never facilitated. In Pea and Kurland's unsuccessful study on the transfer of planning from Logo, for example, no mention nor demonstration of the utility of planning outside of the Logo activity is provided before the transfer task is given. On the other hand, the use of techniques similar to those seen, for instance, in successful reading programs can also lead to improvements in mathematics.

The example of the West Virginia Department of Education's mathematical problem-solving program is cited by Charles and Lester (1984) for its complete process-oriented instructional program which includes not only instructional materials and a teaching strategy for problem solving but also a set of guidelines for organizing the classroom. Use of classroom discussions to prepare, organize,

---

4. Some significant improvements due to Logo have been obtained in teaching problem-solving skills to first-graders (Lehrer and Randle 1987) and second-graders (Rieber 1987). However, in general, the poor transfer of problem-solving skills should not be read as an indication that learning to make connections is not possible through Logo. Lehrer, Guckenberg, and Lee (1988) recently showed that improvements in learning to integrate new with old information (Flavell, Green, and Flavell 1985), and other metacognitive skills such as comprehension monitoring (Markman 1981), which is often seen as an important effect of Logo (Clements 1986; Lehrer and Randle 1987; Miller and Emihovich 1986), do not appear when Logo is used to teach general problem- solving and planning strategies but do indeed result from the work done on mathematics or geometry topics. This result powerfully demonstrates that general thinking skills (e..g., planning) and metacognitive skills (sometimes also called critical thinking skills; Greeno 1989) should not be confused.

and reflect on the problem-solving process and use of a so-called problem-solving guide (or checklist) that presents strategies based on Pólya's (1957) work, such as those used by mathematicians, are its key features. Pre- and post-tests, as well as two intermediate tests, are given to evaluate the program on the dimensions of understanding the problem, planning the solution, and getting the correct result. The program appears to have successfully developed students' understanding and planning skills.

In addition to the reading and writing programs of Palincsar and Brown (1984) and Scardamalia, Bereiter, and Steinbach (1984), there is Schoenfeld's (1985) work on how to solve problems by modeling the behavior of advanced mathematical problem-solvers. He points out how their approach differs from the way solutions are usually presented in mathematics textbooks. Learning how to use heuristics and how to monitor the steps of a solution are the objectives of the program. Classroom discussion is conducted to analyze the steps and the key points of each solution and to observe the limitations and generalizations of both the result and the approach used to obtain it.

Another recent tendency in mathematics education is to pay more attention to the kind of meanings pupils confer on their mathematical knowledge. Special attention is given to teaching the students how to link what they are currently doing in the mathematics classroom to what they had studied earlier in the class, and to what they do in other school disciplines or even to non-school-related activities. The teaching is no longer oriented exclusively toward problem solving; it also includes the sharing and discussion of mathematical meanings and connections (see Bishop 1985). How to make sense of one's mathematical activity is a central concern here (Resnick 1989).

To help students "practice connecting together their fragmentary knowledge into systems of meaningful mathematics," Brown and his colleagues tried to adapt their "reciprocal teaching technique" to mathematics, and they report that this improved students' comprehension (see Brown et al. 1992). Modeling and monitoring were alternately employed throughout the successive steps of defining the problem, planning the solution, solving the problem, checking the work, reflecting on the checked solution, and extending the solution to a class of similar problems. A so-called reflection board is used in which preorganized general information about the main tasks to be accomplished in each step, as well as general metacognitive hints, are combined with all relevant information progressively extracted in the process of solving the problem at hand. The technique has started to be used for teaching word problem solving and early arithmetic.

Engaging the students to make connections is also a key element of Lampert's (1986) technique for teaching elementary school mathematics. To give meaning to basic arithmetical operations such as multiplication, Lampert asks the pupils to build stories and to draw pictures illustrating their own understanding of the studied operation. By putting on the blackboard each of these representations and by leading classroom discussion around them, she tries to make clearer the connections between the four types of knowledge she believes should be tied into the students' understanding of a mathematical operation: intuitive (locally working and handy procedures and representations), concrete (rules governing object manipulations), computational (symbol manipulation), and principled (the reasons why the operation works the way it does).

Characteristics of Programs Successfully Teaching How to Build Bridges

Three main characteristics seem to be present in most programs designed to teach students to make connections in order to improve their understanding and performance.

Understanding over Procedure

Clearly programs that successfully teach students to make bridges focus on understanding the sense of texts, the meaning of concepts or mathematical operations over learning of skills or procedures. Programs in reading focus on improving comprehension, not mere reading skills. Scardamalia, Bereiter, and Steinbach's (1984) program in writing aims at improving understandability of students' essays over stylistic considerations. Lampert's (1986) technique tries first to help pupils to make sense of mathematical operations before asking them to learn the corresponding algorithms.

Large Group Discussions

Almost all the above programs in reading, writing, and mathematics make important use of classroom or group discussions. Such discussions have two main objectives. They allow each pupil to share, revise, and monitor his or her own understanding of the topic discussed by comparing it with that of his or her peers and teacher. They also help students to evaluate their mastery of the specific "sense or connection-making" procedure taught by the program.

Checklist

Finally, all the 3-R programs described here also make use of some sort of checklist to help students monitor more thoroughly their comprehension, and sometimes control their activity.

The presence of these three characteristics in almost all of the programs designed to develop a look-for-bridges attitude in students seems to indicate that they all contribute to the programs' successes. It would seem that all three should be incorporated into any attempt to foster such an attitude in Logo.

Looking for Bridges with Mathematics as Part of Logo Teaching

Helping the students to see a connection with mathematics when such help is needed, or reminding them of a Logo activity to illustrate a new, somewhat difficult, idea in the mathematics class is now regarded as a productive way to use the existing connections between Logo and mathematics. Few attempts have been made, however, to make the development of a look-for-bridges attitude a systematic part of Logo teaching. In fact most Logo classes do not present the three characteristics just mentioned. Very often, understanding is not required, as long as the correct picture is obtained. Pairing-up, or even individual work on personal projects, is often seen as the optimal solution. This could, however, be counterproductive when learning to build bridges between Logo and mathematics is a major concern (Lemerise, chapter 7 in this volume; Lepper and Gurtner 1989). The checklists in a Logo class generally only display a list of basic commands or a set of possible projects, and not metacognitive prompts focusing on monitoring one's comprehension and the progress of one's activity.[5] Moreover Logo classroom checklists are "read-only" devices, whereas those used by Brown et al. (1992), Lampert (1986), or Resnick (1989) in their programs are built to allow the filling of a preexisting structure with dynamically evolving information coming from the work done. Contrasting with these "standard" Logo situations are the few programs that have tried to teach bridging Logo with mathematics where one can find specific attempts to focus on understanding, classroom discussion of the work done, and metacognitive prompts. Globerson and Mioduser (1985) and Jones and Neville (1987) relate two experiences they explored along these lines with adult students. Both programs

---

5. In chapter 6 (this volume) Weir suggests in her conclusion that ensuring that some metacognitive reflection occurs is a crucial requirement of all Logo teaching.

involved group work and classroom discussion of the way in which the Logo work was conducted. They encourage reflections on personal thinking processes and investigate possible generalizations of the strategies used to problems in other domains.

Two programs going in the same direction have been designed for children. Delclos, Littlefield, and Bransford (1984) describe a *mediational* technique that they used on a regular basis in which "the teacher makes specific and conscious attempts to frame what is learned in the Logo lesson in a broader context and to bridge specific principles learned to other situations where the same type of strategy would apply" (p. 6). The importance of relating the new work to past experience is also explicitly and systematically taught. Before starting a Logo course, students are familiarized with various specific contexts other than Logo in which the usefulness of general skills—breaking problems into parts, identifying errors, or planning ahead, for instance—is emphasized and to which reference will be made during the work in Logo (Littlefield et al. 1988). The teacher then elicits a collective search for other contexts in which the same skills could prove useful. At the end of each practice session, classroom discussion is conducted to reflect on the kinds of problems encountered during the work and to extract the "summary principle for the day," which is intended to be kept in mind for further work. "Sometimes it is easier to complete a task if you analyze its component parts" is the example they give to illustrate what such a principle could look like.

Comparisons of this method with unstructured and structured teaching shows that such a mediational teaching program leads to higher levels of mastery of the Logo language than the unstructured method and to a comparable level with the structured method (Littlefield et al. 1988). It was, however, more effective even than the structured method in producing transfer on a near-transfer test involving such abilities as learning to give and follow directions or to identify and correct errors in given sets of directions presented in a map test. Moreover this transfer does not depend on the student's level of mastery of Logo. Understanding the directions in a problem is clearly a major difficulty in mathematics. One can therefore reasonably expect that adoption of a mediational approach to Logo might prove helpful in improving this ability in mathematics. None of the teaching methods was successful in inducing far transfer to problem-solving tests, showing here again that no important benefit is to be expected in this respect.

The Thinking with Logo curriculum, sponsored by the Calgary Board of Education and intended for grades 1 through 6, goes one step further in the direction of teaching children to adopt a consistent look-for-bridges attitude (Missiuna et al. 1987). In the Logo classes, before pupils turn to their computers and start typing in their programs, they are asked collectively and clearly to define the problem proposed by the task of the day, to review the possible strategies for solving it, and to come to a consensus on which strategy would fit better and should therefore be used. They are also asked to anticipate likely difficulties in employing this strategy and to discuss possible ways to overcome them. After realization of the program in Logo, the teacher summarizes the work and derives a so-called metacognitive principle. Based on the day's work in Logo, this principle is supposed to be general enough so that it can be applied beyond the Logo context (e.g., "If data are organized, it helps us to see patterns"). Having made sure that each pupil has understood the principle, the teacher then starts a second collective discussion asking the students to "bridge" the principle with daily life situations and to find school opportunities to practice it. Recently implemented, this whole program is still under proper evaluation.

None of these programs consider work in Logo to be completed when the correct picture sits on the students' screens or when the solution process has been discussed. They systematically and very clearly teach students to extend their Logo activity to daily life situations and to school mathematics in particular. The Thinking with Logo program even tries to encourage the pupils to look toward mathematics at the start of the Logo work, when possible strategies are reviewed and evaluated. With appropriate input from the teacher, such techniques seem likely to elicit a mathematical approach to Logo work and suggest a way to reconcile perceptual and analytic strategies (e.g., how much to turn at a particular point or how many repetitions of a pattern should be done to complete the figure correctly).

4 CONCLUSION

Probably the most interesting feature of Logo is the numerous potential connections it offers with mathematics. Research shows, however, that students seldom use ideas, concepts, or strategies that they have employed in their Logo sessions in their mathematics classes; they also tend not to take an apparently obvious geometrical approach to figure out angles and lengths in their work with Logo.

Two kinds of reasons were postulated for explaining why students do not use these seemingly obvious connections between Logo and mathematics. First, certain key features of Logo that are designed to help the students deal with complex mathematical problems may impede students from connecting their work in

Logo with mathematical or geometrical ideas with which they are already familiar when the problems are less complex. In line with the metaphor of bridges, it was proposed to call these features *tunnels*, since they help a progression within the Logo field but restrict access to the surrounding mathematics. Four such tunnels were identified. The apparent simplicity of Logo tasks tends to lower students' investment of mindful effort and to prevent assimilation of so-called easy-looking tasks into the difficult mathematical domain. The constant availability of immediate feedback favors the adoption of trial-and-error strategies and dispenses with the need for real checking of one's results against the data. Differences in formalism also hinder the making of connections. The same concepts are sometimes formalized completely differently in Logo and in mathematics; for example, the expression of the relations between two quantities in Logo and the relations between two variables in mathematics. The same symbols may have different meanings in the two domains (e.g., the equal sign). Finally, by not explicitly drawing attention to the embedded mathematics, the adoption of a do-math-without-noticing-it philosophy of Logo also deters the student from making connections that *we* might consider obvious. I have given some suggestions on how one could open windows in these tunnels.

Insufficient information on why and how to build bridges represents a second reason why connections with mathematics are often not made in standard Logo situations. Presenting structured tasks, using appropriate microworlds, or making explicit interventions in the course of the student's work are three ways that are increasingly used to provide assistance in building bridges between Logo and mathematics. Developing special programs to teach explicitly the importance of bridging and how to build such bridges is another solution that has received only limited attention in Logo despite success in other domains such as in memorizing, reading, and writing or to a smaller degree in mathematics. Learning to build bridges between pieces of knowledge is part of higher-order thinking skills, and this is often presented as the ultimate goal of teaching. However, for such skills to become widely used by students, isolated instruction in thinking skills is rarely sufficient (Resnick 1987). Practice in using these skills needs to be extended across subject matter and to "suffuse the school program from kindergarten on" (Resnick 1987, p. 48). Learning to build bridges between Logo and mathematics from the beginning thus represents a necessary step in this direction, but it is a step that can prove successful only if other steps are taken to bridge mathematics with science, science with history, and so on.

To conclude, the bridge metaphor views mathematics and Logo as the two banks of a river or a canyon with good places to build bridges all along its length;

these allow passage back and forth for the most interesting views of the river (the problem) and for facilitating one's progression across it. In contrast to the more classical transfer model, in which practice is usually necessary in one domain before any transfer can be obtained, useful bridges can be built from the beginning, as soon as work has started in both domains. The fact that the most critical effect of Logo can be seen even at the kindergarten level speaks in favor of establishing such connections early on at the elementary school level, at the age when children begin learning mathematics.

ACKNOWLEDGMENTS

This chapter was prepared while the author was visiting at Stanford University, supported by the Swiss National Foundation for Scientific Research, Fellowship No. 81.353.0.86. I would like to thank C. Hoyles, J. Hillel, M. Lepper, R. Noss, and an anonymous reviewer for their helpful comments on earlier drafts of this chapter.

REFERENCES

Bishop, A. 1985. The social construction of meaning-a significant development for mathematics education? *For the Learning of Mathematics* 5: 24–28.

Brown, A. L., Campione, J. C., Reeve, R. A., Ferrara, R.A., and Palincsar, A. S. 1992. Interactive learning and individual understanding: The case of reading and mathematics. In L. T. Landsmann (ed.), *Culture, Schooling and Psychological Development*. Hillsdale, NJ: Lawrence Erlbaum Associates.

Charles, R. I., and Lester, F. K., Jr. 1984. An evaluation of a process-oriented instructional program in mathematical problem solving in grades 5 and 7. *Journal for Research in Mathematics Education* 15: 15–34.

Chase, W. G., and Simon, H. A. 1973. The mind's eye in chess. In W. G. Chase (ed.), *Visual information processing*. New York: Academic Press, pp. 215–281.

Clements, D. H. 1987. Longitudinal study of the effects of Logo programming on cognitive abilities. *Journal of Educational Computing Research* 3: 73–94.

Clements, D. H. 1986. Effects of Logo and CAI environments on cognition and creativity. *Journal of Educational Psychology* 78: 309–318.

Coté, B., and Kayler, H. 1987. Geometric constructions with turtle and on paper by 5th and 6th grade children. *Proceedings of the Third International Conference for Logo and Mathematics Education*. Department of Mathematics, Concordia University, Montreal.

Davey, B., and McBride, S. 1986. Effects of question-generation training on reading comprehension. *Journal of Educational Psychology* 78: 256–262.

Delclos, V. R., Littlefield, J., and Bransford, J. D. 1984. Teaching thinking through Logo: the importance of method. Technical Report Series, Report No. 84.1.2. George Peabody College for Teachers, Vanderbilt University, Tennessee.

Dewitz, P., Carr, E. M., and Patberg, J. P. 1987. Effects of inference training on comprehension and comprehension monitoring. *Reading Research Quarterly* 22: 99–119.

Flavell, J. H., Green, F. L., and Flavell, E. R. 1985. The road not taken: Understanding the implications of initial uncertainty in evaluating spatial directions. *Developmental Psychology* 21: 207–216.

Glaser, R. 1984. Education and thinking. The role of knowledge. *American Psychologist* 39: 93–104.

Globerson, T., and Mioduser, D. 1985. Learning Logo mindfully: A model course. Logo85, MIT, 162–163.

Greeno, J. G. 1989: A perspective on thinking. *American Psychologist* 44: 134–141.

Gurtner, J. 1988. EquaLogo. In C. Hoyles (ed.), *Proceedings of the Working Group on Logo*, ICME-6, Budapest.

Gurtner, J. 1987. Success and understanding while solving geometrical problems in Logo. *Proceedings of the Eleventh International Conference for the Psychology of Mathematics Education*. Montreal.

Hayes, J. R. 1981. *The Complete Problem Solver*. Philadelphia: Franklin Institute Press.

Hillel, J. 1984. Mathematical and programming concepts acquired by children aged 8–9 in a restricted Logo environment. *Proceedings of the Ninth International Conference for the Psychology of Mathematics Education*. Holland.

Hillel, J. 1988. Linking Logo to school geometry: A prototype for a learning environment. In Proceedings of ICME-6.

Hillel, J., Kieran, C., and Gurtner, J. 1989. Solving structured geometric tasks with a computer. The role of feedback in generating strategies. *Educational Studies in Mathematics* 20: 1–39.

Hillel, J., Gurtner, J., and Kieran, C. 1988. Structuring and destructuring a solution: An example of problem-solving work with the computer. *Proceedings of the Twelfth International Conference for the Psychology of Mathematics Education*. Budapest, July, 20–25, pp. 402–409.

Hillel, J., and Kieran, C. 1987. Schemas used by 12-year-olds in solving selected turtle geometry tasks. *Recherches en Didactique des Mathematiques*.

Horan, R. D. 1985. Logo, a problem-solving tool. Ed. dissertation. Columbia University Teachers College. DAI 8602053.

Hoyles, C., and Sutherland, R., 1989. *Logo Mathematics in the Classroom*. London: Routledge.

Jones, T., and Neville, L. 1987. Problem solving for teachers. Proceedings of the Third Conference for Logo and Mathematics Education. Dept of Mathematics, Concordia University, Montreal.

Kelly, G. N., Kelly, J. T., and Miller, R. B. 1987. Working with Logo: Do 5th and 6th graders develop a basic understanding of angles and distances? *Journal of Computers in Mathematics and Science Teaching* 6: 23–27.

Kieran, C. 1984: A comparison between novice and more expert algebra students on tasks dealing with the equivalence of equations. *Proceedings of the Sixth Annual Meeting of the North American Chapter of the International Group for the Psychology of Mathematics Education.* Madison, Wisconsin.

Kynigos, C. 1986. Constructing a conceptual pathway from intrinsic to extrinsic geometry. *Proceedings of the Second International Conference for Logo and Mathematics Education.* Department of Mathematics, Statistics and Computing, University of London, Institute of Education.

Lampert, M. 1986. Knowing, doing, and teaching multiplication. *Cognition and Instruction* 3: 305–342.

Lehrer, R., Guckenberg, T., and Lee, O. 1988. Comparative study of the cognitive consequences of inquiry-based Logo instruction. *Journal of Educational Psychology* 80: 543–553.

Lehrer, R., and Randle, L. 1987. Problem solving, metacognition and composition: The effects of interactive software for first-grade children. *Journal of Educational Computing Research* 3: 409–427.

Lepper, M. R., and Gurtner, J. 1989. Children and computers: Approaching the twenty-first century. *American Psychologist* 44: 170–178.

Leron, U. 1982. The group of the turtle. *Byte* 7(8, August): 330–331.

Littlefield, J., Delclos, V. R., Lever, S., Clayton, K. N., Bransford, J. D., and Franks, J. J. 1988. Learning Logo: Method of teaching, transfer of general skills, and attitudes toward school and computers. In R. E. Mayer (ed.), *Teaching and Learning Computer Programming: Multiple Research Perspectives.* Hillsdale, NJ: Lawrence Erlbaum Associates.

Markman, E. M. 1981. Comprehension monitoring. In W. P. Dickson (ed.), *Children's Oral Communication Skills.* New York: Academic Press.

Miller, G. E., and Emihovich, C. 1986. The effects of mediated programming instruction on pre-school children's self-monitoring. *Journal of Educational Computing Research* 2: 283–297.

Missiuna, C., Hunter, J., Kemp, T., and Hyslop, I. 1987. Development and evaluation of the "Thinking with Logo" curriculum. Calgary Board of Education.

Newell, A. 1980. One final word. In D. T. Tuma and F. Reif (eds.), *Problem Solving and Education: Issues in Teaching and Research.* Hillsdale, NJ: Lawrence Erlbaum Associates, pp. 175–189.

Noss, R. 1986. Constructing a conceptual framework for elementary algebra through Logo programming. *Educational Studies in Mathematics* 17: 335–357.

Noss, R., and Hoyles, C. 1987. The dialectic of process and content. *Proceedings of the Third International Conference for Logo and Mathematics Education.* Department of Mathematics, Concordia University, Montreal.

Palincsar, A. S., and Brown, A. L. 1984. Reciprocal teaching of comprehension-fostering and monitoring activities. *Cognition and Instruction* 1: 117–175.

Papert, S. 1980. *Mindstorms: Computers, Children and Powerful Ideas.* New York: Basic Books.

Pea, R. D., and Kurland, D. M. 1984. Logo programming and the development of planning skills. Technical Report No. 16, The Center for Children and Technology, Bank Street College of Education, New York.

Pólya, G. 1957. *How to Solve It: A New Aspect of Mathematical Method.* 2d ed. Princeton, NJ: Princeton University Press.

Pressley, M., McDaniel, M. A., Turnure, J. E., Wood, E., and Ahmad, M. 1987. Generation and precision of elaboration: Effects on intentional and incidental learning. *Journal of Experimental Psychology: Learning, Memory and Cognition* 13: 291–300.

Resnick, L. B. 1987. *Education and Learning to Think.* Washington, D. C: National Academy Press.

Resnick, L. B. 1989. Teaching mathematics as an ill-structured discipline. In R. I. Charles and E. A. Silver (ed.), *The teaching and Assessing of Mathematical Problem Solving.* Hillsdale, NJ/ Reston, VA: Lawrence Erlbaum Associates and National Council of Teachers of Mathematics.

Retschitzki, J. 1987. Retombées cognitives d'une initiation à la programmation en Logo. *Proceedings of the Eleventh International Conference for the Psychology of Mathematics Education.* Montreal.

Rieber, L. P. 1987. Logo and its promise: A research report. *Educational Technology* 27: 12–16.

Salomon, G. 1988. AI in reverse: Computer tools that turn cognitive. *Journal of Educational Computing Research* 4: 123–139.

Salomon, G., and Perkins, D. N. 1987. Transfer of cognitive skills from programming: When and how? *Journal of Educational Computing Research* 3: 149–169.

Scardamalia, M., Bereiter, C., and Steinbach, R. 1984. Teachability of reflective processes in written composition. *Cognitive Science* 8: 173–190.

Schoenfeld, A. H. 1985. *Mathematical Problem Solving.* New York: Academic Press.

Sutherland, R. 1987. What are the links between variables in Logo and variables in algebra? *Recherches en Didactique des Mathématiques* 8: 103–130.

Wood, D., Bruner, J., and Ross, G. 1979. The role of tutoring in problemsolving. *Journal of Child Psychology and Psychiatry* 17: 89–100.

Expressing Mathematical Structures III

In this part, we draw together four contributions, each of which raises what we take to be a central question for existing and future Logo research and curriculum development: namely, the extent to which Logo can form a medium through which children and adults may express mathematical ideas and structures. In contrast to the preceding contributions, the authors are more concerned to focus on mathematical and computational ideas and are less interested in the pedagogical framework within which such ideas may be expressed effectively. Some of the chapters deal with mathematics which, ostensibly at least, takes us out of the realms of school mathematics and into the college and university. Yet the power of these contributions lies in the indication they provide of the possibilities of *change* in the curriculum, of introducing mathematical ideas into the school classroom which would be difficult, if not altogether impossible, without a medium such as Logo. These contributions provide useful ammunition against those who persist in believing that Logo is either only geometrical or only for young children.

Bruno Vitale (chapter 10), an Italian theoretical physicist now living and working in Geneva, Switzerland, builds on his interests in dynamical systems and mathematical modeling to focus on *processes* as a way of integrating the study of computer science into mathematical education. The strong mathematical and computer science interests of Uri Leron and Rina Zazkis (chapter 11), from Haifa, Israel, underpins their analysis of the turtle group. Their chapter provides mathematical insight that has educational implications for the teaching and learning of elementary group theory. Trevor Fletcher (chapter 12), for many years the staff inspector for mathematics in England and Wales, now describes himself—in retirement—as a "nonconforming Logo enthusiast." As in the previous chapter, his focus is on group theory, and he describes how Logo can be used to explore a range of ideas in this field. The final chapter (chapter 13), by Brian Harvey adopts the perspective of the computer scientist and argues that functional programming is both technically powerful and pedagogically sensible. Harvey worked on the design and implementation of many Logo versions and is currently at the University of California at Berkeley.

Vitale's tour of a wide range of mathematical ideas, some of them on the edge of current mathematics research, sets the tone for this part of the book by illustrating just how broad a range of mathematical ideas can be illuminated by expressing them in a programming language such as Logo. Leron and Zazkis, and then Fletcher, address one mathematical structure, namely, the notion of *group*. These two contributions differ in style and approach, and together provide food for thought on the ways in which Logo might transform the mathematics curriculum. Harvey's contribution sounds a salutary note of heresy. He argues that one of the barriers to Logo's acceptance is the heavy reliance it places on recursion as a control mechanism—and one that, perhaps surprisingly for some readers, he argues is unnecessary. Thus Harvey's contribution serves as an antidote to the headiness of Fletcher's paper: Both are concerned with the expression of sophisticated mathematics, but they adopt very different mechanisms for achieving it.

Vitale's central argument is that structure is a pervasive mechanism within mathematics and that understanding of *processes*[1]—a hitherto neglected area within the educational arena—can be facilitated by constructing and studying programs that model them. Vitale sees modeling at the heart of the matter and suggests that in the absence of the computer, the modeling process itself has often been simplified "to the brink of triviality." In fact the difficulty of modeling any but the most trivial (and artificial) examples has been one of the reasons why the process of modeling has received relatively little pedagogical attention. Even in terms of Logo, there have been only a few serious attempts to move beyond the pioneering work of Abelson and diSessa's book *Turtle Geometry*.

One of the most important points to which Vitale returns throughout his chapter is his firm belief (and illustration) that programming is an exploratory activity. This belief is summarized by his approving reference to Weizenbaum's dictum: "One programs just as one writes, not because one understands, but in order to understand." Nevertheless, this bears repeating. The recent history of mathematical programming in educational settings has been beset by a debate on this question, which has missed Weizenbaum's point by setting up a false dichotomy between exploratory process and modeling product—the former often typecast as educational romantics in danger of reducing mathematics to trivial tasks such as rotations of regular Logo polygons; the latter, as hard-nosed modelers who believe that the construction of an effective algorithm is both a litmus test for mathematical understanding and a mechanism for achieving it. Vitale's contribution effectively lays bare the inadequacies of both stereotypes by illustrating the nontrivial mathematical possibilities of even simple Logo programs

---

1. Vitale is not using the word in the sense of *process* as opposed to *content* (an area that is far from neglected in the literature). Rather, he is referring to the construction of formal descriptions of how things work.

ranging from predator/prey problems to stochastic processes and by emphasizing the genuinely exploratory nature of the programming process.

Vitale does, however, stress the importance of keeping the computer in its pedagogical place (a theme taken up by several authors in this volume; e.g., see chapter 3 by Loethe. Vitale poses the problem sharply: The computer is *only* useful after learner's intuitions have been developed by off-computer activities such as discussion and manipulation of concrete models (he would doubtlessly agree that there are exceptions to this rule—notably those for whom programming has become in itself a "concrete" form of manipulation.) Thus Vitale is concerned with pedagogical questions, although his main focus in the chapter is to illustrate the potential of programming for expressing "in the simplest possible way our representation of the problem" rather than observe how learners generally behave during such activities. His rationale for doing this is characteristically straightforward: In a mathematical analogue of Bruner's well-known aphorism, Vitale states that "I do not think that there are *problems* that are specifically suited to young children, or for adolescents, or for adults." He sees these problems as "ageless" in both senses: The crucial factor is just how they are introduced. One important issue is that the power of the medium to express nontrivial models allows consideration of nontrivial meaningful (and social) problems, including ecological processes, dynamical systems, and the spread of the AIDS virus.

Group theory lies at the core of the contributions of both Leron and Zazkis and of Fletcher. Leron and Zazkis weave a thread between euclidean and turtle geometries by building the group isomorphism between them, via their FLIP command, which flips the turtle onto its back. Their contribution is at once based on epistemology and pedagogy: That is, while their prima facie concern is to develop a system with mathematical integrity by constructing their turtle group, they are simultaneously concerned with the increase in expressive power, which they argue is achieved by doing this. Leron and Zazkis maintain that this represents a more intuitive way to express geometrical ideas, although, on their own admission, their evidence for this claim is somewhat limited.

Leron and Zazkis show convincingly what it *means* to say that the expressive power of the language is increased by the introduction of FLIP, which constitutes the turtle primitives (FD, RT, etc.) into a group. Having formed a group, they are able to build procedures to translate, rotate, and reflect that have essentially the same structure—a nice illustration of the way in which mathematical structure can be exhibited by a program *if the right level of expressive tools exists*.

There are other illustrations: A particularly telling one is the reexpression of Abelson and diSessa's program for the Hilbert curve, again a program that makes more visible the mathematical structure that is being modeled. In other words, the formalization of the group concept (which forms the major part of the early sections of the chapter) structures *and is structured by* the expressive power of the programming language.

From a pedagogical point of view, Leron and Zazkis do not claim that the children engaged in such activities are doing group theory or even that they are in any way aware of the group nature of their activities: "We do believe, however, that it is valuable for researchers and teachers to be aware of these connections." This is not as farfetched as it may seem: Leron and Zazkis argue, for example, that the idea of conjugation, though an important idea tying mathematics and computing together, might also prove an effective heuristic for debugging certain classes of program. It is also possible to interpret (of course, from the vantage point of mathematics!) certain common student behaviors as attempts to locate identity elements of a group or the construction of particular subgroups. Once again, it is not part of Leron and Zazkis' argument that this is conscious; our interpretation of their position is that it might be that teacher awareness of what Gérard Vergnaud calls *theorems in action* might (at some time in the future) lead to an awareness of the theorem itself.

This final point is made tellingly by the authors who argue that if students have had enough experience playing around (at some level of consciousness) with ideas such as order, conjugacy, extensions, normal subgroups, homomorphisms, and isomorphisms, then learning the concepts themselves "may amount to little more than just *naming* familiar notions." This is a bold (and unsubstantiated) claim, although it merely mirrors Papert's claim of twenty years ago that programming in Logo may lay the conceptual frameworks on which to base subsequent formalized instruction—with the result that such instruction becomes almost trivial.

Fletcher's approach contrasts with that of Leron and Zazkis in a number of ways. Primarily, his is a contribution that, while still placing the expression of mathematical structures as a prime concern, is more concerned with seeing how mathematical structures might be *used* in the construction of programs. He maintains that a major difficulty with the introduction of group theory into schools is that pupils learned "to act on groups but could not act *with* groups." Leron and Zazkis start by defining and clarifying the mathematics and go on to think about programming suitable mathematical programs. Fletcher, on the other hand, develops "suites" of programs in order to solve his (mathematical) problems. On the way he encounters a lot of mathematics. As he puts it, "Group ideas may be the final destination, but we must not neglect the scenery on the way."

Considering Fletcher's strip ornaments, for example, it is interesting that his concern is primarily with the programming of the solution, not with the mathematical elegance that underpins it. That is not to say that what distinguishes the approaches is merely that Leron and Zazkis's is mathematical while Fletcher's is computational. Leron and Zazkis are concerned with the construction of an abstraction barrier[2] (FLIP) that allows the code to reflect the geometrical ideas by simultaneously constructing mathematical and computational structures and illustrating the interplay between them. Fletcher's intention is different; he uses Logo to build and exhibit the mathematical (geometrical) structures: "procedures. . . are the direct embodiment of the geometrical symmetries." As an example of this distinction, Fletcher is happy to solve the problem of left- and right-handed flags without the elegance of a FLIP by writing the code to switch RTs and LTs. This is a nice application of list processing that contrasts with the mathematical aesthetic proposed by Leron and Zazkis.

A further difference between the two contributions is in the focus on groups themselves. Leron and Zazkis concentrate on the construction and implications of a single group—that of the turtle. In doing so, they are working essentially with a paradigmatic case, and one that they argue encapsulates many of the more general issues that a group-theoretic approach raises. Fletcher's claim is that there exists a symbiotic relationship between Logo and group theory more generally: He suggests that knowing groups helps to program and that programming helps to make explicit the group structures. He argues that the computer allows the general to be seen in the particular: ". . . group ideas provide the mathematician with an excellent filing system—but before a filing system can be developed, it is necessary to be clear about the things that have to be filed." From a pedagogical point of view, an outstanding problem has been that most people only clarified what had to be filed and had no appreciation of the filing system itself. He presents a wide variety of challenging examples, ranging from semiregular tessellations to some tantalizing permutation-based puzzles and culminating in an application of list processing to the construction of a self-

---

2. See Abelson and Sussman's *Structure and Interpretation of Computer Programs* (MIT Press, 1985).

modifying program which, he claims, embodies the levels of abstraction to be found in modern algebra.

Harvey's contribution provides respite from the galaxy of mathematical ideas presented in the preceding chapters. Consider, for example, what heavy use Fletcher makes of recursion in his programs. Harvey, in contrast, argues that this is avoidable. His rationale for doing so is straightforward: His experience suggests that students find nontrivial recursive programs very difficult either to interpret or construct. On an epistemological level, his rationale is similarly clear. He argues that the expressive power of Logo for mathematics is derived from the fact that (like LISP) it is a *functional* language. Programs are viewed "as a collection of mathematical functions that can be applied to arguments and composed with other functions to create more complicated functions." Harvey makes a convincing case that this style of programming is technically more powerful and pedagogically more sensible "especially when computer programming is to be used as a vehicle for teaching mathematical ideas." But the problem is recursion: This is Logo's principle control structure, and there is no doubt that it is a pedagogical obstacle to learners' understanding.

Harvey argues that Logo's functional style and its use of recursive control structures can and should be separated. The key to the functional style of programming is the construction of procedures without "side effects": Procedures that OUTPUT their results in a way that can be composed with other functions. But there is a pedagogical problem: ". . . without recursion, the number of interesting functions you can compute is small." So students either have to confront OUTPUT and recursion simultaneously—this causes difficulties—or use OUTPUT in essentially trivial ways. Harvey's answer is initially to sidestep recursion completely.

His approach is based on the programming language APL, and also on mature versions of LISP—namely, to build higher-level functions that undertake many of the required functions to which recursion is applied, thus simultaneously increasing the expressive power of the language (this time from a computer-science perspective) and masking the (recursive) workings of these particular procedures themselves.

For those of us who have become convinced of the mathematical aesthetics of recursion, this is a thought-provoking approach, not least because it challenges us to ask ourselves whether the fashion for recursion is based upon the intrinsic properties of the idea or simply because it is the means to the end of Logo programming. In fact, as Harvey shows, we often do not need it.

Nevertheless, there are two caveats that Harvey makes to his own position. First, that recursion is an interesting idea that, for the purposes of *mathematics* teaching, may well need to be introduced, whatever the difficulties. As Harvey points out, his approach does not negate this: On the contrary, the learner could be encouraged to look inside the procedural "tools" and see how they work (although there are easier ways to see recursive structures operating).

Second, there *are* projects that are recursive in structure and that benefit immensely from a recursive approach (e.g., the evaluation of a determinant, which is the sum of subdeterminants which are themselves the sum of subdeterminants. . .). In such cases the existence of recursion as a control structure is not only helpful; it serves to express—in programming terms—the underlying mathematical structure of the solution.

Processes: A Dynamical Integration of Computer Science into Mathematical Education   10

Bruno Vitale

It is a heretical doctrine to think that in essence water does not run, and the tree does not pass through vicissitude. The Buddha's way consists in the form that exists and the condition that exists. The bloom of flowers and the fall of leaves are the conditions that exist. And yet unwise people think that in the world of essence there should be no bloom of flowers and no fall of leaves.
—Dogen (1200–1253): Shobogenzo, Hossho (transl. H. Nakamura)

1   INTRODUCTION

Students of mathematics usually encounter only mounted and stuffed Dragons—formidable mathematical problems which have been defined and solved. But the real game—and the greatest fun—lies in the chase, in the snaring and slaughter of these frabjous beasties.
—Cohen (1973)

Mathematical education at all levels moves in three domains of abstraction: that of essences (in this context called *mathematical structures*), that of *closed problems* (as opposed to the open character of most physical and biological problems), and that of *rigor* (traditionally associated with the transparency of the logicomathematical realm, as opposed to the muddy status of the realm of causality).

Essences have played an essential role in the development of mathematical thinking but, when thoughtlessly thrown into mathematical education, have also contributed to making the subject lifeless. In the static teaching approach there is no state of fruition, no maturation. *Closed problems*, where every pertinent aspect of a solution is already known to the teacher, are historically important but boring. They can be used, however, to build new, open, and stimulating models to represent our experiences. *Rigor*, as implied in the steps of theoretical proofs in mathematics, allows for practice in developing disciplined thinking but often very misleadingly creates an unjustifiable hierarchy where theoretical thinking is considered superior to empirical thinking, or the experimental approach of physics and biology.

An interdisciplinary approach that emphasizes the conceptualization and the representation of the *processes* of *time* and *change* (and sometimes, *chance*) would help to lift mathematical education out of these three domains of abstraction. In the correspondingly interesting realm of our causal experience, mathematical structures would not be lost, for they underly all aspects of our construction of reality. Historical solutions to classical problems would not be forgotten, since they would form the underlying structure of our representation of physical and biological phenomena. Rigor would be tempered by an understanding of the empirical and formal limitations of our mathematical models.

I will mention briefly here the main ideas that will be developed in this chapter. A simple example, "the hunt for hidden treasure" in section 2, will be used to help in defining the roles of processes and programming in any interdisciplinary approach that includes mathematical education. Section 3 will go back to the more general issues and show how they will be developed in various projects presented in sections 4 through 7. Section 8 will give a short summary of the results and a few caveats on using computers and programming to teach mathematics.

1.   *Processes are important and should be included in mathematical education.* Time, or any other one-dimensional evolution parameter, is singularly absent in traditional mathematical teaching. One-dimensional ordering structures and multidimensional classificatory structures are indeed present in mathematical thinking (e.g., the discussion on the "arrows of concepts-space" in Michener 1978), but the *dynamics* inherent in the construction of a theory, the unfolding of an algorithm, the development of a complex configuration from initial axioms, are lost in the mathematics provided in schools. Time as a continuum and the dynamical construct of a model are of course at the very basis of the definition of a *process*.

2.   *Processes provide a much-needed bridge between the logicomathematical conceptual framework and the problems and curiosities stemming from our causal experiences.* To escape the feeling of abstraction and the somewhat breathless atmosphere of the mathematical world, a deep plunge into the world of causality can provide a refreshing alternative. But an analysis of processes quickly convinces us that there is no contradiction between the two worlds. Any conceptualization and representation of a process invokes the necessary, underlying logicomathematical structures.

3.   *Modeling on a computer allows teachers and pupils to tackle in the classroom processes that would otherwise be so simplified as to become dull and uninteresting.* The present fate of dynamical problems and models in the classroom is that they have to be simplified to the brink of triviality in order to be analytically solved. Simple pro-

gramming on a computer enlarges the scope of modeling and mathematical experimenting to problems that have no analytical, closed solutions, or problems whose solutions cannot be obtained by the pupils with the technical instruments at their disposal.

4. *Programming helps in defining the respective roles of variables, parameters, algorithms, and initial conditions in a process.* The separation of a process into variables and parameters is not easy. The procedural approach of a programming language demands that functional choices be made, although other choices might be equally explored by programming. The way the algorithm unfolds can be followed in time, and how the final configuration of a program depends on the initial conditions can be explored in detail.

5. *Programming provides useful feedback on the logicomathematical structures needed to conceptualize and to represent a process in space-time.* Different algorithms can describe the same process; they can make use of radically different logicomathematical structures and geometrical spatialization. These different representations enrich both the model and the process corresponding to it. Both the program and the act of programming help clarify the limits of the model used.

Before going to the first example, Treasure, I want only to add that some relevant Logo procedures can be found in the appendix in their *skeletal form* (which hints only at the essential cognitive and representative steps in the formulation of a project) and in a Logo *dialect*. These skeletons can be reformulated into initialization procedures, coordinate definitions, and the like, and translated easily into other Logo dialects or into LogoWriter. Each skeleton corresponds to only *one of the possible procedural realizations* of a project. It might be interesting to find other realizations based on different conceptualizations. The corresponding graphical representations, given in the figures, are equally skeletal representations providing only the essential dynamics. We can enrich them, but the more we become addicted to beautiful graphical displays, the less our programs will be transparent and the more the learners will convince themselves that these projects cannot be realized by themselves or collectively by working with their classmates.

2 THE HUNTING OF THE HIDDEN TREASURE: AN INTERACTIVE GAME AND AN INTRODUCTION TO PROCESSES AND STRATEGIES

The essence of play is in the dominance of means over ends. This is not to say that play is without goals—witness the toddler building a tower of blocks—but in play the process is more important than the product.
—Sylva et al. (1976)

Children have long played a game in which a treasure is hidden, a child looks for it, and the other children shout delightedly: "cold!" "warm!" or "hot!"—as the case may be—to provide a hint about the distance to the treasure and so to guide the search.

No child would be conscious of the fact that a lot of spatial construction and mastery is at work in this game, nor that the search strategies used are dependent on this mastery. But moving around to look for the treasure, changing the direction toward which to search, and integrating the shouts of others into one's search strategy requires a lot of fine adjustments and an overall appreciation of the spatial relations and their relation to motion.

The introduction of this game into mathematical education might be very productive. The game can actually be played in the playground, and pupils can be made attentive to the individual strategies they develop as they take into account the cues coming from their classmates. It can also be played in the classroom, using a large sheet of paper on which to trace the individual search paths. Finally, it can be programmed in Logo and played on a computer, whose responses would take the place of the children's shouts. (The use of this game in furthering a child's programming skills and exploring images on the computer has been discussed in Dionnet et al. 1987, 1989). A comparison of how this game is played in the playground, in the classroom, and on a computer screen is provided by Klaue et al. (1988).

Nothing is simpler to program than TREASURE1. The position of both the treasure and turtle is chosen at each run by the computer (through RANDOM) within the boundaries of the screen. The field of exploration is supposed to be empty and to coincide with the area of the screen. The player can choose the starting position, ask for the distance from the treasure, move the turtle freely according to intuition or a specific search strategy, and then ask for the distance again, repeating this procedure until the treasure is found. The pythagorean theorem and a few other geometric aids are sufficient.

What is not so easy is obtaining a clear enough *conceptualization* of the problem and of the way to state it so that it can be *translated into a program*: What information do *we* need in order to know the distance? What information does the *computer* need? How will the computer have access to this information, and how will it use it? In our research on this project in France and in a nonacademic environment, we have found that the notion of the computer as *computing or calculating* a specific activity is a difficult and opaque one. For most children only the computer *knows* what happens on the screen (and what is hidden beyond the screen) and *sees* it while it happens. Memory functions, translation of numerical data into graphical representations, and recalling of data, for example, are capabilities that have to be carefully integrated into the preliminaries of Logo programming. Learning a programming language with all its lexical, syntactical, and semantic complexity is just not enough. What we need besides is an efficient, operational representation of the functional anatomy of the computer. (I have dealt with the epistemological and pedagogical aspects of children's approach to computer science in Vitale 1988.)

There are at least two ways of developing this game:

1. To complexify the search space, one can introduce obstacles (walls, doors, etc.) in it so that the search path and strategy takes the presence of the obstacles into account. This creates an interesting cognitive problem related to the representation of projective space and a rather difficult problem related to the programming of the *shadow region* of each obstacle (even for trivial obstacles).
2. To make explicit the need for a consistent search strategy and rationale, one can create on the computer a *search-robot*. Here the interest lies in the problem of choosing a search strategy (by a careful observation of physical and screen action strategies) and translating it into a Logo program.

From TREASURE1 to TREASURE2 to TREASURE3 to . . .

I refer to Dionnet et al. (1987, 1989) for a discussion of our research on TREASURE in which is presented an evaluation based on this game and its programming strategies in the framework of Piagetian clinical interviews. What is useful to recall here is the dynamical aspect of the search strategies developed during the game. Each *search* is a *process* that unfolds in time and integrates in various ways the incoming information on the *change* in D, the distance from the treasure, and—in a very few but surprising cases—the *change in the change* of D; (see figure 1 for an example of this search). Clearly the corresponding program has to be interactive to provide the numerical value of D on demand (several children did not care to ask too often for the distance; they preferred to move the turtle around before asking anew for D).

There were few difficulties in planning a possible Logo program for the empty-screen case (TREASURE1), even if the limited time we had at our disposal for each interview made it impossible to fully implement the plan. (The children were invited to play first with the experimenters' program and, if they wanted, to have a look at it by shifting to the editor.) Things

T R E A S U R E 1

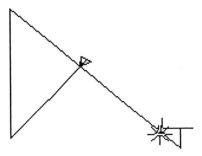

Figure 1 A search path in TREASURE1

T R E A S U R E 2

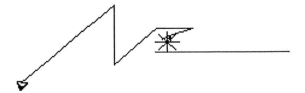

Figure 2 A search path in TREASURE2

became harder when the second and third phases of the project were proposed: to put a linear obstacle on the screen, either touching one of the walls (TREASURE2, figure 2) or free inside the screen (TREASURE3, figure 3). The difficulties were of two types. First, the development of an efficient search strategy needs the decoding of each piece of information on how the distance changes while the turtle moves. This is rather trivial in TREASURE1 (where the only distance is the direct one), more complex in TREASURE2 (where the computer defines D as the direct or the edge-walk distance to take into account the impenetrability of the obstacle), still more complex in TREASURE3 (where the screen topology has qualitatively changed and the choice is between the direct distance, on the one hand, and the shortest of the two edge-walk distances, on the other hand). Second, the programming difficulties grow correspondingly, and the procedural definition and Logo implementation of the *shadow region* of the obstacles require some very careful geometrical thinking, although it is always very elementary geometry (pythagorean), at least as long as one sticks to

T R E A S U R E 3

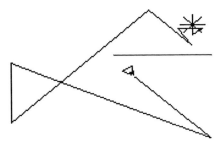

Figure 3 A search path in TREASURE3

linear obstacles. Besides elementary geometry, what is involved here is some very logical thinking and lucid spatial representation to keep straight the rather involved web of conditional statements.

I think that obstacles of arbitrary shape (e.g., defined by a given function on the screen and inside the search program) could lead to more complex Logo programs, but their structure would probably be too opaque for most children. Nevertheless, this could make a challenging research project for an advanced course on geometric problem solving in Logo. It is one of the examples of the rich internal life of models and of their possible development: TREASURE1 can be tackled at the lowest level of Logo instruction, and then at the next level, TREASURE2, and then TREASURE3, and so on.

Hunting the Treasure: From Algorithm to Performance

Among the observed search strategies in the computer version of the game, the most common seems to be the following: Fix an arbitrary starting point and starting heading for the turtle, and then ask for the distance (the independence of the distance from the heading is not as trivial as it seems). Suppose that you get D for an answer, then FORWARD D, ask again for the distance. If you get $D' < D$, FORWARD D' without changing heading; if you get $D' > D$, turn left or right some angle and then FORWARD D'. Continue until the treasure is found.

One of the children (Frédéric, twelve years old), however, consistently used a particular version and modification of this strategy. Independently of the relation of D' to D, at each step he typed RT 90 FORWARD D, OR D', D'' . . . as the case might be, so that (remember that T1 provides the numerical value of D

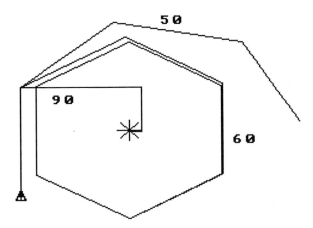

Figure 4 Hunting the treasure with A = 50, 60, and 90

for a given turtle position in TREASURE1) the procedural version of his strategy could have been written REPEAT 1000 [T1 FD :D RT 90].

To our surprise, this very rigid procedure—which did not take into account the way in which D was changing at each step and which Frédéric was unable to justify—worked very efficiently. (It could be that this search strategy is known to treasure hunters, but it was unknown to us.) It took us several runs to be convinced that it was one of the best strategies available and, what is more, that its efficiency was practically invariant for small changes in the turning angle (and of course for the change of LT for RT). RT 65 or LT 130 work almost as well as RT 90.

I have since formalized this strategy in a program HUNT (see figure 4) and discovered that it describes a very interesting one-parameter discrete dynamical system, the parameter being the pivoting angle A. There is of course a fixed equilibrium point corresponding to $D = 0$. When $A < 60$ degrees, all trajectories diverge, so the fixed point is unstable. When $A = 60$ degrees, they all converge toward a hexagon centered on the equilibrium point and whose dimensions depend on the initial conditions (the presence of attracting hexagons is easy to explain because the hexagon is the only regular polygon whose radius—the distance D!—coincides with the side). When $A > 60$ degrees, all trajectories converge toward the equilibrium point, which therefore becomes an attractor. The rate of convergence of course depends on A, and the value chosen by Frédéric (90 degrees) seems to have been the best choice.

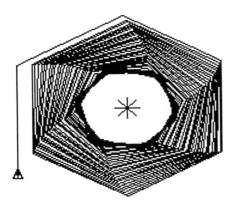

Figure 5 Hunting the treasure with $A = 60.1$, a slow catch

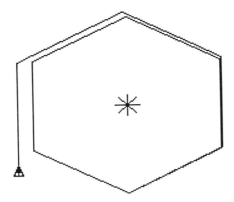

Figure 6 Hunting the treasure with $A = 60.0$, a frustrating waiting in orbit

We encounter here a new important mathematical dragon in our exploration of dynamical processes: a *bifurcation point* in the parameter space defined by A. Around 60 degrees the smallest change in A leads to catastrophic consequences: At A = 59.1 degrees you are swept to infinity, independently of where you start (except if you are sitting right on the treasure); at $A = 60.0$ degrees you run forever on a hexagon, possibly with the treasure just in sight but you are unable to grasp it; at $A = 60.1$ degrees you eventually capture the treasure, but it takes a long time (see figures 5, 6, and 7).

I think that there are several other search strategies that can be described procedurally and then easily programmed in Logo. I am thinking, in particular, of the *acceleration-sensitive* strategy in which the next move is dependent not

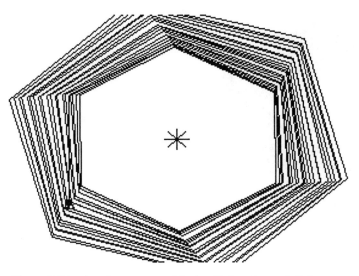

Figure 7 Hunting the treasure with $A = 59.9$, going to infinity

only on how the distance has changed as a consequence of the previous move but also on how much it has changed. (Even if the distance is diminishing with each move, is it diminishing more or less? Is it worth changing direction, and which way?)

In effect, starting from simple play and using a little geometry, some imagination, and the most elementary Logo skills, we have reached the borders of contemporary mathematical thinking and experimenting. This can be repeated with many other children's games. These games should be not spoiled by dry scholarly analysis but rather enriched by thoughtful strategies and procedural methods.

3 THE RICH REALM OF PROCESSES, CHANGE, AND CHANCE: A SURVEY OF POSSIBLE PROJECTS

I propose in what follows a few examples of problems involving, at different levels of abstraction, *processes of change* (see also Vitale 1989, 1989a, 1989b, 1990). These problems are easy to conceptualize and represent with the help of very elementary computer programming (e.g., in Logo or LogoWriter). They start from simple observations of everyday phenomena or games and can be gradually made more complex. The advantage of programming on a computer over traditional solution methods is that this process of conceptual complexification leads to only very slight, and often very trivial, changes in the program.

The reader might think, after looking through the examples given below that they are meant only for adolescent and adult learners. That would be a mistake. I do not think there are *problems* that are specifically suited to young children, adolescents, or adults. As a matter of fact, most of the foundational problems we have to tackle in mathematical, physical, and biological research today are much the same as those identified a couple of thousand years ago by both Chinese and Greek scholars (and perhaps some others). Think, for instance, of the discrete-continuous dichotomy that lead to Zeno's paradoxes and that is still with us despite all attempts at exorcism. What changes with physical age and with historical time is the *level of understanding*, the *level of solution*, and the *complexity of integration* (in a network of interpretations and meanings) of a given problem.

In this sense the projects to be discussed here are ageless. They can be presented over again, in an ever-deepening spiral, at different levels of experience and mathematical competence. A teacher can go very far with these problems because they are *open-ended problems* for which closed, analytical solutions are at best known only in the most simplified cases. We can make them as complex as we want and bring students ever nearer to the actual complexity of causal (physical, biological) situations.

What I am suggesting is that some of these dragons (and there are many dragons hidden in the forest of causal experience and symbolic description, though I do not think that any one of them is more "frabjous" than another) be presented very early to children. This should be done *before any introduction to computers and programming*, if possible in the context of some interdisciplinary course. These dragons should be introduced for what they are: open research projects, born out of curiosity, on the construction of simple models for social problems (the population explosion and control, ecology, etc.), for very complex everyday phenomena (the growth of an organism, the genesis and evolution of forms, etc.), or for games and winning strategies in a game (the extraction of balls from a box, etc.). We can present them at the beginning of secondary school and leave them to ripen, at a higher level of complexity, at the college and university level. All of them can easily develop into significant and sophisticated research projects.

The projects I will introduce in this chapter can all be begun *without a computer* by verbal and gestural analysis and by plotting adequate graphs. Then, if it is possible, they can be simulated on the computer. Qualitative, and sometimes dimensional, analysis can follow (e.g., see Birkhoff 1960). *It is only after the introductory phase that the computer will be useful* and then it should be easy to discover with the children *why* a computer is useful. What is not so easy for both teachers and children is to discover *how* we need to use a computer: *not by making it read some ready-made* (and multicolored) *software* but *by programming in the simplest way our representation of the problem.* (I will not dwell here on the problem of the child-computer relationship that underlies all effective use of a computer in school practice. What do children *expect* of the computer? Which *social and personal representations* of the computer precede their actual acquaintance with it? I refer the reader here to Hofmann et al. 1987 for a discussion of this aspect of introducing Logo into secondary school practice.)

Because of its inherent logic, Logo (as well as any other simple programming language available to children) can act as a *catalyst* in interdisciplinary explorations into new and open domains (Hoyles and Noss 1986, 1989). Very often natural phenomena have been ignored or simplified to dullness in the teaching process, mostly because they would have been too difficult to model in their complete richness and then to *calculate* by the standard tools available. If we could learn to model and then to *program* them, some of the flavor of exploration which is typical of open domains could be experienced. With the help of the computer and simple programming, mathematical education can become a domain of *experimentation* while keeping its privileged status for the development of formal thinking. We would never dream of using Logo programming to *prove* mathematical theorems, but through Logo we could explore the complex phenomenology that leads to theorems and to the construction of pertinent formal structures in our representation of causal experience.

I will give only a few pertinent references for each project: For a careful presentation of mathematics as conceptual understanding and problem solving (with some comments on *discovery learning*), see, in particular, Resnick et al. (1981). For the general problems associated with modeling and the transition from the conceptualization of a project to the choice of a possible representation for it, see, in particular, Janvier (1987) and diSessa (1987). There is also a recent paper by Johanson (1988) on the delicate question of *transferring* the competences acquired in the practice of a procedural language (e.g., Logo) or a declarative language (e.g., PROLOG) to problem solving and other cognitive and curricular domains. Equally interesting is a review on this subject by Krendl et al. (1988).

And now a few preliminary words from a mathematical perspective of the projects in the remaining sections of this chapter:

1. (Section 4) Population growth and predator-prey interaction provide an ideal framework in which to introduce *discrete time*, model *step-by-step change*; and compare the traditional euler (or possibly improved euler) method in the *continuum approach* with the staircase method in the *discrete approach*.
2. (Section 5) Cellular automata have represented the first historical example of *experimental mathematics*. A one-dimensional organism unfolds under a very simple (local) algorithm, and we discover that it is very hard to foresee the (global) configuration of the system after a few generations, together with its symmetries and possible asymptotic behavior.
3. (Section 6) Trees are a perfect representational support for classifications and a beautiful toy for complex drawing. Playing with the numerical values of the parameters and learning to modify the growth algorithm give us a taste of the complex relationship between *algorithm* (genotype?) and *form* (phenotype?). Linear and recursive programs can be proposed of equal efficacity but quite different conceptual and geometrical content.
4. (Section 7) The extraction of white-and-black balls from an urn leads to new curiosities about the mechanism of chance, the representation of results, the possibility of producing histograms "in real time" and the meaning of *limits* and *asymptotic behaviors* in a stochastic process.

4 POPULATION GROWTH AND DYNAMICAL EQUILIBRIUM AMONG POPULATIONS: AN INTRODUCTION TO ECOLOGICAL THINKING

I would therefore urge that people be introduced to, say, the "logistic" equation early in their mathematical education. This equation can be studied phenomenologically by iterating it on a calculator, or even by hand. Its study does not involve as much conceptual sophistication as does elementary calculus.
—May (1976)

Two of the best exploration fields available for simple Logo programming of an open-ended problem are the time evolution of a population and the growth of two interacting populations. These fields can be considered open-ended mathematically in that analytic solutions are available only in the simplest cases and are often beyond the technical abilities of students. They can also be said to be open-ended from the causal point of view because many of their parameters and interaction functions can only be defined through heuristic reasoning and determined by empirical research. I have recently discussed (Vitale 1988a) the rationale behind the proposal to use these fields as experimental grounds for modeling first-order dynamical systems in the continuum. I will present here both discrete and continuum modeling and will try to assess their respective domains of simple programming and easy representation.

I use the expressions *time* and *population* in their most general and sometimes metaphorical sense. Time can represent any one-dimensional evolution parameter such as temperature, nutrient concentration, and light intensity; population density can represent any variable susceptible to change as a function of a one-dimensional parameter such as chemical concentration at equilibrium, number of plants per square meter, and algae density.

The conceptualization of each case always involves the same psychopedagogical tasks:

1.   The need to make explicit the *deterministic character of the evolution* (e.g., see Freeman 1980)—stochastic models are much harder to deal with formally but can be managed rather easily by programming.
2.   The need to clarify the underlying *multiplicative structures* (as defined and studied by Vergnaud 1980, 1983, where it includes proportions and scaling), *functional dependencies* (e.g., see Thomas 1975), and *limits* and *asymptotic behaviors* (e.g., see Taback 1975).
3.   The need to find and interpret the most suitable *graphical representations* (e.g., see Janvier 1987).

For example for the *time-evolution of a given population*, I will use the *discrete approach*, since it involves only one variable (the population density) whose evolution is easily represented by a *staircase diagram* (see May 1976; Collet et al. 1980; Koçak 1986). Most reproduction models are in fact inherently discrete (alternating reproductive and sterile periods), so the finite-difference method is particularly suited.

Then, for the *interaction of two populations* (as in a predator-prey relation), I will use the *continuum approach* which involves two variables, the population densities. The case of two variables is hard to represent graphically in a *staircase diagram*; nor can it be implemented by a simple Logo program. I will show that the differential method in one of its computational variants (Euler, Runge-Kutta, etc.) lends itself to easy, transparent graphical representations of this example (see Koçak 1986).

The Discrete Case: From Equilibrium to Oscillations to Chaos in the Evolution of a Population

In the discrete case the parameters that characterize the time-evolution of a population measure the change that takes place during a given time interval dt. I will consider here only two: the *discrete linear rate of growth J* and the *discrete quadratic density constant L* (for other parameters, even explicitly time-dependent ones, see Vitale 1988a). The dependence of the numerical values of *J* and *L* on *dt* is, however, not explicit, so no limit *dt*→0 can be taken. In other words, the simplest relation giving $P(n + 1)$, the density of a given population at time $t(n + 1) = t(n) + dt$, as a function of $P(n)$, the density at the previous (discrete) time $t(n)$, is written

$$P(n + 1) = J° P(n) \qquad (J° \text{ a real positive constant}). \qquad (1)$$

It is clear that the numerical values of $J°$ depend on *dt* (e.g., the number of babies born in one week in a given population would be about one quarter of those born in a month), but once we have chosen the time interval *dt* for the problem being modeled, we will not explore *dt* dependence any further. It is only the result of the iteration of equation (1) *for a given value of $J°$* (and therefore *dt*) that will interest us from that point on.

Technically the staircase method for equation (1) is straightforward, but it is difficult to obtain a representation of it. We are used to representation spaces whose dimensions correspond to physical observables (e.g., population densities) and/or to time, namely, to dimensions whose semantic interpretation is stable in time (e.g., distance versus time or dilatation versus temperature). In the staircase diagram the two axes correspond to *the same observable*: the population density. But the *x*-axis corresponds to $P(n)$, and the *y*-axis to $P(n + 1)$. As time evolves, what was the next generation becomes the present generation, so the representative point shifts continually from one of the axes to the other by making use of the diagonal (the meeting point at which present becomes past and future becomes present; a nice philosophical locus!).

It is easy to see that $P(n)$ diverges for $n \to \infty$, if $J° > 1$, and converges to 0 if $J° < 1$. This can be shown by qualitative analysis and confirmed by a simple graph (or by programming equation 1). I will, however, give examples of the staircase method for the slightly more complex equation:

$$P(n + 1) = (1 + J - L * P(n)) * P(n) \qquad (J, L \text{ positive constants}), \qquad (2)$$

which is traditionally called the *logistic equation* (see Peitgen et al. 1986; Lergenmüller 1988). A possible program is skeleton 4 in the appendix at the end of this chapter. The density constant *L*, when different from 0, introduces a quadratic negative effect that can be very weak at low density but becomes significant

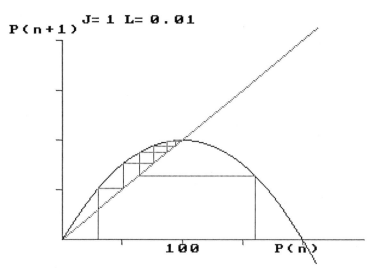

Figure 8 The staircase diagram: $P(0) = 30$ and 160, steady approach to the equilibrium point $P = 100$

enough at high densities to check the exponential growth of a population. Again, this can easily be shown by qualitative analysis and, less easily, by graphing the functional dependence expressed in equation (2). As we will see, in the continuum case there are not many surprises, and it is easy to predict that the asymptotic value of the population will be given by $P(\text{asympt.}) = J/L$ and that the limit will be reached, after a transient period, monotonically. But the discrete case provides some very interesting surprises: Keeping the value of J/L constant, for small values of J we observe the simple *monotonic behavior* discussed above; for larger values of J we start finding an *oscillatory behavior* around J/L that has no counterpart in the continuum case; for larger values still we enter an incredible realm of *instability and chaos* (see figures 8, 9, and 10 for examples of each of the three cases).

There are two further points that are worth noticing: First, purely dimensional analysis of equation (2) leads to the interesting result that it is *possible* to construct a function of the *building blocks* of the model—namely, the initial density $P(0)$, J, and L—with the dimension of *time*. We can therefore expect the occurrence of oscillations and the *period* of oscillation to be a function of the building blocks (even if it turns out to be a constant, as in the harmonic oscillator). We do not find oscillations (and therefore their periods) in the continuum case, and we might think that this dimensional potentiality of the dynamical

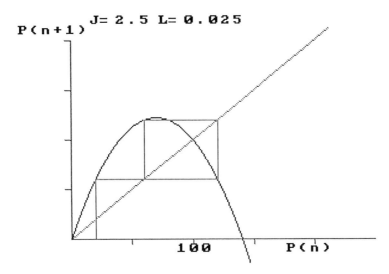

Figure 9 A two-cycle oscillation around the equilibrium point

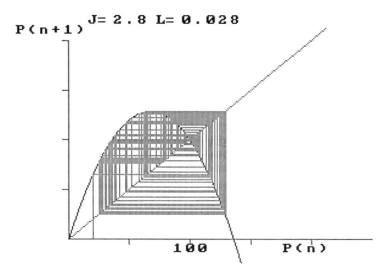

Figure 10 Chaos around the equilibrium point

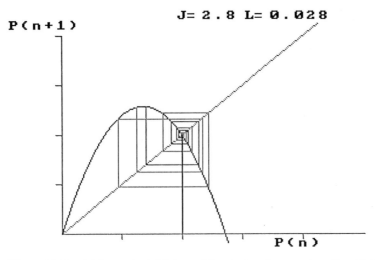

Figure 11 Sensitivity to the initial condition in the chaos region: $P = 99.999$, 100.000, and 100.001

system (2) is not realized by its solution. But for a given range of values of J and L the discrete case provides the missing period of oscillation. The lesson is that qualitative analysis gives only necessary, though insufficient, hints on the behavior of a dynamical system; it can happen that some behaviors are realized only by one of the two models (discrete and continuous) and not by both. Oscillations are not the awkward result of the use of discrete time intervals, an artifact quickly corrected by the use of the continuum model. Rather, they are present in several biological and ecological systems for which the discrete model is the only realistic one. (For more details on the differences to be expected between the results of the discrete and the continuum approaches, see, in particular, May 1974, app. III, pp. 200–203.)

Second, the chaotic behavior of equation (2) around the equilibrium attractor J/L for large enough values of J, and the corresponding sensitivity of its orbits to the initial condition $P(0)$ (figure 11), is not due to stochastic mechanisms and correspondingly nondeterministic dynamics. It is rather quite consistent with the totally deterministic dynamics expressed by the discrete time evolution of equation (2). The lesson is that chaos is not only born out of chance in wild uncontrolled systems but can also be quietly brewed by perfectly respectable and innocent-looking deterministic systems.

In sum, a simple cognitive analysis of the step-by-step growth of a population and of possible limitations to its growth, along with some dimensional and qualitative analysis and a smattering of very elementary Logo programming, has led us into the very core of contemporary discrete dynamical system theory: staircase representation, attracting equilibrium points, attracting dynamical cycles, and chaotic behavior. Can we still keep to the notion that "dynamical systems are for advanced students only," or that "Logo is for children only," as we are sometimes told?

The Continuum Case: From Smooth Cycles to Spirals to Computer Overflow in the Interaction of Two Populations

I refer the reader to Vitale (1988a) for a detailed psychocognitive analysis of the continuum model and for examples of its Logo programming (by the euler method) when the growth of a single population and the interaction of two populations are studied. In the continuum model, equation (2) is changed to

$$P(t + dt) = (1 + J*dt - L*P(t)*dt)*P(t) \qquad (J, L \text{ positive constants}). \qquad (3)$$

Iteration of equation (3) for increasingly small dt leads to successively better approximations (this, however, makes the computing time longer). The examples illustrated in Vitale (1988a) were calculated on a PC (Olivetti M24) for a fixed $dt = 0.001$, which led to very smooth orbits and did not require an unreasonable amount of time.

Once the modeling of *a single population* through equation (3) is accomplished, other parameters (cubic, periodic, etc.) can be introduced to describe growth or the interaction between two populations, or both. The simplest (Lotka-Volterra) model for two populations, predators P and preys p in the (P, p) plane, predicts *equilibrium cycles* around an *indifferent equilibrium point*. In the (P, t) and (p, t) planes this behavior leads to regular oscillations. More sophisticated models, with predator- and prey-density terms and possibly periodic parameters, result in *spiraling* activity toward an *attracting equilibrium point* (correspondingly, damped oscillations toward equilibrium) and explosive resonance, eventually leading to computer overflow.

This simple model can be used for studying the behavior of very diverse ecological systems. One example of contemporary interest is the behavior of the human AIDS virus, where the variables are the virus density V and the immune response I. In this case we would use a slightly modified Lotka-Volterra model. The HIV, however, starts out as the *prey* of the immune system (the *predators* being the leucocytes) and then becomes the *predator* (by feeding on the T4 lymphocytes which become the *prey*). (See Redfield et al. 1988 for a very interesting representation of this complex relationship in (P, t) and (p, t) planes.)

A final word on populations and time. I have used these ecological metaphors to explore one of the many subject areas where mention is made of *change*. Change is present everywhere, in physics (even in statics), chemistry, and biology, where the presentation of *processes* involving observable and measurable quantities should precede any formal analysis of *structures* and *relations between structures*. Change is surely present in economics, geography, history, and music. The representational and programming tools discussed in this section therefore have much greater application than in the study of population growth and interaction. Once developed and conceptually acquired, these tools can be stored in a special file to be used and enriched by each pupil and by the classroom over the years.

5 CELLULAR GROWTH AND MORPHOGENESIS: ORDER OUT OF THE ITERATION OF ARBITRARY RULES

The other side of the coin is the belief that one cannot program anything unless one thoroughly understands it. This misses the truth that programming is, like any form of writing, more often than not experimental. One programs, just as one writes, not because one understands, but in order to understand.
—Weizenbaum (1984)

Cellular automata have recently provided an almost inexhaustible source of models and metaphors in physics, biology, and ecology (see Demongeot et al. 1985 for a recent review of the applications, and Wolfram 1987 for a detailed presentation of the underlying mathematical and logical problems). A particular two-dimensional version, Conway's Life, has proved successful in modeling growth processes (see Gardner 1970, 1971, and Berlekamp et al. 1982 for a presentation of the game, and Finney 1986 for its PASCAL programming).

A cellular automaton simulates the growth of an initial set of *cells* (which can assume a number of *qualities*, among these, life, death, and quiescence) embedded into an *n*-dimensional lattice. The growth takes place according to a set of (largely arbitrary) *growth rules*. For instance, a living cell surrounded by too many living neighbors will die, an isolated cell will equally die, and a dying cell surrounded by two or three living ones will start living again.

This fascinating growth game permits us to explore the difficult *local–global relationship* that hampers our understanding of most processes. The local rule is simple: In the one-dimensional case the whole "organism" is represented by a line, and each "cell" is made to interact only with its second or fourth nearest neighbor. Constraints can be added—for instance, left-right symmetry, or the rule that a three-cell neighborhood of dying cells will produce only dying cells in the next generation. Once the first generation is arbitrarily given, the object is to find answers to these questions: How will the process unfold? Which internal structure, if any, will the strings of cells present? How will symmetry in the rules be felt in the ever-continuing succession of generations? Will there be an initial configuration of living cells (e.g., triads) that multiply into more identical configurations in next generations? And, if so, for which rules? Will there be initial configurations (called *Garden of Eden*) that will never again be reached during the growth process for a given rule?

For some of these questions there are no closed, analytic answers yet. If we want to *understand* what the global effect will be of a local rule and of a specific restriction of the rule, the only thing to do is to experiment with it: a very nice introduction to *experimental mathematics*. (It is not surprising that the first examples of experimental mathematics can be found in the first papers on cellular automata; see Ulam 1962 and Burks 1970.)

Skeleton 5 in the appendix gives the outline of a simple Logo program for cellular automata in the one-dimensional case. (The two-dimensional case, such as Life, can be tackled in Logo, but it is hopelessly slow and should be left to other languages and computers. See, however, Silverman 1986.) One can start from an initial configuration of randomly chosen cells (alive or dead; see figure

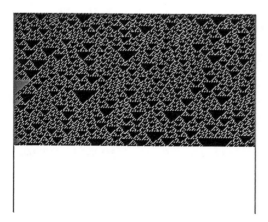

Figure 12 The initial configuration chosen at random

Figure 13 The initial germ L–L–L–L–L

12) or from a small *germ* of, say, five cells in a given configuration (e.g., L–L–L–L–L in figure 13). One has to choose a growth rule (indicated by a code at the top of the figures) and then let the run start. The initial configuration and the iteration of the rule produces interesting and sometimes very surprising patterns.

The *two-dimensional unfolded cellular automaton* (the pattern created on the screen by the growth of the initial one-dimensional configuration) is an interesting type of game: the initial germ can just die, it (or one of the next configurations) can reproduce itself in a periodic process, or *chaos* can be established after a few generations. Even if all *finite* cellular automata are periodic, as seems to be the case, the period can be so large that suicidal, converging, periodic, or chaotic behavior can be very well defined for the first hundred generations; think, for instance, of a one-dimensional cellular automaton with 200 cells and calculate the largest possible period! We find here a situation not very different from that encountered in section 4 in the modeling of population growth and interaction. For discrete processes, a smooth growth can change into a periodic one and then into a chaotic one—and all that for a small change in the values of the parameters (in section 4) or in the growth rules (this section).

6 TREES, INSECTS, AND BIOMORPHS: AN EXPLORATION INTO THE SPACES OF ALGORITHMS AND EVOLUTION

Every person who programs realizes an astonishing discordance between the local simplicity of a program, on the one hand, and the—often insurmountable—global complexity, on the other hand. Locally each instruction is immediately understandable, but the

global structure of a program appears rather complex . . .; often the surprised user finds it difficult to understand what is really happening.
—Wertz (1981)

Trees are beautiful structures, and their graphical representation can be usefully introduced into mathematical courses at all levels. In this section I will describe two interdisciplinary projects that involve tree programs. The first—an interdisciplinary approach to *experimental geometry, drawing*, and *programming*—enables pupils to use algorithms without knowing it. Trees, plants, and flowers unfold on the screen while pupils explore the spaces of parameters and algorithms. The second—an interdisciplinary approach to *experimental algorithm transformation, biology*, and *programming*—enables pupils to follow the evolution of organisms such as plants and insects, or it can even transform plants *into insects*. The user can model natural selection. By changing a parameter or an algorithm, pupils can create biomorphs that become increasingly more adapted to survival according to the (functional and morphological) criteria chosen.

The World of Trees, Plants, and Flowers

A familiar exercise in drawing classes is drawing *trees*: by observing trees outdoors, by copying another drawing, by drawing trees from memory. In general, drawings of trees have a lot in common, since *trees* are represented distinctively differently from, say, houses or floral bouquets. In particular, drawings of winter trees that have bare branches allow for the introduction of a standard mathematical topic: the definition of a problem in terms of an *algorithm* and the *set and range of variables* and *parameters associated with it*. From this we can then easily progress to an interesting programming project.

Take leafless trees. All of them are different, and yet they have in common a basic *construction*: At each node a branch divides into a number of other branches; this scheme reoccurs over and over again. This is the *algorithm*. The entire tree is defined—at least as a line drawing on paper—by the two plane coordinates up–down, left–right, of the nodes. These are the *variables*. And then there are the parameters: for instance, the length of the initial trunk L and perhaps also of the branches at different development stages, the angle A that each new branch makes at each node with its parent branch, the left–right asymmetry engendered by the presence of a constant wind B, and the number of branches into which the parent branch divides at every node M.

TREE2   70   34   9   7

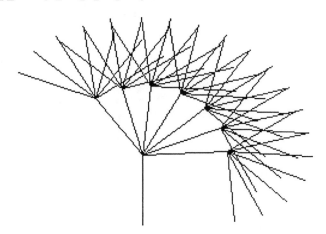

Figure 14 The simplest tree

Skeleton 6 has an interesting and, to me, essential feature: The tree structure is realized by a rather transparent *iterative procedure that follows step by step the construction of a tree instead of the traditional (and completely opaque) nonlinear, nonterminal recursive procedure* that is offered in Logo manuals (see Vitale 1989d for a more detailed, argued analysis of recursive versus iterative procedures in Logo and for an example of recursive tree programs). This allows for the number of branches developing at each node to be given as a parameter M, contrary to what happens in the recursive approach, where one has to change the program to change M and the number of developmental stages is treated as a parameter. In the iterative procedure of skeleton 6 the *user* has to change the program to obtain this number (by stacking TREE2, BRANCH, and TREE1), but this is rather easy because of its clear correspondence to the actual process of drawing a tree. The lesson to be learned here is that breaking up a problem into algorithm, variables, and parameters is not necessarily unique: Different procedural representations of the problem lead to different forms of analysis. It is worth exploring, where possible, several different representations to judge the merits and shortcomings of each.

Figure 14 gives the tree image that was the result of running the tree program with the given values of the parameters (TREE2 of course generates a tree with two developmental stages). The image obtained with a modified algorithm for five developmental stages is given in figure 15. It is easy to appreciate the incredi-

TREE5   20 21 10 2

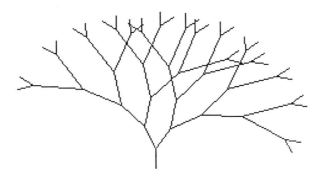

Figure 15 A five-level tree

ble richness of the botanic form, which can be a tree, bush, flower, or herb, that can be obtained just by modifying the values of the parameters. The fact that through drawing and thinking about the creation of a drawing—in terms of the underlying algorithm, pertinent variables and parameters, and simple programming—it is possible to capture the *essence* of a tree should be addressed in classroom discussion, followed by wide and wild experimentation in creating recognizable vegetative forms by changing parameters. (Furthermore the fact that, when the numerical values of *L* change, nothing but the *scale* of the drawing changes can introduce the class to a discussion of *scaling invariance*. Why is *L* such a *qualitatively different parameter* than *A*, *B*, or *M*?) Finally, pupils may discover that when they explore too wildly and change too much the more familiar values of the parameters and/or the structure of the algorithm, they enter a different world: that of *biomorphs*. Biomorphs can have little or nothing to do with what we call usually *trees*; all the same they are engendered by the same *algorithm* (program) or by very similar algorithms.

Evolution and Biomorphs

Dawkins (1986, 1987; see also Dewdney 1988) has simulated on a computer the effects of natural evolution on the shape of an organism. Dawkins's programs are rather elaborate, recursive, and written in PASCAL. I use skeleton 6 in the appendix (any of its derived programs can be used as well) to obtain much the same effect in a more transparent way, more accessible to a secondary-school pupil. The game is easy and can become an exciting class project. It starts out

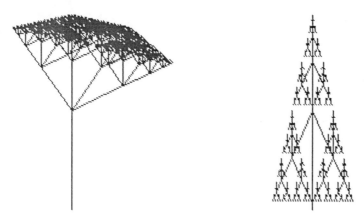

Figure 16 Changing angle, wind strength, and number of branches per node

with a tree, and the players have to change it by altering by a small, definite amount *one* of the parameters such as the angle *A*. Then they must decide, by finding some rationale for it, which of the forms obtained is the best suited for survival in a given environment (e.g., in a dense forest the form that leads to a more compact vertical tree). Now this form becomes the starting tree, and the players proceed to change it by altering by a small, definite amount *another* parameter such as the constant-wind asymmetry *B*. Again, among the forms obtained, they decide which is the best suited for survival in a windy environment. So the game proceeds. Which will be the fittest forms on which the players will settle? Will these forms resemble the initial tree, or will they tend toward quite different biomorphs? (A challenge here would be to program the *algorithm change* itself and let the program take care of the different evolutionary steps.)

Figure 16 shows the transition from one tree morphology to another that is the result of changing parameter values in a program. Figure 17 shows how, by again changing only parameter values, one is led from the world of botanic morphology to the world of insect morphology. The player can easily change the program structure as well as escape into a fantasy world of new, intriguing biomorphs.

7 ENTER CHANCE: PICKING UP WHITE AND BLACK BALLS

Showing my friend how to ride a bike seemed to be of little value to her. My advice "Watch me and then do what I did" caused more anxiety than help. Problem solving is similar insofar as no description, no matter how carefully worded to include all the key

Figure 17 With angle change, plants changed into insects

components, can express its complexity, subtlety, and high personal nature.
—Lester (1983)

The preceding remark is particularly appropriate to the Eggenberger-Pólya urn problem to be discussed presently. Several different representations are possible, each of them useful and clarifying in some way, yet it would be difficult to assess which of them is richer than the others.

 The highly personal nature of the representational problem manifests itself very clearly in the urn problem, and a teacher should be careful to let the different conceptualizations grow independently and then compare them. The problem is a curious one, extremely simple to state, to make operational, and to program, yet it is strangely difficult to solve formally in the context of probability theory. Its formal aspects are dealt with in Blackwell et al. (1964), and some of its epistemological aspects are discussed in Milgram (1983) together with the possible metaphorical implications for the biological and the social sciences.

 Take an urn containing a white ball and a black ball (initial configuration: $[W\ B]$, the order being immaterial inside the list; ratio white/black $= R = 1$). Then, without looking, extract one of the balls. If it happens to be a white one, put two white balls inside the urn; if black, put two black ones inside. The first-step configuration can therefore be either $[W\ B\ W]$ $(R = 2)$ or $[W\ B\ B]$ $(R = 0.5)$.

 What would happen if one iterates this procedure an arbitrary number of times? Presumably when there are very many balls inside the urn, the addition of a single white or black ball should not significantly alter R. One could therefore reasonably expect R to tend to some stable value in the open interval $(0, +\infty)$, say, R(asympt.). Then, when the game starts up again, would the same asymptotic value R(asympt.) be obtained or a different one, equally stable after the initial fluctuations? In the latter case, what would be the distribution of R(asympt.) after several rounds when there is enough information about these nearly stable asymptotic limits?

This problem is a tricky one, since the probability of a white or black ball being inside the urn *changes with the number of extractions* in a stochastic way, making the standard branching-process method of probability theory inapplicable. One could go into a classroom with a box full of black and white balls and start extracting them according to the above rule. Inferring the near stability of the asymptotic values of R requires some complex conceptualization, in particular recognition of the *weight* that an event can have on a given configuration and the kind of *fluctuations* to be expected, (though fluctuations can cumulate stochastically and the stability of R can be threatened at any moment along the iteration chain). The probability of getting a *different asymptotic value of R* with every run is harder to justify, except perhaps by a symmetry argument: Why should *one* value of R be preferred with respect to other values? (This argument could also lead to the plausible but false assumption that asymptotically $R = 1$ because of the equal distribution of black and white balls at the beginning of the game.) Some remarks at the beginning of each run about the role of very large fluctuations might help to clarify this point. This approach can be even more effective if the game is actually played by hand, with real balls inside a real urn, and each step is discussed before proceeding to the next step. The distribution of asymptotic values of R is harder to visualize: A flat R between 0 and $+\infty$ is improbable, so it must be weighted toward the smaller values, but how?

No doubt after a few hundred extractions of balls from an urn, teachers and pupils will be exhausted. But *why* use real balls and urns? Why not juggle letters like W and B? Why not use filled-in circles in a diagram? Why not *program* the extractions and the chosen symbols and let the program run and tell us what is happening? Here is where different conceptualizations of the problem can suggest a number of different representative paths. We can choose among several possibilities, for instance:

1.   Represent, after the nth extraction, the *contents of the urn*, and print the corresponding values of n and $R(n)$.
2.   Represent only R as a function of n in order to follow graphically its fluctuations up to some predefined n (e.g., n(max) = 1,000).
3.   Represent as a function of R the frequency with which a given value of R has been reached (e.g., at the 1,000th extraction).

Playing Only with Letters

In using letters to stand for the balls, no graphical representation is needed. At, say, the thirteenth extraction the output will be something like

$n = 13, [W\ B\ B\ B\ W\ B\ W\ W\ B\ B\ B\ W\ B\ W\ W]$,
$R = 7/8 = 0.875$.

But how does the computer know if the extracted ball is white or black? In this procedure there is an *identification step* (other procedures are of course possible, as will be presented below) that enables the computer to check whether the extracted item is W or B (see skeleton 7 in the appendix). After a few tens of extractions the letters on the screen can become unwieldy. Clearly there is a need for a more compact, graphical mode of representation.

Following the Fluctuations

I now use a different *identification step*: At the nth extraction, when there are $n + 2$ balls ($n(W)$ of them white, $n(B)$ black) in the urn, the computer chooses at random a number x between 0 and $n - 1$. If $x < n(W)$, the new ball will be white (and therefore $n(W) \leftarrow n(W) + 1$); otherwise, $n(B) \leftarrow n(B) + 1$ (skeleton 8 in the appendix).
     This program is particularly useful when we want to follow the fluctuations in R for the first few extractions of each run (figure 18), as well as its relative stability around its asymptotic value for a large enough number of extractions and for each run (figure 19). The discussion is open at this point: Can we really speak of asymptotic *values* in this case? Could not a fluctuation (though decreasing in probability) upset at any moment the convergence toward the asymptotic value? In what sense, and with what limits, can we speak of *convergence*?

Integrating the Limit Values of R into a Histogram

The construction *in real time* of a histogram is for me the most challenging representation. It does not need a whole collection of data on R to be supplied beforehand but uses the information on the *color* under the turtle position to climb the y-axis (skeleton 9 in the appendix).
     One must decide beforehand of course at which number of extractions one feels satisfied that an almost stable limit value of R has been reached (figure 19 shows that $n = 10,000$ is not even enough). Then one must decide about

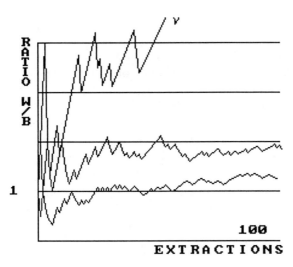

Figure 18 Three runs showing large initial fluctuations

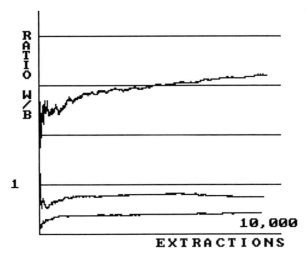

Figure 19 Three runs showing the relative stabilization of *R*

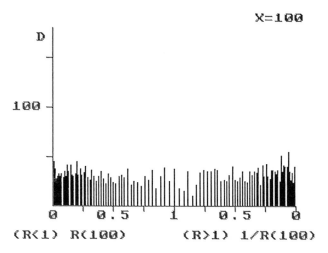

Figure 20 Distribution in *R* for 2,500 runs of 100 extractions each

the *R*-axis. Going from 0 to ∞ along the *x*-axis would lead to a clumsy and asymmetric representation; we can presume that, statistically, there will be as many values of *R* in the open interval (0, 1) as in the open interval (1, ∞) (the value *R* = 1 will be present only if the number of chosen extractions for each run is even). I chose in figure 20 to represent *R* when $0 < R < 1$, and $1/R$ when $1 < R < ∞$, so that the histogram would be symmetric.

Logo on a PC is not well suited for this task because a PC is too slow (the *n* = 100 cutoff value in figure 20 is much too small and was used only to minimize computing time; it falls right in the middle of large fluctuations). If done on a PC, the project might be useful in whetting the pupils' and teacher's appetite for a more powerful language and access to a faster computer.

8 CONCLUSION

I find myself compelled to extend the domain of mathematics so that it will provide room, provide closure, for all the mapping operations of a teacher. Mathematics so considered will obviously overlap with other parts or aspects of the curriculum. A child tracing the flow of coloured water through a transparent siphon is not being a mathematician, or physicist, or town engineer, nor simply delighting in the intuition of colour motion. What he is being is a matter of his momentary trajectory of learning.
—Hawkins (1973)

What we can do with Logo is perhaps not so much to extend the domain of mathematics as to make explicit the logicomathematical aspects of all formalized experience and description of the world of causality. When we are confronted with a new phenomenon, a new game, a new cognitive puzzle, the underlying logicomathematical frame gives relevance and coherence to an apparently disordered scattering of data. An essential component of this logicomathematical frame is the integration into a *process* (into the *time* dimension) of a set of experimental data that (without time ordering) would only be a dust of unrelated points in a space of arbitrary topology. (See Marmo et al. 1985, pt. 1, for a discussion of the relation of time ordering to topology for a dynamical carrier space.)

Time ordering creates processes and also makes possible conceptualizations and graphical representations of these processes. As I have tried to show in the examples of this chapter, the study of processes and their programming in an easy formal language such as Logo can enrich the learning experience of mathematics. The examples I use are only a very small sample of the large number of processes that can be analyzed, discussed, and explored on the computer and in the classroom at all levels, beginning with secondary school. In particular, there are the processes associated with *transformations* (e.g., one of the most important being *aging*). Transformations lead to groups and symmetries (see Freudenthal 1973 for an appreciation of the study of groups and symmetries in problem solving), and when associated with *chance*, they can lead to stochastic *fractals* (Mandelbrot 1982). We are again at the very core of contemporary mathematics!

I am tempted to say that no mathematical dragon can withstand the strength of Logo programming. Eventually it may turn out that this is not the case. The limitations and slowness of the language and of elementary programming—even if one disregards, for instance, nonterminal and nonlinear recursion—make Logo unsuitable for projects requiring in-depth exploration. The discrete, approximate, time-bounded approach of the computer and the intrinsic limitations of a procedural language make all considerations on limits, asymptotic behaviors, divergences, and so on, purely *heuristic*; they will not take the place of the much needed and always stimulating *formal* results. *Nor will we ever prove theorems with Logo*. But each new dragon, even an untreatable one, provides a nice challenge, one that can contribute to and enliven the generally heavy atmosphere of a mathematics classroom.

APPENDIX: SKELETON PROGRAMS IN IBM-PC LCSI LOGO[2]

Skeleton 4 (The Staircase Method, Figures 8–11)

```
TO POPULATION1 :J :L
    WINDOW MAKE "A :J MAKE "B :L MAKE "X 0 MAKE "Y 0
    P1
END

TO P1
    SETPOS LIST :X FX1 :A :B MAKE "X :X + 1
    P1
END

TO FX1 :A :B
    OUTPUT :X * (1 + :A − :B * :X)
END

TO VIA :X0
    PU SETPOS LIST :X0 0 PD MAKE "X :X0
    VIA1
END

TO VIA1
    MAKE "Y FX1 :A :B SETPOS LIST :X :Y SETPOS LIST :Y :Y MAKE "X :Y
    VIA1
END
```

Skeleton 5 (Development of a 200-Cell One-Dimensional Organism,
Figures 12 and 13)

```
TO CELLAUTOM :A :B :C :D :E
    FS CS PU SETH 90 SETPOS [−100 100] PD REPEAT 200 [MAKE "H RANDOM
    2 IF :H = 0 [SETPC 1] [SETPC 2] DOT POS FORWARD 1]
    GO1
END
```

---

2. Procedures CP1, CP2, CP3 and STAMP1 require a version of Logo which has a primitive
COLORUNDER (IBM Logo II) or its equivalent.

```
TO GO1
    MAKE "N 1 REPEAT 200 [MAKE "M 1 REPEAT 200 [SETPOS LIST
    (−100 + :M) (100 − :N) DRAW MAKE "M :M + 1] MAKE "N :N + 1]
END

TO DRAW
    MAKE "L [ ]
    CP1 CP2 CP3
    IF :L = [1 1 1] [SETPC :A]
    IF :L = [1 1 2] [SETPC :B]
    IF :L = [1 2 1] [SETPC :C]
    IF :L = [1 2 2] [SETPC :D]
    IF :L = [2 1 1] [SETPC :B]
    IF :L = [2 1 2] [SETPC :E]
    IF :L = [2 2 1] [SETPC :D]
    IF :L = [2 2 2] [SETPC :2]
    DOT POS
END

TO CP1
    MAKE "C1 COLORUNDER LIST (XCOR − 1) (YCOR + 1) MAKE "L LPUT :C1
    :L
END

TO CP2
    MAKE "C2 COLORUNDER LIST XCOR (YCOR + 1) MAKE "L LPUT :C2 :L
END

TO CP3
    MAKE "C3 COLORUNDER LIST (XCOR + 1) (YCOR + 1) MAKE "L LPUT :C3
    :L
END
```

Skeleton 6 (Trees using a Nonrecursive Approach, Figures 14–17)

```
TO TREE2 :L :A :B :M
    SETPC 3 PU SETPOS LIST 0 −:L SETH 0
    PD FORWARD :L
    MAKE "PX [ ] MAKE "PY [ ] MAKE "PH [ ]
```

```
   BRANCH
   REPEAT :M [TREE1] MS
END

TO BRANCH
   PD LEFT :A
   REPEAT :M [FORWARD :L MAKE "PX LPUT XCOR :PX MAKE "PY
   LPUT YCOR :PY MAKE "PH LPUT HEADING :PH BACK :L RIGHT 2 *
   :A/(:M − 1) + :B]
   SETH 0 PU
END

TO TREE1
   SETPOS LIST (ITEM 1 :PX) (ITEM 1 :PY) SETH ITEM 1 :PH MAKE "PX BF
   :PX MAKE "PY BF :PY MAKE "PH BF :PH
   BRANCH
END
```

Skeleton 7 (Ball Extractions and Letter Display)

```
TO BALLS1
   MAKE "NW 1 MAKE "NB 1 MAKE "A [W B]
   (PRINT :A 1)
   B11
END

TO B11
   MAKE "X COUNT :A
   MAKE "C ITEM (1 + RANDOM (:X − 1)) :A
   MAKE "A LPUT :C :A
   IF :C = "B [MAKE "NB :NB + 1] [MAKE "NW :NW + 1]
   MAKE "R :NW/:NB
   (PRINT :A :R)
   B11
END
```

Skeleton 8 (Ball Extractions and Graphical Display, Figures 18 and 19)

```
TO BALLS2
   FS WINDOW HT MAKE "W 1 MAKE "B 1 MAKE "M 0
```

```
      PU SETPOS [−100 −100] PD
      SORT
END

TO SORT
      MAKE "H RANDOM (:W + :B)
      IF :H < :W [MAKE "W :W + 1] [MAKE "B :B + 1]
      MAKE "R :W/:B MAKE "M :M + 1
      SETPOS LIST (−100 + :M ) (100 + 50 * :R)
      SORT
END
```

Skeleton 9 (Real Time Histograms for White/Black Ratio after X Ball Extractions, Figure 20 with x = 100)

```
TO BALLS3 :X
      MAKE "W 1 MAKE "B 1 MAKE "C 0 MAKE "F 0 MAKE "CW 0 MAKE "CB 0
      SETPC 1 PU SETPOS [0 − 100] PU
      B1
END

TO B1
      MAKE "D RANDOM (:W + :B)
      IF :D < :W [MAKE "W :W + 1] [MAKE "B :B + 1]
      MAKE "C :C + 1
      IF :C < (:X − 1) [MAKE "M 0 MAKE "R :W/:B STAMP1 STOP] [B1]
END

TO STAMP1
      IF :R < 1 [SETPOS LIST (100 * :R − 100) (:M − 100)] [SETPOS LIST (100 * (1 − 1/
      :R)) (:M − 100)]
      IF COLORUNDER = 3 [MAKE "M :M + 1 STAMP1] [PD SETPC 3 DOT POS PU
      BALLS3 :X]
END
```

REFERENCES

Berlekamp, E. R., Conway, J. H., and Guy, R. K. 1982. *Winning Ways for Your Mathematical Games*. New York: Academic Press.

Birkhoff, G. 1960. Modeling and dimensional analysis. *Hydrodynamics: A Study on Logic, Fact and Similitude*. Westport: Greenwood Press, ch. 4

Blackwell, D., and Kendall, D. 1964. The Martin boundary for Pólya's urn scheme, and an application to stochastic population growth. *Journal of Applied Probability* 1: 284–297. (The problem was first discussed in Eggenberger, F., and Pólya, G. 1923. Über die Statistik verketteter Vorgänge. *Zeit. angew. Math. Mech.* 3: 279–289.)

Burks, A. W. (ed.). 1970. *Essays on Cellular Automata*. Urbana: University of Illinois Press.

Cohen, H. A. 1973. *A Dragon Hunter Book*. Victoria: Hanging Lake Books.

Collet, P., and Eckmann, J. -P. 1980. *Iterated Maps on the Interval as Dynamical Systems*. Boston: Birkhauser.

Dawkins, R. 1986. Creation and natural selection. *New Scientist*, 25 September 1986.

Dawkins, R. 1987. *The Blind Watchmaker*. London: Norton.

Demongeot, J., Golès, E. and Tchuente, M. (eds.). 1985. *Dynamical Systems and Cellular Automata*. New York: Academic Press.

Dewdney, A. K. 1988. A blind watchmaker surveys the land of biomorphs (computer recreations). *Scientific American* 258 February: 84–87.

Dionnet, S., Guyot, J., and Vitale, B. 1987. Les aspects psycho-cognitifs de l'animation informatique. In M. Descolonges and F. Enel (eds.), *Les Activités d'animation informatique dans un contexte non scolaire*. Paris: Ministère de la Culture et au Ministère de la Jeunesse et des Sports, 148–176.

Dionnet, D., Guyot, J., and Vitale, B. 1989. Gioco, simulazione e ambiente di apprendimento; La caccia al tesoro. In G.Marucci (ed.), *Computer e software didattico*. Perugia: Giunti e Lisciani, 139–148.

diSessa, A. A. 1987. Artificial worlds and real experience. In R. L. Lawler and M. Yazdani (eds.), *Artificial Intelligence and Education*. Vol. 1: *Learning Environment and Tutoring Systems*. Norwood, NJ: Ablex, 55–78.

Finney, C. 1986. On counting in the game of life. *Computers and Education* 10: 315–325.

Freedman H. I. 1980. *Deterministic Mathematical Models in Population Ecology*. New York: Dekker.

Freudenthal, H. 1973. What groups mean in mathematics and what they should mean in mathematical education. In *Procęeding of ICME-2*. Cambridge: Cambridge University Press, 101–114.

Gardner, M. 1970. Mathematical recreations. *Scientific American* 223: 120–123.

Gardner, M. 1971. Mathematical recreations. *Scientific American* 224: 112–117.

Hawkins, D. 1973. Nature, man and mathematics. In *Proceedings of ICME-2*. Cambridge: Cambridge University Press, 115–135.

Hofmann, B., deMarcellus, O., Rey, F., and Vitale, B. 1987. *TATUE. Le Rapport élèveordinateur: Une Évaluation formative du cours d'informatique du Cycle d'orientation*. Geneva: CRPP.

Hofmann, B., deMarcellus, O., Rey, F., and Vitale, B. 1989. *Observation de cours d'initiation à l'informatique: Complément à la recherche "TATUE."* Geneva: CRPP.

Hoyles, C., and Noss, R. 1986. How does the computer enlarge the scope of doable mathematics? In C. Hoyles, R. Noss, and R. Sutherland (eds.), *Proceedings of the Second International Conference for Logo and Mathematic Education*. London: Institute of Education, 142–153.

Hoyles, C., and Noss, R. 1989. The computer as a catalyst in children's proportion strategies. *Journal of Mathematical Behaviour* 8: 53–75.

ICME-2. 1973. *Developing mathematical education. Proceedings of Second ICME*, Exeter, 1972. Cambridge: Cambridge University Press.

Janvier, C. (ed.). 1987. *Problems of Representation in the Teaching and Learning of Mathematics*. Hillsdale, NJ: Lawrence Erlbaum Associates.

Johanson, R. P. 1988. Computers, cognition and curriculum: Retrospect and prospect. *Journal of Educational Computing Research* 4: 1–10.

Klaue, K., and Marti, E. 1988. Private communication.

Krendl, K. A., and Lieberman, D. A. 1988. Computers and learning. A review of recent research. *Journal of Educational Computing Research* 4: 367–389.

Koçak, H. 1986. *Differential and difference equations through computer experiments* (with 2 disquettes containing PHASER: An animator/simulator for dynamical systems for IBM personal computers). New York: Springer. (Chs.1 and 7 deal with differential equations; chs. 3 and 8 with difference equations.)

Lergenmüller, A. 1988. Rekursionen, ein andwendungsorientierter Einstieg in die Analysis. *Mathematikunterricht* 34: 43–67.

Lesh, R., and Landau, M. (eds.). 1983. *Acquisition of Mathematical Concepts and Processes*. New York: Academic Press.

Lester, F. K. 1983. Trends and issues in mathematical problem solving research. In R. Lesh and M. Landau (eds)., *Acquisition of Mathematical Concepts and Process*. New York: Academic Press, 229–264.

Mandelbrot, B. 1982. *The Fractal Geometry of Nature*. San Francisco: Freeman.

Marmo, G., Saletan, E., Simoni, A. and Vitale, B. 1985. *Dynamical Systems; A Differential-Geometric Approach to Reduction and Symmetry*. New York: Wiley.

May, R. M. 1974. *Stability and Complexity in Model Ecosystems*. Princeton: Princeton University Press.

May, R. M. 1976. Simple mathematical models with very complicated dynamics. *Nature* 261: 459–467.

Michener, E. R. 1978. The structure of mathematical knowledge. DSRE Working Papers No. 3. Cambridge: MIT.

Milgram, M. 1983. Les Formalismes du hasard. In P. Dumouchel and J. P. Dupuy (eds.), *L'Auto-organisation de la physique au politique*. Paris: Seuil, 201–212.

Peitgen, H. -O., and Richter, P. H. 1986. *The Beauty of Fractals: Images of Complex Dynamical Systems*. New York: Springer.

Redfield, R. R., and Burke, D. S. 1988. HIV infection: The clinical picture. *Scientific American* 258 (October): 70–79.

Resnick, L. B., and Ford, W. W. 1981. *The Psychology of Mathematics for Instruction*. Hillsdale, NJ: Lawence Erlbaum Associates.

Rosskopf, M. F. (ed.). 1975. *Children's Mathematical Concepts: Six Piagetian Studies in Mathematical Education*. New York: Teachers College Press.

Silverman, B. 1986. Life game and beyond. In *LOGO'85*. Cambridge: MIT Press, 208.

Sylva, K., Bruner, J. S., and Genova, P. 1976. The role of play in the problem solving of childrens 3–5 years old. In J. S. Bruner, A. Jolly and K. Sylva (eds.), *Play: Its Role in Development and Evolution*. Harmondworth: Penguin, 244–257.

Taback, S. 1975. The child's concept of limit. In M. F. Rosskopf *Children's Mathematical Concepts: Six Piagetian Studies in Mathematical Education*. New York: Teachers College Press, 111–144.

Thomas, H. L. 1975. The concept of function. In M. F. Rosskopf (eds.), *Children's Mathematical Concepts: Six Piagetian Studies in Mathematical Education*. New York: Teachers Collage Press, 192–208.

Ulam, S. M. 1962. On some mathematical problems connected with patterns of growth of figures. *Proceedings of the American Mathematical Society* 14: 215–224.

Vergnaud, G. 1980. Didactics and acquisition of "multiplicative structures" in secondary schools. In W. F. Archenhold, R. H. Driver, A. Orton, and C. Wood-Robinson (eds.), *Cognitive Development Research in Science and Mathematics*. Leeds: University of Leeds, 190–200.

Vergnaud G. 1983: Multiplicative structures. In R. Lesh and M. Landau (eds.), *Acquisition of Mathematical Concepts and Processes*. New York: Academic Press, 127–174.

Vitale, B. 1988. Epistemology and pedagogy of children's approach to informatics (International Congress on Education, Bilbao, 1987). In M. Aguirregabiria (ed.), *Technología y educación*. Madrid: Narcea, 138–148.

Vitale, B. 1988. Psycho-cognitive aspects of dynamical model-building in Logo: A simple population evolution and predator/prey model. *Journal of Educational Computing Research* 4: 227–252.

Vitale, B. 1989a. L'Intégration de l'informatique à la pratique pédagogique, 1: Considérations générales pour une approche transdisciplinaire. Geneva: CRPP.

Vitale, B. 1989b. L'Intégration de l'informatique à la pratique pédagogique, 2: Les Projets. Book I: Jeux (ou, plus sérieusement, psychologie expérimentale). Geneva: CRPP.

Vitale, B. 1989c: L'intégration de l'informatique à la pratique pédagogique, 2: Les Projets. Book III: Croissance et changement. Geneva: CRPP.

Vitale, B. 1989d. Elusive recursion: A trip in recursive land. *New Ideas in Psychology* 7(3): 253–276.

Vitale, B. 1990b. The exploration of the space of informatics and the realm of open mathematics. In W. Blum, M. Niss, and I. Huntley (eds.), *Modelling, Applications and Applied Problem Solving: Teaching Mathematics in a Real Context*. Chichester: Horwood.

Weizenbaum, J. 1984. *Computer Power and Human Reason: From Judgement to Calculation*. Harmondsworth: Penguin.

Wertz, H. 1981. Some ideas on the educational use of computers. Los Angeles: *Proceedings of the Annual Conference of the ACM*, 101–107.

Of Geometry, Turtles, and Groups 11
Uri Leron and Rina Zazkis

1 INTRODUCTION

This chapter touches upon topics from mathematics, computer science and education. To describe our approach, we use the metaphor of "building bridges" among the different disciplines as well as among the various topics within each discipline. The mathematical aspects involve euclidean geometry, turtle geometry, and group theory. There are three possible bridges between the various pairs of these topics, and it turns out that all are interesting to study. The bridge-spanning euclidean geometry and group theory (via transformations) has long been established through Klein's *Erlangen Programme*. The other two bridges—the *geometry bridge* connecting turtle geometry and euclidean geometry and the *turtle bridge* connecting geometrical and algebraic aspects of turtle mathematics—form a major part of the present study. A major tool in building both of these bridges is the *turtle group*—roughly the group of all turtle motions.

For example, in studying the geometry bridge, we determine the turtle analogues of translations and rotations of the euclidean plane. (Contrary to the initial intuition of many, these are not simply FORWARD and RIGHT.) The question then naturally arises as to what is the turtle analogue of line *reflections*. It turns out that the turtle group does not contain the appropriate turtle operation; that is, the analogue of reflection cannot be obtained as a combination of the usual turtle operations.[1] The problem is solved by adding a new turtle operation FLIP that flips the turtle on its back.[2] Formally these connections are summarized by saying that the turtle group is isomorphic to the group of direct trans-

---

1. Throughout the chapter we use "turtle operation" in its mathematical rather than computational sense. That is, operation as transformation or mapping, rather than a procedure (or function) that outputs a Logo object. For example, FD 50 is a turtle operation in this terminology.

2. This is quite different from Edwards's FLIP (chapter 5 in this volume). Edwards's FLIP is a transformation of the euclidean plane (a reflection); ours is a turtle operation. In fact, assuming Edwards's L-shape is fixed so that the "long side" lies on the *y*-axis, our FLIP is the element in the turtle group corresponding to her FLIP in the euclidean group.

formations of the euclidean plane (i.e., the group generated by translations and rotations but no reflections). The extended turtle group (with FLIP added) is isomorphic to the full euclidean group.

A further "math-cs bridge," connecting turtle mathematics and Logo programming, has received much attention in the Logo literature (e.g., Abelson and diSessa 1980; Papert 1980). In this context we view Logo as a language for expressing mathematical entities (processes, relations, objects) and relate this view to the mathematical issues mentioned above. For example, we have seen that the turtle group has no turtle analogue to line reflection in the euclidean plane. In computer science terms, we could say that the original turtle language is not rich enough to express the notion of reflection. However, just as we can extend the turtle group by adding a new operation, so can we extend the turtle language by adding the new command FLIP. We will show that this extension significantly increases the *expressive power* of the language.[3] We discuss this bridge in section 11.4.

The potential implications of the above "bridges" for mathematics education will be discussed in section 7. Here we mention briefly three kinds of possible contributions. First, there are some new insights (into both content and methods) for the teaching of the traditional topics of geometry and group theory. Second, by exploring the relations between turtle geometry and euclidean geometry, showing in a sense their equivalence, the two geometries can be seen as complementary rather than rivals: turtle operations as a stepping stone toward, rather than a replacement for, transformations of the euclidean plane. Finally, there is the issue of conflicting mental imagery concerning transformations. Here we are concerned with the gap between the intuitive, real-life origin of transformations—actions on physical objects—and the formal mathematical definition of them as mappings of the entire plane onto itself. Experience shows that this gap is the source of many problems in learning about transformations (cf. "mental models of the plane" in Edwards, chapter 5 in this volume). Presumably good understanding of transformations involves both intuitive and formal views, and most important, the ability to easily shift back and forth between them. We conjecture that transitionally considering plane transformations as "acting on a turtle" (a view that gets its mathematical justification here) can be helpful in achieving an integrated view.

---

3. The "expressive power" of programming languages is a central issue in current views of computer science. See Abelson and Sussman (1985), pp. 52, 69, 72, and 73.

2 INFORMAL OVERVIEW

The Group of the Turtle

On an intuitive level the elements of the turtle group are the turtle operations FORWARD (FD) and RIGHT (RT), with all possible real inputs and their combinations. These elements can be represented by sequences of FDs and RTs. For example, the sequence <FD 50 RT 90 FD 36 RT 14 FD −70 RT −56> represents a group element. The group operation is composition of functions, and it can be represented by concatenation of the respective sequences. Note that the turtle operations LEFT and BACK are also included via FORWARD and RIGHT with negative inputs.

In this intuitive view turtle operations are just that: physical (or computational, or mental) *actions* on a physical (computational, mental) object—the turtle; and their precise mathematical nature is left unspecified.

The Two Geometries Related

We proceed to establish, still on an intuitive level, the fundamental correspondence between the two geometries. That is, we construct an isomorphism (a one-to-one structure-preserving map) from the turtle group onto the group of direct isometries of the euclidean plane.

The basic idea is simple: The turtle corresponds to a particular isosceles triangle in the euclidean plane, and turtle motions to triangle motions. More explicitly, given a turtle operation (i.e., an element of the turtle group), we first consider its effect on the turtle. Next, we view the turtle as an isosceles triangle in the euclidean plane and look for the isometry producing the same effect on the triangle. Finally, we map this isometry to the given turtle operation.

A Turtle View on Plane Isometries

We now apply the above scheme to finding explicit interpretations of turtle operations in terms of plane translations and rotations, and vice versa. For a start we work out the plane isometry that corresponds to the element <FD 50> of the turtle group. Following the three steps outlined above, we first view the effect of FD 50 on the turtle in its HOME position. Next, we view the same effect as resulting from a motion of a triangle in the euclidean plane (figure 1). Finally, we determine the plane isometry that would produce this same motion, in this case

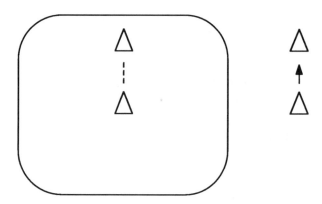

Figure 1 FD 50 as plane translation

the translation of fifty units along the (positive) *y*-axis. Thus our isomorphism maps <FD 50> to this plane translation. Similarly we see that the isomorphism maps all turtle operations of the form <FD *a*> onto the translations along the *y*-axis.

Applying the same scheme to RT 90, we find that the isomorphism carries it to a 90-degree rotation about the origin. Similarly the isomorphism carries all the operations of the form <RT *a*> onto the rotations of the plane about the origin. Since the elements of the form <FD *a*> and <RT *b*> generate the turtle group, we are now in the position to easily calculate the plane isometry corresponding to each element of the turtle group. However, it is not yet clear what the *reverse* correspondence is. In particular, what turtle operation corresponds to an arbitrary translation? To answer this, we pick a particular translation, such as a fifty-unit translation in a 45-degree clockwise direction from the positive *y*-axis, and consider its effect on our chosen triangle.

As can be seen from figure 2, the operation that accomplishes the same effect on the turtle is <RT 45 FD 50 LT 45>. Since a translation shifts the triangle parallel to itself, we can expect the same from the corresponding turtle operation. In turtle terms this means that the operation should be *heading-preserving* (i.e., the turtle's initial and final headings should be the same).

In general, there is a bijective correspondence between translations and heading-preserving turtle operations. The turtle can only move in the direction it is facing. To execute a heading-preserving operation, it needs first to *turn* toward its destination, then to *move* there, and finally, to *turn back* by the same amount. Thus these operations are characterized by their special form <RT *a* FD *b* LT

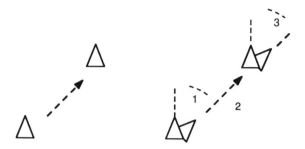

Figure 2 A plane translation (*left*), and translation as turtle operation (*right*)

a>. By a similar (though somewhat more involved) argument it can be shown that turtle operations corresponding to a rotation by *a* about *any* point have the form <RT *s* FD *t* RT *a* BK *t* LT *s*>. This is related to the important general issue of *conjugacy* which will be taken up again in section 5.

Turtle Reflections

We have now found (through the isomorphism) turtle interpretations for two of the fundamental types of plane isometries—translations and rotations. It is therefore natural to ask what in the turtle world corresponds to (line) *reflections*? More formally, how can we extend the turtle group to a group isomorphic to the *entire* group of plane isometries?

In searching for an answer, we turn back to our isosceles triangle—the euclidean object corresponding to the turtle—and consider the effect of a reflection on the triangle. Since this transformation interchanges left and right, it is called an *indirect* isometry. A natural mental image of this operation is that of physically lifting the triangle out of the plane, flipping it over, and then putting it back into the plane. But this description lends itself easily to formulation in turtle terms. We call the corresponding new turtle operation FLIP. Intuitively, FLIP can be described as "turning the turtle on its back" or, equivalently, "interchanging its right and left."

Actually FLIP corresponds to one particular reflection—reflection in the *y*-axis. As before, we can obtain *any* reflection by a suitable combination of FLIP, FDs, and RTs. This too will be discussed more fully in relation to conjugation. We wrap up this overview by asserting that the *extended* turtle group, the one generated by FDs, RTs, and FLIP, is isomorphic to the entire group of plane isometries.

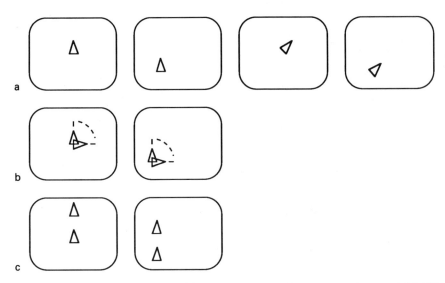

Figure 3 (a) Some turtle states, (b) RT 90 as state-change operation, and (c) FD 100 as state-change operation (*left to right*)

3 THE TURTLE GROUP REVISITED

We now give a fuller and more rigorous account of the turtle group. In view of the intuitive introduction given previously, this section can also be considered an exercise in mathematization and formalization. The exercise is interesting in its own right, since it is typical of the way one is all but forced to abandon the intuitive view of operations as acting on a concrete object when moving to consider these operations as forming a group. (Other examples of the same phenomenon are permutations and vectors.) In our experience the gap between the original intuitions and the eventual formal system has considerable educational implications, since it typically causes serious difficulties for learners.

To make our former intuitive approach more rigorous, we need several changes in the way we view turtle operations. First, we need to view FOR-WARD and RIGHT as operating on the turtle *state* rather than the turtle itself. Second, we need to view these operations as acting on the whole (infinite) *set* of turtle states rather than on a single state.

The *turtle state* then consists of the turtle's position and heading. Analytically we define the turtle state to be the triple (x, y, h), where (x, y) are the coordinates of the turtle's position in a cartesian system, and h is its heading, measured

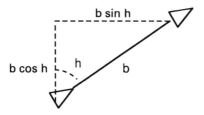

Figure 4 FD *b* as state-change operation

in degrees clockwise from the north. We denote by S the set of all turtle states and call it the *turtle plane*.

Figure 3 shows the turtle in four different states:

$$(0, 0, 0) \text{ (“home”)}, \quad (-50, -50, 0), \quad (0, 0, 45), \quad (-50, -50, 45).$$

In the figure we observe what happens to these states under the turtle operations RT 90 and FORWARD 100. It can be seen that RT 90 transforms these states as follows:

$$(0, 0, 0) \rightarrow (0, 0, 90), \quad (-50, -50, 0) \rightarrow (-50, -50, 90),$$
$$(0, 0, 45) \rightarrow (0, 0, 135), \quad (-50, -50, 45) \rightarrow (-50, -50, 135).$$

In short, RT 90 leaves the position invariant and increases the heading by 90. It can also be seen that FD 100 transforms these states as follows:

$$(0, 0, 0) \rightarrow (0, 100, 0), \quad (-50, -50, 0) \rightarrow (-50, 50, 0),$$
$$(0, 0, 45) \rightarrow (71, 71, 45), \quad (-50, -50, 45) \rightarrow (21, 21, 45).$$

In short, FD 100 leaves the heading invariant and changes the position in a way (to be specified presently) that depends on the heading.

Formally, given real numbers a and b, <RT a> and <FD b> are transformations of the turtle plane, defined for all (x, y, h) in S as follows (see figure 4):

$$<\text{RT } a>: (x, y, h) \rightarrow (x, y, h + a)$$
$$<\text{FD } b>: (x, y, h) \rightarrow (x + b \sin h, y + b \cos h, h)$$

These formulas, incidentally, explain the numbers in the above examples (approximately $21 = -50 + 100 \sin 45$).

Finally, having defined formally what FD and RT are, we now define the *turtle group* to be the group generated by the set {<FD a>, <RT b> | a, b real numbers}. More precisely we start with the group of all invertible (i.e., one-to-one and onto) transformations of the turtle plane and define the turtle group to be the subgroup of this group generated by the above set. We denote the turtle group by **G**.

Remarks and Examples

1.   As is always the case in transformation groups, the group operation is the composition of maps, which in turtle geometry is simply represented by the concatenation of sequences of turtle commands. For example,

if $g_1 = $ <FD 50 RT 90>
and $g_2 = $ <FD 70 RT 30 FD −42>
then $g_1 \circ g_2 = $ <FD 50 RT 90 FD 70 RT 30 FD −42>.

Note: To accommodate to the Logo convention of performing a chain of commands from left to right, we define $g_1 \circ g_2$ as "first g_1 then g_2." This definition, which goes together with writing the operations on the right of the operand, is often adopted by algebraists. Thus

$$t(g_1 \circ g_2) = (tg_1)g_2.$$

2.   The unit element is the identity operation I (i.e., the operation that "does nothing"). In terms of the turtle this is the operation that does not change the turtle state; hence it can be represented as <FD 0> or <RT 0>, for example.

3.   The inverse of <RT a> is <LT a>, which is the same as <RT $-a$>. The inverse of <FD b> is <BK b>, which is the same as <FD $-b$>. The inverse of any sequence of FDs and RTs is the sequence of their inverses taken in reverse order. For example, if $g = $ < FD 10 LT 80 BK 30 RT 120>, then $g^{-1} = $ < LT 120 FD 30 RT 80 BK 10>. In general, the statement that $g \circ g^{-1} = I$ means in turtle terms that by "doing" g and then "doing" g^{-1} (i.e., "undoing" g), the turtle returns to its initial state.

4.   Two elements f and g of **G** are considered equal if they are equal as functions, that is, if $f(s) = g(s)$ for all turtle states s. Thus f and g are equal if they produce the same net change in the turtle state. In terms of the turtle this means that applying f and g to the turtle in any initial position and heading will carry it to the same final position. (Abelson and diSessa 1980 call such operations "state-change equivalent.") In particular, we emphasize that f and g can produce different drawings and still be equal as group elements. For example,

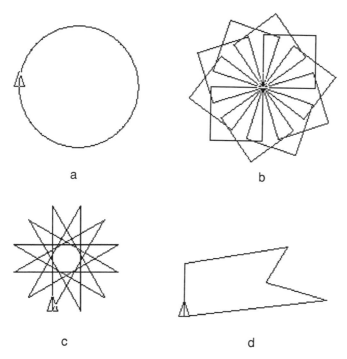

Figure 5 Different representations for the unit element

<LT 120> = <RT 240>
<RT 180 FD 100 RT 180> = <BK 100>
<FD 20 RT 90 FD 50> = <RT 90 FD 50 LT 90 FD 20 RT 90>,

and the following elements are all equal to the unit element *I*:

<RT 360>, <FD 30 BK 30>, REPEAT 4 [FD 50 RT 90],
REPEAT 360 [FD 1 RT 1]

(REPEAT 4 [FD 50 RT 90] is understood here as an abbreviation to [FD 50 RT 90 FD 50 RT 90 FD 50 RT 90 FD 50 RT 90], and thus it has meaning in the group.) More generally, all *state-transparent* sequences of turtle commands—sequences that leave the turtle state unchanged—are equal to *I* (figure 5).

5.   Since we are interested here in mathematics, not technology, we assume that the screen on which the turtle moves is infinitely large and has infinite resolution. This assumption is implicit in the definition of turtle state and in the choice of inputs to FD and RT, both of which involve all real numbers.

In terms of the *Erlangen Programme*, we can summarize the foregoing by saying that the "points" of turtle geometry are the turtle states, the transformations are sequences of FDs and RTs, and the transformation group is the turtle group as defined above. The remaining question of the invariants will be taken up briefly later in this section in our discussion of transitivity and intrinsicness.

The Canonical Representation

The previous examples point to the fact that elements in G may have many representations in terms of FDs and RTs. Each such representation corresponds to a path leading from the initial turtle state to its final state. Intuitively the most efficient way to effect such a change is as follows: First *turn* the turtle toward its final position, then *move* it in a straight line to that position, and finally, *turn* it again to fix its final heading. Thus we may expect each element of G to have a representation of the form <RT a FD b RT c>. It can be proved that this indeed is the case, and further that this representation is essentially unique. We note that uniqueness must be qualified in view of examples such as <RT 0 FD 50 RT 0> = <RT 180 FD −50 RT 180> and <RT 10 FD 0 RT 70> = <RT 11 FD 0 RT 69>. To ensure unqualified uniqueness, we add the requirement that $b \geq 0$ with equality holding only if $c = 0$. We call this representation the *canonical representation*. For a complete proof of the existence and uniqueness of the canonical representation, see Zazkis (1989).

Turtle Illustrations as Decompositions of Group Elements

From the definition of equality in G, it follows that the graphic productions on the screen that result from turtle procedures are not directly represented in the turtle group. Thus two elements that produce quite different drawings will be considered equal as long as the net change in the turtle state is the same. We now ask: What in the group corresponds to turtle drawings? The answer is that each turtle drawing represents a particular *decomposition* of the corresponding group element as a product of other elements. Thus the three illustrations in figure 6 are produced by different decompositions of the same group element, namely,

$$<\text{RT } 90 \text{ FD } 50 \text{ RT } 90> = <\text{FD } 50 \text{ RT } 90 \text{ FD } 50 \text{ RT } 90 \text{ FD } 50>$$
$$= <\text{RT } 30 \text{ FD } 50 \text{ RT } 120 \text{ FD } 50 \text{ RT } 30>.$$

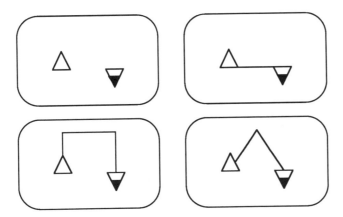

Figure 6 Different decompositions of the same group element

Transitivity and Intrinsicness

Given two turtle states s and s' we can always move from one to the other by an appropriate sequence of turtle commands. For the turtle group this means that there always exists an element g in G such that $g(s) = s'$. Because of this property G is said to be a *transitive group*. It can also be proved that this g is unique.

The transitivity of G has the following significance: As mentioned above, two elements of G are considered equal (as is always the case with functions) if they have the same effect on all turtle states. From the last uniqueness assertion it follows that for two elements to be equal it suffices that they coincide on any *one single state*. That is, for any two elements g and h in G, if $g(s) = h(s)$ for some s, then $g = h$.

Not only is the whole operation determined by its action on a single state, but its *shape* is determined as well. This is due to the intrinsic nature of turtle operations. Thus applying g to any state s has the same geometric effect as applying g to any other element s'. That is, the relation between s and $g(s)$, as expressed in terms of distance and turning, is the same as that between s' and $g(s')$. Returning momentarily to Klein's *Erlangen Programme*, we may now add that these invariants (the relation of s to $g(s)$) are the fundamental invariants of the group G. Graphically the invariants include all turtle drawings generated by intrinsic turtle procedures.

We have now come full circle with our mental image of turtle operations. Initially our naive view of commands such as FD 50 was that of simply moving the turtle. A more sophisticated mathematical view—and one that we had to adopt in order to turn these operations into a group—was as operations acting on the whole set of turtle states. The observations of the last paragraphs allow us legitimately to return to our original naive view of FD 50 as acting on a single turtle, since we have seen that this action determines the image of all other states. As is so often the case in mathematics (e.g., vectors, infinitesimals), one needs a whole piece of sophisticated machinery to enable both views—the naive but intuitively appealing and the complex but mathematically sound—to coexist peacefully.

REPEAT, Power and Order

In our exploration of correspondences between constructs of the Logo language and group theory, we now arrive at the control command REPEAT. We have been abbreviating the sequence of turtle commands:

<FD 50 RT 90 FD 50 RT 90 FD 50 RT 90 FD 50 RT 90>

as REPEAT 4 [FD 50 RT 90]. Viewing that same sequence as an element in the turtle group, we see that it can be represented as the fourth power of <FD 50 RT 90>. Thus REPEATing in Logo corresponds to raising to a power in the group.

The discussion of powers leads naturally to the order of an element. The *order* of a group element g is defined to be the minimal natural number n such that $g^n = I$. If no such n exists, we say that g has infinite order. For example, the order of <FD 50 RT 90> is 4 while the order of <RT 15 FD 30 RT 45> is 6. In turtle terms this means that both REPEAT 4 [FD 50 RT 90] and REPEAT 6 [RT 15 FD 30 RT 45] bring the turtle back to its initial state. In general, the order of g is the minimal n such that the command REPEAT n [g] brings the turtle back to its initial state (position and heading). In what follows we determine the order of all elements of **G**.

It turns out that the order of g depends only on the fundamental property called *total turning*. Abelson and diSessa (1980) define the total turning along a turtle path as the sum of all turtle turns along the path (left turns counting as negative turns). For the turtle group the total turning of a group element g is the net change in the turtle heading effected by g. If g is given in its canonical representation <RT a FD b RT c>, its total turning is $a + c$. Denoting the total turning of g by T, it follows from the Poly Closing theorem (Abelson and diSessa 1980, p. 26) that the order of g is the minimal natural n such that

$$n\,T = 360k \quad \text{for some natural number } k. \tag{1}$$

In case of an integer T, $\mathrm{ord}(g) = \mathrm{lcm}(T, 360)/T$, where "ord" and "lcm" stand for "order" and "lowest common multiple," respectively. In general, equation (1) is solvable for an integer n—hence g is of finite order—if and only if T is a nonzero rational number.

We note that g can fail to have finite order for two different reasons. The first, corresponding to the case $T = 0$, is exemplified by <FD 50> or, more generally, by any element of the form <RT a FD b RT $-a$>. In this case, increasing the powers of g sends the turtle off to infinity, so it can never return to its initial position. In the second case, that of irrational T, the turtle keeps going around its initial position as the powers of g are successively increased, but it can never exactly hit the initial heading.

4   THE STRUCTURE OF THE TURTLE GROUP

For any significant application of the turtle group (or, for that matter, any group), we need to know more about its structure—mainly how it is built from its subgroups and how it relates to other more familiar groups. We begin by studying the subgroups of G and continue, in the next subsection, with its relation to other groups.

Subgroups of G

In Logo work with children and even with beginning adults, it is common to use turtle commands with a restricted subset of inputs. For example, the RT command is most often used by beginners with inputs of 90, 45, or 30. Two famous instances of this phenomenon are the INSTANT environments for very young children (e.g., Abelson 1982, p. 152) in which educators create a "protected" environment with restricted inputs, and the case of Deborah (Turkle 1984, p. 144) who chose on her own to limit her use of turtle turns to just inputs of 30.

In our own experiments (Leron 1981) we have recorded the case of Hanna, who chose to restrict her drawing to a right-angled grid so as "not to lose the north," as she put it. Unlike Deborah's arithmetical rule, Hanna's rule seems to have been of a geometrical nature. With this restriction she set out to draw her

name with the turtle. Happily her inputs were sufficient for writing the (Hebrew) letters of her name.

From our perspective these examples demonstrate two major ways, algebraic and geometrical, in which subgroups of **G** arise: (1) restricting the set of generators or the inputs to these generators, and (2) specifying a particular geometric effect. In what follows we list some naturally occurring subgroups of **G**, describing them from both the geometric and the algebraic perspectives.

The simplest two subgroups that come to mind are "trips" and "turns." The former is defined by the set $F = \{<\text{FD } a> \mid a \text{ real}\}$, and the latter is defined by $T = \{<\text{RT } a> \mid a \text{ real}\}$. Restricting the turtle commands to **F** only, keeps the turtle moving along a straight line. Restricting the turtle commands to **T** only, keeps the turtle turning in its place.

Another simple family are the *cyclic* subgroups, obtained by restricting the generators to a single element. For example, the subgroup generated by <FD 50 RT 90> has order 4 (as does its generator) and corresponds to a drawing of a square. In general, the geometric image of the cyclic subgroups is an "ornamented POLY" (Abelson and diSessa 1980, p. 35).

Perhaps the most interesting subgroup from a geometrical viewpoint is the subgroup **H** of *heading-preserving operations*. These are the elements of the turtle group that leave the turtle's heading invariant. That is, a turtle operation g is an element of **H** if and only if s and $g(s)$ have the same heading for all s in **S**. Using the canonical representation, we can easily find the general form of the elements of **H**. Indeed, since the total turning of <RT a FD b RT c> is $c + a$, it follows that the elements of **H** are precisely those having the form <RT a FD b RT $-a$> or, equivalently, <RT a FD b LT a>. Recall that heading-preserving operations have already appeared in the first part of this chapter, namely, as the turtle operations corresponding to translations of the euclidean plane.

It turns out that **H** has an important role in describing the structure of **G**. To see this, we first note that **H** is a normal subgroup.[4] This follows from the fact that if h is heading-preserving, then so are both <FD a> h <FD $-a$> and <RT b> h <RT $-b$>. Since the FDs and RTs generate the group, it follows that ghg^{-1} is in **H** for all g in **G**. A second observation is that **H** and **T** have only the identity element in common, and together they generate the whole group **G**. It

---

4. That means that for all h in H and g in G, ghg^{-1} is in H. Equivalently it means that for all h in H and g in G, there is an h' in H so that $hg = gh'$.

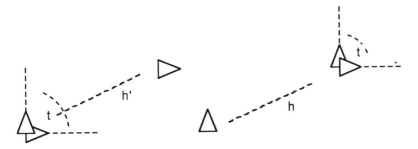

Figure 7 Two versions of semidirect decomposition

follows that **G** is a *semidirect product* of **H** and **T** (Rotman 1973). For our purposes this means that every element in **G** can be uniquely represented as a product *ht* with *h* in **H** and *t* in **T**. Intuitively this can be interpreted as follows: To move from one turtle state to another, first perform a "crab walk" to move to the new position without changing the heading, and then perform a turn to set the heading (figure 7, left panel). Alternatively, we could first set the heading (by the same *t*) and then do a (different) crab walk to set the position (figure 7, right panel). This corresponds to the alternative representation of *g* as *th'*, whose existence can also be seen algebraically from the fact that **H** is normal.

Extending the Turtle Group

Adding Pen State
In defining the turtle group we have given central place to the turtle commands FD and RT. It is natural to inquire whether we could extend the group to accommodate additional turtle commands. We consider first the commands PENUP (PU) and PENDOWN (PD). Intuitively PU and PD appear as inverses of each other, so we might attempt to adjoin them to **G** as such. However, a closer look reveals that not only are they not inverses of each other, but they are not even invertible, so they cannot belong to any group. Indeed, no matter how we try to mathematize these as functions, they turn out not to be one to one. This follows, for example, from the property that PU always has the same outcome, independent of whether the pen was up or down to begin with.

To include the pen operations in the group, we need therefore to introduce invertible versions. This is accomplished with the new operation CHANGEPEN (CP) that switches the state of the pen from "up" to "down," and vice versa. More formally we first extend the turtle state to a 4-tuple (x, y, h, p), where p is a pen-state variable and can assume the values "up" and "down." Next we define the operation CP as follows:

$$CP(x, y, h, \text{down}) = (x, y, h, \text{up}), \quad \text{and}$$
$$CP(x, y, h, \text{up}) = (x, y, h, \text{down}).$$

The former operations FD and RT are extended to act on the new state in the obvious way.

Finally, the extended turtle group GP is the group generated by all FDs, all RTs, and CP. It is the direct product of G and the two-element group $\{I, \text{CP}\}$. In a similar fashion, we can extend the group to include visibility operations (the invertible analogs of ST and HT). (We can also stick with the original commands PU and PD if we are willing to abandon the group. The mathematical framework for such "quasi-invertible" elements, as well as some related psychological issues, are discussed in Leron 1986.)

Adding Pencolor State

We now take up the analogous but somewhat more intricate question of adjoining the pencolor commands to the group. These too are noninvertible, so we need to look for invertible analogues. However, the solution we adopted in the PU/PD case is not good enough, since pencolor assumes more than just two values (in fact four to sixteen values or more, depending on the particular Logo implementation). Thus our previous "binary switch" solution needs to be modified. Our solution is to permute the pen colors *cyclically*. Formally, we extend again the turtle state by adding a new pencolor component pc and define the new command TURNPC *step*, which adds to the current pencolor *step* modulo the number of available colors. For example, assume that the number of available colors is 6 and that the current pc value is 4. Then TURNPC 1 will give the pc value 5, while TURNPC 5 will give it the value 3. (Note that this solution actually reduces to the previous "switch" solution in case there are only two colors.)

Some Remarks on Invertibility

Having seen two examples of finding invertible analogues of turtle commands, it is time to explain the meaning of this term. Intuitively we consider two (sets of) turtle commands as equivalent if they produce the same set of turtle motions (i.e., the same set of transitions of turtle states). More formally, two sets A and B of turtle commands are *equivalent* if, given any pair s and s' of turtle states, we can reach from s to s' by a sequence of commands in A if and only if the same is true of B. In this sense the set {PU, PD} is equivalent to {CHANGEPEN}, and the command SETPC with all possible inputs is equivalent to TURNPC with all its inputs.

So far we have used equivalence to introduce invertible analogues to non-invertible Logo primitives. Mathematically it is no less interesting to find equivalences among existing primitives. Thus it is easy to see that RIGHT is (an invertible) equivalent to (the noninvertible) SETHEADING. Moreover RIGHT stands to SETHEADING in precisely the same relationship as TURNPC to SETPC.

As a last example we ask: What is the invertible analogue of SETPOS? As it turns out, the invention of turtle graphics is in a sense just the answer to this question! In fact, while SETPOS did not differ radically from commonly existing computer graphic commands of the time, its invertible analogue—the commands FD and RT with all possible inputs—is the heart and soul of the turtle.

The last dramatic statement should be slightly modified, namely, there are other, nonturtle solutions to the problem of finding an invertible analogue to SETPOS. In fact commands to increment the turtle x- and y-coordinates will also do the trick. The more precise statement is that turtle graphics is the solution that is both invertible *and* intrinsic. The relationship between invertibility and intrinsicness is an interesting issue that merits further research.

5   THE TWO GEOMETRIES RELATED ONCE AGAIN

In this section, we give a fuller treatment of the main formal relationship between the turtle and euclidean geometries, namely, the isomorphism between the turtle group and the group of direct isometries in the euclidean plane. This relationship has already been discussed in the informal overview where we established a correspondence between motions in the two geometries by viewing the turtle as an isosceles triangle in the euclidean plane. However, to make this idea precise, we need to move from the correspondence between motions to a correspondence between transformations. This is accomplished with the aid of the following two theorems:

1.   Given two turtle states, there is a unique element in the turtle group carrying one to the other.

2.   Given two congruent triangles with corresponding vertices, there is a unique plane isometry carrying one to the other (see, e.g., Coxeter 1961).[5]

We can now describe the correspondence as consisting of three stages, the middle of which is the intuitive idea mentioned above. First, we fix an arbitrary turtle state, say, the HOME state $(0, 0, 0)$, and view elements of the turtle group as acting on a *single* turtle (in its HOME state) via theorem (1). Second, we view turtle motions as motions of the corresponding isosceles triangle as described above. Third, we view motions of the isosceles triangle as plane isometries by theorem (2). Inverting this three-step process, we can find turtle operations corresponding to each translation and rotation. Thus our map is one to one and *onto*.

For a more formal treatment of the isomorphism, we use the structure of the turtle group as semidirect product $G = HT$, where H is the normal subgroup of heading-preserving operations and T is the subgroup of turns. According to this decomposition each element g in G can be uniquely decomposed as $g = ht$, with h in H and t in T. The isomorphism maps any element $g = ht$ of G to the corresponding product of a translation and a rotation. Specifically, let $h = $ <RT a FD b RT $-a$> and $t = $ <RT c>, so that $g = $ <RT a FD b RT $-a$ RT c>. Then we define

$$F(g) = \text{TRANS}(b, a) \circ \text{ROT}(c),$$

where TRANS (b, a) is the plane translation of length b and direction a (measured in degrees clockwise from the positive y-axis), and ROT (c) is the clockwise plane rotation by c degrees about the origin. Note that, as in the intuitive mapping described in section 2, heading-preserving operations are mapped to the corresponding translations, and turns are mapped to rotations about the origin.

A proof that F is indeed an isomorphism can be found in Zazkis (1989).

Conjugacy—Doing the Same Thing in a Different Place

We recall that heading-preserving operations were given two equivalent definitions: (1) operations that leave the turtle's heading invariant and (2) operations

---

5. What we actually need is a variant of this last theorem, namely, that given two congruent *isosceles* triangles, there is a unique *direct* isometry that does the job.

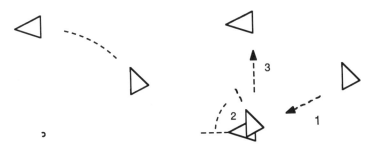

Figure 8 A plane rotation (*left*), and (*right*) rotation as turtle operation

whose canonical representation has the form <RT a FD b RT $-a$>. We have also seen that they form a normal subgroup of the turtle group G, isomorphic to the subgroup of translations of the euclidean plane.

Although the equivalence between these two definitions of heading-preserving transformations is obvious in turtle terms, interpreting it back in the group of isometries yields an interesting insight, namely, that every translation can be obtained by conjugating a translation along the y-axis by an appropriate rotation. (Recall that the *conjugate* of B by A is the transformation ABA^{-1}.) As can be seen from this example, this is a formal way to express the intuitive notion of "doing the same thing in a different place" (Leron 1986; Mason 1984; see also a similar use of conjugation with "tile patterns", as discussed by Fletcher in chapter 12 of this volume, especially his remarks following the HEX procedure).

A similar line of reasoning helps in finding the turtle analogue of a *general* rotation in k degrees (not necessarily about the origin), that is, the inverse image of the rotation under the isomorphism F. As can be seen from figure 8, this analogue has the form of a conjugate of RIGHT k by a suitable heading-preserving operation, namely,

<RT a FD b RT $-a$> <RT k> <RT a FD $-b$ RT $-a$>.

Interpreting this back in the euclidean plane yields a representation of a general rotation as the conjugate of a rotation about the origin by a translation. Note that the translation is precisely the one that shifts the center of rotation to the origin. This is a typical demonstration of how such an isomorphism can be useful: Properties that are quite obvious in one system can yield interesting insights when interpreted through the isomorphism in the other system.

FLIPing Once Again

We have introduced the new operation FLIP as the turtle analogue of line reflection. Before going on to explore the implications of this construct, we pause to set it on firmer foundations. To define FLIP formally, we extend the turtle state to include a fourth component—the flip state—which can take on two values: facedown and faceup. FLIP is now defined as the operation that switches the values of the flip state while leaving all other components of the state invariant. (Appropriate shapes for a FLIPable turtle are discussed in the next subsection.)

Having completed the definition of FLIP, we next move to substantiate the statement that the extended turtle group—the one generated by FDs, RTs, and FLIP—is isomorphic to the entire group of plane isometries. To extend the isomorphism, we only need to specify its value for FLIP, since the extended group is the direct product of G and the subgroup $\{I, FLIP\}$. The motivation for the definition comes once more from the trick of identifying the turtle with an isosceles triangle. Thus we define the image of FLIP under the extended isomorphism to be the reflection in the y-axis. It is now a matter of routine to check the details that this establishes the desired extended isomorphism.

The question naturally arises as to what in the extended turtle group corresponds to an *arbitrary* reflection. For the answer we use conjugation to reduce a general reflection to the special reflection in the y-axis. That is, we write $R_L = A \circ R_y \circ A^{-1}$, where R_L and R_y are the reflections in an arbitrary line L and in the y-axis, respectively, and A is a suitable direct transformation that brings the two lines together. Carrying out the calculations, we obtain the following expression for the turtle analogue of R_L:

<RT a FD b RT $-a$> <RT k> <FLIP> <RT $-k$> < RT a FD $-b$ RT $-a$>.

Here FLIP is first conjugated by <RT k>, where k is the angle between the two lines of reflection, then conjugated again by a heading-preserving operation, which corresponds as always to a translation of the plane. In case the two lines intersect, this is the translation that shifts the point of intersection to the origin. If the lines are parallel, this is any translation that maps L on the y-axis. Looking at the turtle expression above, we can see that the parallel case is actually obtained as a special case where $k = 0$.

As a by-product of the above considerations, a somewhat nonstandard set of generators for the euclidean group emerges. These are the analogues of the

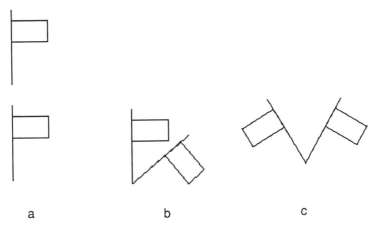

a   b   c

Figure 9 Flags: capturing congruent patterns with FLIP

"natural" generators of the extended turtle group, and they consist of the trans-lations parallel to the *y*-axis, the rotations about the origin, and the single reflec-tion in the *y*-axis.

The Power of FLIP

The need for introducing FLIP has been presented through purely mathematical considerations. However, now that we have it as part of the turtle's vocabulary, we can demonstrate the resulting increase in the *expressive power*[6] of the lan-guage.

We start with a very simple example, just to demonstrate what is meant by "increase in expressive power." Of course FLIP is not really necessary to pro-gram this example. In fact, increase in expressive power does not mean increase in *computational* power. The point of the enriched language is not *more* descrip-tions but *better* ones, in the sense that they better capture our concepts and perceptions.

Consider the three pairs of "flags" in figure 9. We'd like to express in our programming language the notion that the two members of each pair are "the same." More precisely we would like our procedures to reflect the idea that each pair is composed of two congruent flags with varying mutual orientation. Thus a natural form for all the procedures ought to be something like the following:

---

6. See footnote 2.

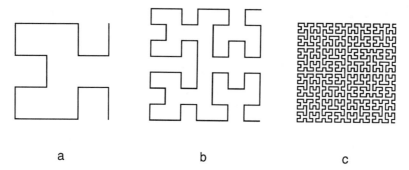

a   b   c

Figure 10 The Hilbert curve

```
TO FLAGS
  FLAG
  MOVE
  FLAG
END
```

In fact, it is easy to write a procedure FLAGS of the desired form for the first two pairs, but not for the third one. It turns out that the original turtle language is not rich enough to describe the two flags in figure 9c as being the same. In this sense it is lacking in "expressive power." The standard solution for this problem is to write separate procedures RIGHT.FLAG and LEFT.FLAG. A better solution (in the sense of yielding a better description) is to extend the language so that it can express our geometric perceptions rather than the limitations of the given language. Specifically, if we substitute "FLIP RT 45" for MOVE, we obtain the desired picture.

It is interesting to compare this treatment to Fletcher's (chapter 12) version of working with left and right flags without FLIP where one is forced to define two separate procedures and keep track of the face state of the turtle (cf. "strip ornaments in Logo" in Fletcher's chapter). The difference between the versions is obviously not in the mathematics, and not even in the amount of programming required; it is rather that FLIP enables us to erect an "abstraction barrier" separating the purely geometrical issues from the details of implementing them in the programming language (Abelson and Sussman 1985; Leron 1987).

Our second example is the HILBERT curve (figure 10) discussed in Abelson and diSessa (1980, p. 96). Their first version is composed of two "mirror" procedures, LHILBERT and RHILBERT that recursively call themselves and each other.

```
TO LHILBERT :SIZE :LEVEL        TO RHILBERT :SIZE :LEVEL
  IF :LEVEL = 0 [STOP]            IF :LEVEL = 0 [STOP]
  LT 90                           RT 90
  RHILBERT :SIZE :LEVEL − 1       LHILBERT :SIZE :LEVEL − 1
  FD :SIZE                        FD :SIZE
  RT 90                           LT 90
  LHILBERT :SIZE :LEVEL − 1       RHILBERT :SIZE :LEVEL − 1
  FD :SIZE                        FD :SIZE
  LHILBERT :SIZE :LEVEL − 1       RHILBERT :SIZE :LEVEL − 1
  RT 90                           LT 90
  FD :SIZE                        FD :SIZE
  RHILBERT :SIZE :LEVEL − 1       LHILBERT :SIZE :LEVEL − 1
  LT 90                           RT 90
END                             END
```

Their second, more elegant, version takes advantage of the similarity between LHILBERT and RHILBERT, uniting them into a single procedure. This elegance, however, is achieved at the cost of introducing a rather unnatural mathematical trick, namely, an additional variable called PARITY that takes on the values 1 and −1 and, accordingly, keeps or reverses directions.

```
TO HILBERT :SIZE :LEVEL :PARITY
  IF :LEVEL = 0 [STOP]
  LT 90*:PARITY
  HILBERT :SIZE :LEVEL − 1 − :PARITY
  FD :SIZE
  RT 90*:PARITY
  HILBERT :SIZE :LEVEL − 1 :PARITY
  FD :SIZE
  HILBERT :SIZE :LEVEL − 1 :PARITY
  RT 90*:PARITY
  FD :SIZE
  HILBERT :SIZE :LEVEL − 1 − :PARITY
  LT 90*:PARITY
 END
```

We now introduce another solution using FLIP, which seems to us to represent more faithfully the geometrical relationships involved. Instead of distinguishing right from left or introducing extraneous tricks, we observe that conjugating LHILBERT by FLIP actually yields RHILBERT. Thus the basic similarity of the two can be captured in our enriched language as

```
TO HILBERT :SIZE :LEVEL
  IF :LEVEL = 0 [STOP]
  LT 90
  FLIP HILBERT :SIZE :LEVEL − 1 FLIP
  FD :SIZE
  RT 90
  HILBERT :SIZE :LEVEL − 1
  FD :SIZE
  HILBERT :SIZE :LEVEL − 1
  RT 90
  FD :SIZE
  FLIP HILBERT :SIZE :LEVEL − 1 FLIP
  LT 90
END
```

Three Remarks on FLIP

1.   The way we have presented FLIP (by identifying the turtle with a triangle in the plane) makes it appear quite a natural (not to say trivial) discovery. It may therefore be of some interest to note that the idea of FLIP as a new command for the plane turtle, only occurred to us following a prolonged involvement with *space* turtles, where FLIP emerged as ROLL 180.[7] Apparently our thinking had been bound too strongly to the "flatland" of the screen turtle.

2.   To be able to experiment with the enriched turtle language, a computer simulation may be desirable. Perhaps the simplest way to achieve this is to enter in Logo any standard simulation of a 3-D turtle (e.g., Abelson and diSessa 1980, p. 144ff), define FLIP as ROLL 180, redefine RIGHT as YAW, and ignore PITCH and TRAVEL.

3.   What is the effect of adding the FLIP operation on the shape of the turtle? In fact, what are the considerations for an acceptable representation of the turtle on the computer screen in general? Consider, for example, two representations of the standard turtle (figure 11) What these two shapes (and many others) have in common is that they give a faithful, visible representation of the turtle's state, namely, that a change of state is

---

7. Editors' note: See Loethe's chapter 3 in this volume for further discussion of space turtles.

Figure 11 Two shapes for the standard turtle

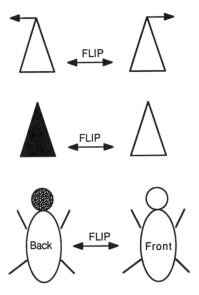

Figure 12 Suggested shapes for a FLIPable turtle

clearly indicated. In contrast, an equilateral turtle fails to represent heading, and the effect of, say, 120-degree rotation is not visible. Similarly the effect of FLIP is not distinguishable on the standard shape, since the flip state is not represented. Figure 12 shows some acceptable shapes for a FLIPable turtle.

6 3-D TURTLES AND OTHER ANIMALS

Since there are many kinds of turtles, there are correspondingly many turtle groups. Considering the totality of all possible turtle groups raises deep and complex mathematical issues, such as how to formalize the concept "turtle," and how to tell whether a given (abstract) group can be represented as a turtle group for some turtle. Even the mere definition of a turtle group (or the decision whether one exists) in some cases is not easy. This seems to be the case, for example, for turtles on a cube or the dynaturtle (diSessa and White 1982). Here we will contain ourselves to a few remarks on some simple turtle groups arising from the turtle "escaping the plane" (to borrow Abelson and diSessa's phrase).

We first consider the *space turtle*, a turtle moving in three-dimensional euclidean space. The definition of the space turtle group is quite similar to the plane turtle, after taking into account the required changes in the turtle state and operations. Recall that the turtle state here consists of its position and orientation. The position is given by a point or a vector in 3-D space and can be represented as a triple (x, y, z). Unlike the plane case, heading is not enough here to determine the orientation. Instead, we use a right-hand orthogonal triad of unit vectors: $\mathbf{h}$ (for heading), $\mathbf{l}$ (for left), and $\mathbf{u}$ (for up). The fundamental turtle operations are TRAVEL (replacing FORWARD), ROLL (rotation about $\mathbf{h}$), PITCH (rotation about $\mathbf{l}$), and YAW (rotation about $\mathbf{u}$, identical to LEFT). For a fuller treatment refer to Abelson and diSessa (1980, p. 140ff). We remark that the third orientation vector $\mathbf{u}$ is used here for convenience only, since it is completely determined by $\mathbf{h}$ and $\mathbf{l}$.

The resulting turtle group turns out to be isomorphic to the group of direct isometries in euclidean three-dimensional space. Continuing the analogy with the plane turtle, we ask for the turtle analogue of a 3-D *reflection* (i.e., reflection in a plane). It is an easy matter to mimic formally our plane solution, adjoining a HYPERFLIP operation to the group, thus extending it to one isomorphic to the full group of isometries in euclidean space. Thus we can define HYPERFLIP in the following way:

$$\text{HYPERFLIP}\,(\mathbf{h}, \mathbf{l}, \mathbf{u}) = (\mathbf{h}, -\mathbf{l}, \mathbf{u}).$$

Normally when we discussed any of the turtle operations, we first presented it in intuitive turtle terms, and only later in formal analytical terms. The new operation HYPERFLIP is the first exception to this rule. It has been first introduced analytically through the above formula. We did this for a reason. It turns out that the natural question of what the turtle should do in order to execute HYPERFLIP is not entirely trivial.

To see why, we return once more to the two-dimensional case and examine our intuitions about congruent figures in the plane. According to these intuitions, two figures are congruent if we can put one on *top of* the other so that the two coincide. Note that this image definitely involves moving into the third dimension, so we may expect difficulties when dealing with three-dimensional congruence. Indeed, our mental imagery breaks down when trying to imagine two congruent solid bodies moved until they physically coincide. It is even harder to imagine how two solid bodies that are congruent via *indirect* isometry (e.g., a left and a right shoe) can be made physically to overlap. Kasner and Newman (1979) remark in this connection that "modern science has as yet devised no relief for the man who finds himself with two left gloves." In contrast, the two-dimensional version of this problem, faced by the inhabitants of Flatland (Abbott 1952), is easy for us 3-D creatures to solve. We simply lift the flat glove clear out of the plane, flip it over, and put it back in the plane. Flatland inhabitants, being two-dimensional creatures, cannot even imagine such an operation, let alone carry it out. According to Kasner and Newman, it is possible that a four-dimensional Gulliver could just as easily solve our three-dimensional problem of the two left shoes, though we lack the ability to imagine his solution: He would simply "lift" the glove into the fourth dimension, hyperflip it, and put it back in our space.

Similarly we could claim that the physical realisation of HYPERFLIP goes through the fourth dimension. But perhaps we should settle more modestly for saying that HYPERFLIP transforms the turtle into its mirror image relative to a mirror in the (**h**, **u**)-plane.

Another interesting nonplanar turtle is the turtle moving on the sphere (Abelson and diSessa 1980, chs. 5 and 7). We will not go into details here, except for mentioning that the spherical turtle group turns out to be isomorphic to the group of rotations of the sphere. In this isomorphism the turtle operations TRAVEL and TURN (analogues of FD and RT) correspond to rotations of the sphere about two perpendicular axes through its center. The intuitive picture of the isomorphism corresponds to the two ways of viewing a change in the turtle state either as a chain of turtle operations or as a rotation of the sphere "under the turtle's feet." In particular, since the turtle group is generated by the operations TRAVEL and TURN (with all possible inputs), it follows that the group of rotations of the sphere is generated by rotations in two fixed perpendicular axes. This is one more example of how the isomorphism helps translate a property that is quite easy to see in one system, into a nontrivial property of the other.

7   A GROUP THEORY PERSPECTIVE ON CHILDREN'S LOGO WORK

In this section we have collected some examples of group theoretical contents that can be observed in children's spontaneous Logo work. Clearly it is not our

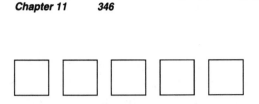

Figure 13 A SQUARES procedure

claim that the children are in any way doing group theory or are aware of the group-theoretic nature of these activities. We do believe, however, that it is valuable for researchers and teachers to be aware of these connections. Moreover in some cases the general patterns involved have proved to be useful in programming, especially in debugging. These will be pointed out in the appropriate places.

Inverses and Conjugates

A child is trying to draw the line of squares appearing in figure 13. One way to write the finished product is as follows:

```
TO SQUARES
  REPEAT 5 [SQUARE MOVE]
END

TO SQUARE
  REPEAT 4 [FD 40 RT 90]
END

TO MOVE
  RT 90 PU FD 50 PD LT 90
END
```

Let us consider in more detail the structure of the MOVE procedure. The "main step," FD 50, is conjugated here twice: first by PU with its "inverse" PD,[8] and second by a RT 90 with its inverse LT 90. Typically the role of conjugation is to provide the right set up for the "main action" and avoid undesirable side effects (Leron 1986). Thus the RT 90/LT 90 pair ensures motion in the proper direction while the PU/PD pair is needed to avoid leaving a trace.

---

8. As we saw in section 4, PU is not really invertible. We have chosen to use it rather than its invertible equivalent CHANGEPEN in order to remain within the familiar Logo environment.

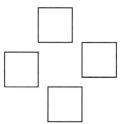

Figure 14 A buggy SQUARES procedure

A frequent bug observed in children's programming is to leave out the second member of a conjugating pair, such as the LT 90. This is understandable since the LT 90 is not really needed for the move itself but in preparation for later drawing. This tiny omission has the surprising effect shown in figure 14. Debugging this is a nontrivial task for beginners. (In particular, it is not clear who "swallowed" the fifth square.) Experience shows that awareness of the conjugation pattern (ABA^{-1}) can help a lot here, as well as prevent bugs in the future.

Identity and Order

When children learn that the instruction REPEAT 4 [FD 50 RT 90] draws a square and that the instruction REPEAT 3 [FD 50 RT 120] draws a triangle, they then look for a number to complete the form REPEAT 5 [FD 50 RT __] in order to draw a pentagon. From our perspective we can describe their activity as looking for a number x such that the element <FD 50 RT x> in the turtle group has order 5. (We recall that the completed pentagon expression is equal to the identity element, since there is no net change of state.)

Another activity in which the order of the element is typically involved is drawing a circle. When children are involved in the activity of "playing turtle" (Papert 1980, p. 59), the following form for a circle naturally arises:

REPEAT <a lot> [FD <a bit> RT <a bit>].

As for the "bits" appearing in this expression, the number 1 seems quite a natural choice for most children. However, they show a large variety of choices for values for "a lot." Children who choose 400 or 500 are happier than those who choose 100 or 200. The problem of making the circle precisely close becomes prominent only later, such as when the circle is used as a subprocedure in a larger project. From our perspective the search for the "magic number" 360 that makes

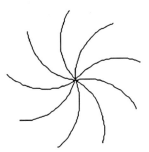

Figure 15 A SPIDER procedure

the circle close can be interpreted as the search for the order of the element <FD 1 RT 1> in the turtle group.

Subgroups

Subgroups of the turtle group appear naturally in children's work when they choose to restrict themselves to a limited set of inputs, such as 30 or 90 for the RT command. See the cases of Deborah and Hanna discussed in section 4.

On Spiders and Bugs

In one of our favorite activities we present children (or teachers, or college students) with the following SPIDER procedure and the picture it produces (figure 15):

```
TO SPIDER
  REPEAT 9 [ARC RT 40]
END
```

```
TO ARC
  REPEAT 20 [FD 4 RT 4]
  --------------------
END
```

We then ask them to complete the missing line so that the procedure SPIDER will produce the correct picture. Clearly the first line in the ARC procedure draws the arc, while the missing line is supposed to bring the turtle back so as to make ARC state-transparent.

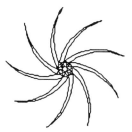

Figure 16 A buggy SPIDER procedure

The first attempt to "bring the turtle back" is most frequently the following instruction:

REPEAT 20 [BK 4 LT 4]

which produces, to the programmer's great surprise, the lovely but unexpectedly inflated spider shown in figure 16. The bug may be nontrivial to discover but is quite clear when looked at from the group-theoretic perspective. Thus, in order to invert the product <FD 4 RT 4>, we need to take the product of the inverses *in reverse order*, namely, the missing line should be

REPEAT 20 [LT 4 BK 4]

(We have also used the fact that "the inverse of a power is the power of the inverse," which people do seem to be using intuitively in the context of the turtle.) Interestingly, we have seen this bug occurring even to college students who had taken a group theory course and could quote the relevant theorem when asked to. Presumably they were not thinking of the turtle commands in group terms (functions, compositions, inverses, etc.) and thus failed to draw upon the relevant knowledge.

8   DIRECTIONS FOR FUTURE RESEARCH AND DEVELOPMENT

The topics discussed in the previous sections have educational implications in several directions. While the implementation of these ideas will certainly require much further research and development, we will survey briefly some promising directions. In what follows we discuss possible benefits to the teaching and learning of the topics of Logo, geometry and group theory.

We have seen that the turtle group provides a useful perspective on many Logo activities. While we certainly do not advocate making all these insights explicit to children, we think it may be helpful for teachers to become aware of them. Using appropriately simple formulations, they may better guide the children to see some general structures in programming, especially in debugging.

As for geometry, the turtle group provides a fresh outlook on euclidean geometry in two ways. Mathematically turtle geometry can be considered as giving an *intrinsic* view of euclidean geometry. As examples we cite the reduction of a general rotation to a rotation about the origin and the reduction of a general translation to a translation along the *y*-axis. In both these cases the turtle version of the relationship involved appears to be simpler and more intuitive than the euclidean one. Even if you are ultimately interested in the teaching of euclidean (transformation) geometry, the turtle might serve as an effective stepping-stone via a careful application of the connections indicated in this chapter.

Psychologically turtle geometry provides different mental images with which to view plane isometries. Viewing isometries as turtle operations (through the isomorphism) brings back and legitimizes our original intuitions of acting on physical objects, intuitions that are all but lost when working with transformations of the whole plane. In the Logo literature turtle geometry is often considered as an alternative to euclidean geometry. Our discussion of the isomorphism between the two groups establishes a different relationship between the two geometries: turtle geometry as adding another, perhaps more intuitive, view of euclidean geometry rather than replacing it. The words of Abelson and diSessa (1980, p. 185) are appropriate here:

. . . whenever we have two different representations of the same thing we can learn a great deal by comparing representations and translating descriptions from one representation into the other. Shifting descriptions back and forth between representations can often lead to insights that are not inherent in either of the representations alone.

Finally we discuss the educational implications for the teaching and learning of elementary group theory. It is customary to preface the abstract theory of groups with explorations in one particular group—most often groups of symmetries or permutations—in which the learner can explore and construct group-related concepts. We propose that the turtle group is particularly suitable for such explorations because it offers a rich variety of topics for demonstrations and explorations, as well as interesting activities for carrying out the explorations. As examples of such topics, we may mention the order of an element, conjugacy, subgroups, normal subgroups, extensions, homomorphism, and isomorphism—all of which can be amply found in the turtle group. The abundance of interesting activities stems from the graphical connotations and the possibility for the students to program their hypotheses and try them out on the computer. The feedback from the computer can then be used for refining old hypotheses and stimulating new ones. Finally the turtle group has the desirable feature of not being too specific. By this we mean that if students are to develop lots of intuitions about groups by exploring one particular "generic" example, this example had better not be part of a more complex structure (e.g., a field), or be commutative or finitely generated, among other things.

In conclusion, one can envision an elementary group theory course for students who have had a rich previous experience with Logo and the turtle. The course would be built around examples from the turtle group and related programming activities. In such a course many introductory group-theoretic concepts could be naturally built on that experience. In fact with a strong activity-based intuitive background, learning concepts like closure, inverse, order, subgroup, noncommutativity, and transitivity may amount to little more than just *naming* familiar notions.

REFERENCES

Abbot, E. A. 1952. *Flatland: A Romance of Many Dimensions*. Mineola, NY: Dover.

Abelson, H. 1982. *Logo for the Apple II*. New York: BYTE/McGraw-Hill.

Abelson, H., and diSessa, A. 1980. *Turtle Geometry: The Computer as a Medium for Exploring Mathematics*. Cambridge: MIT Press.

Abelson, H., and Sussman, G. J. 1985. *Structure and Interpretation of Computer Programs*. Cambridge: MIT Press.

Coxeter, H. S. M. 1969. *Introduction to Geometry*. New York: Wiley.

Coxford, A. F. 1973. A transformation approach to geometry. In *Geometry in the Mathematics Curriculum*. 36th yearbook. Reston, VA: NCTM.

diSessa, A., and White, B. 1982. Learning physics from a dynaturtle. *BYTE* 7,8 (special Logo issue).

Kasner, E., and Newman, J. 1979. *Mathematics and the Imagination*. Harmondsworth. Penguin.

Leron, U. 1981. Final report of the Nesher School Logo project (in Hebrew). Unpublished.

Leron, U. 1986. State transparency and conjugacy. *Micromath* 1,3: 45–47.

Leron, U. 1987. Abstraction barriers in mathematics and computer science. In J. Hillel (ed.), *Proceedings of the Third International Conference for Logo and Mathematics Education (LME3)*. Concordia University.

Mason, J. 1984. Review of *Bypasses* by Z. A. Melzac. *Mathematics Teaching* 109.

Papert, S. 1980. *Mindstorms: Children, Computers and Powerful Ideas*. New York: Basic Books.

Rotman, J. J. 1973. *The Theory of Groups: An Introduction*. Boston: Allyn and Bacon.

Thompson, P. W. 1985. A Piagetian approach to transformation geometry via microworlds. *Mathematics Teacher* 78,6: 465–471.

Turkle, S. 1984. *The Second Self—Computers and the Human Spirit*. London: Granada.

Zazkis, R. 1989. Transformation geometry and turtle geometry: A group theoretic perspective. Unpublished doctoral thesis. Technion-Israel Institute of Technology, Haifa.

Patterns, Permutations, and Groups

Trevor Fletcher

12

1 INTRODUCTION

This chapter is about using Logo to investigate various elementary ideas in group theory. Chapter 11 by Leron and Zazkis and chapter 5 by Edwards are concerned with related questions and provide complementary discussions on many matters.

At the Second International Conference on Mathematical Education, Hans Freudenthal gave an invited paper entitled "What Groups Mean in Mathematics and What They Should Mean in Mathematical Education" (see Freudenthal 1973). In this paper he emphasized the use of groups to help in the study of some system that is already familiar and whose properties merit further investigation. He explained that this was the way in which groups came into mathematics in the first place, and he contrasted this approach with the way in which the ideas were being introduced into schools, with the emphasis on the group and with the multiplication table as a primary object of attention. He claimed that the school approach makes some issues more difficult, as well as ignoring the historical development of mathematics.

Freudenthal summarized his position as, "Groups are important because they arise from structures as systems of automorphisms of those structures." The *automorphisms* of a system are the ways in which it can be related to itself. Groups are important because they give a description of the symmetries of a system and show how the symmetries interrelate and combine. On first acquaintance the word *group* need be no more than the appropriate collective noun for a family of automorphisms.

In the situations that arise in elementary geometry the groups involved are sometimes infinite and sometimes finite. An overt appreciation of the significance of group ideas first came into geometry with Klein's work in 1872, and here the groups were infinite. He showed how geometries can be classified according to the transformations (automorphisms) that do not alter the properties under discussion. In two-dimensional euclidean geometry these are translations, rotations, and reflections. If we are concerned with changes of scale, then dilations are to be included as well. In projective geometry the automorphisms are the perspective transformations that are used by artists, or that occur in a photograph.

The transformations that Klein was discussing were to be seen as affecting the space as a whole, but transformations *may* be considered as only affecting particular figures. The groups in this case may be finite. Books describing elementary approaches to Logo give many procedures, usually using the RE-PEAT command, which draw symmetrical patterns such as regular polygons. Patterns are patterns precisely because they have symmetries, and the symmetries, taken together, form a group. A square has eight symmetries altogether because a square piece of card can be fitted eight ways into a square frame. If we are given just one-eighth of a pattern with this symmetry we can construct the rest if we know where the axes of symmetry are. A regular polygon with n sides has $2n$ symmetries, and its group is of order $2n$. (These groups are called *dihedral* groups.) Elementary investigations in Logo are also much concerned with drawing spiral patterns, and these sometimes display unexpected symmetries. Some of these designs have rotational symmetries but not mirror symmetries. If there is an n-fold symmetry of this kind the corresponding group is the cyclic group of order n.

Automorphisms occur in other mathematical systems. The symmetries of a polygon, which are reflections or rotations, rearrange the vertices among themselves and do the same for the sides. The transformations permute certain objects. In the new context the automorphisms are these rearrangements. A rearrangement of a rearrangement is a rearrangement, and, as always, the automorphisms of the system combine with one another in a natural way.

At first sight it is mysterious that geometrical systems and, say, the permutations of a set of objects may be quite different mathematical systems but yet embody the same group structures. There are twenty-four permutations of four letters in sequence. There are twenty-four ways in which a cube may be placed on a square table (assuming that a face of the cube just fits the tabletop). Is there any correspondence between rearranging the letters and rotating the cube? Label the eight vertices of the cube with the letters, using each letter twice and placing it at vertices that are at opposite ends of a long diagonal of the cube. Now each of the twenty-four positions of the cube gives a different arrangement of letters at the four corners of the table, and the correspondence is immediately clear.

The last example can be used to underline what is a recurring source of confusion to the beginner who is striving to master group ideas. The automorphisms in the group are not the arrangements of the letters, nor are they the positions of the cube—they are the in between movements. The *rearranging* is an automorphism in the one case; the *rotating* is an automorphism in the other. Likewise the group is not made up of the arrangements of the letters or the positions of the cube; the group is the family of automorphisms of the structure and not the structure itself.

Group ideas are involved in the build-up of the number system, whether they are made explicit or not. A very full explicit account may be found in Griesel (1971), and his approach has been embodied in school texts in Germany. A particularly interesting example is provided by the way in which many traditional school texts introduce the integers. The properties of integers are demonstrated by using a line of points, extending indefinitely in both directions. The addition of integers is demonstrated by successive displacements along the line. Some authors appear to identify integers with the points on the line, and label the points accordingly. This representation has certain uses and does convey some properties of the integers correctly. But a more adaptable model, which conveys properties that the earlier one does not, is obtained by seeing the integers as translations of the whole of the line along itself. An integer is to be seen not as a point on the line, but as an automorphism of the whole set of points.

This is harder to appreciate. But the properties of the integers are genuinely hard to appreciate, as the difficulties experienced by generations of school pupils show. The ideas have to be presented so that the difficulties may be mastered progressively. The integers are a structure that every school child is expected to master. From the point of view of this chapter, they are a particular group of automorphisms. They exemplify difficulties that occur repeatedly in the learning of mathematics; the learner looks at individuals instead of looking at the entire set. The teacher is talking about the forest—the child is looking at a tree.

Let us consider two further examples. The first example is from Vergnaud (1988):

When counting a set of elements, most five or six-year-olds count: one, two, three, four, five, six, . . . six! Not only do they have to establish one-to-one correspondence between the objects to be counted, the gestures of the finger, the movements of the eyes and the number-words, but also they feel the need to say the word "six" twice. The first utterance refs to the sixth element of the set, the second utterance refers to the cardinal of the set: the double utterance means that the concept of cardinal has been recognised (p. 30).

This is success! A short while before this child was at the familiar stage of attaching the name "six" to the last object counted. The point at issue is the distinction between a set and one of its members—it is a question of the level of abstraction. Group ideas are not involved in this example; they are in the next.

Consider the notion of a *vector*. On some views a vector is a line segment, but on other views a vector is an equivalence class of line segments. (That is to say, it is an entire set of line segments, equal and parallel to one another.) Textbooks display much confusion on this point. There is a continuing, and sometimes bitter, controversy in didactical circles. It is the view of the author that in the long term the vector should be seen as the equivalence class, but this makes things harder to teach in the initial stages. A lot of work has to be done with line segments before the final formulation of the theory can be understood.

When vectors are regarded as equivalence classes, they are automorphisms of the plane, and the difficulties in teaching vectors exemplify difficulties that arise when teaching groups in general. Much experience is needed with individual transformations before the properties of the family as a whole can be appreciated.

The examples that follow are in sympathy with Freudenthal's approach. The introduction of group ideas is gradual. Group ideas may be the final destination, but we must not neglect the scenery on the way. The intention is to use Logo for tasks for which it is well suited, in situations that have some intrinsic interest (for the most part geometrical patterns or permutational puzzles), and to display a two-way relationship between groups and Logo, each helping the other. On the one hand, an appreciation of the group structure helps to write Logo procedures; on the other, writing Logo procedures leads to an understanding of how the parts of a structure fit together and to an appreciation of the structure as a whole. Initially, therefore, the emphasis on group ideas is slight; groups are implicit in the discussion rather than explicit. Later the groups themselves receive more attention. Group ideas provide the mathematician with an excellent filing system. But before a filing system can be developed, it is necessary to be clear about the things that have to be filed.

Freudenthal's talk began with some geometrical patterns drawn with compasses by an eight-year-old girl. She drew the familiar sixfold floral pattern, and then extended it by constructing further circles in successive layers. We will consider a Logo approach to this problem later, but with Logo it is easier to draw polygons than circles, and so we start with these.

2   TILE PATTERNS

Let us consider some of the tiling designs made up of regular polygons that can be found in decorative art from all parts of the world from very early times. One very common design consists of octagons and squares (see figure 1). Each square is surrounded by four octagons, and each octagon is surrounded by four squares and four more octagons arranged alternately. This forms the basis for a recursive method of drawing the pattern. Squares and octagons have to be drawn in such a way that the drawing of each square somehow leads to the drawing of four neighboring octagons, and the drawing of an octagon somehow involves drawing four neighboring squares. The simplest way to draw a square is to say

```
TO S :SIDE
  REPEAT 4 [LT 90 FD :SIDE]
END
```

and the simplest way to draw an octagon is to say

```
TO O :SIDE
  REPEAT 8 [RT 45 FD :SIDE]
END
```

These procedures have to be modified[1] so that, when the turtle gets to each corner of a square, it draws an octagon and, when it gets to every other corner of an octagon, it draws a square. So try

---

1. I conform to the convention, adopted in this book, of printing all Logo procedures and variable names in uppercase with great reluctance. Logo is not simply a code that makes machines run. Logo is also a vehicle for human communication. I may write a Logo procedure to explain an algorithm to someone, perhaps with no intention of actually running it; I may write Logo to explain mathematics to people, or to explain computing to people, or even to explain Logo to people. I can also write Logo to explain people's thought processes, and the Logo procedures that appear in my writing are an essential part of the prose. Restriction to uppercase is as irksome as the compulsion to write the mother tongue exclusively in uppercase. The option of using lowercase for variable names and for procedure names (in certain cases) in the interests of clarity is one that I would wish to exercise.

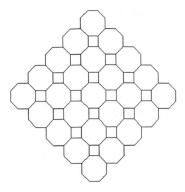

Figure 1 A tiling pattern made up of octagons and squares

```
TO S :SIDE
  REPEAT 4 [LT 90 FD :SIDE O :SIDE]
END
```

and

```
TO O :SIDE
  REPEAT 4 [RT 45 FD :SIDE RT 45 FD :SIDE S :SIDE]
END
```

As things stand these procedures never finish. There is a standard way of dealing with such difficulties. Start with a certain amount of patience and gradually use it up. When patience is exhausted, stop! This means putting a patience parameter into the procedures and reducing it at each recursive call. So the procedures become

```
TO S :SIDE :P
  IF :P = 0 [STOP]
  REPEAT 4 [LT 90 FD :SIDE O :SIDE (:P - 1)]
END
```

and

```
TO O :SIDE :P
  IF :P = 0 [STOP]
  REPEAT 4 [RT 45 FD :SIDE RT 45 FD :SIDE S :SIDE (:P - 1)]
END
```

There are many other ways of drawing this tessellation, some of them more economical than the one just used. For example, the squares can be seen as merely gaps between octagons; so draw octagons only! There is a minor difficulty to overcome because the previous method drew octagons and squares clockwise and counterclockwise, respectively. What is to be done if the method is based on just one type of polygon? If left turns are used then the octagon being drawn is on the left of the turtle—so to pass onto an adjacent octagon, turn rightabout, draw it, and then turn back again.

To indicate yet another possibility, consider drawing the pattern with the minimum number of instructions to draw line segments, but liberal use of recursion. There are just two types of line segment in the pattern. Some lines have an octagon on each side, and the others have an octagon on one side and a square on the other. How does this lead to a Logo construction? It is essential to go forward, turn left 45, and then go forward again. But it is necessary to make suitable recursive calls. The solution involves careful inspection of the figure and an appreciation of subtleties of the pattern that are easily overlooked. One method is as follows, but it is profitable to look for others:

```
TO O :P
  IF P = 0 [STOP]
  FD :SIDE RT 180 O (:P - 1) LT 180
  LT 45 FD :SIDE LT 45 O (:P - 1) RT 45
  BK :SIDE RT 45 BK :SIDE
END
```

A value of "SIDE has to be specified.

Recursive algorithms, such as these, can be very inefficient as computer programs, but they are extremely interesting if you enjoy seeing a lot of computer drawing from very short procedures. Many other approaches are possible; for example, one may devise methods for constructing tessellations layer by layer, but these are somewhat more complicated than the present methods.

The familiar tiling pattern based on hexagons surrounded by triangles provides similar opportunities for experiment (figure 2). Another well-known tessellation is made up of dodecagons and triangles. This can be drawn with

```
TO D :P
  IF :P = 0 [STOP]
  REPEAT 6 [RT 30 FD :S RT 30 FD :S T (:P - 1)]
END
```

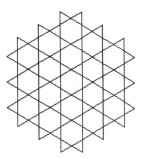

Figure 2 A tiling pattern made of hexagons surrounded by triangles

```
TO T :P
 IF :P = 0 [STOP]
 REPEAT 3 [LT 120 FD :S D (:P - 1)]
END
```

Once again, there are many other methods, including a method using dodeca-gons only, leaving the triangles as the gaps in between.

The various possible tile patterns are described in a number of references (Cundy and Rollett 1952; Kraitchik 1943; Steinhaus 1950), and these offer many opportunities for turtle geometry. The familiar tilings of the plane by equilateral triangles, by squares and by hexagons are called *regular tessellations*, and only these three exist. The other tessellations considered so far are members of the family of *semiregular* tessellations.

A *semiregular* tessellation is defined as one in which each face is a regular polygon and all the vertices are congruent to one another. These are the plane analogues of the semiregular archimedean solids. There are just eight of them. A semiregular tessellation involves faces (tiles) of different shapes, but the vertices are all congruent (by definition). Therefore it is profitable to concentrate on this defining feature and to devise construction methods based on it. The tessellation is a set of vertices linked by edges, and it may be drawn by drawing the vertices rather than by drawing the polygons. The set of edges radiating from a vertex is called the *vertex figure*. Since all the vertices are congruent, we can devise a construction for a semiregular tessellation by writing a procedure that draws the vertex figure and calls itself recursively at the end of each edge. The difficult part is to orient the turtle properly before making the recursive call and to restore it properly afterward.

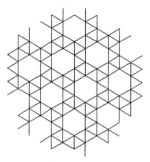

Figure 3 A *semiregular* tessellation of hexagons and triangles

In the regular tessellation of hexagons the vertex figure consists simply of three lines inclined at equal angles. To set the heading of the turtle at the end of a radiating segment in such a way that the pattern continues to propagate over the plane, 60 degrees is a suitable rotation. (Are there any others?) This has to be done three times, and this gives the procedure

```
TO HEX :P
 IF :P = 0 [STOP]
  REPEAT 3 [FD :SIDE LT 60 HEX (:P - 1) RT 60 BK :SIDE LT 120]
END
```

Once more this employs the fundamental principle

make some movement (in this case LT 60),
carry out the procedure you are interested in,
do the inverse of the original movement (in this case RT 60),

in order to get the turtle appropriately positioned and oriented for the next stage. This process, which has already been used in many of the previous procedures, is sometimes called *conjugation*. (Leron and Zazkis, chapter 11 in this volume, give a most helpful discussion of conjugacy and related matters.)

In many of the tessellations orienting the turtle is simple enough, but in some cases care is necessary. The most complicated of the semiregular tessellations is one composed of a particular pattern of hexagons and triangles (figure 3). (Incidentally this pattern is not identical to its mirror image—it can exist in right- and left-handed forms.) In all of these situations we consider the pattern as extending indefinitely over the plane. There are infinitely many lines of symmetry and infinitely many centers of symmetry, and the group is an infinite group. We are using Logo to define a small number of basic operations that will generate all the rest. We are therefore using in an informal way the ideas that are central to the development of group theory on the lines of a book such as Grossman and Magnus (1964) or, at a more advanced level, Coxeter and Moser (1965).

We may write a Logo procedure to construct a 60-degree arc and investigate how it may be called recursively to produce drawings of the kind made by the little girl described by Freudenthal in his ICME address. She used compasses to draw the familiar pattern of flower petals produced by overlapping circles. There is no doubt that the child was thinking recursively, but just how was she thinking? There are usually many different recursive constructions for the same geometrical pattern. Logo may be used as the vehicle for sophisticated recursive algorithms, but it can also be used to mimic the unprompted thinking actually employed by children. The algorithm that the child thought out (albeit intuitively) was almost certainly more efficient for a human being than the algorithms in the preceding paragraphs, but it might be rather more difficult to write down.

3 STRIP ORNAMENTS IN LOGO

The tessellations just described are classified according to the geometrical properties of the polygonal faces and the vertices. Geometry developed over many centuries looking at regular plane figures, solids, and tessellations from this point of view, without explicit reference to their symmetry groups. The same was true of the ornamental patterns that we consider next. But in recent times the value of group ideas in the classification of these patterns has been realized, and nowadays geometers usually discuss them from this point of view. The important idea is that the patterns are classified by their overall symmetries, whereas when they are constructed step by step, the local properties are the immediate concern.

Edwards, chapter 5 in this volume, describes the TGEO microworld. Her chapter introduces many of the ideas that follow, and her discussion of the relations between the "local" action of the turtle and "global" actions of the transformations is especially relevant. We go on to give methods whereby teachers and students may produce a variety of microworlds that are subsystems of the TGEO microworld. Chapter 11 by Leron and Zazkis also relates to this material. In what follows we are concerned with discrete subgroups of the turtle group and the euclidean group. There are many applications of conjugation, and of the use of flips.

First, consider strip ornaments, or frieze patterns. These are plane patterns along an axis. The pattern is taken to extend indefinitely in both directions. All the patterns have translational symmetries along the axis, and this axis may also be an axis of mirror symmetry, or it may be a glide axis (which means that there is reflection plus a translation of half an interval, as with the pattern of footsteps in snow). The patterns may also have mirror symmetry about equally spaced lines perpendicular to the axis; and they may also have centres of twofold symmetry (half-turns) equally spaced along the axis.

Geometry books explain how there are just seven distinct cases. Each strip pattern belongs to one of just seven families, and each family is characterized by its own particular group of symmetries. From this point of view a row of Ts and a row of Ms have the same symmetries. Translations, to the right or to the left, superimpose the pattern onto its former position; the axis of the pattern is not itself an axis of symmetry, but there are axes of symmetry perpendicular to it, which go alternately through the center line of a letter and through a space between letters. (Throughout this discussion we assume that the letters are drawn symmetrically where possible, and that the issue is not complicated by serifs or thick and thin strokes, etc.)

A row of Bs or Ds has a new group of symmetries. This time the main axis of the row is an axis of mirror symmetry, and there are no axes of symmetry perpendicular to it. A row of Ns or Ss has no mirror symmetries, but there are centers of symmetry. The center of each letter is a center of symmetry, and the points halfway between these are centers of symmetry also. Some other cases come later.

Any pattern consists of repetitions of a fundamental motif, and to appreciate the theoretical points involved, we take a motif that is itself devoid of any internal symmetry. (A practical designer may proceed differently.) Logo therefore has to provide procedures to draw the motif and procedures to move it to its various positions. The procedures that produce the movements are the direct embodiment of the geometrical symmetries. The whole point is that we do not need a separate procedure for every symmetry. We need just a few fundamental symmetry operations, from which all the rest can be generated. A flag provides a suitable motif, and for patterns with reflectional symmetry we need right- and left-handed versions.

```
TO RFLAG :ANG :LEN
  RT :ANG FD 2 * :LEN RT 120 FD :LEN
  RT 120 FD :LEN LT 60 FD :LEN RT 180 - :ANG
END
```

A similar procedure can be defined, with right and left interchanged to draw the left-handed versions. These procedures are complicated by the consideration that it is not just a question of drawing a flag. It is frequently the case with Logo that you have to end a procedure by bringing the turtle back to the starting point and restoring its original heading before you move on. Conjugation is at work once again, and this accounts for many of the moves that are needed.

When reflections are involved, it is necessary to keep track of the orientation of the motif, that is, to determine whether the right- or left-handed version has to be drawn. (Here we are concerned with the *flip* used by the writers just quoted.) For this purpose define a two-state variable, call it "FACE, and let it take values +1 and −1. We can then define

```
TO FLAG
  PD IF :FACE = 1 [RFLAG 40 30] [LFLAG 40 30] PU
END
```

Initially :FACE may be specified as 1.

Now we define the movements that are used in generating patterns. Many of these are very like common turtle movements, but it is useful to have them all in a standard form of code. Translations along the axis are required, so define

```
TO F
  FD :STEP
END
```

This takes the turtle forward by one unit. "STEP has to be given a suitable value. It is useful to include the inverse operation also, so define

```
TO FINV
  BK :STEP
END
```

With the commands F, FINV, and FLAG, one can produce patterns that contain translational symmetries only (similar to patterns with a row of Ps or a row of

Js). As always with Logo, commands may be entered singly or in batches. If a practically useful suite of procedures is to be written, it is helpful to have the axis of the strip horizontally across the screen and to write a START procedure to set the turtle up accordingly, with suitable parameters.

```
TO START
 CS RT 90 MAKE "STEP 50 MAKE "FACE 1
END
```

Some strip ornaments contain half-turn symmetries, so define

```
TO C
 RT 180
END
```

Using C with the previous commands enables a new lot of patterns to be constructed. These have the symmetries of a row of Ss or a row of Ns.

Some patterns can be reflected in the axis of the ornament, so define

```
TO R
 MAKE "FACE − 1 * :FACE
END
```

If R is used alone with F and FINV (and of course FLAG) patterns with the symmetries of a row of *B*s or a row of *C*s are produced. IF R and C are both used, we get patterns with the symmetries of a row of *X*s or a row of *O*s. These also contain reflectional symmetries about lines perpendicular to the axis of the pattern. A separate procedure to produce these symmetries can be defined very simply,

```
TO M
 C R
END
```

Use of M (only) with F and FINV produces patterns with the same symmetry as a line of Vs.

Patterns can have both half-turn symmetries and reflections in lines perpendicular to the axis. There are two separate cases of this. The half-turn centers may be on the mirror lines (as with the line of Xs mentioned before), or they may be halfway between (as with a line of Vs pointing alternately upward and downward, forming a zigzag). Patterns of the latter type can be generated by introducing a procedure N:

```
TO N
  FD :STEP / 2 M BK :STEP / 2
END
```

(Conjugation again!)

If N is used with C, patterns of the zigzag type arise, and the operations F and FINV are not needed explicitly because they arise from combinations of N and C.

It is possible for patterns to have glide-reflection symmetries only, so define

```
TO G
  FD :STEP / 2 R
END
```

with its inverse

```
TO GINV
  BK :STEP / 2 R
END
```

G and GINV (on their own) generate patterns with the symmetry of a line of footsteps in the snow; combined with half-turns they give another way of generating zigzag patterns.

The world's decorative art bears witness to the immense range of experiments possible with these procedures (Jones 1856). The various operations combine with one another in fascinating ways, and we see, for example, that patterns that contain some types of symmetry necessarily contain others because they arise by combination. One can find different sequences of operations that always produce equivalent results (just as above it was possible to define M as C followed by R). This setting exemplifies many of the things that happen whenever a group is defined by means of a set of generators—alternative definitions may be possible and there are many equivalences between different sequences of operations.

Some patterns occur as subpatterns of others. This introduces the subgroups of a group and illustrates how subgroups relate to one another and to the parent group. This situation not only offers many lines of approach into the ideas of group theory, it also presents opportunities for experimenting with Logo techniques. Procedures may be written to draw patterns automatically, perhaps by selecting operations at random from some list, or patterns may be constructed by adapting the tree search procedures that are described below.

4   THE SEVENTEEN PLANE SYMMETRY GROUPS

Repeating patterns that cover the plane have been known since earliest recorded history, and these designs are part of the heritage of many cultures. Only comparatively recently has it been known that these designs are of just seventeen types, and there can only be these seventeen types. (It is claimed that all seventeen may be found in the decorations in the Alhambra Palace, in Granada, Spain.) The seventeen plane symmetry groups are a treasure house of elementary geometry. The ideas are developed below in a way that is intended to bring out the geometrical theory while developing Logo strategies that have more general application. If the prime purpose were to develop a design tool for artists, then it might be better to proceed differently.

It is necessary to be more careful about the underlying geometrical theory than before. Perhaps the easiest way to analyze the patterns is to see them as generated by the movement of a template that carries a motif (Coxeter and Moser 1965; SMP 1966,1968). The template is moved according to various sets of rules; each of the seventeen groups is a self-contained system with its own set of template-moving rules. The template may carry any motif whatever, and we imagine it moved around and used as a stencil.

The template is moved according to *local* rules; it is moved with reference to points or lines that it carries around with it. But the patterns generated are classified according to their *global* symmetries; they are symmetric with respect to points and axes that remain fixed as the template moves about. The designing skill, or the applied group theory (depending on your point of view), consists in arranging that the template always falls appropriately on the global axes and points of symmetry as it moves about.

Since the intention is to produce a set of procedures to assist investigation or classroom demonstration, it is useful to develop some drawing techniques that show what is happening in a convenient way. The current positions of the template and the flag will be drawn in one color, and the past positions will be left as traces in other colors. (Some versions of Logo permit more sophisticated coloring schemes.) These groups are usually known by international symbols which

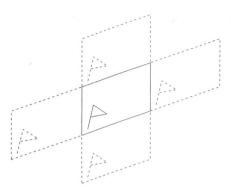

Figure 4 An example of the plane symmetry group *p1* acting on a parallelogram

were originally introduced by crystallographers. The simplest one of the family is called *p1*.

5 THE GROUP p1

With the simplest and most familiar of the seventeen groups, the patterns are produced by translating a fundamental motif in two independent directions. The template is a parallelogram, which may be translated along its sides (figure 4). Since this is the first case to be studied, it is necessary to define certain procedures for general use. We take the basic motif as a flag, and the procedure introduced above can be used to draw it. When writing procedures, it is an advantage to anticipate future complications. With some symmetry groups the flag has to be drawn in both right- and left-handed versions, so we need the parameter "FACE again. With the group *p1*, "FACE always has the value 1.

```
TO START
  SETCONSTANTS CS SETPC 3
  DTEMP FLAG LOOP
END

TO SETCONSTANTS
  MAKE "U 30 MAKE "V 50 MAKE "ANGUV 70
  MAKE "ANG 25 MAKE "LEN 20 MAKE "FACE 1
END

TO LOOP
  MAKE "INPUT RL SETPC 1 DTEMP SETPC 2 FLAG
```

```
    RUN :INPUT SETPC 3 DTEMP FLAG LOOP
END
```

START is the same for each symmetry group, but SETCONSTANTS is different each time. The current position of the template will be shown in one color, and imprints of the template will be made as it is moved around under the control of the user. The loop is a standard working cycle, and it does a number of interesting things. It waits for an instruction, it changes the colors of the template and the flag, and then it draws them in their new positions.

The template is a parallelogram, and one of its angles we will call "ANGUV.

```
TO DTEMP
    PD REPEAT 2 [FD :U RT :ANGUV FD :V RT 180 - :ANGUV] PU
END
```

```
TO FLAG
    PD IF :FACE = 1 [RFLAG :ANG :LEN][LFLAG :ANG :LEN] PU
END
```

The template and flag have to be given vector displacements in two directions. One direction may be taken up the screen, so define the translation UP by

```
TO UP
    FD :U
END
```

and the inverse transformation UN by

```
TO UN
    BK :U
END
```

Likewise, define a translation VP, with inverse VN, by

```
TO VP
    RT :ANGUV FD :V LT :ANGUV
END
```

```
TO VN
    RT :ANGUV BK :V LT :ANGUV
END
```

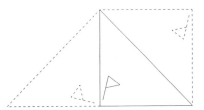

Figure 5 An example of the plane symmetry group *p4* acting on a right-angled isosceles triangle

To produce a design, call the procedure START, and then use the commands UP, UN, VP, VN either one at a time or in batches.

6   THE GROUP p4

Next consider the group called *p4*. This can be generated by using the familiar 45-, 45-, 90-degree setsquare as a template. The fundamental operations are a half-turn about the midpoint of the hypotenuse and a quarter-turn about the right-angled vertex (figure 5).

Before attempting the computer program, take a setsquare and move it about in this way. Check that the repeated use of just these two movements will take the template all over the plane and that the replications of the motif will generate a pattern if you use it as a stencil. The pattern consisting of swastikas at the vertices of a square lattice is an example of *p4*. Note that these rules do not allow the template to be turned over, and so there are no mirror symmetries in the pattern. We need new procedures to set constants and to draw this particular template.

```
TO SETCONSTS
  MAKE "S 40 MAKE "D :S * SQRT 2
  MAKE "ANG 25 MAKE "LEN 20 MAKE "FACE 1
END
```

There are no reflections in this group, but MAKE "FACE 1 is a precaution to ensure that the template and flag are correctly oriented. START is as before.

```
TO DTEMP
  PD FD :S RT 135 FD :D RT 135 FD :S RT 90 PU
END
```

The procedure for the quarter-turn is very simple.

```
TO S
  LT 90
  END
```

It is also simple to do a half-turn, but the half-turn has to be made about the right place. A satisfactory definition is

```
TO T
  RT 45 FD :D RT 135
END
```

and conjugation is needed once again. But there are alternatives. For instance, use the program, enter the command START, and experiment with the operations S and T. Composite operations can also be used. For example, type S T S before typing <*return*>. This opens up a further area for experiment. As with the familiar FD RT, etc., of ordinary turtle geometry, composite operations can be given a special name. Thus one could, for example, define

```
TO U
  S T S
END
```

and experiment with the use of the pair of instructions T and U. In this way the study of subgroups, alternative sets of generators, and other more advanced topics becomes easily accessible. With these programs can be introduced some of the features discussed in relation to strip ornaments—random selection of the turtle moves or the generation of patterns using tree searches.

7 THE GROUP cm

The previous group was generated by rotations. The group *cm* is generated by a glide reflection and an ordinary reflection parallel to it. The template is an isosceles triangle, and the operations are a reflection in the base and a glide reflection along the segment joining the midpoints of the two equal sides (see figure 6). (In the present context there is no harm in thinking of reflection as flipping the template over, but in other contexts it may be essential to distinguish between reflecting a lamina in a plane and turning it by 180 degrees about an axis.)

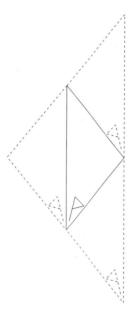

Figure 6 An example of the plane symmetry group *cm* acting on an isosceles triangle

Suitable constants can be set with

```
TO SETCONSTS
  MAKE "HYP 40 MAKE "ROT 50 MAKE "GLIDE :HYP * COS :ROT
  MAKE "ANG 25 MAKE "LEN 20 MAKE "FACE 1
END
```

This group has reflections, so the value of "FACE alternates. So we define RS
(reverse side) with

```
TO RS
  MAKE "FACE - 1 * :FACE
END
```

The template is an isosceles triangle

```
TO DTEMP
  PD FD 2 * :GLIDE RT (180 - :ROT) * :FACE
  FD :HYP RT 2 * :ROT * :FACE FD :HYP RT (180 - :ROT) * :FACE PU
END
```

This comparatively short definition embodies a great deal of geometry. Note particularly how the directions of the rotations depend upon which face of the template is uppermost. This exemplifies the principle noted earlier—the geometrical operations performed are local operations on the template, but they have to fit onto the global symmetries of the pattern.

The first generating movement is a glide reflection about the line joining the midpoints of the two equal sides of the template.

```
TO P
  RT :ROT * :FACE FD :HYP LT :ROT * :FACE RS
END
```

This moves the template forward by the appropriate distance and then reflects it. We define also the inverse move

```
TO Q
  LT :ROT * :FACE BK :HYP RT :ROT * :FACE RS
END
```

In the previous notation Q = PINV. The other permitted move in this group is a reflection in the base (i.e., the unequal side of the template). This is very simple.

```
TO R
  RS
END
```

Once again, START places the template in its initial position, and then the commands P, Q, and R drive the template and generate the pattern.

The remaining symmetry groups can be investigated by adapting the techniques used so far. In sections 8 and 9 are two examples of interesting patterns with extremely simple procedures that carry out the turtle movements.

8 THE GROUP p4g

This group is also generated by a template in the form of a 45-, 45-, 90-degree setsquare, but this time the permitted movements are reflection in the hypotenuse and a quarter-turn about the right-angled vertex. An example of the pattern is provided by alternate right- and left-handed swastikas situated at the vertices of a square lattice (figure 7).

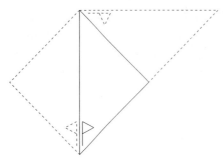

Figure 7 An example of the plane symmetry group *p4g* acting on a right-angled isosceles triangle

The procedures SETCONSTANTS and DTEMP are much as earlier,

```
TO SETCONSTANTS
  MAKE "S 32 MAKE "D :S * SQRT 2
  MAKE "ANG 10 MAKE "LEN 10 MAKE "FACE 1
END
```

```
TO DTEMP
  PD FD :D RT 135 * :FACE FD :S
  RT 90 * :FACE FD :S RT 135 * :FACE PU
END
```

and the two geometrical transformations are

```
TO S
  FD :D RT 90 * :FACE
END
```

```
TO A
  RS
END
```

9   THE GROUP p6m

This group is generated by a template in the form of a 30-, 60-, 90-degree set-square, with reflections in the three sides. An example of a pattern with this symmetry group is provided by six-petaled flowers at the vertices of a lattice of equilateral triangles (figure 8).

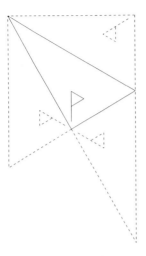

Figure 8 An example of the plane symmetry group ***p6m*** acting on a right-angled triangle

```
TO SETCONSTANTS
  MAKE "S 40 MAKE "H ( :S / 2 ) * SQRT 3
  MAKE "ANG 20 MAKE "LEN 8 MAKE "FACE 1
END

TO DTEMP
  PD FD :H RT 150 * :FACE FD :S
  RT 120 * :FACE FD :S / 2 RT 90 * :FACE PU
END
```

Below are the geometrical operations.

```
TO A
  RS
END

TO B
  RT 180 RS
END

TO C
  RT 60 * :FACE FD :H LT 120 * :FACE RS
END
```

10 CAYLEY GRAPHS

Logo can be used very effectively for another approach to group theory. Associated with any given group there are structures called *Cayley graphs*. An elementary exposition of these, with a great deal of detail, may be found in Grossman and Magnus (1964). A Cayley graph is a set of links joining nodes, just as in the tile patterns in an earlier section of this chapter. The links of the network are interpreted as operations of the group, and the links are colored in such a way that a separate color is associated with each of the operations under consideration. A Cayley graph is a useful way of showing the interrelationships between some generators of a group. All of the tessellations in the earlier section can be converted into Cayley graphs by appropriately coloring the links. Generally speaking, each of the tessellations can be colored in a number of ways, so producing different Cayley graphs from the same network. For example, with suitable colorings, the edges of the tessellation of octagons and squares studied above give Cayley graphs of *p4, p4g, p4m,* and *cmm* (Coxeter and Moser 1965). The tessellation itself has group *p4m*.

The graphs so produced are graphs of the seventeen symmetry groups considered in section 9. But the Cayley graph should not be confused with a pattern having the symmetry group whose structure the graph represents; these may not be the same. This is explained in detail by Coxeter and Moser (1965). Logo offers a very convenient way of illustrating this whole area of group theory, but Logo only provides convenient ways of drawing the Cayley graphs once the structure of the graph has been understood. It does not provide an algorithm to produce the graph automatically from the defining relations of the group. In the next section we now consider groups in a quite different context.

11 GROUPS OF PERMUTATIONS

Group ideas arise naturally in the study of permutations. That is to say, in any situation where the interest is in arranging objects in order in different ways, we find a corresponding mathematical group. The group shows how the different arrangements are interrelated.

Permutational problems often occur as sliding block puzzles, or as puzzles about deformable solids. The Rubik Cube is the most outstanding example. The eventual aim in this section is to investigate a puzzle that was once on sale in toyshops, called the Tantalising Seven. This puzzle is somewhat complicated, so we will study some simpler problems first. The first problem is not very interesting in itself, but it serves to introduce methods to be developed later. The main method is the use of a search tree, and this has applications in any situation involving a finite group, and more widely in any problem that involves finding a suitable sequence of choices.

Consider four girls, standing in line left to right.

Sue   Ann   Jo   Pat.

The game is to move them about by giving just two commands, P and Q. On the command P the girl on the right is moved to the left-hand end, and all the others move up one place, giving

Pat   Sue   Ann   Jo.

When the command Q is given, the girl on the right stands still, the third girl moves over to the left, and the other two move up. So that if the command Q is given with the original lineup, they move to

Jo   Sue   Ann   Pat.

The problem is to give commands that reverse the order of the lineup—that is, arrange the girls in the order

Pat   Jo   Ann   Sue.

(This example is artificial, but problems of a similar kind arise when using certain kinds of programmable calculators or certain programming languages.) We will write a Logo program that searches for solutions. The Logo instruction ITEM :N :MYLIST picks out the *N*th item of a given list. Since ITEM is going to be used a number of times, it is convenient to write a separate procedure to do this.

```
TO I :N
  OP ITEM :N :MYLIST
END
```

This can be used to write procedures to carry out commands P and Q,

```
TO P :MYLIST
  OP (LIST I 4 I 1 I 2 I 3)
END
```

```
TO Q :MYLIST
  OP (LIST I 3 I 1 I 2 I 4 )
END
```

Typing commands such as

PRINT P [Sue Ann Jo Pat]

PRINT P P P [Sue Ann Jo Pat]

produces different permutations of the girls. Using P four times over restores the original state. P followed by Q must be typed in as

PRINT Q P :MYLIST

that is to say, the operators must be read from right to left. The order in which operators are to be read requires constant attention in mathematics and in Logo. Simple sequences of commands in Logo work in the natural order of writing, from left to right, whereas when operators take input values, these are printed to the right of the operator. Therefore the succession of operators, which work on some initial input(s), perforce operates right to left. This can present difficulties to the inexperienced. There is no universal solution to the problem, and the difficulties have to be overcome if the student is to proceed.

We will now devise a tree search to hunt for the solutions to permutation problems. Tree searches are an adaptation of the recursive methods used above to draw tessellations.[2] The use of these methods to generate solutions to various combinatorial problems is described in Fletcher (1988).

In a given situation we have at our disposal the two commands P and Q. So we start a tree with a P-branch and a Q-branch. The procedure is to be recursive, so we need a depth (patience) parameter, "D. We compile a list of the operators as we go along. We call this list "OPLIST, and we examine the various sequences that are produced. If we arrive at the target position, we FINISH—and a separate procedure has to be given for this. If we have not finished, we see if we are to search any further. If $D = 0$, we stop searching on the branch along which we

---

2. It is worth experimenting with various ways of formatting the output on the screen so that tree searches can be displayed as they take place. Different versions of Logo handle ASCII control codes differently, so formatting methods are often system specific and they will not be pursued here.

are traveling and go back. But if we have to continue, we start further branches with TRYP and TRYQ.

```
TO TREE :D :OPLIST :POSN
  IF :POSN = :TARGET [FINISH]
  IF :D = 0 [STOP]
  TRYP TRYQ
END
```

```
TO FINISH
  PRINT :OPLIST STOP
END
```

What is involved in trying P and trying Q? In each case another tree has to be generated, using an updated operator list and an updated position of the girls.

```
TO TRYQ
  TREE :D - 1 ( FPUT "Q :OPLIST ) ( Q :POSN )
END
```

```
TO TRYP
  TREE :D - 1 ( FPUT "P :OPLIST ) ( P :POSN )
END
```

It is convenient to write a short calling procedure to set things off.

```
TO T :D :START :TARGET
  TREE :D [   ] :START
END
```

Now, given the command

T 6 [Sue Jo Pat Ann][Ann Jo Pat Sue]

the machine searches for sequences of commands that change :START into :TARGET and prints them out as they are found. In this case it searches to six deep.

There are twenty-four permutations of four objects, and the operations P and Q defined above will generate all twenty-four permutations, starting from any arbitrary position. We say that P and Q generate a group of order 24. It is called the *symmetric group*, **P4**.

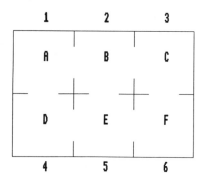

Figure 9 The furniture-moving puzzle

Q produces a cyclic permutation of the three left-hand elements. If the definition of P is changed, so that instead of permuting all four elements it permutes the right-hand three, a different situation arises. The new P and Q generate only one-half of the twenty-four permutations. Algebra texts explain how permutations may be classified as odd and even, by counting the number of pairwise interchanges needed to produce a given permutation from the standard order. In the new situation P and Q generate only the even permutations. This is easy to verify, although an algebraic proof involves some tedious detail. The twelve even permutations of four objects form a group called the *alternating group*.

12 *MOVING FURNITURE*

Recently a popular television programme included the puzzle illustrated in figure 9. A house contains six rooms. Room 5 is empty, and the other rooms each contain pieces of furniture. We will use the letters A, B, C, D, F to denote the pieces of furniture, and the letter E to denote the empty room space. The furniture has to be moved about, and for the purposes of the puzzle no room is allowed to contain more than one piece of furniture at any time. The puzzle, as originally set, was to interchange the pieces of furniture B and F, but we will investigate the situation more fully to see what arrangements can be produced within the given constraints.

It is possible to regard this as a problem about the arrangements of the six objects A, . . . , F, but certain moves in the puzzle are forced. If room 2 or 5 is empty, there is a choice for the next move. But if any of the others is empty, one must either retract the last move or proceed with a move that is forced. There are many ways of using Logo on the problem. One way is to consider the sequences of four or six moves between one position in which room 5 is empty and the next position in which room 5 is empty. This means working with the cyclic permutations that permute either the objects in the four left-hand rooms or the objects in the four right-hand rooms, or with the cycles that rotate all the objects clockwise or counterclockwise.

To carry out an analysis, it is sufficient to consider the operation of rotating the furniture in rooms 1, 2, 4, and 5, and the operation of rotating the furniture in rooms 2, 3, 5, and 6. A rotation of all of the objects through the rooms can be regarded as a combination of these two moves. The procedures of the previous examples can now be adapted to the new problem. They will compute the effect of sequences of moves, or they will carry out searches for moves to produce desired transitions. There is much opportunity for experiment. For example, the puzzle specified only the final positions of certain items, so the FINISH condition may be modified by specifying a comparison of :POSN and :TARGET that affects only the specified items.

Experiment (or the theory of odd and even permutations) will show that not all of the 120 possible permutations of the five objects A, B, C, D, F can be produced within the constraints. Only the sixty even permutations can be generated. The puzzle as set demanded the interchange of B and F. This can only be done if two other items are interchanged as well. The puzzle concerns the alternating group $A5$ and not the symmetric group $P5$.

13 THE TANTALISING SEVEN

The same techniques apply to another puzzle that was on sale in the shops a few years ago. The Tantalising Seven puzzle consists of a plastic frame carrying a track in a form equivalent to a figure of eight within which seven counters slide. A pin can be removed from the side of the track, and the counters can be taken out and rearranged in any order. The pin is then replaced. The puzzle is to bring the counters to some desired position, moving them within the imposed constraints. The counters carry the numbers 1 to 7, and the standard positions on the track are numbered the same way (figure 10).

It is possible to move the counters around the outer loop in either direction, or around the upper and lower loops in either direction. These moves are not truly independent because experiment shows that, for example, displacing the counters in positions 4 through 7 by a clockwise move round the lower loop produces exactly the same effect as displacing everything around the outer loop

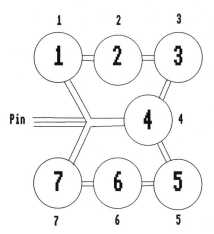

Figure 10 The "Tantalising Seven" puzzle

(clockwise) and then displacing everything in the upper loop counterclockwise. We have to analyze what is possible within these constraints. The approach employed on the previous puzzle can be used with very little modification, but here is an analysis in which P is a clockwise rotation around the outer track, and Q is a clockwise rotation around the lower loop.

The notation on the puzzle as sold uses numbers to label both the sliding counters and the fixed positions, although using the same labels for both can be a source of confusion. Different labels can, if you wish, be used to denote the counters. Procedure I is just as before.

```
TO I :N
  OP ITEM :N :POSN
END
```

Rotating all of the counters in a clockwise direction has the following effect:

```
TO P :POSN
  OP (LIST I 7 I 1 I 2 I 3 I 4 I 5 I 6)
END
```

The notation means that item 7 of the old list occurs in the first position of the new list, item 1 of the old list occurs in the second position of the new list, and so on.

Rotating in a clockwise direction around the lower loop produces the change

```
TO Q :POSN
  OP (LIST I 1 I 2 I 3 I 7 I 4 I 5 I 6)
END
```

TREE may be used just as before, but the experiment shows that extensive searches are needed. These have to be at least twelve deep and up to eighteen deep. This means that economy should be exercised where possible. If the operation P is performed seven times in succession, the original positions are restored. Therefore TRYP should not be used more than six times in a row. Likewise TRYQ should not be used more than three times in a row. Therefore introduce two new variables, "PCOUNT and "QCOUNT, and incorporate them into the TREE procedure in the following way:

```
TO TREE :D :OPLIST :POSN :PCOUNT :QCOUNT
  IF :POSN = :TARGET [FINISH]
  IF :D = 0 [STOP]
  IF :PCOUNT < 6 [TRYP]
  IF :QCOUNT < 3 [TRYQ]
END
```

More measures to remove redundancies could be undertaken, but they are perhaps more trouble than they are worth. The next procedures are much as before, but for convenience they are given again.

```
TO FINISH
  PRINT :OPLIST STOP
END
```

```
TO TRYP
  TREE (:D - 1) ( FPUT "P :OPLIST ) (P :POSN) (:PCOUNT + 1) 0
END
```

```
TO TRYQ
  TREE (:D - 1) ( FPUT "Q :OPLIST ) (Q :POSN) 0 (:QCOUNT + 1)
END
```

A calling procedure can save typing

```
TO T :D :START :TARGET
  TREE :D [   ] :START 0 0
END
```

Now typing T 18 [1 2 3 4 5 6 7][7 6 5 4 3 2 1] finds methods of rearranging the counters in reverse order, using P and Q no more than eighteen times.

There are 5040 possible positions. Is it possible to move between any two, or do the constraints of the puzzle prohibit this? It would take a long time to decide this by using a tree search for every case. Can some human thinking save computer searches? Is there any way of interchanging just two adjacent counters while leaving the rest in their original positions? A search will show that methods can be found; alternatively, the reader who is experienced in calculating with permutations may be able to find a way by hand.

But if any two adjacent counters can be interchanged, then so can any other adjacent pair. To see this, suppose that a method is known to interchange the counters in positions 1 and 2. Then to interchange some other adjacent pair, slide all the counters round until the desired pair is in positions 1 and 2, do the interchange, and then slide back. (Conjugation again.) There may be quicker methods, but this argument shows that the interchange of any adjacent pair is possible. But if you can interchange 1 and 2 and interchange 2 and 3, then you can interchange 1 and 3. (How? Conjugation again!) So the argument now shows that any pair may be interchanged, and if this can be done, then any desired arrangement can be attained by the successive interchange of pairs. This shows that however the counters are initially placed in the track, they may be moved to any desired positions. This puzzle is therefore concerned with the symmetric group *P7*, and not just with the alternating group *A7*. This differs from the furniture puzzle, and the reason again involves the parity of the permutations. The techniques that have been described so far merely use Logo procedures to assist searches; it is a further, much more complicated, challenge to use Logo to do the algebraic calculations that decide the size of the group which the given operations generate.

14 LOGO AS A SELF-MODIFYING LANGUAGE

It is often said that Logo is a self-modifying language. Logo is a language for handling lists, and since the definitions of Logo procedures are themselves lists, Logo can modify its own definitions. But it is difficult to find in the literature examples that persuade one to use this feature of the language.

Before introducing some elementary examples of Logo procedures that alter other procedures and that may indeed alter themselves, we will consider some of the features of the structural ideas that were much discussed when "modern mathematics" was introduced in the 1960s. Some innovators supported the strategy of introducing such ideas as groups, rings, and fields early in the mathematics course without realizing the Pandora's box that was being opened. These ideas of abstract algebra do not merely classify mathematical systems at one particular level, they open up unlimited possibilities of extending the system hierarchically. A group of automorphisms (which exists at some level of abstraction) has its own automorphisms with their own group structure (at a level of abstraction one stage up). Groups can describe groups.

It is easy to regard this as pure mathematicians' fantasy which is irrelevant to elementary teaching. But if one looks into the structure of the number system, going no further than the rational numbers and the negative numbers that are taught almost universally to all pupils, we find that these structural principles are already involved. It has not been demonstrated to the general satisfaction of teachers that an explicit recognition of these sophisticated aspects of the number system actually helps in the early stages of teaching—but pupils and teachers have regular and continuing difficulties with the number system when it is taught without an understanding of these subtleties.

A number of mathematics educators consider it an acceptable middle way to approach integers as operators on counting numbers (in the way described above) and to approach rational numbers as operators, either on counting numbers or on integers. This is the beginning of a hierarchical account of the number system, and as one goes on, the hierarchy is extended—each new mathematical entity is described in terms of operations on the level previously known. This gives rise to the aphorism,

Algebra consists of operations on operations.

Elementary mathematics has these hierarchical features, and Logo can be used hierarchically in various ways. All elementary introductions to Logo describe the use of procedures that call other procedures, but there are further possibilities. Logo procedures can modify, or even construct other procedures. As an introductory example consider a standard way of drawing an octagon:

```
TO O1 :S
 REPEAT 8 [FD :S LT 45]
END
```

There are many ways in Logo of extending this simple procedure to create a variety of patterns. One way is to observe that the definition involves turning left. But an octagon can also be drawn by turning right; so define

```
TO O2 :S
  REPEAT 8 [FD :S RT 45]
END
```

O1 and O2 both produce octagons, but the successive commands O1 O2 produce two octagons that are not superimposed. They stand side by side. It is natural to extend the pattern by introducing

```
TO O3 :S
  REPEAT 8 [BK :S LT 45]
END
```

which gives another octagon; once again in a different position with respect to the starting point. It is natural to complete the pattern with

```
TO O4 :S
  REPEAT 8 [BK :S RT 45]
END
```

A pleasant pattern arises from the consecutive use of the four procedures, which extends to a table mat design if it is repeated four times with rotations of 45 degrees in between. A consideration of the steps involved in creating this comparatively simple design leads to unexpected depths in geometrical symmetry and in the language itself.

There are obvious geometrical relationships between the four procedures. They embody a very common set of geometrical relationships, and we have an example of the four-group. The last three procedures are modifications of the first one. Can we devise procedures to make these modifications automatically within the resources of the language?

15 PROCEDURES TO HANDLE PROCEDURES

Leron and Zazkis (chapter 11) discuss the operation FLIP. We now consider a procedure that provides one method of carrying it out.

When deriving O2 from O1 the problem is simply to change LT into RT. A more general problem is to change every occurrence of LT in a procedure into RT and every occurrence of RT into LT. We do not know how many occurrences we might find, and we do not know how complicated the procedures may be because of having REPEAT loops or IF conditions. We have to be able to cope with every complication, so the obvious way is to proceed recursively!

A Logo definition is a list. Take any procedure, such as O1, and ask the machine to SHOW TEXT "O1. The machine prints out the definition of O1 as a list. The command TEXT changes the definition of the procedure into a list, and conversely, the command DEFINE turns a list into a definition. To illustrate this,

DEFINE "LOCT TEXT "O1

defines a new procedure called LOCT, which is an exact copy of the procedure "O1. This is of no value, but it opens the way to transforming one procedure into others. The immediate problem is to take a list of symbols and to turn every LT into RT and every RT into LT. We need a procedure that will take as input :MYLIST and output something that we may call REFLIST. So it needs to start with

TO REFLIST :MYLIST

It is necessary to provide for various contingencies. The simplest case is to have no list at all! This gives the first line of the procedure.

IF :MYLIST = [   ] [OP :MYLIST]

Various cases now arise. The first item of the list may be LT, in which case it must be changed to RT. The first item may be RT, in which case it must be changed to LT. The first item may itself be a list, in which case the procedure must act recursively and change this (sub)list before going on. There is also the possibility that the first item in the list needs no modification, in which case the procedure has to pass on to the next item. A line has to be written to cover each contingency, and furthermore the lines have to be placed in an order that ensures that they carry suitable priority. Many interesting points of recursive programming are involved. A suitable procedure is

```
TO REFLIST :MYLIST
  IF EMPTYP :MYLIST [OP :MYLIST]
  IF LISTP FIRST :MYLIST [OP FPUT REFLIST FIRST :MYLIST REFLIST BF
    :MYLIST]
  IF "LT = FIRST :MYLIST [OP FPUT "RT REFLIST BF :MYLIST]
  IF "RT = FIRST :MYLIST [OP FPUT "LT REFLIST BF :MYLIST]
  OP FPUT FIRST :MYLIST REFLIST BF :MYLIST
END
```

Now DEFINE "O2 REFLIST TEXT "O1 produces the definition of O2 from the definition of O1.

In a similar way one can write a procedure REVLIST to change every occurrence of BK into FD, and vice versa. This will produce O3 from O1. O4 can be produced from O1 by using REVLIST and REFLIST in sequence. It is a further challenge to compare REFLIST and REVLIST. These two procedures are very similar in construction, so there is a superprocedure that will transform these two into one another. A procedure that operates on procedures that operate on procedures, and so on.

Here there is opportunity for much investigation into the possibilities of the language. What happens if procedures are applied not only to other procedures but also to themselves? Are

TEXT "REFLIST and REFLIST TEXT "REFLIST

the same? It may be surprising, but they are. Every occurrence of RT in TEXT "REFLIST is changed to LT, and vice versa, but there are no such occurrences. The symbols occurring are "RT and "LT, and since Logo obeys instructions to the letter, these two are not interchanged. However, the procedure REFLIST can be extended by adding instructions to interchange "RT and "LT as well. Call the extended procedure REFLISTX. What happens if we compare

TEXT "REFLIST and REFLISTX TEXT "REFLIST

We could also compare

TEXT "REFLISTX and REFLISTX TEXT "REFLISTX

What happens now?

Here is another procedure that modifies itself, and it does so in an interesting way.

```
TO GROW
  PRINT [WATCH ME GROW]
  MAKE "OLDTEXT TEXT "GROW
  MAKE "NEWTEXT FPUT [  ] FPUT ITEM 2 :OLDTEXT BF :OLDTEXT
  DEFINE "GROW :NEWTEXT ERN [OLDTEXT NEWTEXT]
END
```

When the procedure has been defined, if you type GROW, it prints out "WATCH ME GROW." But run it again, and it types the sentence twice. Indeed, each time it is run the procedure grows. Look again at the definition itself. You will see that the definition now contains more print lines, depending on how many times it has been run. The definition in the work space continually enlarges itself, but if there is a version of the procedure in the editor, this remains unchanged until you reenter the editor and alter it.

The microcomputer is a remarkable device, and Logo is a remarkable language. Logo has unexpected depths, and to use its power to the full calls for unfamiliar ways of thinking. Logo provides an opportunity for teachers of mathematics and teachers of language to meet on common ground, which so far neither party has explored. Specialists in language teaching sometimes dismiss programming as "merely coding," but Logo programming involves more than this, if only because it demands choice of language and sensitivity to style. In addition the possibilities of self-reference in Logo raise questions that are far more than matters of coding; they are a challenge to think in quite different ways. Furthermore Logo procedures can refer to and modify themselves, and this invites us to think about how we think.

APPENDIX: THE SEVENTEEN SPACE GROUPS OF TWO-DIMENSIONAL CRYSTALLOGRAPHY

This list gives a fundamental region (template) and a possible set of generators for each of the seventeen symmetry groups of plane ornaments. In the groups that are not generated entirely by reflections, there is some choice of the fundamental region. (This was exploited most remarkably by Escher.) The regions below are as discussed in Coxeter and Moser (1965); the generators are taken from Coxeter (1961).

p1   parallelogram, with translations along the sides

p2   Any triangle, with half-turns about the midpoints of the sides

pm   A rectangle, with reflections in a pair of opposite sides and a translation along them

pg   A rhombus, with two parallel glide relections (these are along lines parallel to one of the diagonals and one-half its length)

cm   An isosceles triangle, with a reflection in its base and a glide reflection along a line parallel to the base and of half the length

pmm   A rectangle, with reflections in the four sides

pmg   An isosceles triangle, with a reflection in its base and half-turns about the midpoints of the equal sides

pgg   A rectangle, with glide reflections along the two center lines

cmm   An isosceles right-angled triangle, with reflections in the two perpendicular sides and a half-turn about the center of the hypotenuse

p4   An isosceles right-angled triangle, with a half-turn about the midpoint of the hypotenuse and a quarter-turn about the right-angled vertex

p4m   An isosceles right-angled triangle, with reflections in the sides

p4g   An isosceles right-angled triangle, with a reflection in the hypotenuse and a quarter-turn about the right-angled vertex

p3   A 120-degree rhombus, with rotations of 120 degrees about the 120-degree vertices

p3m1   A 120-degree isosceles triangle, with a reflection in the base and a rotation of 120 degrees about the vertex

p31m   An equilateral triangle, with reflections in the sides

p6   A 120-degree isosceles triangle, with a half-turn about the midpoint of the base and a rotation of 120 degrees about the vertex

p6m   A 30-, 60-, 90-degree triangle, with reflections in the sides

REFERENCES

Abelson, H., and diSessa A. 1980. *Turtle Geometry*. Cambridge: MIT Press. Note especially the general remarks on implementing turtle graphics in chapter 3.

Budden, F. 1972. *The Fascination of Groups*. Cambridge: Cambridge University Press. At the end of the book the seventeen groups are described from a point of view close to that adopted here.

Coxeter, H. S. M. 1961. *Introduction to Geometry*. New York: Wiley.

Coxeter, H. S. M., and Moser, W. O. J. 1965. *Generators and Relations for Discrete Groups*. 2d. ed. Berlin: Springer.

Cundy, H. Martyn, and Rollett, A. P. 1952. *Mathematical Models*. Oxford: Oxford University Press.

Fletcher, T. J. 1963. *Some Lessons in Mathematics*. Cambridge: Cambridge University Press. Gives an appropriate background of transformation geometry.

Fletcher, T. J. 1988. Trees and beyond. Paper presented to the section on Logo and Mathematics Education, ICME-6, Budapest.

Freudenthal, H. 1973. What groups mean in mathematics and what they should mean in mathematical education. In *Developments in Mathematical Education*. Proceedings of the Second International Congress on Mathematical Education. Cambridge: Cambridge University Press.

Griesel, H. 1971. *Die neue Mathematik für Lehrer und Studenten*. 3 vols. Hannover: Schroedel.

Grossman, I., and Magnus, W. 1964. *Groups and Their Graphs*. New York: Random House. This was one of a series of books published for the Monograph Project of the School Mathematics Study Group.

Jones, Owen. 1856. *Grammar of Ornament*. London: Day.

Kraitchik, M. 1943. *Mathematical Recreations*. London: Allen and Unwin.

SMP. 1966. *Additional Mathematics*, Part 1. *Teacher's Guide* 1968. Cambridge: Cambridge University Press. Do the seventeen groups from a point of view closely related to the view taken here.

Steinhaus, H. 1950. *Mathematical Snapshots*. Oxford: Oxford University Press.

Vergnaud, G. 1988. Theoretical frameworks and empirical facts in the psychology of mathematics education. In *Proceedings of Sixth International Congress on Mathematical Education*. Budapest: Malev.

Zazkis, R., and Leron, U. 1992. Capturing congruence with a turtle. *Logo Exchange*, to appear.

Avoiding Recursion

Brian Harvey

13

1 INTRODUCTION

It is traditional to understand a computer program as a *sequence* of instructions. The computer carries out these instructions one after another. Various *control structures* allow the programmer to change the order in which these instructions are carried out. There are conditional structures that allow a choice between subsequences, and looping structures that allow the repetition of a sequence.

In contrast to this idea of sequential programming, there is a more recent model called *functional programming* (Backus 1978; Allen 1984; Abelson 1985). In this approach a program is viewed as a collection of mathematical functions, which can be applied to arguments and composed with other functions to create more complicated functions. The emphasis is on the input-output behavior of a function rather than on the sequence of events by which the computer determines the output value. Programming languages such as LISP, Logo, and APL emphasize the functional model, while BASIC, Pascal, and C emphasize the sequential view. (This division is not absolute; any program can be written in any language, more or less. But each language encourages a certain natural style of programming.)

In this chapter, I begin by arguing that functional programming is not only more powerful technically but also more sensible pedagogically, especially when computer programming is to be used as a vehicle for teaching mathematical ideas. Why then is secondary school programming done almost exclusively in BASIC and Pascal? Why not in Logo? Although there are several answers to this question, I want to focus attention on one technical reason: Teachers are put off by Logo's heavy reliance on recursion as the principal control mechanism. I will discuss the relationship between functional programming and recursion, show how the two can be separated, and suggest specific approaches to sample mathematical programming problems.

Recursion is itself an interesting mathematical idea because of its connection with proof by induction. I do not mean to suggest that mathematics teachers should wish to avoid recursion in every situation. Indeed, later we will consider examples, such as computing the determinant of a matrix, for which the use of recursion is naturally connected with the task. Logo is of course an excellent vehicle for the study of recursion when that is desired. But not every topic is inherently recursive, and the value of functional programming will be enhanced if the issue of recursion can be separated from that of functions.

2 SEQUENTIAL AND FUNCTIONAL PROGRAMMING

Consider the problem of adding two matrices:

$$\begin{bmatrix} 2 & 3 & 4 \\ 5 & 6 & 7 \end{bmatrix} + \begin{bmatrix} 87 & 0 & 14 \\ -6 & 28 & 9 \end{bmatrix}.$$

The result is a matrix with the same shape as the two addends. Each element of the result is formed by adding the corresponding elements of the addends. In sequential programming this leads to six assignment instructions, which can be arranged in two nested loops to reflect the two-dimensional structure of the matrix. For now let us ignore the matter of reading these particular numbers into the computer, and suppose we have two arrays A and B containing the addends. A BASIC program to add these matrices might be written as follows:

```
10  DIMENSION A(2,3), B(2,3), C(2,3)
20  FOR I = 1 TO 2
30  FOR J = 1 TO 3
40  C(I,J) = A(I,J) + B(I,J)
50  NEXT J
60  NEXT I
70  END
```

This is a simple enough program. It has two main weaknesses. One has to do with the use of arrays to represent the matrices. The problem is that the particular dimensions, two rows by three columns, must be built into the program, both in the array declarations and in the control structures (the FOR statements) that control the sequence of events. The second weakness is that this program expects to find its data in fixed places, the arrays A and B, and leaves its result in a third predetermined location C. This is fine if we only want to compute $A + B$, but what if we want to solve a slightly different problem, like $A + 2B$? What if we want to check that addition of matrices is truly commutative, by adding first

$A + B$ and then $B + A$? Or, having computed C as the sum of A and B, what if we want to use that result as part of a larger computation, like $C + B$? In each case we would have to rewrite the program.

A better interactive system for students to use in exploring matrix arithmetic would supply functions whose domain and range are matrices. We should be able to enter instructions like

```
PRINT ADD(A,B)
PRINT ADD(A, ADD(B,B))
LET C = ADD(A,B)
PRINT ADD(C,B)
IF ADD(A,B) = ADD(B,A) THEN PRINT "IT'S COMMUTATIVE."
```

(In this fanciful example, I am using the syntax of BASIC but asking for computations that are beyond the powers of most versions of BASIC. Many versions do allow this sort of functional notation, but only for certain functions of single numbers, not array-valued functions.)

Although functions are one of the central ideas of mathematics, they are not limited to the narrow school version of mathematics as "stuff about numbers." Consider the functions

```
plural(box) = boxes
French(book) = livre
capital(England) = London
AtomicWeight(silver) = 107.87
```

I will resist the temptation to explore possible pedagogic uses of functional programming in the areas suggested by these simple functions. A serious effort to translate English into French, for example, would need much more sophistication than the word-for-word translation function illustrated above. The point is that no matter what a computation is about, the ability to define, invoke, and compose functions is a natural and convenient tool.

Computer scientists are excited about functional programming for reasons unconnected with pedagogy. To a computer scientist, what distinguishes this methodology from traditional approaches is that a function has no "side effects." That is, when a programmer asks for the value of $f(7)$ the value returned is always the same. This computation does not cause a permanent change in the computer's memory that might affect later computations. (For example, there are no assignments to global variables.) This is important for two reasons. First, it is easier to carry out formal reasoning about a program without side effects. One branch of computer science is concerned with program *verification*: the attempt to provide formal proof of the correctness of a program. Functional programs lend themselves to this attempt more readily than traditional sequential programs that are heavily dependent on long-term variable assignment. Second, if the computation of a function has no side effects, then it makes no difference which of two desired computations is done first; each is guaranteed to be independent of the other. Recent developments in computer hardware include *parallel* processors in which the two computations might actually take place at the same time. Functional programs can easily take advantage of this parallelism; traditional programs require detailed analysis before any subtask can be split off for parallel computation.

For our pedagogic purposes, however, the important points about functional programming are different. A student who wanted to use the BASIC instructions shown above to add two matrices in a larger program would have to remember that the result is in the array C and write the rest of the program accordingly. Two such addition problems with different matrices would require two copies of the instructions or reuse of the same arrays for different purposes. A function that can be applied to any two matrices, and whose return value can be used as part of a larger expression instead of being tied to a specific result array, allows the student to think about the mathematics instead of tripping over the programming language.

3 FIRST-CLASS DATA AGGREGATES

Consider now the problem of entering the actual matrix values into the program. In most programming languages the facilities for dealing with individual numbers (scalars) are much more flexible than the facilities for arrays. It is as if numbers are "real things," while collections of numbers are less real. For example, in BASIC or PASCAL a scalar constant can be directly assigned to a variable ($X = 3$) or can be part of a larger expression ($X = Y + 3$), but you cannot say

$A = 2, 3, 4, 5, 6, 7$

to assign a value to an entire array at once. Instead, getting this value into the computer is a sequence of events in itself:

```
10  DIMENSION A(2,3)
20  FOR  I = 1 TO 2
30  FOR  J = 1 TO 3
40  READ  A(I,J)
50  NEXT  J
60  NEXT  I
70  DATA  2, 3, 4, 5, 6, 7
80  END
```

Logo's list processing makes matrix manipulation much more convenient. For one thing, the size of a list need not be declared in advance; we can write matrix functions that work on matrices of any size or shape. Also a list is a "first-class" entity. Like a number it can be used as part of an expression, as an input to or output from a function, as the value assigned to a variable, or as something to be read or printed.

We will represent a matrix as a list of lists. Each of the sublists will be one row of the matrix. We can solve the addition problem posed above by assigning matrix values to variables:

```
MAKE "A [[2  3  4] [5  6  7]]
MAKE "B [[87  0  14] [−6  28  9]]
SHOW ADD :A :B
```

or we can use the matrix values directly as inputs to the addition function:

```
SHOW ADD [[2  3  4] [5  6  7]]  [[87  0  14] [−6  28  9]]
```

The brackets that delimit the sublists make the two-by-three shape of the matrix immediately clear to a human reader as well as to the computer program.

4   ADDING MATRICES IN LOGO

I have indicated some of the reasons why Logo is a good language in which to add matrices, but I have not yet written the actual program. I will now do so, in a traditional Logo style. The two-dimensional nature of a matrix is reflected in a two-procedure program structure. The top-level procedure goes through the two input matrices row by row, adding pairs of rows to produce a row of the result. The subprocedure that adds a row has the same general structure; it goes through two vectors (i.e., what a row of a matrix is) element by element, adding pairs of numbers.

```
TO MATRIX.ADD :M1 :M2
 IF EMPTYP :M1 [OUTPUT [ ]]
 OUTPUT FPUT  (VECTOR.ADD FIRST :M1 FIRST :M2)
                  (MATRIX.ADD BUTFIRST :M1 BUTFIRST :M2)
END

TO VECTOR.ADD :V1 :V2
 IF EMPTYP :V1 [OUTPUT [ ]]
 OUTPUT FPUT (SUM FIRST :V1 FIRST :V2)
                  (VECTOR.ADD BUTFIRST :V1 BUTFIRST :V2)
END
```

I have called the top-level procedure MATRIX.ADD rather than just ADD to make sure there is no confusion about which is which. The procedure SUM that is used by VECTOR.ADD is Logo's built-in addition function for scalars.

? SHOW MATRIX.ADD [[2 3 4] [5 6 7]] [[87 0 14] [−6 28 9]]
[[89 3 18] [−1 34 16]]

These procedures are *recursive*. That is, each of them includes an invocation of the same function applied to different inputs. Defining a function in terms of itself is a familiar trick to mathematicians:

$$n! = \begin{cases} 1 & \text{if } n = 0, \\ n \times (n-1)! & \text{if } n > 0. \end{cases}$$

But mathematicians also know that it is hard to get students to understand these inductive definitions at first.

There are many reasons why Logo is not widely used in teaching mathematical topics such as matrix arithmetic. BASIC is popular because it often comes free with personal computers. Pascal is popular, in the United States, because of the Advanced Placement Exam in Computer Science. Logo, because of its widespread use in elementary schools, has an undeserved but nearly universal reputation as a language suitable *only* for very young students doing trivial problems. Many people believe that Logo can only do graphics, like a paint program. But even people who see past these misunderstandings often consider Logo list processing difficult because of the frequent use of recursion.

Why is a recursive definition needed here? Later I will suggest that the use of recursion is *not* truly necessary; by providing a larger functional programming "toolkit" we can express the desired computation without writing self-referential procedures. Still, there is a connection between the functional approach and the use of recursion. To simplify the discussion, consider the subprocedure VECTOR.ADD. The sequential view of programming would express the job of this procedure as a sequence of events, one for each element of the result vector:

LET C(1) = A(1) + B(1)
LET C(2) = A(2) + B(2)
LET C(3) = A(3) + B(3)

In this illustration I am supposing that we are adding vectors of length three. Sequential programming languages generally provide a looping mechanism so that a string of similar events can be encoded without explicit repetition:

FOR I = 1 TO 3
LET C(I) = A(I) + B(I)
NEXT I

In the functional programming model, we are trying to get away from this idea of a sequence of events. For one thing, we have no predetermined place, like the array C in the sequential version, to put the result. Still it is possible to express the output value in terms of composition of built-in functions. We must use the addition function SUM, but also functions that select particular elements from a vector or combine elements into a new vector:

TO VECTOR.ADD :V1 :V2
 OUTPUT (LIST (SUM ITEM 1 :V1 ITEM 1 :V2)
              (SUM ITEM 2 :V1 ITEM 2 :V2)
              (SUM ITEM 3 :V1 ITEM 3 :V2))
END

Again, in this illustration I am assuming three-element vectors. I have used the built-in function ITEM to select one element from a vector and the function LIST to combine several elements into one vector. (I have formatted this procedure to indicate the groupings clearly, but in most microcomputer versions of Logo the OUTPUT instruction must be entered as a single, long line.)

   The difficulty comes in generalizing this definition to work with vectors of any length. Formal mathematical notation has no trouble with

$$(a_1, a_2, a_3) + (b_1, b_2, b_3) = (a_1 + b_1, a_2 + b_2, a_3 + b_3),$$

but when we want to generalize, we must resort to ellipses:

$$(a_1, \ldots, a_n) + (b_1, \ldots, b_n) = (a_1 + b_1, \ldots, a_n + b_n).$$

This notation is flexible on paper but not quite what we want for a computer program. The mathematician's solution is an inductive definition: Imagine that we know how to add n-element vectors, and use that to define addition of vectors with $n + 1$ elements. To do this, we need a function "adjoin" that takes a number and a vector as inputs, giving as its output a slightly longer vector including the new number. Then we can say

$$\text{adjoin}(a_0, \mathbf{a}) + \text{adjoin}(b_0, \mathbf{b}) = \text{adjoin}(a_0 + b_0, \mathbf{a} + \mathbf{b}).$$

The Logo equivalent of adjoin is called FPUT, for "first put." It takes two inputs. The first can be anything, but the second must be a list. The output is a new list consisting of the old list with the new thing put in front. Taking apart a vector is accomplished with the functions FIRST, to extract the first element of a list, and BUTFIRST, whose output is a list equal to its input with the first element removed.

The recursive definition of VECTOR.ADD, then, expresses the sum of its input vectors in terms of the sum of two smaller vectors, namely, the BUT-FIRSTs of the inputs, with one extra number adjoined, namely, the ordinary numerical sum of the FIRST elements of each vector. Like any inductive definition, it needs a base case. This one says that the sum of two zero-length (empty) vectors is the empty vector. The analysis of MATRIX.ADD is similar, except that a matrix is a list of vectors rather than a list of numbers.

5   WHY IS RECURSION HARD?

There are several aspects to the difficulty that students have in coming to understand recursive programming style. One of these is also found in learning to accept inductive proofs: the sense of unfairness in any self-referential definition. "You're assuming what you're supposed to be proving!" But in some ways the difficulty is greater in the case of programming.

An inductive proof can be presented "ground up." We show explicitly that the theorem is true for $n = 1$. Then, by the inductive step, we can see that it must be true for $n = 2$. Then, by induction again, it must also be true for $n = 3$. The advantage of this perspective is that each step is taken from a firm footing, with nothing hanging in the air. That is, by the time we consider the case $n = 3$, we are completely satisfied that the theorem has been demonstrated for $n = 2$.

By contrast, in the programming context the more usual situation is that we have to work backward. For example, we are presented with a pair of three-element vectors to add. That is our starting point. We then say, "we can do this if we know how to add two-element vectors." The initial problem must be suspended while we consider this subproblem. By the time we get down to the base case, there are three such suspended problems. This state of affairs is a challenge not only to our faith but to our memory. It is very easy to lose the thread of contexts in which subproblems arose. The difference between the proof and the program arises because in the proof we are not specifically concerned with any concrete example; the goal is a general truth, and it makes as much sense to start small as not. But we wrote the program because we wanted to solve a particular problem, and most often not a trivial base-case problem.

For teaching purposes it is possible to introduce recursion from the ground up. We can introduce a general problem and then decide to start by solving the simplest possible case. This is the method I prefer in my own teaching. The advantage is that it avoids the sense of hanging in midair, but there are two costs. First, it means that the use of recursion cannot be motivated by a problem that really arises in class; such problems will not be so simple. Second, although the students do not feel strained, they do feel foolish during the beginning stages of the explanation. The recursive style seems like an overcomplicated approach to such simple problems. Then the more complicated cases can feel like rabbits suddenly pulled from a hat.

Another problem in learning recursion is faced by students who have previous experience in the sequential programming style. They are strongly tempted to interpret the recursive invocation as a loop, an instruction to "do it again." That interpretation can sometimes work for recursive Logo commands (programs with side-effect instructions) but is almost never appropriate for recursive operations (functions that return values, like VECTOR.ADD). The actual sequence of events in the computer is not what these students would predict, in which the first invocation computes the first element, then the second takes over. It would be more nearly accurate to say that the sequence happens backward; the first invocation cannot do its job until the second is complete, and so on. So it is the *last* invocation, the one for the base case, that really happens first!

A problem related to the "do it again" misunderstanding concerns the nature of local variables. In a loop, such as the FOR–NEXT examples seen earlier, there is one single loop variable whose value keeps changing. In a recursive procedure the relevant variable names (the procedure inputs, like V1 and V2) do not correspond to a single box into which changing values are placed. Rather, each invocation of the procedure creates a new set of variables. Several such variables can exist at the same time. Students have to work out how the program decides which variable to use when such a name appears in an instruction.

6 FUNCTIONAL PROGRAMMING WITHOUT RECURSION

One language specifically designed for matrix manipulation is APL. To add two matrices in APL, we can simply use the built-in + operation. Addition in APL is defined to work for scalars, vectors, matrices, or higher-dimensional arrays. The APL programmer avoids both looping and recursion. (Of course there is some kind of repetition going on behind the scenes if the APL program is running on a conventional computer that can only perform one arithmetic operation at a time. But this repetition is invisible to the programmer, just as every language makes certain details invisible.)

APL encourages a functional programming style. The addition operator is a function; it can be composed with other functions to build new, more complex functions. Because the primitive functions all work on arrays as well as scalars, many problems can be solved using "one-liners," programs with no visible control structures at all. There is no looping construct in APL. When a control mechanism is needed, the APL programmer can choose between two extremes, Logo-like recursion and an unstructured "goto" operation. But many mathematical problems can be solved without raising the issue of control, which is advantageous for a math teacher.

Unfortunately, APL is not widely available. The largest obstacle is that it uses a notation very close to that of ordinary mathematics, full of Greek letters and other strange symbols. These are not part of the standard computer character set, and special hardware is required to display them. (Indeed, there are not enough keys even on the APL keyboard. Some symbols are formed by overprinting two other symbols. This approach was designed for hardcopy computer terminals, which backspace and overprint naturally. It is not suitable for most current display devices, which allow only one character in any screen position.)

Can we use, in Logo, the APL idea of operating on a vector or matrix "all at once," rather than explicitly manipulating each element individually? Tools for this programming metaphor have long been part of LISP, Logo's parent language. It is an easy matter to extend Logo (by writing procedures in Logo and loading them for students) with such tools.

7 AVOIDING RECURSION IN LOGO

Let me begin by defining a few simple arithmetic procedures.

```
TO SQUARE :X
 OUTPUT :X * :X
END

TO NEXT :X
 OUTPUT :X + 1
END

TO DOUBLE :X
 OUTPUT :X * 2
END
```

Now consider these interactions with Logo.

```
? SHOW MAP "SQUARE [2 3 4 5]
[4 9 16 25]
? SHOW MAP "NEXT [7 8 9]
[8 9 10]
? SHOW MAP "DOUBLE [5 3 20 6 1]
[10 6 40 12 2]
```

The procedures SQUARE, and so on, are defined to operate on scalars. The general tool called MAP allows these functions to work on vectors, by arranging to apply a function to each element of the vector. The output from MAP is another vector with the same number of elements, but with values computed by the function being mapped.

Logo is an extensible language. This means that a user-defined procedure is invoked in exactly the same way as a primitive procedure. MAP happens not to be a Logo primitive, but if it is included in a startup file, it can be presented to students just as if it were a primitive. Its purpose is immediately clear and should present no conceptual problems to students. The same idea can be extended to functions of two inputs.

```
? SHOW MAP.2 "SUM [1 2 3] [40 50 60]
[41 52 63]
? SHOW MAP.2 "PRODUCT [5 6] [7 8]
[35 48]
? SHOW MAP.2 "EQUALP [1 4 6 7] [30 4 5 9]
[FALSE TRUE FALSE FALSE]
```

MAP.2 requires three inputs, a function and two lists. The two lists must have the same length, and the output will have that length also.

We are now in a position to return to the problem of matrix addition with which we began:

```
TO MATRIX.ADD :M1 :M2
 OUTPUT MAP.2 "VECTOR.ADD :M1 :M2
END

TO VECTOR.ADD :V1 :V2
 OUTPUT MAP.2 "SUM :V1 :V2
END
```

That's all there is! I find this version simpler than the original BASIC program with nested FOR loops. There are no auxiliary variables I and J; there is no need to build the size or shape of the matrices into the procedures. Once the general idea of MAP is understood, its application to this problem is straightforward.

The MAP and MAP.2 procedures themselves are, naturally, a little more complicated. They are defined recursively, using some of the more advanced capabilities of Logo. If students (or teachers) want to understand the inner workings of these tools, they must face the challenge of recursion. I think this is fine. People who are interested in programming must eventually understand recursion. The point is that that understanding no longer has to come first. The mathematics can be studied and the programming issues can be postponed. (The Logo definitions of all the tools presented in this chapter are collected in an appendix.)

8 TEMPLATES

One problem with the mapping tools as I have presented them above is that we must define a named scalar function in order to use that name as an input to MAP. For example, when I first introduced MAP, I had to detour through definitions of SQUARE, NEXT, and DOUBLE in order to have something to map over the vectors in the examples. It is not so bad to have names for these functions, since the functions are useful in themselves and the names are sensible. But sometimes we need an *ad hoc* function just for one particular mapping operation. The problem will become clearer if we consider an example.

We would like to be able to multiply a matrix by a scalar. That is, we want to be able to say

? SHOW MATRIX.SCALE 3 [[1 2 3] [4 5 6]]
[[3 6 9] [12 15 18]]

The function MATRIX.SCALE (I am saving the name MULTIPLY for multiplication of a matrix by a matrix) takes two inputs, a number and a matrix. Its output is a matrix with the same shape as the input, but with each element multiplied by the number.

It may be tempting to write MATRIX.SCALE as follows:

```
TO MATRIX.SCALE :NUM :MAT                ;incorrect!
 OUTPUT MAP.2 "VECTOR.SCALE :NUM :MAT
END

TO VECTOR.SCALE :NUM :VEC
 OUTPUT MAP.2 "PRODUCT :NUM :VEC
END
```

This looks like a straightforward application of the same ideas that we used in MATRIX.ADD, but the parallel does not work. The problem is that MAP.2 requires two *lists* of equal length so that it can inductively step through them, applying the function input to pairs of elements. Here we are trying to use a single number :NUM repeatedly.

There is really only one matrix input in this problem, not two, and so we need a solution using MAP, not MAP.2. It would be easy enough to do this for any specific scale factor:

```
TO TIMES3 :X
 OUTPUT 3 * :X
END

TO MATRIX.SCALE3 :MAT
 OUTPUT MAP "VECTOR.SCALE3 :MAT
END

TO VECTOR.SCALE3 :VEC
 OUTPUT MAP "TIMES3 :VEC
END
```

But it is not obvious how to generalize this into the desired MATRIX.SCALE function. We would have to be able to invent the functions like TIMES3 "on the fly."

The problem we are experiencing here turns out to be similar to the problem that encouraged us to switch from BASIC to Logo as the medium for matrix manipulation. In BASIC we were unable to compute the sum of two matrices without putting the result in a specific named array C. Without a name an array could not exist as a real object on its own. Logo lists, by contrast, are first-class objects that can be entered directly as arguments to functions like MATRIX.ADD without the intermediate step of assigning them as the value of a named variable. What we need now is *first-class functions*. We want to be able to say "the function 3 times *x*" as an input to MAP.

First-class functions are one of the central ideas of LISP, the language from which Logo was developed. Logo itself does not include LISP's mechanism for this purpose, but it does include other mechanisms that allow us to implement first-class functions within Logo. We can put a Logo expression in a list, like

[3 * :X]

and then we can ask Logo to RUN the list. That is, the function RUN takes an expression list as its input and gives the value of the expression as its output.

It may seem that this is all we need. We could write

OUTPUT MAP [3 * :X] :VEC

instead of

OUTPUT MAP "TIMES3 :VEC

and just design the MAP procedure so that it runs the expression list for each element of the vector. This is almost the right thing, but there is a mathematical confusion involved. An expression is not the same thing as a function. In mathematical notation, we do not say $f = 3x$; we say $f(x) = 3x$. In this particular example the difference may not seem important; x is the only variable around, and so it is obvious what is meant. But consider the difference between $f(a, b) = 2a + b$ and $g(b, a) = 2a + b$. These two functions are not equivalent, even though they are defined by the same expression $2a + b$.

A similar naming problem arises in the SCALE problem. If we just want to scale by 3, then we could say that there is only one variable around. But we are going to want to write something like

```
TO VECTOR.SCALE :NUM :VEC
 OUTPUT MAP [:NUM * :X] :VEC
END
```

In this situation it's not obvious how MAP should know that the variable NUM has a particular value assigned to it externally, while the variable X is the one into which it should plug the elements of the vector. The traditional LISP solution is to represent a function as a *lambda expression* that contains the names of the input variables as well as the defining expression. So in LISP we might say

```
(DEFINE F (LAMBDA (A B) (+ (* 2 A) B)))
(DEFINE G (LAMBDA (B A) (+ (* 2 A) B)))
```

(LISP uses prefix form (* 2 A) rather than infix form (2 * A) to represent arithmetic operations. But the important point for our purposes is to notice the difference between F and G, namely, the list of parameter names following the word LAMBDA.)

It would be possible to invent this precise mechanism for Logo. Then we could say

```
TO VECTOR.SCALE :NUM :VEC
 OUTPUT MAP [LAMBDA [X] [3 * :X]] :VEC
END
```

The trouble is that this notation seems needlessly obtrusive. If we present this to students, their attention will be focused on the meaning of the notation, rather than on matrix arithmetic. I wanted to find a better alternative. A quick-and-dirty solution would be to say that the parameter to every function must be called X; for two-input functions we could reserve X and Y. That would work, but it seems ugly to me. It would prevent the use of those names for other purposes. (For example, what if I had wanted to call the scale factor X instead of NUM?)

I took my inspiration from an earlier problem in mathematics education that seems closely related. Some of the early New Math experimenters wanted to use algebraic ideas with elementary school students, presenting very simple equations like

$$x + 3 = 7.$$

They found that the underlying idea of "what plus three is seven?" was not too difficult, but that the x notation was a problem for some students. Their solution was to present the equation in the form

$$\Box + 3 = 7$$

Pedagogically the box seems to suggest "this is a slot to be filled" without raising the difficulties about names and values that students find with x. Unfortunately, there is no box character in the ASCII sequence, but I wanted to come as close as possible to this ideal of a graphically obvious slot indication. My solution was to use a question mark:

```
? SHOW MAP [3 * ?] [2 3 4]
[6 9 12]
? SHOW MAP [? * ?] [2 3 4 5]
[4 9 16 25]
? SHOW MAP [IFELSE (? < 0) [−?] [?]] [2 −3 12 0 −14]
[2 3 12 0 14]
```

An expression list with a question mark slot to be filled is called an *expression template*.

We can now solve the SCALE problem:

```
TO MATRIX.SCALE :NUM :MAT
 OUTPUT MAP [VECTOR.SCALE :NUM ?] :MAT
END
```

```
TO VECTOR.SCALE :NUM :VEC
 OUTPUT MAP [:NUM * ?] :VEC
END
```

We have redesigned MAP to accept templates instead of named functions. What about MAP.2? We need a way to express templates with two slots. My solution is to name the slots ?1 and ?2.

```
? SHOW MAP.2 [?2 − ?1] [1 2 3] [15 20 30]
[14 18 27]
```

This does not seem quite so compelling as the unadorned question mark, just as New Math equations with boxes and triangles seem more cluttered and less obvious than the ones with only boxes. Still the notation clearly indicates which slot is which.

By the way, are you tired of having to write MATRIX and VECTOR versions of everything when you really only care about the matrix version? You can invent two-level mapping tools that will allow direct definition of the matrix functions.

```
TO MMAP :FN :MAT                ;matrix map
 OUTPUT MAP [MAP :FN ?] :MAT
END

TO MMAP.2 :FN :M1 :M2
 OUTPUT MAP.2 [MAP.2 :FN ?1 ?2] :M1 :M2
END

TO ADD :M1 :M2
 OUTPUT MMAP.2 [?1 + ?2] :M1 :M2
END

TO SCALE :NUM :MAT
 OUTPUT MMAP [:NUM * ?] :MAT
END
```

The definitions of ADD and SCALE now embody the mathematical ideas quite directly, with very little programming language noise. You may find the definitions of MMAP and MMAP.2 a little tricky, but the structure of nested MAPs is exactly analogous to the nested FORs in the sequential version of matrix programming.

9 MORE FUNCTIONAL PROGRAMMING TOOLS

I would like to define an exponentiation function. That is, I want to take a given base to a given power, using repeated multiplication. (The power must, of course, be a nonnegative integer.) This is an example of composition of functions, in which the function [? * :BASE] is invoked :EXP times, with the result from one invocation filling the slot for the next invocation. (The first invocation is done with 1 in the slot.)

```
TO POWER :BASE :EXP
 OUTPUT CASCADE :EXP [? * :BASE] 1
END
```

```
? SHOW POWER 2 5
32
```

CASCADE is a tool for repeated composition of a function with itself. It takes three inputs. First is a number saying how many times we want to invoke the function. Second comes a template indicating what the function is. Third is the initial value used to fill the slot in the first invocation. As another example of its use, here is Newton's method to approximate the square root of a number by repeated composition of a function:

```
TO NSQRT :X
 OUTPUT CASCADE 10 [(? + (:X/?))/2] 1
END
```

Newton's approximation function takes the average of the previous guess and the quotient of x and the guess. In this procedure we start with an initial guess of 1, and we apply the approximation function 10 times. This constant number of invocations is too simple; fewer invocations would do for small values of x, while more are needed to get a good approximation for large values. (For example, try NSQRT of a million.) To fix this problem, CASCADE accepts as its first input either a number or a *predicate template*, that is, an expression template whose value is TRUE or FALSE. The repeated composition continues until the value of the predicate template is TRUE.

```
TO NSQRT :X
 OUTPUT CASCADE [LESSP ABS (:X-?*?) 0.00000001] [(? + (:X/?))/2] 1
END
```

```
TO ABS :X
 OUTPUT IFELSE :X < 0 [-:X] [:X]
END
```

It is sometimes convenient for the function being cascaded to know how many times it has been invoked so far. For example, the factorial function is like the power function except that each new multiplication is by a larger number, instead of always by the same :BASE. Therefore CASCADE templates can include another special symbol, #, indicating the number of invocations.

```
TO FACTORIAL :N
 OUTPUT CASCADE :N [? * #] 1
END
```

The template is first invoked with 1 in the question mark slot (because the third input to CASCADE is 1) and also 1 in the number sign slot (because this is the first invocation). The result is 1. Next time, ? is 1 because that is the result of the first invocation, but # is 2. The third time, ? is 2 and # is 3.

The function being cascaded is not limited to a scalar domain or range. We can use list processing operations to generate the vector of all the integers from 1 to *n*:

```
TO FROM1TO :N
 OUTPUT CASCADE :N [LPUT # ?] [ ]
END
```

```
? SHOW FROM1TO 5
[1 2 3 4 5]
```

Here the initial value is an empty vector, and each invocation of the template appends the next integer in sequence. (LPUT means "last put"; it is like FPUT except that the new element is adjoined on the right instead of on the left.) Just as there is a MAP.2 for two-input functions, we sometimes need CASCADE.2 for two-input functions. The parallel is not exact, however. In this context we need not only two initial inputs but also two functions, one to specify the next value of ?1 and one to give the next value of ?2. CASCADE.2 therefore takes five inputs.

CASCADE.2 end.test template.1 initial.1 template.2 initial.2

For example, here is how to compute the *n*th Fibonacci number:

```
TO FIB :N
 OUTPUT CASCADE.2 :N-1 [?1 + ?2] 1 [?1] 0
END
```

The final output from CASCADE.2 is the final value of ?1.

Because I'm presenting so many examples so briefly, the overall point may be in danger of being lost, so let me take a moment to review where we are. I started by presenting the idea of functional programming in which the focus is on the input-output behavior of a procedure rather than on the exact sequence of events through which the computer produces the desired output. I suggested that functional programming is much better suited to mathematics teaching than traditional, sequential programming. If this is true, teachers should prefer a functional language like Logo rather than a sequential one like BASIC or Pascal. One stumbling block has been the need to teach recursion in order to program even the simplest mathematical ideas, but this obstacle can be avoided by providing tools that are the functional analogues to the looping construct in sequential programming.

So far I have introduced two such tools, MAP and CASCADE, in one-input and two-input versions. With this small toolkit I have been able to write procedures that are not self-referential for a variety of mathematical functions. In my experience, students quickly understand MAP with hardly any explanation and can use it correctly themselves. CASCADE is a little harder, perhaps just because it has more inputs and the procedures are therefore harder to read. But the effort to understand the metaphor behind CASCADE (composing a function with itself) pays off in more expressive power than students of traditional languages get from similar effort put into FOR, WHILE, UNTIL, and so on. I now want to introduce two more functional programming tools.

We want to take the dot product of two vectors. To do this, we must multiply pairs of corresponding elements and then add up all the products. The first part of this is clearly a job for MAP.2, but we need a tool for the second part.

```
? SHOW REDUCE "SUM [2 3 4]
9
? SHOW REDUCE "PRODUCT [2 3 4]
24
```

```
TO DOTPROD :V1 :V2
 OUTPUT REDUCE "SUM (MAP.2 "PRODUCT :V1 :V2)
END
```

Because the function I want to map over the two vectors happens to be included as a Logo primitive, I have just given MAP.2 its name, as I did in the earliest examples, instead of a template with question marks. We will write these tools so that either form is allowed. REDUCE, the new tool in this example, takes a two-input associative function and applies it to all the elements of the indicated list. (We insist that the function be associative to avoid questions about the precise grouping of the elements of the list.)

It may be time for a reminder that functional programming tools can be applied to nonnumerical computation as well:

```
TO ACRONYM :NAME
 OUTPUT REDUCE "WORD MAP "FIRST :NAME
END
```

```
? SHOW ACRONYM [AMERICAN CIVIL LIBERTIES UNION]
ACLU
```

```
TO PIGLATIN :WORD
 OUTPUT WORD (CASCADE [MEMBERP FIRST ? "AEIOU]
                      [WORD BUTFIRST ? FIRST ?]
                      :WORD)
          "AY
END
```

```
? SHOW PIGLATIN "SPAGHETTI
AGHETTISPAY
```

The last tool is used to select a subset of the members of a list, based on a predicate template.

```
? SHOW FILTER [EQUALP (REMAINDER ? 2) 0] [1 2 3 4 5]
[2 4]
? SHOW FILTER [EQUALP (SQRT ?) (INT SQRT ?)] [1 2 3 4 5]
[1 4]
```

Suppose that we want to know if a number *n* is perfect. We need to find all the factors of *n* and then add them up.

```
TO PERFECT? :N
 OUTPUT EQUALP :N
                  REDUCE "SUM
                         FILTER [EQUALP (REMAINDER :N ?) 0]
                                FROM1TO :N-1
END
? SHOW PERFECT? 6
TRUE
? SHOW PERFECT? 7
FALSE
```

In this procedure FROM1TO gives us a list of all the numbers that might be factors of *n*. FILTER selects the ones that actually are factors by checking the remainder of dividing *n* by each candidate. REDUCE adds all the factors, and EQUALP checks whether the sum is equal to *n*.

You may be wondering if there will be REDUCE.2 and FILTER.2 procedures. It turns out that these would not be meaningful. Functions can have more than one input, but they are only allowed one output. If we tried to select elements from two lists in parallel, we would end up with two sublists. Which would we output?

10 SOME PROBLEMS REALLY ARE RECURSIVE

Suppose we want to find the determinant of a square matrix. The well-known algorithm requires us to select a single row or column of the matrix; then for each element of that row or column, we must compute *the determinant of a submatrix* formed by removing the row and column containing that element. (Next we multiply by plus or minus the element, and we add up all the results, but those are the easy parts.) The words in italics are a self-referential part of the definition of the determinant. The use of recursion to solve this problem is not an accidental result of missing features in the programming language. It is a naturally recursive problem.

It will turn out to be easiest if we choose the leftmost column of the matrix as the one to treat specially. If we chose the top row, which would be more traditional, then for each element of that row we must extract a submatrix in which its column is removed. If we start with a column, then for each of its elements the submatrix is found by removing a row. The latter operation is easier, since we store matrices as lists of rows. The left column of a matrix is found with the expression

MAP "FIRST :MATRIX

which selects the first element of each row. Similarly the expression

MAP "BUTFIRST :MATRIX

returns a (nonsquare) matrix with the first column eliminated. This latter matrix will be used as the basis from which rows will be eliminated to form each submatrix.

```
TO DET :MATRIX
 IF EMPTYP BUTFIRST :MATRIX
     [OUTPUT FIRST FIRST :MATRIX]              ; base case, 1 × 1
 LOCAL "RIGHTPART
 MAKE "RIGHTPART MAP "BUTFIRST :MATRIX        ; all but 1st col
 OUTPUT "REDUCE "SUM
              MAP [(PRODUCT ? (SIGN #)
                             (DET ALLBUT # :RIGHTPART))]
 END                     MAP "FIRST :MATRIX

TO ALLBUT :N :MAT                              ; all but nth row
 OUTPUT FILTER [NOT EQUALP # :N] :MAT
 END

TO SIGN :N
 OUTPUT IFELSE (EQUALP REMAINDER :N 2 0) [−1] [1]
 END
```

Even though recursion is necessary in this problem, I have continued to use the nonrecursive functional tools wherever possible. To make this work, I had to extend the # notation in templates, which I originally intended only for CASCADE, to work in MAP and FILTER as well.

Since DET is defined recursively, it must have a base case. In this problem the base case is that the determinant of a matrix with one row and one column is the single number in the matrix. We say FIRST FIRST because the number is the first element of the first row. For other cases the program is more complicated. First we create a local variable RIGHTPART and assign to it the nonsquare matrix with the first column of the original matrix removed. The reason for this step is to avoid repetitive computation of the same matrix for every row, which would result if we just said

```
OUTPUT REDUCE "SUM
MAP [(PRODUCT ? (SIGN #) (DET ALLBUT # MAP "BUTFIRST :MATRIX))]
     MAP "FIRST :MATRIX
```

without using the extra variable. Now we can pick apart the long OUTPUT instruction to see how it embodies the definition. We know from the use of REDUCE that we are going to compute a list full of numbers and then add up the numbers. What is the list? Well, it is computed by

```
MAP [ . . . ] MAP "FIRST :MATRIX
```

which means "compute some function of each element of the first column of the matrix." So far, so good. What function do we compute for each element of the first column? It is a product of three factors: the element itself, either positive or negative 1 depending on which element it is, and the determinant of a submatrix. That submatrix is computed by selecting all but a particular row from the matrix :RIGHTPART.

This is a complicated problem, and the complexity of the procedure reflects that. Still, the use of functional programming has allowed us to solve the problem without introducing auxiliary index variables. The procedure exactly reflects the structure of the definition of determinant.

Since we cannot avoid recursion in the definition of DET, it might be worthwhile to compare this version with the way it would traditionally be written in Logo, relying even more heavily on recursion:

```
TO DET :MATRIX
 IF EMPTYP BUTFIRST :MATRIX [OUTPUT FIRST FIRST :MATRIX]
 OUTPUT DET1 (FIRSTS :MATRIX) (BUTFIRSTS :MATRIX) 1 1
END
```

```
TO DET1 :COL :REST :N :SIGN
 IF EMPTYP :COL [OUTPUT 0]
 OUTPUT SUM (PRODUCT (FIRST :COL) :SIGN
            (DET ALLBUT :N :REST))
            (DET1 (BUTFIRST :COL) :REST :N+1 −:SIGN)
END


TO FIRSTS :LIST
 IF EMPTYP :LIST [OUTPUT [ ]]
 OUTPUT FPUT (FIRST FIRST :LIST) (FIRSTS BUTFIRST :LIST)
END


TO BUTFIRSTS :LIST
 IF EMPTYP :LIST [OUTPUT [ ]]
 OUTPUT FPUT (BUTFIRST FIRST :LIST) (BUTFIRSTS BUTFIRST :LIST)
END


TO ALLBUT :N :LIST
 IF :N=1 [OUTPUT BUTFIRST :LIST]
 OUTPUT FPUT (FIRST :LIST) (ALLBUT :N−1 BUTFIRST :LIST)
END
```

To someone familiar with recursion, the procedures DET and DET1 in this version may seem less intimidating than the earlier version. It would be possible to compromise, using MAP and FILTER to define FIRSTS, BUTFIRSTS and ALLBUT as in the first version, but using DET and DET1 from the second version.

On the other hand, to a reader who is not intimidated by the first version, it makes the structure of DET more plainly apparent. In the second version the fact that the determinant is a sum of products is buried inside DET1, and you have to notice that one of the inputs to SUM is a recursive call in order to see that several products will be added. The first version says

OUTPUT REDUCE "SUM MAP [(PRODUCT. . . .

right up front.

Computing the determinant is a hard problem, and the program will be complex no matter how it is written. Here is an easier problem that is still most convenient in recursive form: Compute the *transpose* of a matrix. That is, interchange the rows and the columns. The trick is to see that the first row of the output will be the first column of the input, while the remaining rows of the output will be the *transpose* of the remaining columns.

```
TO TRANSPOSE :MAT
 IF EMPTYP FIRST :MAT [OUTPUT [ ]]
 OUTPUT FPUT (MAP "FIRST :MAT) (TRANSPOSE MAP "BUTFIRST :MAT)
END
```

```
? SHOW TRANSPOSE [[1 2 3][4 5 6]]
[[1 4][2 5][3 6]]
```

As a third example in which recursion is helpful, let us return to the question of MATRIX.ADD and VECTOR.ADD. My first implementation defines one in terms of the other. Later, by inventing a special tool for two-dimensional mapping, I was able to define the matrix version directly. But now suppose that I want to be able to add vectors, matrices, and even multidimensional arrays. I do not want to have to define a separate ADD procedure for every possible dimension. Instead, I want one ADD procedure that will work on scalars, vectors, matrices, or any other array.

```
TO ADD :A :B
 IF NUMBERP :A [OUTPUT :A + :B]
 OUTPUT MAP.2 "ADD :A :B
END
```

This procedure extends the pattern of vector and matrix addition to any number of dimensions by mapping *itself* over its inputs!

Perhaps it is time for another review of our journey so far. In principle there is no need for any control mechanism other than recursion in a programming language. Any problem can be solved using recursive procedures without explicit looping mechanisms. However, the idea of recursion is hard for beginning students, so in order to make functional programming practical, it is helpful to provide tools that are analogous to looping constructs but consistent with the functional style. I have shown four such tools: MAP, CASCADE, REDUCE, and FILTER. These tools are adequate for many problems, but not for all problems. If a problem is fundamentally self-referential, then the student must understand recursive programming to solve it.

11   CONTINUING DEVELOPMENT

Until the writing of this chapter I had never written a determinant procedure. This is the first example I have found in which MAP and FILTER templates need the # mechanism to let the function know the position of its argument in the original input list. Therefore the procedure definitions at the end of the chapter are somewhat different from earlier published versions. Since these tools are language extensions written in Logo itself, I can make this change without having to rewrite the Logo interpreter. Other teachers can also invent their own tools so that their students have exactly the necessary tools for whatever projects are relevant to their topic. For example, for a computer-based linguistics course (Goldenberg 1987) Paul Goldenberg invented a tool to make systematic changes in the spelling of a word:

```
? SHOW REPLACE [M O] [P A] "MOMMY
PAPPY
```

The first input is a list of letters to look for in the word, and the second input is a same-length list of replacements.

Recently I have found myself, in certain situations, wanting something more like the LISP lambda notation with explicit names for the slots in the template. For example, here is a program to multiply two matrices.

```
TO MULTIPLY :A :B
 LOCAL "TB
 MAKE "TB TRANSPOSE :B
 OUTPUT MAP [MULROW ? :TB] :A
END

TO MULROW :ROWA :TB
 OUTPUT MAP [DOTPROD :ROWA ?] :TB
END
```

Each element of the product is the dot product of a row of :A and a column of :B. (The program uses TRANSPOSE because we store matrices by rows, and a row of the transpose is a column of the original matrix.) The subprocedure MULROW computes a single row of the answer; the entire answer is found by mapping MULROW over the rows of the first input matrix.

I do not like having to have the auxiliary procedure MULROW. I would rather use two nested MAPs, as in the MMAP tool. But if I try that, I end up with the instruction

OUTPUT MAP [MAP [DOTPROD ? ?] :TB] :A

One of those question marks refers to the slot in the inner template, while the other refers to the slot in the outer one. This cannot work. (Nor would it help to use ?1 and ?2. We are not using MAP.2 to map over two lists in parallel; we are using the single-slot MAP twice.) To render the two slots unambiguous, I have to be able to give each one a name explicitly. The notation does not actually require the word LAMBDA, which LISP uses for historical reasons; if the first thing in a template is a list in square brackets, I want to take that as a list of names of slots. Then I can say

OUTPUT MAP [[ROWA] MAP [[COLB] DOTPROD :ROWA :COLB] :TB] :A

I have written tools that accept this format, but I have not yet tried teaching it to anyone.

Another annoyance I would like to eliminate is the need for separate procedures MAP and MAP.2. What if I want to map a three-input function over three lists of inputs? I would like a single MAP that can take any number of inputs, just as certain Logo primitives do, inside parentheses. This change, unfortunately, does require modifications to the Logo interpreter. One published version of Logo (Object Logo, for the Macintosh, distributed by Paradigm Software) allows user-defined procedures with variable numbers of inputs. I hope the idea is extended to other dialects.

12 TEACHING EXPERIENCE

When I published the first volume of *Computer Science Logo Style* (Harvey 1985), I introduced mapping tools near the end of the book, *after* the reader was familiar with recursion, because my emphasis was on the implementation of the tools. I wanted to make the point that Logo is an extensible language by showing how to extend it. I had considered introducing the tools earlier, without showing their definitions, to allow readers to write interesting functional programs in the early chapters. What dissuaded me, at that time, was that I was trying to make the book usable without a teacher by readers who might have any of half a dozen versions of Logo at home. Each dialect is slightly different from the others. I felt that I could not use tool procedures unless I provided the definitions on diskette, and that seemed like too much trouble.

As it turned out, the biggest complaint I heard from people who taught courses based on that book was about the difficulty their students had in the chapter on recursive operations. Their confusion was not only about recursion but about the more fundamental issue of writing operations at all. They were uncomfortable with OUTPUT and with list manipulation. The reason for this, I decided, was that until that chapter they had had very little practice writing operations at all. Without recursion, the number of interesting functions you can compute is small. By presenting tools like MAP earlier, it would be possible to present more and better examples of functional programming in the early chapters.

In the fall semester of 1988 I taught a Logo programming course to a small group of Berkeley undergraduates using this approach. I have not revised the book, but in the early weeks of the course I supplemented it with handouts and class discussion showing the mapping tools. (The tool procedures I used were the versions in Harvey 1987, which are slightly different from the ones in this chapter.) My experience was that the students were, as expected, easily able to apply functional programming ideas to problems that could be solved without recursion. Their early efforts could focus on what it means for a procedure to output a value without being confused by the additional issues of self-reference. On the other hand, I had hoped that with this basis they would find recursion itself easy when we got to it; in that respect I was disappointed. Recursion was still a big hurdle. By the end of the semester almost all of the students could understand recursive procedures that I presented, but not all could reliably write their own recursive procedures.

One mistake that I made was to try to motivate the use of recursion by starting with quite complicated examples that could not be done using the iterative tools the students already knew. I was overreacting to the anticipated question, "Why don't we just use MAP?" I would now begin with simpler examples and announce by fiat that the iterative tools may not be used this week. I would explain that they are going to learn how things like MAP can be written in Logo, and to understand that, they have to pretend that MAP is not available. (By the way, I have of course done something similar in this chapter, in section 10 which explains why recursion is still sometimes necessary. But I trust that the reader is not new to Logo and has already seen simpler examples of recursion.)

Many Logo teachers have noticed that students find recursive operations more difficult than the command-heavy style of programming used in turtle graphics applications. Some have responded by restricting their Logo teaching to graphics. Others, wanting to preserve the ability to explore natural language issues, have introduced word processing commands into Logo so that English text can be processed in the easier command-heavy style. (See, for example, Tempel and Michaud 1986 for a description of this approach in LogoWriter.) I am unwilling to withhold from students the powerful idea of functional programming; the work described here is an attempt to preserve the functional style while allowing students to take smaller steps than the enormous intellectual leap that seems to be required in moving from commands directly into recursive operations.

APPENDIX: THE IMPLEMENTATION

Resist the temptation to use shorter variable names in these procedures. It's important that these names be different from any variable names used in other parts of the program that invokes these tools.

```
TO MAP :MAP.TEMPLATE :TEMPLATE.LIST
 OUTPUT MAP1 PREPARE.TEMPLATE :MAP.TEMPLATE
        :TEMPLATE.LIST 1
END

TO MAP1 :MAP.TEMPLATE :TEMPLATE.LIST :TEMPLATE.NUMBER
 IF EMPTYP :TEMPLATE.LIST [OUTPUT [ ]]
 LOCAL "TEMPLATE.VAR
 MAKE "TEMPLATE.VAR FIRST :TEMPLATE.LIST
 OUTPUT FPUT (RUN :MAP.TEMPLATE)
             (MAP1 :MAP.TEMPLATE (BF :TEMPLATE.LIST)
                  1+:TEMPLATE.NUMBER)
END

TO PREPARE.TEMPLATE :TEMPLATE
 IF LISTP :TEMPLATE [OUTPUT :TEMPLATE]
 OUTPUT SENTENCE :TEMPLATE "?
END

TO ?
 OUTPUT :TEMPLATE.VAR
END
```

```
TO #
 OUTPUT :TEMPLATE.NUMBER
END

TO MAP.2 :MAP.TEMPLATE :TEMPLATE.LIST1 :TEMPLATE.LIST2
 OUTPUT MAP.21 PREPARE.TEMPLATE.2 :MAP.TEMPLATE
               :TEMPLATE.LIST1 :TEMPLATE.LIST2 1
END

TO MAP.21 :MAP.TEMPLATE :TEMPLATE.LIST1 :TEMPLATE.LIST2
                        :TEMPLATE.NUMBER
 IF EMPTYP :TEMPLATE.LIST1 [OUTPUT [ ]]
 LOCAL [TEMPLATE.VAR1 TEMPLATE.VAR2]
 MAKE "TEMPLATE.VAR1 FIRST :TEMPLATE.LIST1
 MAKE "TEMPLATE.VAR2 FIRST :TEMPLATE.LIST2
 OUTPUT FPUT (RUN :MAP.TEMPLATE)
             (MAP.21 :MAP.TEMPLATE (BF :TEMPLATE.LIST1)
                  (BF :TEMPLATE.LIST2) 1+:TEMPLATE.NUMBER)
END

TO PREPARE.TEMPLATE.2 :TEMPLATE
 IF LISTP :TEMPLATE [OUTPUT :TEMPLATE]
 OUTPUT SENTENCE :TEMPLATE [?1 ?2]
END

TO ?1
 OUTPUT :TEMPLATE.VAR1
END

TO ?2
 OUTPUT :TEMPLATE.VAR2
END

TO CASCADE :CASCADE.LIMIT :CASCADE.TEMPLATE
           :TEMPLATE.VAR
 OUTPUT CASCADE1 PREPARE.LIMIT :CASCADE.LIMIT
               PREPARE.TEMPLATE :CASCADE.TEMPLATE
               :TEMPLATE.VAR 1
END
```

```
TO CASCADE1 :CASCADE.LIMIT :CASCADE.TEMPLATE
            :TEMPLATE.VAR :TEMPLATE.NUMBER
IF (RUN :CASCADE.LIMIT) [OUTPUT :TEMPLATE.VAR]
OUTPUT CASCADE1 :CASCADE.LIMIT :CASCADE.TEMPLATE
            (RUN :CASCADE.TEMPLATE)
                  1+:TEMPLATE.NUMBER
END

TO PREPARE.LIMIT :LIMIT
IF NUMBERP :LIMIT
   [OUTPUT SENTENCE [GREATERP :TEMPLATE.NUMBER] :LIMIT]
OUTPUT PREPARE.TEMPLATE :LIMIT
END

TO CASCADE.2 :CASCADE.LIMIT
            :CASCADE.TEMPLATE1 :TEMPLATE.VAR1
            :CASCADE.TEMPLATE2 :TEMPLATE.VAR2
OUTPUT CASCADE.21 PREPARE.LIMIT.2 :CASCADE.LIMIT
            PREPARE.TEMPLATE.2 :CASCADE.TEMPLATE1
                              :TEMPLATE.VAR1
            PREPARE.TEMPLATE.2 :CASCADE.TEMPLATE2
                              :TEMPLATE.VAR2 1
END

TO CASCADE.21 :CASCADE.LIMIT
            :CASCADE.TEMPLATE1 :TEMPLATE.VAR1
            :CASCADE.TEMPLATE2 :TEMPLATE.VAR2
            :TEMPLATE.NUMBER
IF (RUN :CASCADE.LIMIT) [OUTPUT :TEMPLATE.VAR1]
OUTPUT CASCADE.21 :CASCADE.LIMIT
      :CASCADE.TEMPLATE1 (RUN :CASCADE.TEMPLATE1)
      :CASCADE.TEMPLATE2 (RUN :CASCADE.TEMPLATE2)
      1+:TEMPLATE.NUMBER
END

TO PREPARE.LIMIT.2 :LIMIT
IF NUMBERP :LIMIT
   [OUTPUT SENTENCE [GREATERP :TEMPLATE.NUMBER] :LIMIT]
OUTPUT PREPARE.TEMPLATE.2 :LIMIT
END
```

```
TO REDUCE :REDUCE.TEMPLATE :TEMPLATE.LIST
 OUTPUT REDUCE1 PREPARE.TEMPLATE.2 :REDUCE.TEMPLATE
                   :TEMPLATE.LIST
END


TO REDUCE1 :REDUCE.TEMPLATE :TEMPLATE.LIST
 IF EMPTYP BUTFIRST :TEMPLATE.LIST [OUTPUT FIRST
                   :TEMPLATE.LIST]
 LOCAL [TEMPLATE.VAR1 TEMPLATE.VAR2]
 MAKE "TEMPLATE.VAR1 FIRST :TEMPLATE.LIST
 MAKE "TEMPLATE.VAR2 REDUCE1 :REDUCE.TEMPLATE
                              BUTFIRST :TEMPLATE.LIST
 OUTPUT RUN :REDUCE.TEMPLATE
END


TO FILTER :FILTER.TEMPLATE :TEMPLATE.LIST
 OUTPUT FILTER1 PREPARE.TEMPLATE :FILTER.TEMPLATE
                   :TEMPLATE.LIST 1
END


TO FILTER1 :FILTER.TEMPLATE :TEMPLATE.LIST
            :TEMPLATE.NUMBER
 IF EMPTYP :TEMPLATE.LIST [OUTPUT [ ]]
 LOCAL "TEMPLATE.VAR
 MAKE "TEMPLATE.VAR FIRST :TEMPLATE.LIST
 IF (RUN :FILTER.TEMPLATE)
    [OUTPUT FPUT :TEMPLATE.VAR
                FILTER1 :FILTER.TEMPLATE BF :TEMPLATE.LIST
                       1+:TEMPLATE.NUMBER]
 OUTPUT FILTER1 :FILTER.TEMPLATE BF :TEMPLATE.LIST
                1+:TEMPLATE.NUMBER
END
```

REFERENCES

Abelson, H., and Sussman, G. 1985. *Structure and Interpretation of Computer Programs*. Cambridge: MIT Press.

Allen, J., Davis, R., and Johnson, J. 1984. *Thinking about [TLC] Logo*. New York: Holt, Rinehart and Winston.

Backus, J. 1978. Can programming be liberated from the von Neumann style? *Communications of the ACM* 21: 613–641.

Goldenberg, E. P., and Feurzeig, W. 1987. *Exploring Language with Logo*. Cambridge: MIT Press.

Harvey B. 1985, 1986, 1987. *Computer Science Logo Style*. 1985: Vol. 1: *Intermediate Programming*. 1986: Vol. 2: *Projects, Styles, and Techniques*. 1987: Vol. 3: *Advanced Topics*. Cambridge: MIT Press.

Tempel, M., and Michaud, N. 1986. Beyond turtle graphics? *Logo 86 Proceedings*, Massachusetts Institute of Technology.

Afterword

IV

The chapters in part III remind us of the potential for mathematical expression that Logo presents to students. Taken together with the curricular issues of part I and the social/affective issues raised in part II, they offer us a thought-provoking array of ideas and approaches that *could* transform the ways in which children think and feel about mathematics. Yet, as various authors have implied, the path from theory to practice has not been easy—there are many outstanding questions that collectively stand in the way of Logo's potential being realized in classrooms. In the final chapter we attempt as an afterword the task of explaining why this has been so, and of synthesizing some of the cognitive and social issues that have been raised by other authors in this volume into a tentative theoretical framework for conceptualizing children's Logo work. We look back and forward at the role of Logo in the learning of mathematics.

Looking Back and Looking Forward

14

Richard Noss and Celia Hoyles

1 INTRODUCTION

Despite Papert's early recognition of the importance of the creation of a computer culture, this recognition merely took the form of an existence theorem, and very little has been actually proposed in ways that can be implemented in the classroom. In our view, much of the discussion around the theme that "Logo did not deliver what it promised" has centered on two problems: a resistance to focus on a knowledge domain and an inadequate synthesis of the psychological and the social. On the first point, the view that suggests that Logo provides an "all-purpose learning environment" has raised a range of unrealistic expectations concerning the development of general problem-solving skills which, except in very tightly constrained circumstances, have not been fulfilled (see, e.g., Pea and Kurland 1984; De Corte et al. 1990). As to the second point, there has been a generalized failure to address the nontechnical aspects surrounding Logo use in any serious way: There has been little adequate description and analysis of the influence on pupil strategies and learning outcomes of the social, cultural, and pedagogical context into which Logo is inserted—an influence that we will argue is crucial. Nevertheless, Logo-based research and curriculum development in the context of mathematics, has—as is evident in this volume—begun to produce careful analyses of what can be expected as outcomes of Logo activity within a range of mathematical microworlds.

In this chapter we wish to explore the mathematical nature of Logo programming. We aim to take a wide perspective within the problematic of mathematics education, one that weaves together the social with the psychological, drawing on our own work as well as some of the contributions in this book as supporting evidence and illustration of our case. We begin by stating our agenda: We would like to know the extent to which Logo provides a *mathematical* environment and whether there are properties of the environment that are inherently mathematical. To answer these questions, we need to clarify our own terms. What do we mean by a mathematical environment? What do we mean by "inherently mathematical"? We also look closely at three related issues. What meanings do pupils bring to the environment? How are these meanings made explicit and shared with the teacher? How far does Logo programming *only* constitute a mathematical environment in the context of the school mathematics classroom where the pedagogical agenda is to push toward abstraction and generalization?

In addressing these questions, we intend to draw parallels between the way mathematics is used (or avoided) in a Logo programming environment and the way mathematics enters (or does not enter) into everyday practice. We are thus able to draw upon significant research in this latter field. Our initial focus, however, is to review the range of mathematical activities with which children can engage in a Logo setting and to sketch our current understanding of how Logo operates as a medium for children to express their mathematical ideas.

2 DOING LOGO AND DOING MATHEMATICS—AN EXAMPLE

There is considerable evidence that Logo provides a computational environment in which mathematics can, at some level, take place and that it can provide access to otherwise unattainable mathematical ideas (Hoyles and Noss 1989). Papert has talked about developing a "mathland" where children can roam freely, encountering mathematical "nuggets" as they go. We have, in the past, referred to this as an environment in which to "do" mathematics (Noss 1986) or in which mathematical ideas can be "used" (Hoyles 1986). The main rationale for this view was derived from the way in which the Logo environment can provide pupils with an opportunity to engage in mathematical problem posing and solving, during which they develop control over their own learning—where they, rather than their teachers, ask the questions and answer them in their own way and in their own style. We wanted pupils to develop the confidence to test out ideas and hypotheses and thus to build upon or debug the mathematical intuitions already developed either within or outside school, and we wanted the Logo activity to be a catalyst for more open and cooperative styles of working. Our approach was predicated on the well-supported belief that a major problem of mathematics education is the imposition by the school curriculum of formal algorithms that do not connect with pupils' mathematical intuitions.

This view still retains much of its initial force. Logo can undoubtedly provide a rich and exciting environment in which children involve themselves in projects during which they engage in some mathematics in a way that is meaningful to them; mathematics can be brought into operation by pupils as a necessary intellectual tool for the successful completion of their projects. Moreover our own

Figure 1 STAR

observations of children over many years lead us to the view that children programming in Logo can enjoy sustained pleasure working on personally motivating activities over considerable periods of time. There is of course a considerable literature that concurs with this view (as well as one that does not). While we have no wish to gratuitously add further anecdotes to this already impressive reservoir of material, we do wish to problematize the issues that arise from these observations and reports. To this end we present an example of two children's interactions with the computer. Since it will serve as a paradigmatic case for some of what follows, we discuss the incident in some detail (the original episode is reported in Hoyles and Sutherland 1989, pp. 18–22).

Sally and Janet are twelve-year-old girls regularly using Logo in their mathematics lessons. Janet does the typing; Sally plays a relatively minor role in the proceedings. At the beginning of their second year of learning Logo, after approximately twenty hours of Logo, Sally and Janet decided to define a procedure to draw a star. They succeeded in doing this and defined STAR (see figure 1):

```
TO STAR
    REPEAT 4 [FD 40 LT 144]
    FD 40
END
```

Why did they choose this asymmetric formulation of the procedure? It arose as a result of the way it had been constructed: as a series of direct-drive commands aimed at a screen effect, which were subsequently tidied up using REPEAT (in the editor).[1] This resulted in a STAR procedure that was not state transparent.[2] They had, we can be fairly sure, no explicit awareness of the tur-

---

1. They had used the very same strategy previously when working on a project to draw a rotated polygon pattern.

2. A state-transparent procedure in turtle graphics is one in which the turtle orientation and position is the same at the beginning and end of the procedure.

Figure 2 SS

Figure 3 FS version 1

tle's final state in relation to its initial state, and yet, as we will see, they *used* this to great effect in their subsequent exploration. Sally and Janet entered STAR, STAR, STAR, STAR, STAR, counting as the pattern emerged until it closed. Employing their familiar strategy, they then defined a procedure in the editor (see figure 2):

```
TO SS
    REPEAT 5 [STAR]
END
```

Janet referred to the procedure STAR as an "upside-down star" and Sally as a "backward star" and between them they decided to draw a "forward star." They again worked in direct drive and drew a non-state-transparent star, turning right instead of left when they came to write it in the editor. For some reason, at the point of defining their new procedure FS (see figure 3), they made it state transparent (can we be so sure now that they were unaware of the turtle's state?):

```
TO FS
    REPEAT 5[FD 40 RT 144]
END
```

Figure 4 SFS version 1

Figure 5 SFS version 2

They then defined "superforward star," SFS, with the same structure as SS (see figure 4):

```
TO SFS
  REPEAT 5 [FS]
END
```

However, they soon discovered that SFS did *not* give them a rotated pattern as expected. For the SFS procedure to work in the same way as SS, the *internal* structures of the two procedures would have had to be similar: That is, the girls would need to pay intention to the structures of FS and STAR, respectively. But of course these are different: FS is state transparent and STAR is not. Instead, the generalization (perfect in the formal sense) focused only on the *external* structures of the procedures. Not surprisingly, Sally and Janet had difficulty debugging their procedure; their first attempt simply added a FD 40 to the last line of SFS, a relatively unreflective attempt at patching the code (see figure 5):

```
TO SF
  REPEAT 5 [FS]
  FD 40
END
```

When this still did not give a rotated star the pair *did* reflect on the internal structure of FS compared with STAR and finally modified FS to the following (see figure 6).

Figure 6 FS version 2

Figure 7 SDS

```
TO FS
    REPEAT 4 [FD 40 RT 144]
    FD 40
END
```

When they tried this out, it drew their desired image. However, since they had not deleted the final line FD 40 from SFS, this procedure itself was not state transparent (unlike the procedure of which it was a generalization, SS)—by chance they had incorporated an interface into SFS! Nevertheless, they now had two modules to play with (SFS and SS), and once again the pair wanted to make sense of them by running them and seeing what might happen. Janet entered SS, and then SFS, so the two stars were drawn one on top of the other. At this point the researcher intervened to suggest that they define a procedure for this new module. This was the first time that they had defined a superprocedure with two levels of nested subprocedures, and they called it SDS—"superduperstar" (see figure 7):

```
TO SDS
    SS
    SFS
END
```

Because of the lucky chance of the FD 40 left on the end of SFS, the interface for another superduperstar was set up!

Janet then used the new module SDS in direct drive. But surprisingly perhaps, having typed SDS, she then entered SS, SFS—the subprocedures of SDS—rather than SDS itself. That is, she appeared to ignore or avoid (we do not know how conscious she was of her strategy) using the new expressive power she and Sally had just developed by constructing SDS (recall that this was the first time that they had used a superprocedure of this kind). SDS was a word in their vocabulary, but its full expressiveness was not yet apparent. Janet typed:

```
SDS
SS
SFS
SS
SFS
```

So now the chance bug (i.e., the apparently unplanned FD 40 at the end of the SFS procedure) generated a new exploratory activity by moving each successive call of the modules through a translation. The key point here is that the bug meant that the interface between modules did not have to be considered *explicitly* (at least in its formalized sense). We do not claim, however, that the girls were unaware of it: They were in fact using it to good effect.

Watching the new pattern emerge on the screen and looking at the structure of the code, Janet said (with great excitement and delight): *"Wait a minute . . . that is Superduperstar SDS . . . so the next one that's got two can be Superduperduperstar SDDS . . . the next one can be Superduperduperduperstar SDDDS."* She saw a generalization of her pattern and invented a language to describe it—a language which now incorporated *Superduperstar*.[3] This enabled Janet to operate within the symbolic discourse of Logo, moving beyond thinking at each stage of what the symbols referred to, and thus gaining in mathematical expressiveness. She defined procedures SDDS and SDDDS immediately, without trying them out in direct drive (figures 8 and 9).

```
TO SDDS
    REPEAT 2 [SDS]
END
```

3. We will argue below that this is not a one-way process. Equally, the language structured Janet's awareness of the generalization.

Figure 8 SDDS

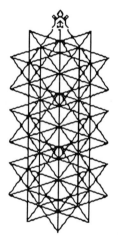

Figure 9 SDDDS

```
TO SDDDS
    REPEAT 3 [SDS]
END
```

At this point we intervened to show them how to define a general procedure:

```
TO SDNS :N
    REPEAT :N [SDS]
END
```

This formalization exactly matched the pair's activity, and the girls accepted it quite naturally. We encouraged them to make sense of this new procedure by trying it out with different inputs.

There is little doubt that this episode illustrates beautifully the development of a project during on-computer activity: Sally and Janet were working with the computer, using it as a medium that structured and was structured by the ways in which they thought about their project. A generalization emerged naturally, a generalization from which they derived both power and pleasure and which is clearly mathematical—at least in some sense, which we now consider in more detail.

Let us begin with the most obvious point: That this episode has been chosen to illustrate how effectively such kinds of generalizations can take place. Yet we know that many children fail to discover this kind of expressive power, even after considerable experience. There are many issues that arise out of this observation, and we will pursue some of them later. We might note in passing the two interventions in the episode above, and ponder the ways in which the exploration might have developed (or stagnated) had those interventions not taken place (or different interventions made). Here we wish to look a little more deeply at the Sally and Janet episode, or at least at the issues that are thrown up by it.

There are three issues we wish to pursue that emerge from Sally and Janet's exploration. First, consider the way in which they made use of the turtle's state without apparently reflecting on the idea to any extent—at least at the symbolic rather than visual level. This issue was precisely what gave the exploration its richness, yet even in the phrase "made use of state transparency" there is an implicit intentionality implied that might have been lacking in reality. Second, we notice that at one point Sally and Janet at first explicitly avoided using their SDS procedure, *even though they had constructed it themselves*. Nevertheless, we should notice too that Janet soon came to see SDS as an expressive device because of the regularities of the visual image that it produced and the pattern within the formal code. Third, we might notice that Sally and Janet succeeded in a beautiful generalization that gave them enormous pleasure. Their need for generalization emerged as a result of a synthesis of visual and symbolic, and developed to the extent of inventing a language in which to express it, yet there is no evidence that they employed any kind of mathematical analysis (why should they?) to work out, for example, the state of the turtle in relation to their subgoals—or even that they had explicit subgoals (they worked in a negotiating style that tends to be characteristic of girls, see Turkle 1984). Again we should make clear that this is not a criticism of the pair, merely an observation: One of the interesting issues of Logo is the scope it provides for just such exploratory, non-goal-oriented activities. Nevertheless, if we are examining the relationship between Logo activities and mathematics, this is an issue we can hardly ignore.

3 LOOKING BACK

Our intention here is to explore the issues raised by Sally and Janet's episode and to raise them in more general form in the context of existing Logo-based research as a preliminary step toward the construction of a theoretical framework in which to understand them. We should stress that our analysis here is both provisional and largely empirical: We intend to survey retrospectively issues that have arisen in our own and others' research, and we will try to fix some of our less precise ideas in the succeeding sections.

Our overall contention is that there is a need to be more precise as to what can be learned given certain contexts and conditions, and to reevaluate our earlier unproblematic conceptualization of the relationship between Logo and mathematics: Specifically we query whether much of what we previously saw as "doing mathematics" was merely our interpretation of what took place, rather than a description of reality.

Unreflective Use of Tools

It is clear that children's Logo productions are structured by the software tools they have for expressing them, the programs and metaphors available; moreover we will argue later that these productions are structured in a mathematical way. Nevertheless, it is an open question as to how far this structuring and the relationships involved are recognized by the pupils. Consider as a preliminary example how this perspective helps in interpreting beginning Logo activities, starting with the very simple Logo tools in the subset of turtle graphics consisting of FD, BK, RT, and LT. These primitive tools and the graphical feedback available almost inevitably shape children's behavior in ways that ensure that they bump up against a range of mathematical concepts, and one could hypothesize that children would develop an intuitive sense of these as a result of unguided (in a pedagogical sense) exploratory activities. The following might be an unordered and partial list of such embedded notions: turtle turn/angle, estimation of lengths/turns; symmetry, regular polygons, variation, trial and improvement methods, ordering and logical sequencing, and possibly tail recursion.[4] However, the question remains as to how far pupils are *aware* of the nature of the tools they are using, how far they are thinking about the mathematics used, and to what extent their activity is seen *by them* to be mathematical. This issue is brought into stark focus by a further example from the Logo Maths Project:

Throughout the whole of their first year of programming in Logo, Linda and Jude restricted their input to turtle turns to multiples of 45 which were less than or equal to 180. This strategy for angle input influenced the shapes they chose to produce squares, cubes, rectangular letters—and enabled them to cope easily with parallel lines or symmetrical slanting lines. At the beginning of their second year it was suggested that they draw a regular hexagon in order to provoke them to think about turn and use of a wider range of inputs. The pair immediately tried FD 40 RT 45 repeated 6 times and produced an incomplete octagon. This provoked surprise and then experimentation until eventually they came to use a turn of 60 and produced the regular hexagon. When asked why they had always before used multiples of 45 for angle input Linda replied: *"Dunno . . . 'cos we didn't want to explore any different angles I suppose."*

After they had finished their hexagon, they were asked to draw an octagon. They had achieved this *many* times before using their 45-degree strategy. Their actions at this point indicated that they had obviously not reflected on the octagon's construction—that is the relationship they were applying between the turn and the number of sides. To use 45 degrees was not now their first inclination and they tried to use "6 sides for 60 degrees" so "8 sides for 80 degrees" as described earlier. (Hoyles and Sutherland 1989, p. 184)

In this case pupils were not aware of the nature of the tools that they were using until they were faced with a situation where their present state of awareness would not enable them to complete the task. Essentially the pair were using

---

4. We note in passing that we do not distinguish between content-related ideas (angle) and processes (estimation).

"RT 45" as a tool whose internal structure they could safely ignore. Yet this proved inadequate to draw a hexagon. This inadequacy of the tool to express the desired idea provoked a discrimination among the components of its internal structure—the RT and the 45—and so led to an increased awareness of the meaning of the turtle command RT.

There are other less-detailed examples that illustrate the same point. For example, it is very apparent that pupils using the REPEAT command tend to produce symmetrical figures without necessarily recognizing this symmetry and the structures that underlie its construction; pupils who "undo" a sequence of <FD __ RT __ > commands by a sequence of the form <LT __ BK __ > do not necessarily think about the functional nature of these commands and the order of inverse operations. Sally and Janet were apparently unaware of state transparency in the STAR example described earlier and yet used it effectively. It is not clear that pupils spontaneously come to see the strengths and weaknesses of these strategies (Weir, chapter 6 in this volume, calls these "result-producing rituals"—they can be exhibited without understanding, and it is in their sharing that knowledge develops). We need to consider more deeply how the tools available determine the primitive notions of the environment and to simultaneously find ways of encouraging pupils to become aware of how the tools are structuring their activities.

The examples in the preceding paragraph concern Logo primitives—RT, LT, REPEAT, and so on. However, if we design more sophisticated microworlds, we face exactly the same issues as those raised above. With careful epistemological analysis, it is not difficult (though not trivial) to design the technical component of a microworld, that is, the set of software tools that provides the pupil with a representational system of some mathematical structures and relationships. But how far are pupils *aware* of this structuring and how far *can* they be helped to awareness if they cannot recognize the mathematics they are expected to discover? This is in our view the essential problematic of microworld design, the *play paradox*. We would like pupils to play with ideas as a way of experiencing their power *before* they are taught them formally, as the converse approach is devoid of experiential meaning. Yet when they are playing, they are unlikely to be playing with the *same* ideas that we had mind, (i.e., mathematical ones). The play confers meanings to the activity but blurs the specificity of the *intended* meaning.

As an example of this phenomenon, in a recent study (Hoyles and Noss 1987a) we investigated how pupils progressively became aware of and generalized the embedded relationships within a parallelogram microworld. Pupils were given the following procedure SHAPE:

```
TO SHAPE :SIDE1 :SIDE2
    FD :SIDE1 RT 40
    FD :SIDE2 RT 140
    FD :SIDE1 RT 40
    FD :SIDE2 RT 140
END
```

They were asked to use and explore SHAPE in various structured and exploratory tasks (e.g., to make a tiling pattern). Our main interest here is to comment that although the pupils constructed tiling patterns with their SHAPE procedure, they did not necessarily discriminate the salient features of its internal structure, that is, the variants and invariants if the output was to be a parallelogram. Additionally even the most mathematically successful pupils labeled the interior angles of their drawings with the values of their turtle turns.

There are higher levels of mathematical embedding that exhibit the same phenomenon, and several are given in this volume. For example, Leron and Zazkis (chapter 12) and Fletcher (chapter 12) provide in rather different ways a medium in which to express the ideas of group theory; Loethe (chapter 3), Kynigos (chapter 4), and Edwards (chapter 5) construct tools that embody in some sense specific notions of geometry. The point is that simply by interacting with software, pupils cannot be expected spontaneously to generate fully developed discriminations or generalizations of the mathematical notions embodied. On the contrary, we see it as a positive yet problematic feature of the Logo environment that it is possible to use such notions effectively but unreflectively.

Bypassing of Logo Tools

We have observed that pupils not only used tools in an apparently unaware manner but also sometimes consciously bypassed the use of tools of which they were aware: An example was Janet failing at first to use her SDS procedure. Similarly, when the pupils in the parallelogram study were asked to draw a series of parallelogram shapes, they frequently reverted to direct mode, despite having had time to explore and become familiar with the SHAPE procedure. For example, in drawing the four parallelograms shown in figure 10, Nicola—a twelve-year-old pupil with considerable Logo experience—failed to use the SHAPE procedure.

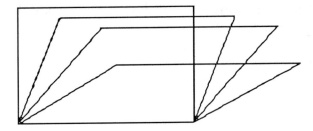

Figure 10 Nicola's four parallelograms

She wrote a non-state-transparent procedure REC for the rectangle (did she not realize that a rectangle was a particular case of a parallelogram?) and then adopted a more immediate drawing mode for the other parallelograms and wrote the following procedure:

```
TO PAT
    REC
    RT 135
    FD 100
    RT 45 . . . etc.
    FD 200
    RT 135
    FD 100 . . . etc.
```

Our provisional interpretation of this phenomenon is that in cases such as these, the new, "higher level" tool is not *owned* by the pupil; he or she does not feel confident of its power and possibilities. That is not to say that he or she does not "recognize" or "understand" it, only that it is not sufficiently part of his or her understandings to displace existing knowledge and strategies (see the "investment principle" proposed by Minsky 1988). The outcome to be constructed on the screen is not uniquely determined by which tool or tools are available. From the pupil's perspective it makes sense to use whatever is at hand and whatever minimizes cognitive demand. Elegance, efficiency, and mathematical aesthetics are not *necessarily* on the pupils' agenda!

In Nicola's case the eschewed tool was prewritten and not a Logo primitive. But there are other examples that are more primitive (in the sense of being built into Logo) as well as being higher level in terms of sophistication. For example, Leron (1985) has shown that when pupils think of Logo as a drawing tool, they do not naturally adopt a modular approach to their programming. Similarly Harvey's suggestion (chapter 13 in this volume) is that students appear to have a "natural" aversion to the idea of recursion.

From the mathematical point of view, this needs some explanation. To stay with Harvey's example for the moment, using recursion provides an elegant and powerful means of exploring and solving problems. Then why do so many pupils (and adults) avoid it and, more important, invent alternative strategies? Of course, it may be that recursion is an inherently difficult idea (not an explanation), that it runs counter to people's everyday intuitions about how processes work (perhaps true), or that the Logo community has not yet had sufficient experience to teach the idea effectively (entirely possible). But whatever the explanation(s), the fact is that the *practice* of Logo does not (contrary to our initial expectations) encourage the use of one of its most powerful ideas. In referring to Logo as a practice, we hint at a central issue, namely, that Logo is best understood as a practice with its own rules of discourse. We will have more to say on this later.

Avoidance of Mathematical Analysis

It has frequently been observed that children fail to bring mathematical analysis to bear on their Logo work. For example, children have almost instinctive ideas as to what they would like to create in a graphical mode; these ideas frequently seem to involve closed shapes. Yet Logo does not make this so easy (except in the case of regular polygons)—the tools are not readily available (although, of course, they can be created: see Loethe, chapter 3). In such cases there are two paths open for pupils: either to use an analytic method to work out *in advance* what the unknown(s) must be, given the structure of the required figure, or adopt an intuitive approach based on visual feedback. It has been found, for example, that pupils will very often adopt the latter approach and use "homing in" (see Noss 1985) as an alternative to calculation: This is the way, familiar to every Logo teacher, in which children juggle the turtle to its desired heading or position by edging their way toward it, rather than "working out" how to get there—*even when the latter method would be mathematically straightforward.*

This kind of behavior is a rather elementary example of the more general phenomenon of the use of a perceptual as opposed to an analytic strategy described by Hillel (chapter 1) and Gurtner (chapter 9) in this volume. Perceptual strategies produce success, at least at some level acceptable to the pupil (and that

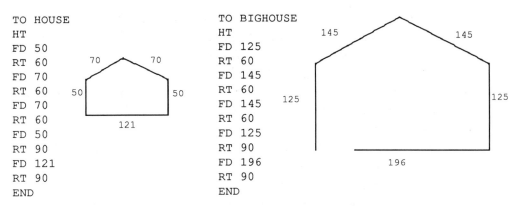

```
TO  HOUSE                     TO  BIGHOUSE
HT                            HT
FD  50                        FD  125
RT  60                        RT  60
FD  70                        FD  145
RT  60                        RT  60
FD  70                        FD  145
RT  60                        RT  60
FD  50                        FD  125
RT  90                        RT  90
FD  121                       FD  196
RT  90                        RT  90
END                           END
```

Figure 11 HOUSE (*left*), and BIGHOUSE adopting an additive strategy (*right*)

is what counts!). This of course represents one of the powerful aspects of Logo as a learning environment in terms of motivation—beginning pupils rarely fail to achieve their goals. However, *pupils'* goals may not be *mathematical* goals: They often concern the production of screen effects that involve quite different intentions.

Let us take an example from the Microworlds Project[5] (Hoyles, Noss, and Sutherland 1990). Pupils were given a procedure for a closed shape—HOUSE (see figure 11) and the procedures STEP and JUMP which, respectively, moved the turtle (without drawing) up and across the screen. We made these procedures available in order to avoid pupils having to confront the problematic issues of interfacing procedures and turtle orientation (as these were not the main items on our agenda). Pupils were asked to build bigger and smaller HOUSEs that were all in proportion. We hoped that pupils' attention would be drawn to the *necessity* of using multiplicative scalar relationships, since unclosed or overlapping shapes would be produced as a result of adopting nonmultiplicative strategies. Our model was thus based on the idea of informative and surprising feedback triggering cognitive conflict which would lead to a reevaluation of pupils' strategies. Figure 11 illustrates computer feedback from the adoption of an additive strategy and the obvious mismatch between the intended and actual outcomes.

In practice, however, some children did *not* experience cognitive conflict at all! They did of course notice that the outcome was not a "HOUSE" but de-

---

5. A three-year research project (1986–89) funded by the Economic and Social Research Council (UK).

bugged this perceptually, simply closing the gap by homing-in along the base after the figure had been drawn. This made the visual outcome "look all right." These pupils focused on the HOUSE as a drawing, choosing to ignore the mathematical requirements for the construction of a proportional product. Their goal was not the same as ours.

We certainly do not want to underestimate the importance of the visual components of the Logo environment: We have abundant evidence that learning and motivation is supported by the provision of reasonable outcomes for pupils at an early stage and the possibility of increasing refinement. Nevertheless, the pattern of avoiding mathematical analysis is too prevalent to ignore, and it adds a further twist to the story of just what understandings pupils bring to—and take away from—their Logo activities.

4   THE PUPILS' PERSPECTIVE OF MATHEMATICS

We have identified three major and pervasive obstacles to learning mathematics in a relatively unstructured way by activity in Logo-based microworlds: unreflective use of tools, bypassing of tools, and avoidance of mathematical analysis. All these obstacles have been observed in other school environments and, more pertinently, in extraschool settings where there is no teacher intervention. Thus, in order to make sense of the results from Logo research, we intend to draw upon investigations of mathematics used outside school. In doing so, we have chosen to view Logo activity as in some ways comparable to doing "informal mathematics"; that is, using mathematical fragments for a practical purpose.

We start from an idea in a related domain—that of physics. DiSessa (1983) has argued that people's notions about physical situations are based on intuitions derived from experience—*phenomenological primitives* or *p-prims* ("a rich but heterarchical collection of recognizable phenomena in terms of which they see the world and sometimes explain it"). These intuitions are *phenomenological* because they are derived from day-to-day interaction with the environment, and *primitive* because they are indivisible pieces of knowledge that are applied in a range of (sometimes inapplicable) situations. Is there an equivalent notion for mathematics?

First, we might ask whether there are primitive mathematical notions that children develop and apply outside school? Taking just a few, the genesis of mathematical ideas like counting are clearly to be found in childhood activities, and in this sense we might think of them as being derived from experience. But more complex intuitions have to be derived from thought experiments rather than from activities:[6] They are abstractions from experience rather than purely phenomenological.[7]

We propose the term *situated abstractions* to attempt to capture the ways in which people make mathematical sense of everyday activities. These are sense-making devices that are *situated* in that they are derived from experiences within specific mathematizable situations. They are *abstractions* in that they are not isomorphic with these experiences: That is, they are generalized abstractions of already mathematized situations. Since they derive from everyday practice and not from mathematics, they involve "misconceptions" when viewed from the perspective of mathematical discourse—but they *work*. A provisional list might include

1. the belief that operations are "do it" buttons: (4 + 8 *makes* 12),
2. division means sharing (so dividing by one makes no sense),
3. shapes that *look* different are *different (the definition of a shape is dependent on its orientation)* and shapes whose *names* are different *are* different,
4. "getting bigger or smaller" overrides anything else in the situation and is made to refer to the *object* of the experience (e.g., "the rate of inflation is getting smaller" means inflation is going down).

Our objective in focusing on the situatedness of activity allows us to interpret pupil behavior "not as activity in some mental realm, but as a pattern of be-

---

6. We note here that our rejection of a phenomenology of mathematics has as a corollary a rejection of the "ethnomathematical" movement that has recently become the vogue in the mathematics education community. Since we cannot divert the reader for too long on this topic we simply state the central thesis of ethnomathematics, namely, that within a range of human activities there is mathematics that is "frozen" (Gerdes 1986) and those who participate in such activities are, at some level, "doing mathematics" (D'Ambrosio 1985). We cannot agree with this position. In our view, mathematics exists in the head, not in the street (markets). To be sure, as Keitel (1986) points out, there is a wide range of activities that can serve as starting points for mathematical teaching, but that is not the same as arguing that the mathematics is in some sense "already there" waiting to be unpacked. See Noss (1988) and Hoyles (1991) for further discussion of this issue.

7. It could be argued, as indeed does Mason (1987), that this distinction is unwarranted, that in both scientific and mathematical thought "primitive images" are psychological constructions, an ideal world. In that sense Mason sees much in common between them. He, in fact, goes further and argues that there really is nothing knowable—there is only our construction of reality rather than reality itself. We do not accept this view as a useful philosophical foundation, but it is beyond our scope to discuss this issue here.

haviour that is relevant to the functioning of the person or organism in its world" (Winograd and Flores 1988, p. 71). The important point here is that the intuitions that are called up *are dependent on the practice that is being engaged in.* In arithmetic the child's early experiences are with natural numbers: Their abstractions tend to stay with these. Thus decimals are seen just as whole numbers with a point in them (e.g., 0.2, 0.4, 0.6, 0.8, 0.10); fractions are seen as one number on top of another—so "when you add them, you just add the tops and add the bottoms." The crucial issue here is that there is no everyday setting in which children have experience of decimal addition or manipulation as such (in case money is thought to be such an example, consider how difficult it is for children to use money as a paradigm for decimals in mathematics). Thus, when the number system is extended, the abstractions stay situated with the natural numbers— this remains the paradigm. It is true that new paradigms are introduced as teaching strategies (e.g., temperature for negative numbers), but these are *merely* school devices, and not surprisingly, many children simply try to extend their existing abstractions to the new situation. *In terms of Logo a question we will have to address is: What are the situated abstractions that children construct while engaged in Logo activities?*

Among the many classes of explanation that have been preferred for the situatedness of thinking, there are two that deserve mention.[8] The first, essentially an idea from cognitive science, has argued that knowledge is itself domain specific and that, in Minsky's phrase, the use of intuitive notions in inappropriate situations is due to the wrong frame being retrieved (e.g., see Minsky 1988). The other has stressed the importance of "context," and has attempted to graft on context (as Valerie Walkerdine critically puts it) into an essentially psychological framework. More recently a strand of work taking ideas from social anthropology and social psychology has suggested that the setting itself creates problems and structures its own solutions (Lave 1988; Walkerdine 1989). In some situations it actually makes sense to use strategies that superficially appear to be mathematical yet are removed from mathematical practices so that adding in a "best buy" situation is, as Lave argues, a perfectly sensible solution to the real problem. In other situations people can and do use strategies that are nearer to the mathematically acceptable one, but her key finding is that people construct solutions in the course of action and that these solutions are structured

---

8. We deliberately ignore the large "misconceptions" literature which, although interesting on an empirical level, in general fails to provide explanatory power.

by their activity. In other words, people avoid doing arithmetic in the supermarket, not because they cannot or will not do it but because arithmetic and shopping are different kinds of practices—arithmetic in the supermarket does not and cannot look like arithmetic in the classroom.

Thus for a mathematician looking at the practice of supermarket shopping, for example, it is *obvious* that the calculation of ratios is *necessary* in order to decide upon best buys. However, this is generally avoided. Qualitative decision-making takes precedence, and when quantitative reasoning *is* used, it does not reflect the structures of school mathematics but rather a mathematics made possible through the resources of the supermarket (e.g., the comparison in terms of price of the same weights of cheese). Within the mathematics education community, there is a wealth of similar examples of mathematical strategies being developed in everyday practice, in ways that bear little resemblance to school algorithms (e.g., see Carraher and Carraher 1988). *Two more Logo questions arise: What mathematics is made possible through the resources of Logo, and what are the intentions, or goals of pupils while engaged with Logo?*

Within school, attempts are traditionally made to provide experiential situations (e.g., temperature) and then to use these as paradigms for mathematical generalizations. Not surprisingly, these tend not to work. The problem is that generalized experiences are not part of ongoing activity. We have previously used the expression "not meaningful," to capture this mismatch between the ways that mathematics fails to enter into children's thinking. But now we can be a little more precise in our attempt to understand the difficulties of constructing the problem in this way. The difficulty is that the metonymic level (the interrelationships among the symbols of mathematics) is too often seen as an embarrassment rather than as a setting. Understanding in the mathematics discourse is not necessarily grounded in experience, it is not necessarily metaphorical. It also involves understanding of mathematical form, of appreciating mathematics as a discourse in its own right (see Walkerdine 1989). *Is this separation between symbol and meaning still true within Logo, where actions are formalized in the programming language as a necessary part of the activity?*

The main implication of the above discussion is that we must endeavour not to restrict ourselves to *individual* analyses of pupil behaviors within a Logo setting but rather look to a broader interpretative framework. A computational microworld involves constructing a model of some mathematical structures and relationships manipulable in ways that correspond and are consistent with formal rules. Correspondence between the formalism of the computer and the embedded mathematical structures aims to highlight key ideas and repress others. However, activity in the microworld necessarily implies an engagement within it, a move away from being a detached observer. This brings into operation the "play paradox"—involvement in the microworld can allow the learner to ignore just those mathematical nuggets that are placed there so carefully! Above all, it implies that the activities themselves are part of children's social sense—that the goals and subgoals that are naturally posed as part of the microworld not only contain solutions that are feasible for the child but also resonate with the goals and subgoals of the child's social existence within the classroom (and preferably outside it). The issue of the activities into which these tools are embedded is therefore crucial if the pupils are to appreciate the purpose of their computer work from a mathematical point of view. We can better understand the findings of Logo research reported earlier if we continually ask ourselves: What did the pupils think they were doing?

By concentrating on the situatedness of abstractions, we can turn on its head the notion that children's intuitions are misconceptions to be avoided. On the contrary, we see it as a major challenge to expand the range of situated abstractions that children spontaneously derive, to attempt to provide mechanisms for synthesizing and generalizing such abstractions across the boundaries of mathematical objects, and bring them into line with mathematical orthodoxy. It is our contention that Logo provides the opportunity for doing all these things.

5 IS LOGO A MATHEMATICAL ENVIRONMENT?

We now return to our first question: Is Logo programming just another environment for manipulating mathematical objects and bumping up against mathematical ideas, or does it have distinctive features? Let us summarize the argument so far. It is recognized that pupils working with Logo frequently avoid mathematical calculation or mathematical analysis by using other strategies made available by the setting. As we argued above, we see parallels here to the way mathematics is avoided in everyday practice. Nevertheless, our answer to the question is yes; we suggest activity in a Logo environment *does* have distinctive features. Below we propose a number of reasons why this is so.

Avoidance of Intended Mathematics Does Not Imply Avoidance of Mathematics

In contrast to the everyday situation, the avoidance of analytic mathematics within a Logo setting does not necessarily imply avoidance of mathematics.

Within a Logo environment, the pupil is able to slip down[9] toward more intuitive mathematical strategies rather than avoid them altogether. These strategies are available through the structures of Logo which provide the possibility of a dynamic interrelationship between action and visual feedback (see Noss and Hoyles 1988). Thus children are able to express solutions (or pose problems) at a number of different levels: They can mobilize resources from the situation, which are appropriate to their needs precisely because the environment has this flexibility built into it (this is actually *not* usually true for "everyday" activities, such as Lave's supermarket shopping, where the resources are structured externally—by the arena of the supermarket—and are largely inflexible).

When pupils debugged their additive strategy for BIGHOUSE (see figure 11), it is tempting to dismiss their homing-in strategy as an avoidance of mathematical structures and analysis: this is, in fact, how we presented it in our empirical overview. In fact, they avoided *our* mathematical structures in favour of their own: *we* had a clear and (to us) unambiguous agenda concerning ratio and proportion—*they* did not. There is a risk in such analysis of posing adult mathematical strategies as some kind of objective goal on behalf of the children; and thus of undervaluing the pupils' own goals, conceptions and strategies. The classical model of conceptual progress through conflict, only makes sense when there is a mismatch between the results of the pupil's action and *his/her intended and personal* goal (Winograd and Flores, 1988, call these 'breakdowns').

Scaffolding

We suggest that the use of intuitive exploratory Logo strategies can be—unlike other informal activities which are not computationally based—a catalyst for later, more analytic work by allowing children to develop and debug their own intuitions through a process of inductive generalisation. Their symbolic representations can then grow out of their action, rather than being imposed from above, and mediate between thought and action by providing an external representation (as in the SDNS example above; see also Weir, this volume). It is our

---

9. We are deliberately avoiding choosing to name our metaphor here. There are abundant metaphors that have been used to describe the ways in which mathematical thinking develops toward increasingly abstract thought (e.g., spirals, chains of signification; Walkerdine 1989). None of these really captures the interconnectedness of mathematical thought, the fact that it precisely does *not* develop linearly or hierarchically. See Kieren (chapter 8 in this volume) for further discussion of this issue.

contention that Logo can provide *scaffolding*[10] for bridging the gap between actions and generalisations.

In order to explain and justify this claim, we turn to another example where apparently intuitive actions with Logo, subsequently served as the basis for reflection: that is a strategy which initially provided a means to 'avoid' mathematical analysis later provided a bridge for mathematisation.

When pupils start to use general procedures, the declaration of the variable on the title line of the procedure is a first and important step—it forces the pupil to state in explicit form what is varying and then, by default, what is not. However, we have noticed that without pedagogical intervention pupils will often continue 'adding-on variables' for everything that varies and avoid making any necessary relationships among variables explicit (Hoyles, 1987). The procedures are then called with values for the variables which satisfy the relationships— which suggests that at some *implicit* level, the relationship is recognised. We therefore argue that declaration of variables in this way can serve as scaffolding for later analysis, since the way the variables are called can become the focus of reflection, then formalisation (see also chapter 2 by Sutherland). The example we have in mind is that of Noel, a pupil working on the parallelogram task we discussed earlier (Hoyles and Noss 1987a). Noel responded to the invitation to construct a general parallelogram (the figure was supplied) by adopting an "adding-on" strategy for inputs in which he merely appended a new input to his procedure for everything seen to be varying: He typed

TO S :W :L :R :L

We contend that Noel perceived the inputs as related to the *physical attributes* of the figure. That is, :W and :R were not viewed as the values of the inputs but its *different* sides; similarly :L signified the equal and opposite (interior) angles of the figure. This was only a very temporary phase that was perhaps an artefact of the figure (let us call this *stage 1*). As he constructed his procedure, the letters were transformed to represent values rather than objects (*stage 2*). He wrote the following procedure (see figure 12):

TO S :W :M :R :L
   FD :W RT :R

---

10. This term refers to that of Wood, Bruner, and Ross (1979). We clarify its meaning in this context below.

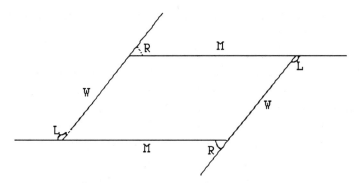

Figure 12 Noel's parallelogram

```
    FD :M  RT :L
    FD :W  RT :R
    FD :M  RT :L
END
```

This program encapsulates the state of Noel's understandings at this point: There was a symmetry in the program (it repeated twice), the opposite sides were equal, and the inputs to the turns were different. He was not able to see the relationship between :R and :L—to capture in some form the fact that :R and :L added up to 180. Later, however, the necessary relationship was finally made explicit by him (*stage 3*) when he made a synthesis between the meanings of the symbolic code he had created and the visual output he received for his attempts. (In Noel's case, there was no pedagogical intervention made during the activity.) What we have here is a play between code and picture, signifier and signified. There is no simple break between the symbolism of the code and that to which it refers: meaning is produced not by the reference of code to object but by *new meanings* that are constructed by the relationships *among* the signifiers.[11]

Our contention is that Noel used the computer as scaffolding at each of the three stages: He used it to provide himself with precisely the degree of support that allowed him to solve his problem, and in a way that seems (as far as we can tell) to have catalyzed his awareness of the implicit relationships encapsulated

11. The origin of the "linguistic" view of meaning is Saussure's. The idea of chains of signification is Lacan's Walkerdine's recent book *The Mastery of Reason* relates these ideas to the construction of elementary arithmetic meaning.

within his formalization. We note here that he erected this scaffolding *himself* (in conjunction with the available resources). This is one place in which our borrowing of the term "scaffolding" is a modification of its original meaning by Bruner and his colleagues—in their meaning of the term, such scaffolding was provided externally by an outside agency (e.g., a parent). Of course this distinction may not be so clearcut. Parents providing scaffolding for their child's linguistic meanings are structuring their own interventions by the child's utterances, and so in some ways the child is eliciting support *from* the parent in much the same way in which Noel elicited scaffolding from Logo. In both cases the scaffolding is produced from the situation.

There is a major corollary here. Namely, there are tasks that children can do with a computer that would be impossible without one. This hypothesis is resonant with Vygotsky's (1978) theory that every stage of a child's development is characterized by an actual developmental level and a potential development level;[12] the child may only be able to exploit his or her potential developmental level with help—commonly by interacting with a more knowledgeable person. In fact we have investigated and confirmed that Logo can play the role of such a person (see Hoyles and Noss 1987a, 1988).

Let us sum up. We argue that the symbolic representation of a computer program can allow the pupil to erect scaffolding around the solution of a problem and only subsequently attend to the elements of the solution on which details need to be filled in (there are echoes here with Leron and Zazkis's discussion of *abstractions*, chapter 11 in this volume). At the heart of this process (at least in turtle graphics) is the way in which pupils are able to switch between symbolic and visual representations of their thinking. We have argued elsewhere that it is this interplay between visual and symbolic forms that is special to computational media (see Hoyles and Noss 1987a): The symbolic form captures just enough of the intended goal—even if the elements of the goal are not completely understood or analyzed—and allows the pupil to attend to local elements without necessarily having to think of the structure of the solution process in global terms. In a Logo environment this forms a rather recurrent pattern precisely because actions *have* to be represented symbolically. (We might in passing note the asymmetry of the visual and symbolic modes in Logo: The pupil cannot

---

12. Vygotsky names the gap between actual and potential knowledge the "zone of proximal development."

manipulate the geometric figure to bring about corresponding changes in the symbolic representation.[13])

The Primacy of Mathematical Relationships over Objects

In an earlier paper (Hoyles and Noss 1987b) we argued that the Logo environment is specifically mathematical. Our justification, among others, was that the interaction with Logo objects could be characterized as mathematizing because the nature of the objects themselves provides the grounds for counting this activity as mathematics—the potential primitives of mathematical structures and relationships. We now want to reassess our own argument: Essentially the qualification we would like to make in retrospect is the too-easy identification of *mathematics* with such activities. We have come to realize that as with other environments, some of which are noncomputational, the Logo environment is rich in premathematical content that might serve as the basis for subsequent reflection or explicit teaching (and that is where mathematics is created): Mathematics is best seen as a separate discourse with its own culture (its own linguistic register, its own practices, and its own rules of the game).

Our previous position stated that an essential qualification for mathematical activity was that the objects of activity were themselves mathematical. Hence despite the mathematical structures that can be imposed on, for example, bell-ringing, bell ringing itself could not qualify as mathematics. While we do not want to change our conclusion, we do want to modify the emphasis of our reasoning. The crucial point is, as we have already pointed out, that mathematics takes place in the head. From this perspective any object can serve as the basis for mathematical reflection, but it does not make sense to identify objects—even mathematizable objects like turtles—with mathematics.

Instead, we now want to focus on the *relationships* rather than objects—or rather on the way that relationships can themselves become objects (of thought). This is a second order phenomenon; it concerns relationships *among* objects. It is precisely because mathematical activity involves such second-order activities that its underlying primitive notions are conceptual rather than phenomenological. *But it is also why Logo programming has mathematical potential, as the essence of programming lies precisely in the need, at some point, to make relationships explicit.*

---

13. This is one of the most promising directions in which new generations of software is moving.

We are now in a position to sum up our conclusion that Logo has particular facets that are mathematical. The key point is that there exists a way in which the nature and combinations of intuitive actions arising from perceptual rather than analytical thinking can be captured in symbolic form and thus become the objects of reflection. Clearly an important mechanism here is that feedback can be matched against intended outcome, and the feedback can be either qualitative or quantitative, allowing correspondingly qualitative or quantitative debugging.

Thus the actions of the children are documented. They can be put together, named, and symbolically represented, and more important, the symbolic representation is amenable to generalization. Logo objects have measures associated with them that are visible, quantifiable, and formalizable. Thus there is scope for the symbolic form matching the intuitive: A key issue here is the boundary of the relationship between intuitive and reflective (see Hoyles 1985 for the importance of a "complementarity" between these two activities). Intuitive and reflective modes of thought are different: They cannot be reduced one to the other. The essence of mathematical thinking is that they need to merge at all levels and be kept in mind simultaneously, and this is clearly no easy task.

6 THE ROLE OF PEDAGOGY

Our wish to place reflection center stage allows us to turn naturally to the second question we posed at the beginning of this chapter: How far does Logo only provide a mathematical environment in the context of school, where the agenda is to push toward abstraction and generalization? In other words, we seek to illuminate the precise role that pedagogy plays in the environment.

It is clear that everyday mathematics has little necessary relationship with either school mathematics or with the activities of academic mathematicians, although we do not ignore the role that schooling and teacher intervention can play in helping to synthesize all the fragments of constructed mathematized reality into a codified mathematical framework for some pupils. It may be that schooling is a catalyst for seeking some generalization in everyday activity (Carraher et al. 1985), although, as we argued earlier, school mathematics *itself* is not applied outside school. There is no evidence that a reciprocal process takes place.

Our original position on teacher intervention (e.g., see, Hoyles and Noss 1987b) was that there is a range of mathematical activities in which children become spontaneously engaged with Logo, and it is a potential environment for meeting rich mathematical ideas. *But this is not necessarily the case.* At one level the extent to which pupils can and will discover mathematical structures and relationships for themselves depends heavily on the pedagogical intervention and the kinds of teaching agendas that the teacher has in mind. These issues are sharply focused in the design of microworlds.

The criteria for the construction of Logo tools in microworlds are pedagogical. If homing-in is deemed to be an important mathematical strategy—for estimation of length and/or for the development of iterative strategies—then it does not make sense to provide pupils with a POST command as Loethe proposes in chapter 3 in this volume. On the other hand, if this is *not* what is important and the teacher wants to build on children's intuitive notion of closing shapes, then POST would certainly be an expressive tool. Essentially, as we have argued, the task in creating such tools and an explicit pedagogy to go with them is to build an intuitive framework around these higher-level concepts—in other words, to design an environment in which these concepts become the objects of study around which relationships may be explored and developed.

A fruitful avenue of recent research has been to illuminate just how these kinds of discoveries can be encouraged and, in particular, the role of the teacher (and more generally, of pedagogical intervention) in doing so. We give as an example of this an episode that aims to provide a paradigmatic case on which to base our subsequent argument. We analyze the episode by focusing on the pedagogical interventions made by the researcher.

Peter and Nigel are two twelve-year-old boys with about fifty hours Logo experience. They had started on a project to draw variably sized squares. At the beginning of the session, they loaded a procedure they had previously built.

```
TO SQS :SIZE :TIMES
    REPEAT 4 [FD :SIZE RT 90]
    SQS :SIZE/:TIMES :TIMES
END
```

They were only using a value of 2 for :TIMES—they were halving the square size at each call of SQS. We present an abbreviated and annotated rendering of the transcript that focuses on the interventions made by one of the researchers (and that leaves out many of the intervening activities):

INTERVENTION(1):   *Why not use other numbers for TIMES?*

They then used 3, 4, 5.

I(2): *Can you get the squares to grow?*

After considerable discussion, the pair introduced decimal numbers for :TIMES. They then returned to their integer inputs.

I(3): *Wouldn't it be nice to make the program stop?*

They then introduced the following (after some syntactical errors which they debugged themselves):

IF :SIZE < 10 [STOP]

They were unsure where to type this line in their program but again were left to sort it out for themselves. After all, they could see after putting it just before the END, that the program still did not stop!

I(4): *Can you predict how many squares will be drawn?*

This caused the two boys to stop and reflect and to work out the size of each square in a step-by-step way.

I(5): *What do you think would happen if you put in a number for :TIMES which was less than 0?*

Peter and Nigel did not have much idea at all about this but were quite fascinated by what happened on the screen and tried to make sense of it.

I(6): *Why does it do "top right" and then "bottom left?"*

They again were not sure but took out their calculators and worked out that the inputs for :SIZE in SQS would alternate from positive to negative so *that must be positive* [pointing to top right] and *that must be negative* [pointing to bottom left].

I(7): *How about stopping it?*

They eventually inserted IF :SIZE < -200 [STOP]. There was considerable discussion as to whether it should be "less than" or "greater than."

By compressing a lengthy and absorbing episode in this way, we run the risk of representing the interventions as more heavy-handed than they actually were.

Nevertheless, we hope it is clear that it was the nature of the interventions that pushed the boys toward *mathematical* activity. Let us consider these interventions in more detail.

I(1) and I(2) served to nudge the boys toward the use of an extended set of numbers as inputs and thus toward generalization. I(3) provoked reflection on the structure and function of the parts of the program and the logical sequence within it. It also necessitated the formulation and construction of a logical connective (IF . . . THEN) and a mathematical relationship (less than/more than).

I(4) operated at a more metacognitive level using the symbolic code as a starting point and inviting prediction as to its effects. It introduced an orientation toward a more precise analysis of the formalization and a particular relationship between the code and visual outcome. Here it prompted the drawing out of a quantitative implication (the number of squares) as a consequence of the program that could then be linked with screen outcome.

I(5) was a further metacognitive intervention, this time starting from the visual output. It attempted to draw attention to a pattern in the screen output (the alternation of the squares between top-right and bottom-left quadrants) and then to nudge the boys to think about why this pattern had been created by reference to the program.

I(6) and I(7) were extensions to I(3) but were intended to introduce another mathematical idea known to be difficult—in a comparison between two negative numbers the numerically larger negative number is the smaller. The rationale for introducing this in this context was to utilize visual feedback as scaffolding for the extension (and the debugging of the incorrect intuitive extension) of the everyday definition of "less than" (with respect to counting numbers) to the mathematical definition with respect to integers.

The agenda of the researchers is probably now clear to the reader! At a general level it was to promote reflection on the relationship between visual and symbolic modes of representation. However, the framework for this agenda was to provoke the pupils to extend the range of numbers used as inputs to their procedures in order for them to develop a more robust understanding of negative numbers.[14] We wanted the pupils to *use* negative numbers and to develop a sense of the effects of operating upon them. We wished them to explore their intuitions as to the meaning of bigger and smaller as far as integers were concerned, by reflecting upon the effects of using them as inputs for length. For example, with

---

14. The pupils had been introduced to integers as part of their mathematics curriculum.

reference to I(5), what was brought to the boys' attention was a *particular* pattern in the visual outcome of the squares which the researcher *knew* arose from the mathematical structure of the integers (a negative number multiplied by a negative number gives a positive number).

It is important to clarify what kind of an example this episode with the two boys represents. Notice first that the critical interventions aim at developing understandings within the Logo setting itself: We are not dealing here with an issue of explicit synthesis *across* domains—the activities take place *within* the practice of Logo. Second, the interventions for the development of the project were those which the researchers judged (from the vantage point of a mathematician) would throw up interesting visual feedback in relation to their mathematical agenda. A similar agenda applied to the suggestions for reflection on the symbolic code or the screen output—they were aimed at giving mathematical meaning to the boys' activity. Third, there was a delicate balance (perhaps not evident in these extracts) between leaving the boys alone and intervening—for example, there was no need to help when they could not insert the STOP command in the correct place since they could and did find this out for themselves by trying out the possibilities. Notice too that the issue is both one of extending a specific project so as to focus on some mathematics (and thus helping the student to recognize it) and at the same time to help to raise any mathematical intuitions and practices to the surface. In short, the pedagogical agenda sought to draw the practices of mathematics and Logo closer together in the context of a pupil-project (see chapter 9 by Gurtner in this volume for a somewhat different perspective).

A further question that we might ask is, What would have happened in this episode *without* intervention? While we cannot, of course, ever answer this question, it is clear that if we feel that the interventions were crucial, then it is an important point in reporting Logo work that we plan, document, and analyze our interventions. In an attempt to systematize the kind of pedagogic practices we have outlined above, we have worked on the design and evaluation of a mathematical microworld for *ratio and proportion* (see Hoyles, Noss, and Sutherland 1990).

In the first place our ratio and proportion microworld involved some careful thought about the kinds of computational objects we offered to the pupils (one, HOUSE, has already been illustrated; see figure 11). We wanted pupils to reflect on quite detailed distinctions (e.g., the difference between *within measure* and *between measure* strategies for proportion), and we were therefore forced to construct not only objects but also pedagogical strategies that held a reasonable promise of pupils encountering these ideas. This in itself proved far from trivial, particularly as we also wanted to ensure that pupils had opportunities for their own explorations (including sidetracks that bore little connection to our intended agendas).

Second, at a few selected points we highlighted particular aspects of mathematics. For example, we stressed what *we* meant by "proportional" and encouraged a specifically *mathematical* usage of the term. That is, we pointed to the *differences* between mathematical usage and everyday usage (this is something of a departure from that conventional pedagogical wisdom which emphasizes only the similarities across discourses, sometimes with disastrous results; see Pimm 1987 for a fuller discussion of this issue).

Third, we made sure that pupils were encouraged to work both on and off the computer. We are aware that by doing so, we were to some extent enforcing a style of working upon the pupils, but we decided that this was a price worth paying if we were to maximize the pupils' chances of encountering the rather subtle pieces of mathematics we intended (this point is considered further in our conclusions). Nevertheless, even with the off-computer activities, there was little in the activities that could be described as explicitly mathematical. At no time throughout the six one-and-a-quarter hour sessions did we "teach" ideas of proportionality or get the pupils to practice arithmetic manipulation. The challenge we set ourselves was to link children's existing intuitions about proportional situations (which turned out not to be especially rich) with new intuitions derived from their Logo activities that could serve as a conceptual framework for understanding within the terms of mathematical discourse.

Fourth, we built into the children's activities class discussions and small-group activities as well as on-computer work. In doing so, we were attempting to gain some homogeneity of intentions across pupils as well as between pupils and ourselves. We wanted pupils to know what we wanted them to do, and reciprocally we wanted to know what the pupils thought they were doing.

A major relevant finding of our work is that although the computational activities and associated pedagogical nudges were crucial in building intuitions and alerting pupils to the contextual clues related to proportionality, the off-computer activities, the class discussions, and the small-group work were significant in engendering shifts in pupil responses toward an appreciation of the *mathematical* requirements of the task, that is, from situated abstractions to mathematical abstractions.

To summarize, we believe that even with our carefully constructed set of procedures, intervention and pedagogic structuring of the activities were important in realizing the mathematical nature of Logo programming *for the pupils* (*we* were convinced of it all along!). It seems as though this kind of intervention is necessary to highlight the embedded structures *and* that intervention is necessary away from the computer to validate those structures that are part of mathematical discourse. How far this can be achieved while maintaining the delight of pupil-controlled work and respect for pupil-determined goals is a complex and crucial question for teachers and researchers. It is a tension that can only be resolved in practice.

7 LOOKING FORWARD

An underlying theme for many chapters of the book concerns the way in which the use of computational tools can potentially structure, amplify, and reorganize thinking (see Pea 1987). We have viewed as problematic the evidence that Logo considered as a set of tools might not empower children in a mathematical sense, that children they sidestep sophisticated tools, are unaware of their nature, and fail to bring mathematical analysis to Logo work. Our search for some theoretical framework led us to consider the analogies between mathematics used in Logo work and mathematics used in everyday practice. This enabled us to incorporate into our interpretation of pupils' Logo behavior pupils' intentions in interaction with the resources of the setting.

Insofar as our intention is to induct pupils into the practice of mathematics and to build intuitions rather than simply dictate formal rules, the best that we can hope for is to provide situations and environments in which fragments of mathematical discourse make sense and are useful in solving the problems that structure and are structured by the setting, that become for pupils *situated abstractions*. We suggest that Logo extends significantly the range of situated abstractions available to pupils and that this range can be further extended by the construction of microworlds. This does not obviate the need for pupils to synthesize across abstractions and bring them into line with mathematical discourse—both processes which, we have argued, can be facilitated through the Logo experience.

We propose that when we think about programming in Logo, it is helpful to distinguish between two ways in which pupils construct meanings. First, we have the situated abstractions that are inevitably encountered while programming in Logo or in suitably designed microworlds. These are the mathematical ideas discriminated through activities that provoke breakdowns and awareness of the available tools and the underlying mathematical relationships. We would argue that within any microworld, the set of primitive tools available can act as scaffolding for the construction of more abstract mathematical ideas that become the new objects of study from prior formalizations. In this way we might begin to exploit the way in which the computational setting creates a dialectic between tools and concepts[15] and so can build a range of abstract mathematical ideas from an intuitive base.[16]

Second, there is the mathematics that is highlighted for pupils through teacher intervention. We see a chain of levels in which pedagogical intervention and structuring of activities is part of the production of meaning at that level. Intervention can help children to create new powers of expression within the medium and can assist in elevating tools to the status of objects through on- and off-computer activities. Of course, there is no unique way to do either of these (cf. in this volume, the approaches of Weir, chapter 6, and Gurtner, chapter 9, with respect to the first issue, and Leron and Zazkis, chapter 11, and Fletcher, chapter 12, with respect to the second). By making this distinction, we do not mean to suggest the existence of two types of mathematical ideas. The distinction simply arises from the extent to which the goals and intentions of the pupils coincide with those of the underlying pedagogical framework of the activities.

At the same time as enriching and extending the range of situated abstractions, we have argued that the Logo environment has other specific features in relation to pupils' mathematical learning: Pupils can move between intuitive and analytic methods, the sidestepping of the teacher's mathematical agenda does not necessarily imply avoidance of mathematics per se, and the programming language itself provides modes of scaffolding from situated abstractions toward generalizations. Writing a program helps to capture variants, invariants, and the relationships between them.

---

15. See Douady (in press) for a detailed discussion of the "tool-object dialectic."

16. We are beginning to investigate these kinds of ideas with BOXER, which is a computational medium developed by Andy diSessa at Berkeley.

In this chapter we have been self-critical of some of our earlier claims, and we end with a final reflection on our earlier position. In our first attempt at addressing the issue of Logo-based microworlds, we proposed that a microworld cannot be defined by the software alone in isolation from its other components: the learner, the teacher, or the context within which it operates. Activity within microworlds, we argued, is shaped by the intuitions of the learner, and by the aims and expectations of the teacher. Evaluation of a microworld necessitates recognizing the multiple agendas of pupils and the range of potential learning. The writing of this afterward has reshaped our thinking about the relationship between the different components and, in particular, has provoked us to elevate the contextual component from its status as an auxiliary consideration to that of a central and pervasive element. We have attempted to be more precise as to how contextual influences are critical in understanding and interpreting pupil interactions with the technical component (the software/hardware combination). The context does far more than modify our interpretation of children's cognition; the setting—that is, the relationship between the participants and the physical context—is central to understanding how children use the medium to express their ideas and how those ideas are themselves structured by the medium. We previously saw context as something we ought to allow for in our observation and interpretation of data, but we now see it as the very medium that we are investigating. We should point out that this observation does not make our task as researchers any easier; it only gives us a clearer idea of where to look!

Perhaps then we should lay to rest our rather loose use of the word "tools" in the preceding pages. Although the idea of a tool is a convenient metaphor, we run the risk of implying that there exists a set of decontextualized tools that can be "applied" across a range of contexts without changing them. We would still like to stay with the idea of using or avoiding tools, but we want to stress here that pupils are not entirely free to choose what tools they use any more than people are free to use whatever language they like.

This book is a testimony to the fact that the potential for mathematical learning inherent in Logo is only currently being tapped. Our concerns in this chapter have been wide-ranging, and we conclude with a brief mapping of some of the key questions that need to be researched and curriculum development issues that need to be addressed. In the first instance we suggest a need for more investigation into the limits and boundaries which Logo presents for mathematical learning.[17] What becomes intuitive in a Logo-rich culture, and what does and does not resonate with school-based knowledge within that culture? What explicit mathematics might be taught—and how easily—to children who have absorbed a range of intuitions from experience of computational media?[18] Should we try to isolate key areas of study in an attempt to circumvent the difficulties presented by the interconnectedness of mathematical ideas? How can we build settings that structure pupils' learning *without* artificially fragmenting the activities, destroying pupils' joy and motivation, and threatening teachers' respect for pupils' own goals?

Researching these questions will necessitate methodologies that recognize their complexity and generality. For our part we are aware that looking at learning mathematics through a Logo lens has broadened our field of view far beyond its initial focus on Logo and has widened it to encompass fundamental issues that include the incorporation of computational media into classrooms and the social, cultural, and pedagogical contexts of mathematical learning itself.

REFERENCES

Carraher, T. N., Schliemann, A. D., and Carraher, D. W. 1988. Mathematical concepts in everyday life. In G. B. Saxe and M. Gearhart (eds.), *Children's Mathematics*. San Francisco: Jossey-Bass, pp. 71–87.

D'Ambrosio, U. 1985. Ethnomathematics and its place in the history and pedagogy of mathematics. *For the Learning of Mathematics 5* (1): 45–48.

DeCorte, E., Verschaffel, L., Hoedemaekers, E., Schrooten, H. and Indemans, R. 1990. Logo and the acquisition of planning skills in sixth graders. In E. Dubinsky and R. Fraser (eds.), *Computers and the Teaching of Mathematics: A World View*. Nottingham: Shell Centre for Mathematics Education, pp. 200–205.

diSessa, A. 1983. Phenomenology and the evolution of intuitions. In D. Gentner and A. Stevens (eds.), *Mental Models*. Hillsdale, NJ: Lowrence Erlbaum Associates, pp. 15–33.

17. There are changes taking place in the software-hardware combination that might well make both subtle and not-so-subtle differences to the activities and mathematical learning of pupils. Some of these are essentially trivial, such as the user-interface (although we do not rule out the fact that these may turn out to be important), some involve changes of the underlying story (changing what it means to "edit" in LogoWriter, or using an object-oriented implementation), and others may necessitate a change in our very conception of what programming means.

18. This is an old question of Papert's that has not really been addressed. A version of it is currently being investigated by diSessa (1989).

diSessa, A. 1989. A child's science of motion: Overview and first results. In U. Leron and N. Krumholtz (eds.), *Proceedings of the Fourth International Conference for Logo and Mathematics Education.* Jerusalem.

Douady, R. 1991. Mathematical ideas as both tool and object. In A. Bishop, S. Mellin-Olsen, and Van Dormolen J. (eds.), *Mathematical Knowledge: Its Growth through Teaching.* Dordrecht: Kluwer, pp. 109–130.

Gerdes, P. 1986. How to recognize hidden geometrical thinking: A contribution to the development of anthropological mathematics. *For the Learning of Mathematics* 6 (2): 10–12.

Hoyles, C. 1985. *Culture and Computers in the Mathematics Classroom.* Inaugural lecture, Bedford Way Paper. London: Institute of Education, University of London.

Hoyles, C. 1986. Scaling a mountain: A study of the use, discrimination and generalisation of some mathematical concepts in a Logo environment. *European Journal of Psychology in Education* 1 (2): 111–126.

Hoyles, C. 1987. Tools for learning: Insights for the mathematics educator from a Logo programming environment. *For the Learning of Mathematics* 7 (2): 32–37.

Hoyles, C. 1991. Computer-based learning environments for mathematics. In A. Bishop, S. Mellin-Olsen, and J. Van Dormolen (eds.), *Mathematical Knowledge: Its Growth through Teaching.* Dordrecht: Kluwer, pp. 147–172.

Hoyles, C., and Noss, R. 1987a. Children working in a structured Logo environment: From doing to understanding. *Récherches en Didactiques de Mathématiques* 8 (12): 131–174.

Hoyles, C., and Noss, R. 1987b. Synthesising mathematical conceptions and their formalisation through the construction of a Logo-based school mathematics curriculum. *International Journal of Mathematical Education in Science and Technology* 18 (4): 581–595.

Hoyles, C., and Noss, R., 1989. The computer as a catalyst in children's proportion strategies. *Journal of Mathematical Behavior* 8: 53–75.

Hoyles, C., and Sutherland, R. 1989. *Logo Mathematics in the Classroom.* London: Routledge.

Hoyles, C., Noss, R., and Sutherland, R. 1990. *The Microworld Project: Final Report to the Economic and Social Research Council.* London: Institute of Education, University of London.

Keitel, C. 1986. Cultural premises and presuppositions in psychology of mathematics education. *Plenary Lectures, Proceedings of the Tenth International Conference for the Psychology of Mathematics Education.* London.

Lave, J. 1988. *Cognition in Practice.* Cambridge: Cambridge University Press.

Leron, U. 1985. Logo today: Vision and reality. *The Computing Teacher* 12: 26–32.

Mason, J. 1987. What do symbols represent? In C. Janvier (ed.), *Problems of Representation in the Teaching and Learning of Mathematics.* Hillsdale, NJ: Lawrence Erlbaum Associates.

Minsky, M. 1988. *The Society of Mind*. New York: Simon and Schuster.

Noss, R. 1985. Creating a Mathematical Environment through Programming: A Study of Young Pupils Learning Logo. Doctoral dissertation. Chelsea College, University of London. London: Institute of Education, University of London.

Noss, R. 1986. How do children do maths with Logo? *Journal of Computer Assisted Learning* 2, (3): 2–12.

Noss, R. 1988. The computer as a cultural influence in mathematical learning. *Educational Studies in Mathematics* 19 (2): 251–268.

Noss, R., and Hoyles, C. 1988. The computer as a mediating influence in the development of pupils' understanding of variable. *European Journal of Psychology of Education* 3 (3): 271–286.

Pea, P. D. 1987. Cognitive technologies for mathematics education. In A. H. Schoenfeld (ed.), *Cognitive Science and Mathematics Education*. Hillsdale, NJ: Lawrence Erlbaum Associates, pp. 89–122.

Pea, R., and Kurland, M. 1984. On the cognitive effects of learning computer programming. *New Ideas in Psychology* 2 (1): 137–168.

Pimm, D. 1987. *Speaking Mathematically*. London: RKP.

Turkle, S. 1984. *The Second Self: Computers and the Human Spirit*. New York: Simon and Schuster.

Vygotsky, L. 1978. *Mind in Society*. Cambridge: Harvard University Press.

Walkerdine, V. 1989. *The Mastery of Reason*. London: Routledge.

Winograd, T., and Flores, F. 1988. *Understanding Computers and Cognition*. Reading, MA: Addison-Wesley.

Wood, D., Bruner, J., and Ross, G. 1979. The role of tutoring in problem solving. *Journal of Child Psychology and Psychiatry* 17: 89–100.

Index